T0290579

A Legal Dictionary
for Museum Professionals

DISCLAIMER

The information provided in this text does not constitute legal advice. All information included is for general informational purposes only. For legal issues that arise, the reader should consult with legal counsel. Information included in this text may not represent the most up-to-date legal information, or it may not reflect the state of the law in any particular jurisdiction. For specific legal matters, readers are advised to consult with appropriate, knowledgeable professionals. Readers should not act or refrain from acting based on the information in this book without consulting with their own attorney or other appropriate professional with knowledge of the laws in the relevant jurisdiction. Only your attorney can ensure that the information contained in this book (and your personal interpretation of that information) is appropriate and applicable to your situation.

A Legal Dictionary for Museum Professionals

2ND EDITION

Heather Hope Kuruvilla

ROWMAN & LITTLEFIELD

Lanham • Boulder • New York • London

Published by Rowman & Littlefield
A wholly owned subsidary of The Rowman & Littlefield Publishing Group, Inc.
4501 Forbes Boulevard, Suite 200, Lanham, Maryland 20706
www.rowman.com

Unit A, Whitacre Mews, 26-34 Stannary Street, London SE11 4AB

British Library Cataloguing in Publication Information Available

Library of Congress Cataloging-in-Publication Data

Names: Kuruvilla, Heather Hope, author.
Title: A legal dictionary for museum professionals / Heather Hope Kuruvilla.
Description: Second edition. | Lanham : Rowman & Littlefield, [2021] |
    Includes bibliographical references and index.
Identifiers: LCCN 2020049510 (print) | LCCN 2020049511 (ebook) | ISBN
    9781538142974 (cloth) | ISBN 9781538142981 (epub)
Subjects: LCSH: Museums--Law and legislation--United States--Dictionaries.
Classification: LCC KF4305.A68 K87 2021 (print) | LCC KF4305.A68 (ebook)
    | DDC 340.03--dc23
LC record available at https://lccn.loc.gov/2020049510
LC ebook record available at https://lccn.loc.gov/2020049511

∞™ The paper used in this publication meets the minimum requirements of American National
Standard for Information Sciences—Permanence of Paper for Printed Library Materials, ANSI/NISO
Z39.48-1992.

CONTENTS

LIST OF TABLES

COMMON SYMBOLS AND THEIR MEANINGS

Symbol	Meaning
©	Copyright
Copr.	Copyright
®	Federally registered mark (trademark or service mark)
SM	Common law service mark
TM	Common law trademark

COMMON ACRONYMS AND THEIR MEANINGS

Acronym	Meaning
AAM	American Alliance of Museums (formerly American Association of Museums)
AAMD	Association of Art Museum Directors
ACHP	Advisory Council on Historic Preservation
ADAA	Art Dealers Association of America
AMICO	Art Museum Image Consortium
ARPA	Archaeological Resources Protection Act
ARS	Artists Rights Society
ASCAP	American Society of Composers, Authors, and Publishers
BCIA	Berne Convention Implementation Act
BMI	Broadcast Music, Inc.
BSI	Blue Shield International
CCC	Copyright Clearance Center

Acronym	Meaning
CFR	Code of Federal Regulations
CITES	Convention on International Trade in Endangered Species of Wild Fauna and Flora
CMP	collections management policy
CPIA	Cultural Property Implementation Act
EIN	employer identification number
FASB	Financial Accounting Standards Board
FIC	found in collection
FMV	fair market value
ICBS	International Committee of the Blue Shield
ICCROM	International Center for the Study of the Preservation and Restoration of Cultural Property
ICOM	International Council of Museums
IMP	independent museum professional
MPLC	Motion Picture Licensing Corporation
NAGPRA	Native American Graves Protection and Repatriation Act
NEPIP	Nazi-Era Provenance Internet Portal
NHL	National Historic Landmark
NHPA	National Historic Preservation Act
NPS	National Park Service
NRHP	National Register of Historic Places
NSAF	National Stolen Art File
PTO	(United States) Patent and Trademark Office
R&R	rights and reproductions
SHPO	State Historic Preservation Office(r)
TPM	time, place, manner restrictions
UBIT	unrelated business income tax
UCC	Uniform Commercial Code
UNESCO	United Nations Educational, Scientific, and Cultural Organization
UNIDROIT	International Institution for the Unification of Private Law

Acronym	Meaning
USC	United States Code
USPTO	United States Patent and Trademark Office
VARA	Visual Artists Rights Act
WIPO	World Intellectual Property Organization

LIST OF STATUTES

Statute Title	Common Acronym or Alternate Name	Citation
Advisory Council on Historic Preservation	ACHP	54 U.S.C. §§ 304101-112
Antiquities Act	National Monuments Act	16 U.S.C. §§ 431-33
Archaeological Resources Protection Act	ARPA	16 U.S.C. § 470aa-mm
Arts and Artifacts Indemnity Act		20 U.S.C. §§ 971 *et. seq.*
Convention on Cultural Property Implementation Act	CPIA	19 U.S.C. §§ 2601-13
Copyright Act of 1976		17 U.S.C. §§ 101 *et. seq.*
Curation of Federally Owned and Administered Archaeological Collections		36 C.F.R. Part 79
Endangered Species Act		16 U.S.C. §§ 1531-44

Statute Title	Common Acronym or Alternate Name	Citation
Federal Insurance Contributions Act	FICA	26 USC § 3101 *et. seq.*
Holocaust Expropriated Art Recovery Act	HEAR Act	Pub. L. 114–308
Internal Revenue Code	IRC	26 U.S.C. §§ 1 *et. seq.*
Justice for Uncompensated Survivors Today Act	JUST Act	Publ. L. 115-171
Lanham Act	Trademark Act	15 U.S.C. §§ 1051 *et. seq.*
National Historic Landmark Program		36 C.F.R. Part 65
National Historic Preservation Act	NHPA	16 U.S.C. §§ 470 *et. seq.*
National Museum of the American Indian	NMAI	20 U.S.C. § 80q
National Register of Historic Places	NRHP	54 U.S.C. §§ 302101-108
Native American Graves Protection and Repatriation Act	NAGPRA	25 U.S.C. §§ 3001-13
Protection of Archeological Resources Uniform Regulations		36 C.F.R. Part 296
Protection of Historic Properties	Section 106 Review	36 C.F.R. Part 800
State Historic Preservation Programs		54 U.S.C. §§ 302301-304
Visual Artists Rights Act	VARA	17 U.S.C. § 106A

PREFACE

Museums exist in a fascinating nexus of important concerns, and the conversations around those concerns have become more varied and developed in the new century. How museums engage with their communities, whom they answer to, who wields authoritative power—these are conversations that have bubbled to the surface across the museum field and continue to push the boundaries of what museological work has been in the past and can be moving forward.

The baseline of many of these conversations touches on the law. And on ethics, most certainly, as ethics and the law tend to intermix in many conversations involving museum work. To be clear, museum law and museum ethics are separate, based on different sources and sometimes with different answers to the same questions. But the fact that they both inform museum work cannot be denied. Sometimes it is the manner in which they exist both in concert and in tension that gives rise to the most interesting and creative answers to the issues and questions presented to the field today.

This text is a step down from that higher level of museological critique and analysis, focusing almost entirely on the legal aspect of the museum profession's work. While ethics do appear throughout, in the end this is a legal text and should be considered in that light. The idea for this book came from the realization that every museum professional, whether a seasoned expert or a student just entering the field, finds herself facing legal issues that require a clear, concise answer. While an in-depth understanding of the deeper legal issue may be helpful, it is not always necessary. Sometimes that professional just needs a quick refresher, or a clear understanding of the difference between two similar but related terms. Should the museum's logo have a ® or ™ symbol after it? What does it mean to be a tax-exempt organization, and is that the same as being a nonprofit organization? Does the museum have to provide a written acknowledgment for donations? Does the museum need a license to reproduce this copyrighted work?

Recognition of that need is what gave rise to this book. *A Legal Dictionary for Museum Professionals* is intended to be a go-to reference book. It provides clear, concise, plain-language definitions for a number of legal topics that relate to the museum profession, covering everything from the art market, cultural property, collections management, nonprofit corporations and tax exemption, boards, and intellectual property. Definitions are presented alphabetically to permit easy lookup, and entries are thoughtfully and thoroughly cross-referenced. In addition to the alphabetical dictionary, this text provides a number of more in-depth chapters, examining some of the more intricate topics while retaining the straightforward approach of the dictionary entries.

The second edition builds on the groundwork laid in the first, expanding and updating the existing resources while adding new entries and chapters to address the ongoing evolution of the profession. In the few short years since the first edition, changes have occurred in how the field approaches deaccessioning and the use of proceeds from disposal, including the issuance of the AAM "Direct Care of Collections" white paper and the AASLH "Valuing History Collections" position paper, both intertwined with the 2019 update from the Financial Accounting Standards Board that now acknowledges "direct care" as an appropriate use of deaccession proceeds.

Aside from deaccessioning, developments in the ongoing issue of Nazi-looted objects before and during WWII continue to emerge. The Holocaust Expropriated Art Recovery Act of 2016 was signed into law mere months after the release of the first edition, and the Justice for Uncompensated Survivors Today (JUST) Act became law the following year. These each have their own entries in the new edition.

Other topics now included in the second edition include worker classification, defining employees and independent contractors, and considering the still-evolving situation in California since the passage of AB5, new entries on issues related to property law and fund-raising, and entries related to various common forms of business structures. These are accompanied by new in-depth chapters on worker classification, business strictures, and the current state of deaccessioning in the field.

A Legal Dictionary for Museum Professionals will be the first stop for any professional seeking plain-language guidance. It a desktop reference guide that presents information in a plain-language, easily digestible format. This reference book will ideally be kept within arm's reach, there to provide guidance and necessary information when a refresher is required on a particular topic, or the simple answer to a question is sought. It is intended to be useful for the museum studies student or the experienced professional and will be a useful addition to anyone's shelf.

A Legal Dictionary for Museum Professionals
Second Edition

ACKNOWLEDGMENTS

This book came about during a strange time, both for myself personally and for the museum profession and wider world. My proposal for this second edition was accepted in late 2019, and work began early 2020. As reports of a new illness began to emerge in the news, I drafted timelines and to-do lists, unaware of how much things would change and how quickly.

Working on this from home while overseeing my daughter's virtual learning was not the vision I had going into this project. Like many others, I found myself wearing multiple hats throughout the day as I shifted between parent, teacher, professional, spouse, and writer. It's been a hard road, but I received so much support throughout that has permitted me to get to this point (even if I did miss my deadline!).

First, a big thank you to my colleagues and friends, who were always willing to listen to me and help flesh out ideas, provide suggestions and guidance, and give support when I needed some assistance or mental fortitude. Most importantly, they helped me stay smiling, laughing, and upbeat with their friendship, support, and often healthy doses of sarcasm. Thank you to Ginny Cascio Bonifacino, Shannon Domigpe, MK Ellis, Liz Lopez, Ashley May, Brooke Novak, Amanda Patterson-Dwyer, Laura Preston, Aaron Rosenthal, Nicole Roth, Linda Sariahmed, and Alison Velea.

And of course, a thank you to Claudia Ocello and Sally Yerkovich, who were both supportive of the idea for this book and have been wonderful colleagues and supportive friends. I must also include with them Charles Harmon, my editor, who has been exceptionally accommodating and provided guidance at every step. My students at Kutztown University of Pennsylvania and the University of Kentucky have continually demonstrated just how engaging, exciting, and complicated these topics can be, and they remind me that there is always a new perspective and more to learn.

Finally, as before, I want to end with thanking my husband, Teddy, who remains my support, my rock, my partner, and my best friend. Without you, I'm not sure if this edition would have happened. And I must close with a hug and a thank you for Isabel, who is growing before our eyes into the smartest, funniest, and kindest person.

CHAPTER 1

MUSEUM LAW DICTIONARY

ABANDONED PROPERTY

Abandoned property is personal property to which the rightful owner intentionally relin-quishes all rights.[1] Real property cannot be abandoned.[2]

These three examples should assist in distinguishing between lost, mislaid, and abandoned property. Imagine a museum visitor brings a 1920s beaded clutch with her to the museum. If she sets the clutch on the visitor information desk while talking to a friend and then walks off without picking it back up, the clutch is mislaid. The visitor did intend to set the clutch down on the desk, but she had no intention to leave it behind. However, if the clutch's strap breaks while she is walking through the galleries, and she does not notice, the clutch is lost. The visitor did not intend to leave the clutch behind in the galleries. In either of these situations, the museum is not the intended recipient of the clutch, and it should be securely stored until it can be returned to the visitor.

Alternatively, if the woman intentionally leaves the clutch at the museum's front door before business hours or at the visitors' desk with an anonymous note inside indicating it is a donation to the museum, it is abandoned. The visitor has intentionally left the clutch behind, has no intention to return and reclaim it, and the museum is the intended recipient.

At common law, abandoned property often became the property of the person who found and took possession of it—the source of the old saying "finders, keepers." Today many states have unclaimed property laws, though many of these only apply in very specific situations, such as regarding monies held in abandoned bank accounts or a landlord's obligations to store personal property left behind by a tenant.[3]

If a museum receives abandoned property that purports to be a donation, the museum does have the option to retain and accession the property, though this may raise issues regarding collections management, especially since the object's provenance is unknown and the museum has no way of confirming the person who left the object was its rightful owner. Questions related to title, copyright, authenticity, or other concerns may exist. If the object is one of cultural heritage, archaeological materials, or contains certain animal products, it is possible the object's acquisition would conflict with certain federal laws. For all these reasons, a museum may want to establish publicized policies that discourage abandonment of objects purporting to be donations.

Compare "Adverse Possession."
See also "Collections Management Policy."
See also "Cultural Heritage."
See also "Donation."
See also "Personal Property."

ABC TEST FOR WORKER CLASSIFICATION

There are two different tests to determine if a worker should be classified as an employee or as an independent contractor. The possible tests to apply are the common law test and the ABC test.[4]

The ABC test was developed at the state level,[5] and as such, it can vary from state to state. In addition, some states only utilized part of the ABC test. The most common criteria under the test are:

(A) that the worker is free from the control and direction of the hirer in connection with the performance of the work, both under the contract for the performance of such work and in fact;
(B) that the worker performs work that is outside the usual course of the hiring entity's business; and
(C) that the worker is customarily engaged in an independently established trade, occupation, or business of the same nature as the work performed for the hiring entity.[6]

Under this test, a worker will be classified as an independent contractor only if all three criteria apply. The ABC test starts with a presumption the worker is an employee and applies the criteria to the worker-employer relationship to determine if the worker should instead be classified as an independent contractor.

See also "Common Law Test for Worker Classification."
See also "Employee."
See also "Independent Contractor."
See also "Worker Classification."

For a more in-depth discussion, see "Chapter 10: Worker Classification: Distinguishing between an Employee and an Independent Contractor."

ACCESSION

As used in the museum profession, the word *accession* has two distinct but related meanings. First, an accession is an object acquired (acquisitioned) by the museum and formally processed into the museum's permanent collection.[7] This definition, therefore, applies to every object in the museum's permanent collection, each of which could properly be referred to as an "accession" interchangeably with terms such as *object* or *collection object*.

Second, "accession" is the process by which an object is processed into the permanent collection.[8] It is the second step after the acquisition of the object.[9] Objects not intended for the permanent collection should not be accessioned. For example, an object that is destined for a handling collection often is not accessioned, as it is likely to deteriorate due to the constant handling by museum visitors and therefore it is not intended that the object will be held in the public trust in perpetuity. Likewise, a donation of office furniture to be used by museum staff would not be accessioned, as it is not intended for the permanent collection.

Objects accessioned into the permanent collection are held and cared for in compliance with the museum's collections management policy.[10] The accessioning process would include everything from object documentation, creation of the object file, photography, creation and application of a unique object number, assignment to a specific collection or department, placement in storage, and any other procedures that must be completed to properly take control over the object.

The process of accessioning an object gives rise to ethical and legal obligations.[11] The museum board must meet its fiduciary duties in relation to the collection, and failure to do so may give rise to legal consequences. Museum professional organizations promulgate professional codes of ethics that discuss the ethical obligations museums have to their collections and to their public. When a museum accessions an object, it should be careful to comply with all applicable obligations.

Compare "Acquisition."
Compare "Deaccession."
See also "Code of Ethics."
See also "Collections Management Policy."
See also "Fiduciary Duty."
See also "Mission Statement."

ACQUISITION

Acquisition is a term used to describe the process by which an object is obtained by a museum. While there is no consistent profession-wide accepted definition, the most commonly accepted use of the term is that an acquisition occurs when title to an object transfers to the museum.[12]

Acquisition is the first step in the accessioning process; however, not all objects that are acquisitioned are intended for accessioning. For instance, objects acquisitioned and intended for an education/handling collection are often not accessioned, as they will likely deteriorate due to the nature of their use. A similar reason applies in a natural history museum that does not accession scientific specimen intended for destructive testing. In both situations, the objects acquisitioned are not to be held in the public trust in perpetuity, and therefore accessioning may be inappropriate, depending on the guidelines found in the museum's collections management policy.

When acquisition occurs with the intention of accessioning the object, such acquisition should be guided by the museum's collecting goals, its mission, and the collection management policy. Additionally, the object's provenance should be considered, as it may impact the appropriateness of the acquisition and accession.

An acquisition may come about by any means whereby legal title transfers to the museum. This includes purchase, donation, gift, or bequest.

Compare "Accession."
See also "Collections Management Policy."
See also "Mission Statement."
See also "Provenance."
See also "Title."

ADVERSE POSSESSION

Adverse possession is a legal mechanism by which ownership of property can be acquired. The rules of adverse possession vary in each state, but generally, the requirement is that the property in question be possessed by an individual other than the owner in a manner that is

Actual, meaning the possessor is in actual possession of the property;

Exclusive, meaning possession is not shared with others, including the owner;

Open and notorious, meaning the property is used in a manner that is so visible as to put the owner on notice of the potential claim on the property;

Hostile, also called nonpermissive, meaning the owner did not give the possessor permission to use the property; and

Continuous for the length of time required in the jurisdiction, which can range from seven to thirty years, depending on the state.

If the requirements of adverse possession are met, then the possessor can acquire title to the possessed property, though the quality of that title depends on the jurisdiction. Some jurisdictions require additional steps, such as a suit to quiet title.

Typically, adverse possession is effective against real property. For personal property, a more appropriate applicable law would be that addressing abandoned property.

Compare "Abandoned Property."
See also "Personal Property."
See also "Real Property."
See also "Title."

ADVISORY COUNCIL ON HISTORIC PRESERVATION

See "National Historic Preservation Act."

AGENT

An agent is one who acts on behalf of another, with that person's permission and authority. The agent has the ability to bind that other person to contracts or other obligations. For example, a donor may conduct the donation of an artwork through the donor's agent.

Imagine a donor, Peggy, wishes to make a large donation to her city's art museum. Peggy is a busy and in-demand businesswoman, often traveling to Europe and Asia to negotiate high-stakes business deals. Peggy may find it more convenient to have her agent conduct the donation transaction with the museum staff, as she cannot guarantee that she will necessarily be in her home city to review donation paperwork or conduct other aspects of the donation process. Peggy has a personal assistant, Agatha, whom she trusts to conduct business on her behalf. Peggy instructs Agatha to maintain communication with museum staff, sign donation paperwork, and make the objects available for crating and transport to the museum. In this relationship, Peggy is the principal and Agatha is Peggy's agent. Agatha has full legal authority to act on Peggy's behalf, including to sign contracts that will be binding on Peggy personally.

An agent may have general legal authority to act, or she may have special legal authority limited to certain areas. Agatha may have the legal authority to act in relation to the specific donation, but she most likely does not have the authority to give away Peggy's entire art collection, nor does she have the authority to sell off Peggy's personal property en masse. Further, an agent's powers may arise from a contract or they may be implied by the relationship of the implied agent to the principal's business. Agatha's agency powers may be contained in her employment contract or other written agreement with Peggy, or they may have arisen through their working relationship and are therefore implied and not express.

ANONYMOUS WORK

Under copyright law, an anonymous work is any work where "no natural person is identified as author."[13] Identification of the author is not a requirement for copyright protection, and these works are entitled to the same level of protection as any other work.

When a creation is an anonymous work, it is entitled to copyright protection for a term of 95 years from the date of its first publication, or a term of 120 years from when it was created, whichever ends first.[14] However, if the author or authors of the anonymous work are at any point identified in registration records filed with the Copyright Office, then the term becomes the standard term for single-creator or joint works as applicable.[15] As with other copyrightable works, the artistic creation must meet the requirements of copyright law and, if it does, copyright protection vests at the time of creation.[16]

See also "Copyright."

ANTIQUITIES ACT

Full Title: Antiquities Act of 1906
Also Known As: "National Monument Act"
Citation: 16 U.S.C. §§ 431-33

The Antiquities Act authorizes the president to "declare by public proclamation historic landmarks, historic and prehistoric structures, other objects of historic or scientific interest that are situated upon the lands owned or controlled by the Government of the United States to be national monuments. . . ."[17] In other words, the president is authorized to create national monuments from publicly held lands in order to protect natural, cultural, and scientific features present on those lands. Since its passage, seventeen American presidents representing both major parties have designated 157 national monuments.[18] Whether a president can unilaterally revoke a monument's designation is currently the subject of litigation in the United States District Court for the District of Columbia, arising out of December 4, 2017, proclamation in which President Trump attempted to dismantle Bears Ears and Grand Staircase-Escalante, two monuments in Utah.[19]

Under this Act, a permit is required to excavate archaeological objects or gather objects of antiquity upon federally owned lands.[20] These permits are acquired from the secretary of the department that controls the land, and they are only available for excavations performed for the benefit of "reputable museums, universities, colleges, or other recognized scientific or educational institutions. . . ."[21]

It should be noted that this Act authorizes the creation of National Monuments, not National Parks, though some Monuments have later been converted or incorporated into Parks.[22]

See also "Curation of Federally Owned and Administered Archaeological Collections."

APPRAISAL (AUCTION HOUSE)

When consigning an object to an auction house, the auction house will often provide an evaluation of the object's fair market value. This fair market value is determined by comparing the object with similar objects that have recently sold at auction. Based on this appraisal, the auction house will determine what the object's presale auction estimate is, and it can also be used to set a reserve price.

The appraisal that is prepared by an auction house in contemplation of consignment for auction is distinct from an appraisal prepared for the purpose of obtaining a tax deduction for the donation of an object to a museum. An appraisal made in connection to a donation must meet certain requirements set by the Internal Revenue Service in order for the donor to take the deduction, while the appraisal prepared in contemplation of an auction is a less formal valuation.

Compare "Appraisal (Donation)."
See also "Auction House."
See also "Disposal."
See also "Fair Market Value."

See also "Guarantee."
See also "Reserve."

APPRAISAL (DONATION)

An appraisal "states an opinion about the value, condition, or importance of something," such as a donation to a museum.[23] A donor may or may not need an appraisal of the donated item in order to receive her tax deduction for the donation. Whether an appraisal is necessary should be determined by the donor, not by the donee museum or any of its employees, and the donee museum is not qualified to provide that appraisal according to the rules of the Internal Revenue Service (IRS).

The IRS will only accept a qualified appraisal made by someone properly knowledgeable and meeting other requirements, called a qualified appraiser.

Compare "Qualified Appraisal."
See also "Deduction."
See also "Donee."
See also "Qualified Appraiser."

ARBITRARY MARK

Trademark law categorizes marks along a spectrum of distinctiveness, with marks that are considered more distinctive receiving more protection than those further down the spectrum. A mark's categorization along the spectrum determines whether it may be registered as a mark with the Patent and Trademark Office (PTO), how strong a mark the PTO will consider it to be, and if it requires acquisition of a secondary meaning.

From most protected to least protected, marks are described as (1) arbitrary/fanciful, (2) suggestive, (3) descriptive, or (4) generic.[24] It is important to understand that a term that falls into one category for a certain product may fall into an entirely different category for another product.[25] The highest level of protection goes to marks that are either arbitrary or fanciful. These categories apply to marks that do not describe the product in any way and are considered inherently distinctive.

A mark is arbitrary when its English language meaning is entirely unrelated to the product it identifies. A famous example of an arbitrary mark is "Apple," used to identify computers. Other arbitrary marks include "Absolut" for vodka and "Comet" for household cleanser.

Arbitrary marks have the advantage of receiving strong protection under the law, but they have the disadvantage that the consumer will have no indication of what goods are being marketed without further information through advertising or other means. Arbitrary marks may be registered with the PTO on their own strength.[26]

Compare "Fanciful Mark."
See also "Secondary Meaning."

See also "Spectrum of Distinctiveness."
See also "Trademark."

ARCHAEOLOGICAL RESOURCES PROTECTION ACT

Full Title: Archaeological Resources Protection Act of 1979, as amended
Also Known As: ARPA
Citation: 16 U.S.C. § 470aa-mm

The Archaeological Resources Protection Act (ARPA) was enacted to protect our nation's irreplaceable heritage. The purpose of ARPA is "to secure, for the present and future benefit of the American people, the protection of archaeological resources and sites which are on public lands and Indian lands, and to foster increased cooperation and exchange of information. . . ."[27] This protection takes the form of regulating access to archaeological resources on public lands, forbidding unpermitted excavation or removal of those archaeological resources, and forbidding the sale or other form of transfer of those archaeological resources. Violation of ARPA may result in civil or criminal penalties, including fines, confiscation, or incarceration. ARPA applies to both public lands, meaning lands owned and administered by the United States or to which the United States owns title,[28] and to Indian lands, meaning lands held in trust by the United States or subject to a restriction against alienation on behalf of Native tribes or individuals, with some limitations.[29]

Under ARPA, "archaeological resources" is defined as "any material remains of past human life or activities which are of archaeological interest. . . ."[30] Examples of archaeological resources within the meaning of this definition include pottery, weapons and projectiles, structures, rock paintings and carvings, and human skeletal materials.[31] Materials must be at least 100 years old to qualify as an archaeological resource, and paleontological specimens are not considered an archaeological resource unless the specimen is found within an archaeological context.[32]

ARPA provides guidelines to obtain an excavation permit or authorization for removal.[33] Also subject to ARPA is the curation of archaeological resources that were removed from public or Indian lands pursuant to the Act.[34]

See also "Curation of Federally Owned and Administered Archaeological Collections."

ART DEALER

See "Dealer."

ARTICLES OF INCORPORATION

As part of the incorporation process on the state level, a corporation must file articles of incorporation with the state. These articles are the primary document that dictates how the corporation will operate, and as such, they are one of the most important documents related to the corporation. The requirements of these articles are governed by local law, and therefore the requirements vary across jurisdictions.

Generally, articles will include information such as the organization's name, the name and address of the corporation's designated agent, and requirements for membership if applicable. If it is intended that the corporation qualify on the state level as a nonprofit organization *and* will later apply for federal tax exemption, the articles must also contain language required by the Internal Revenue Service. Failure to include that mandatory language will result in a denial of federal tax exemption.

Due to the fact that articles of incorporation are filed with the state, they are not easily amended. Often, the amended articles will have to be filed and reviewed by the state in a process similar to the initial filing. Additionally, articles of incorporation are a matter of public record and will be viewable by the general public.

Compare "Bylaws."
See also "Agent."
See also "Nonprofit Corporation."
See also "Tax-Exempt."

For a more in-depth discussion, see both "Chapter 8: Nonprofit Corporations and Tax Exemption" and "Chapter 11: Understanding the Various Forms of Business Structures."

ARTS AND ARTIFACTS INDEMNITY ACT

Full Title: N/A
Also Known As: N/A
Citation: 20 U.S.C §§ 971 *et. seq.*

When an object is imported by a museum, there is the possibility it may be seized by the courts if there is litigation against the lender, even if that litigation is unrelated to the purpose of importation for temporary museum exhibition.[35] In order to prevent such judicial seizure, museums have the opportunity to apply for immunity through the Arts and Artifacts Indemnity Program. The Indemnity Program has international and domestic components.

International Indemnity

Created to minimize the insurance costs associated with international exhibitions, the Arts and Artifacts Indemnity Program allows nonprofit museums to obtain protection for objects imported into the United States for the purpose of temporary exhibition. If indemnity is approved, it will be backed by the full faith and credit of the United States.[36]

Indemnity is available for eligible foreign-owned objects imported to the United States during the course of the temporary exhibition, as well as American-owned eligible objects exported for exhibition abroad, preferably when exported as part of an exhibition exchange.[37]

When an American-owned object is on display within the United States, it may be eligible if there are eligible foreign-owned objects included in the same exhibition and those foreign-owned objects are integral to the exhibition.[38]

Indemnity is only available to eligible objects, and some types of objects are ineligible for indemnity. Eligible objects include:

- Works of art,
- Artifacts,
- Rare documents,
- Books and printed materials,
- Photographs,
- Films, and
- Videotapes.[39]

For the most part, objects ineligible for indemnity are those that are generally fragile, such as chalks, pastels, and works on vellum, or objects that are so large as to be difficult to properly crate and ship.[40]

The current amount of coverage available for a single exhibition, the total dollar amount of all indemnity agreements in effect at one time, and the deductible amounts are all available on the National Endowment for the Arts website.[41] Also available on the site are the current deadlines for submitting an application. Applications may not be submitted more than one year and three months before the desired indemnity period, though applicants may choose to submit preliminary statements about exhibitions for which indemnity will be sought up to four years in advance.[42] If indemnity is granted, credit to the Federal Council on the Arts and Humanities must be included in all published materials and other announcements related to the exhibition.[43]

The application demands a fairly detailed amount of information, all of which should be available through the regular exhibition-planning process. Information includes the locations and dates of exhibition, the total number and value of all objects in the exhibition, the expected importation dates, and a statement to establish the cultural significance of the objects.[44]

Domestic Indemnity

The domestic indemnity program is available for domestic exhibitions on view in American museums. It mirrors the international program in almost all aspects. The main differences are as follows:

- Indemnity is available for exhibitions within the United States, without a requirement that foreign-owned essential objects be included in the exhibition;
- Eligible exhibitions must have a total dollar value for the American loans that exceed $75 million, though the amount requested for indemnification may be lower; and
- The indemnity limits are lower than for international exhibitions (though the deductibles are largely similar).[45]

The types of objects eligible and illegible for indemnity, application submission deadlines, and credit requirements are all the same as with international indemnity.[46]

ASSEMBLY BILL 5

See "ABC Test for Worker Classification."

ATTORNEY GENERAL

The attorney general is the top law enforcement agent of the state (or the federal government, when referring to the U.S. Attorney General).[47] In many states, the attorney general is chosen in a popular election, though the position is appointed by the governor or by some other means in a minority of states. The attorney general has a variety of responsibilities, including oversight of nonprofit organizations.

The attorney general's office is often tasked with oversight of a variety of issues concerning nonprofit and charitable organizations such as museums, including registration of charities, oversight of charitable activities, and providing a means to report inappropriate activities conducted by charities. This oversight arises from the fact that museums are considered public trusts.[48] While museums serve the general public, that public does not generally have standing to sue to enforce the museum's legal obligations. That responsibility falls to the attorney general, who has the responsibility to represent the state's and citizens' interests regarding charitable trusts.[49] Under common law, even if the public only indirectly benefits from the charitable trust, the trust is still subject to public supervision.[50] As a general rule, members of the public do not have standing to directly bring an action against a museum.[51]

In many states, the attorney general's office can serve as a valuable resource for charities and museums, providing informative publications and guidance on how the organization is expected to operate in order to meet its legal obligations.[52] Museums can use this resource to provide guidance in areas such as fund-raising activities and trustee responsibilities.[53]

See also "Charitable Trust."
See also "Fiduciary Duty."
See also "Nonprofit Corporation."

ATTRIBUTION, RIGHT OF

The Visual Artists Rights Act provides two moral rights. One is the right of attribution. This right grants the artist of a qualifying work of visual art two related but different rights regarding the work. First, the artist has the right to claim authorship in the work, allowing the artist to insist her name be associated with the artwork.[54] Secondly and conversely, the artist has the right to prevent herself from being named the author of a work of visual art that the artist did not actually create.[55] This means that a museum may be compelled by an artist to use her name when displaying an artwork, listing her as the creator on exhibition labels or in catalogs, for example. It also means the artist can prevent a museum from naming her as the author of works she did not create. Clearly, this right of attribution creates a right that is in line with museum best practices and accepted modes of professional behavior.

The right of attribution does not apply to reproductions of the work.[56] A more potentially complicated aspect of the right of attribution is the artist's right to effectively disown her own work. The Act provides that an artist has the right to prevent being named the author of a work when the work has been subjected to "a distortion, mutilation, or other modification . . . which would be prejudicial" to the artist's honor or reputation.[57] This right reflects on the source of moral rights, which arise from the belief there is a lingering, ongoing relationship between the artist and her artwork. However, it is easy to think of scenarios in which a museum may want to display an artwork that has been distorted in some way, and the right of attribution may prevent naming the artist as the author of the work.

Ignoring the temporal problems with this hypothetical, imagine that instead of a postcard reproduction of the *Mona Lisa*,[58] Marcel Duchamp had drawn a mustache and beard on one of Jeff Koons's balloon animal sculptures. Now imagine a museum wants to display the work, which could be seen as being distorted or even mutilated by Duchamp's addition. The curator believes the work is a vital component to the exhibit, but Koons does not want his name associated with the altered work. This could create problems for the museum, as it could not properly and completely identify the underlying work and its creator without violating Koons's moral right of attribution. This is a dilemma that could conceivably arise in numerous iterations.

This right to disown is limited in certain cases where the artwork was incorporated into a building in a manner that means its removal would constitute destruction. If the artist consented to that installation prior to June 1, 1991, or if the artist and building owner sign a document specifying the work may be distorted or destroyed upon removal, the artist has effectively waived this right.[59] Further, if the work can be removed without causing destruction or distortion, and the owner has made a diligent, good-faith effort to notify the artist and either that effort was futile or it was successful but the artist failed to remove the work within ninety days, the artist has effectively waived this right.[60]

See also "Moral Rights."
See also "Visual Artists Rights Act."

AUCTION HOUSE

An auction house is simply a company that conducts public auctions. They can vary from small local operations to large, multinational companies. For a museum that deaccessions an object and determines to dispose of the object through sale, selling at public auction may fetch the highest price while also ensuring the sale is conducted publicly. However, sale through an auction house does not guarantee the work will remain available to the public, as it is likely the object will be purchased by a private collector. The auction house collects a commission on the sale, generally set as a percentage of the sale price. Whether a sale at public auction is appropriate should be determined by the museum's collections management policy and code of ethics.

Compare "Dealer."
See also "Code of Ethics."
See also "Collections Management Policy."

See also "Deaccession."
See also "Disposal."
See also "Proceeds from Deaccessioning."

AUTOMATIC CREATION

The Copyright Act provides protection to "original works of authorship fixed in any tangible medium of expression. . . ."[61] When a work satisfies the triple requirement of originality, fixation, and works of authorship, then copyright protection is automatically created.

Under current law, no further formalities, such as affixing a copyright notice or registering with the Copyright Office, are required.[62] It is a common misconception that works without copyright notice, generally the "c" within a circle or © along with an author name and creation date, are in the public domain. This was the law for a long time in America, but it is no longer true. Older works that were published with a missing or insufficient copyright notice, however, may be in the public domain and free to use.

While registration is no longer necessary for copyright protection to vest in a work, registration may be required in certain circumstances, notably in order to bring a civil lawsuit for infringement.[63] Further, registration is a prerequisite for certain enhanced remedies in an infringement suit.[64]

See also "Copyright."
See also "Fixation."
See also "Infringement."
See also "Originality."
See also "Public Domain."
See also "Works of Authorship."

AUTOMATIC REVOCATION

Organizations that have been granted tax-exempt status by the Internal Revenue Service (IRS) are required to file annual reporting forms or risk their tax-exempt status. For all tax years beginning after December 31, 2006, tax-exempt organizations that fail to meet this filing requirement for three consecutive years are subject to an automatic revocation of their tax-exempt status.[65] A failure to file electronically when required to do so is considered a failure to file.[66]

Organizations that find themselves subject to automatic revocation of their tax-exempt status may be required to file applicable tax returns and pay any applicable taxes.[67] Because they are no longer tax-exempt, they will not be eligible to accept tax-deductible contributions from their donors.[68]

An organization may regain its tax-exempt status by reapplying to the IRS.[69] There is no truncated application process, so the organization will need to go through the entire tax-exempt status application process as though it were applying for the first time. Therefore, the disadvantages facing the organization, such as paying taxes and being ineligible for tax-deductible contributions, can continue for an extended period. For this reason, tax-exempt organizations should diligently meet their annual reporting requirements.

See also "IRS Form 990."
See also "Section 501(c)(3)."
See also "Tax-Exempt."

For a more in-depth discussion, see "Chapter 8: Nonprofit Corporations and Tax Exemption."

BAILEE

See "Loans."

BAILMENT

See "Loans."

BAILOR

See "Loans."

BEQUEST

A bequest is the gift of personal property (such as money, fine art, or collectibles) made at the time of death through the deceased's will. As such, it is a donation that is made not during the donor's lifetime but upon the occurrence of the donor's death.

A bequest may simply offer the property to the donee, or it may be accompanied by restrictions, which would then classify the bequest as a restricted gift. Unlike with restricted gifts offered by living donors, the restrictions on a bequest often do not permit negotiation to lessen their terms nor dialogue with the donor to clarify intent or interpretation. Therefore, a bequest in the form of a restricted gift may present difficulties for the museum at a later time that cannot be mitigated or anticipated prior to acceptance.

Regardless if the bequest does or does not have restrictions, it is up to the donee to determine if the bequest will be accepted. The donee is not obligated to accept the bequest. However, if the bequest has restrictions and the bequest is accepted, acceptance of the restrictions is mandatory.

See also "Declaratory Judgment."
See also "Donation."
See also "Gift."
See also "Restricted Gift."

BERNE CONVENTION FOR THE PROTECTION OF LITERARY AND ARTISTIC WORKS

The Berne Convention is an international agreement administered by the World Intellectual Property Organization. It requires signatory countries to recognize the copyright in works created by authors from other signatory countries, giving equal treatment to those foreign-copyrighted works as under national law.[70] Berne was originally signed on September 9, 1886.[71] However, the United States did not join Berne until it enacted the Berne Convention Implementation Act (BCIA) in 1988.[72]

The United States delayed joining Berne in order to avoid certain aspects of the Convention that conflicted with longstanding American copyright law. While many of Berne's requirements are similar to established American law, such as the protected subject matter categories[73] and the protection for translations and adaptations as original works,[74] some aspects of Berne required fairly significant changes to American law.

First, Berne required that no formalities be required to enjoy and exercise copyright's protections.[75] Prior to the passage of the BCIA, American authors were required to meet various formalities before copyright protection would arise, including publication of the work with proper notice affixed[76] or registering the unpublished work with the U.S. Copyright Office.[77] The copyright notice consisted of the word "Copyright," the abbreviation "Copr.," or the "©" symbol, accompanied by the creator's name and the year of publication.[78] Berne prohibited such formalities, and today copyright protection arises from the moment of fixation, assuming certain other requirements are satisfied.

Second, Berne mandated recognition of moral rights, a series of rights that arise from artistic works that are separate and distinct from the economic rights covered by copyright law.[79] Moral rights were not recognized by American law at the time of the BCIA, and legislation was drafted to grant this new category of rights. The resulting Visual Artists Rights Act protects the moral rights of attribution and integrity, but not the *droit de suite* (resale royalty).[80]

See also "Automatic Creation."
See also "Copyright."
See also "Moral Rights."
See also "Visual Artists Rights Act."

For a more in-depth discussion, see "Chapter 4: An Overview of the Basics of Copyright Law."

BILATERAL AGREEMENT

Under the Convention on Cultural Property Implementation Act (CPIA), which authorizes the federal government to implement Articles 7(b)(1) and 9 of the Convention on the Means of Prohibiting and Preventing the Illicit Import, Export, and Transfer of Ownership of Cultural Property, the president's designee is authorized to respond to a request from another State Party to enter an importation restriction agreement on stated archaeological or ethnological material.[81]

The importation restriction may take the form of a bilateral agreement between the United States and the requesting State Party or the form of a multilateral agreement between the United States, the requesting State Party, and one or more additional nations (which may or may not be State Parties themselves).[82]

Regardless of the form of the agreement, it may not have an initial effective period longer than five years.[83] If an extension is sought after the initial five-year term, the Cultural Property Advisory Committee, an eleven-member committee composed of individuals representing fields impacted by the CPIA such as museums, archaeology, anthropology, and the international market in cultural heritage objects,[84] will investigate the restrictions and prepare a recommendation for continued action.[85]

A list of bilateral agreements currently in force is available from the United States Department of State, Bureau of Educational and Cultural Affairs.[86]

See also "Convention on Cultural Property Implementation Act."
See also "Convention on the Means of Prohibiting and Preventing the Illicit Import, Export, and Transfer of Ownership of Cultural Property."
See also "Cultural Heritage."

BLUE SHIELD INTERNATIONAL

The Blue Shield is an emblem intended to provide a protective marking on cultural sites found in locations of armed conflict.[87] It was created under the authority of the 1954 Hague Convention.[88] It consists of a blue and white shield set in a light blue circle.

Blue Shield International (BSI) works to protect our collective cultural heritage by the facilitation of international responses to threats to cultural property.[89] BSI trains national and regional experts on how to prevent and recover from disasters, consults with organizations such as UNESCO, and promotes risk preparedness.[90] On the national level, Blue Shield Committees provide a forum in which professionals, local and national government officials, emergency services, and armed forces representatives can work to raise awareness of threats to the nation's cultural heritage and improve emergency preparedness.[91]

See also "Convention for the Protection of Cultural Property in the Event of Armed Conflict."
See also "Cultural Heritage."

BOARD OF TRUSTEES

The board of trustees (also called officers, directors, or some other term) is the group of individuals who oversee a museum's operations. The board ensures the museum is meeting its legal obligations, upholding and furthering its mission, and maintaining its ongoing institutional and financial health for the present and future. Boards are self-perpetuating, and a board remains in existence for the lifetime of the organization it oversees.

As the board is responsible for ensuring the museum adheres to its charitable or educational mission, it is governed by state law, including fiduciary duties. The executive director reports to the board, and the board oversees how its policies and procedures are implemented by the executive director. Board members provide oversight only and are not expected or required to be involved in the daily operations of the museum. This is due to the board's ability to delegate some of its responsibilities to appropriate staff. Board members themselves may bring their own set of skills the organization otherwise lacks, such as knowledge of financial planning, legal training, or connections with community members and potential donors.

The board answers to the museum's members, donors, and served community. However, those individuals and groups generally do not have the ability to bring legal intervention should the board fail at its responsibilities to the museum.[92] When a board fails to meet its obligations, including when it breaches its fiduciary duty, the attorney general may intervene to protect the public's interests.

See also "Attorney General."
See also "Fiduciary Duty."
See also "Trustee."

For a more in-depth discussion, see "Chapter 9: The Board of Trustees and Their Fiduciary Duty."

BUSINESS STRUCTURES

There are numerous types of ways a business may be formed. The business structures are governed by state laws, and therefore the specifics pertaining to each type of business structure will vary depending on the jurisdiction. Not all business structures are available in all states. The specific business structure elected impacts a number of factors related to the business and the parties involved in it, such as the amount of personal liability carried by those parties and how the taxes are collected from the business and parties. Some business structures can only be operated as a for-profit entity, while others may elect to operate as nonprofit and may be eligible for tax-exempt recognition.

The most widely recognized business structures are sole proprietorship, partnership, corporation, and limited liability company (LLC).

See also "Corporation."
See also "Limited Liability Company (LLC)."
See also "Nonprofit Corporation."

See also "Partnership (General)."
See also "Sole Proprietorship."
See also "Tax-Exempt."

For a more in-depth discussion, see "Chapter 11: Understanding the Various Forms of Business Structures."

BYLAWS

Bylaws are the internal document that outlines the rules, regulations, and procedures of a corporation, including a nonprofit corporation. They should outline all necessary operating procedures, such as the number of members on the board of trustees and their terms thereon, the schedule of board meetings, how many trustees must be present to achieve quorum, the powers allotted to board committees, rules related to membership in the corporation, and any other regulations needed to allow the corporation to function properly.

Unlike the corporation's articles of incorporation, the bylaws are an internal document, generally not filed with the state,[93] and therefore are more easily amended to fit the evolving needs of the corporation. Guidelines to govern the amendment process should be included within the bylaws.

Compare "Articles of Incorporation."
See also "Board of Trustees."
See also "Nonprofit Corporation."
See also "Tax-Exempt."

CALIFORNIA ASSEMBLY BILL 5

See "ABC Test for Worker Classification."

CAPITALIZATION OF COLLECTIONS

As relevant to museums, capitalization is the practice of recording the fair market value of an object or a collection on financial statements. The result is that the collection's fair market value is added to the organization's other financial assets[94] to determine the overall financial strength of the organization. This requires a level of recordkeeping that not all museums do (or can) accomplish regarding their collection, even if such recordkeeping would be expected of a for-profit business of similar size.[95]

As an example, if a museum has a collection valued at $5,000, and the museum capitalizes the collection, that $5,000 would be included in financial statements in addition to other funds such as account balances and endowments to determine the overall financial health of the museum.

When collections are capitalized in this way, they may be considered financial assets. As such, they may be encumbered, such as being used as collateral to secure a loan. If a collection (or part of a collection) is used to secure lending such as a loan and the organization defaults on that loan, the collection could be sold to satisfy the terms of the loan. Capitalized collections may also be sold to satisfy other debts of the organization if they are viewed as financial assets rather than cultural property that is preserved and maintained for a public benefit.

Due to the risk of a capitalized collection being sold to satisfy the organization's financial obligations and the fact that capitalization of collections can present a misrepresentation of the organization's financial health, the American Association for State and Local History[96] and the Association of Art Museum Directors[97] both take the position that collections should not be capitalized.[98]

Despite the guidance from these organizations, a museum that is housed within a larger organization may still find itself in a situation in which it may or must capitalize its collections. When a museum is part of a government entity, capitalization may be done by that entity to secure a favorable bond rating or interest rate by using the fair market value of the collection to increase the overall financial health of that parent entity. Similarly, if the parent entity finds itself in financial difficulties, it may look to the museum collection as a source of income. An analogous situation exists for museums housed within university systems, where the collection may be viewed as a potential financial asset to overcome financial hardships or where the ongoing costs associated with housing and caring for the collection seems out of alignment with the greater educational mission and goals of the school.

Per the 2019 update promulgated by the Financial Accounting Standards Board, a museum may not be required to capitalize its collection if it meets certain obligations regarding policies and practices.

See also "Direct Care of Collections."
See also "FASB Update No. 2019-03."

For a more in-depth discussion, see "Chapter 3: Museum Deaccessioning and Proceeds from Disposal."

CATEGORIES OF LAW

There are numerous categories and sources of law. These may be distinguished from one another by the source of the law's authority or the subjects covered. In the United States, which is a common law country, law can originate from a statute or from case law that establishes legal precedent over time.

Table 1.1. Sources and Systems of Law

Source of Law	Examples	Description
Federal Law		Federal law is ultimately derived from the U.S. Constitution, which empowers Congress to enact statutes to address certain limited purposes. When a federal law conflicts with a state or local law, the federal law prevails.
Statutory Law	• Archaeological Resources Protection Act • Copyright Act • Native American Graves Protection and Repatriation Act	Statutes, passed by Congress and signed into law by the president.
	• Constitutional law • Criminal law	Public laws (those related to the interaction between individuals and the government) are collected in the United States Code (USC).
	• National Historic Landmarks Program • Section 106 review	Congress often grants federal agencies broad rulemaking authority, allowing the agency's specialists to determine the best was to address the real-life situations that arise when operating within the confines of a statute. The regulations generally carry the force of law, and they are codified in the Code of Federal Regulations (CFR).
		States and local governments also have statutes, and when those statutes conflict with federal statute, the federal statute prevails unless it can be shown that the federal statute oversteps Congressional power to enter an area reserved for the states.
Common Law		The law that has developed over time from the ruling of judges in prior cases, called precedent. In the common law system, cases with similar facts should have similar outcomes, as judges are bound to previous decisions. The United States' federal system is a common law system, as it is for all the states except for Louisiana (which has a hybrid of the common and civil law system).
State Law		In the United States, each individual state has the power to create their own laws in the areas they control. While federal law generally deals with issues such as interstate commerce, international agreements, and other trans-national issues, state law tends to deal more with issues facing individual states' citizenry, such as education, family law, and contract law. However, the distinction can be complicated and still regularly comes up in litigation.
Local Law	• Local zoning laws • Local traffic laws	Local law is the law regulating an area smaller than a state, such as a county or city.

Source of Law	Examples	Description
Procedural Law	• Federal Rules of Evidence • Federal Rules of Civil Procedure	Laws having to do with the procedure to be followed by the courts and the parties operating within the court system. Procedural law concerns questions such as the discovery process, timelines for filing motions and responses to the same, and other procedural aspects to make the court system function.
Substantive Law	• Intellectual property law • Labor and employment law • Tort law	The general term for areas of law that go to the actual "substance" of the law. Note that there is no substantive area of "museum law." What is colloquially called "museum law" is really a mishmash of numerous areas of law, including corporate law, intellectual property law, contracts law, trusts and estates law, and others.

There are numerous sources of law, which are distinguished from one another according to the source of authority and the topics covered.

In countries outside the United States, especially in Europe, a different prevailing form of law places less emphasis on precedent and gives judges more authority than under our common law system.

Compare "Equity."
Compare "Ethics."
See also "Civil Law."
See also "Common Law."

CHARITABLE CONTRIBUTION

See "Donation."

CHARITABLE TRUST

A charitable trust is an organization in which an individual, often called a settlor or a trustor, gives property to a trustee. The trustee, who holds legal title to the trust property, is instructed by the settlor as to what purpose the property is to be held and utilized. If the beneficiary of the property is an individual or group of individuals, such as the donor's heirs, then a trust arises. When the stated purpose is charitable, then a charitable trust arises. Unlike with traditional trusts, a charitable trust generally does not have named beneficiaries. Instead, the beneficiaries are some indefinite group of people, or simply "the public."

Just as with unincorporated associations and nonprofit corporations, charitable trusts can qualify for tax exemption under the Internal Revenue Code if they meet the Code's statutory requirements.

A charitable trust is easier to create than a nonprofit corporation, and it allows for more protection than an unincorporated association. It also provides more privacy than nonprofit corporations, as its founding documents are not required to be filed with the state and are not subject to public inspection.

Charitable trusts are governed by the trustees authorized by the original settler, as outlined in the original trust document. Those trustees are generally organized as a self-perpetuating board, though the founding document may dictate a different arrangement. Trustees must meet legal and ethical obligations regarding their relationship to the trust, including maintenance of their fiduciary duties. These fiduciary obligations ensure the trustees do not use the trust property for their own private benefit and that they remain faithful to the settlor's intended purpose for the property.

As the beneficiaries of a charitable trust are an indefinite group or the public, the beneficiaries generally have no standing to sue. Instead, oversight and enforcement fall to the state's attorney general. The attorney general can sue to enforce the charitable trust and to ensure the trustees are using the trust property for the intended charitable purpose.

Compare "Nonprofit Corporation."
Compare "Unincorporated Associations."
See also "Attorney General."
See also "Board of Trustees."
See also "Fiduciary Duty."
See also "Prohibition Against Private Inurement."
See also "Tax-Exempt."
See also "Trustee."

CIVIL LAW

Across the world, there are two main systems of law.[99] The civil law system developed on the European continent and today can be found in a variety of forms in nations formerly colonized by European nations across South America and in parts of Asia (such as Argentina, Brazil, South Korea, and Vietnam).[100] In comparison, the common law system derives from the system developed under the English monarchy and can today be found in a number of former British colonies, including most of Canada, India, and the United States.

The civil law system can be traced back to the Corpus Juris Civilis, laws first compiled by the Roman Emperor Justinian I around 600 B.C.E. The civil laws of various countries, such as in France, Spain, and Germany, were further differentiated at later dates by the adoption of other codes. While the specifics of any one country's civil law system can vary fairly widely, a basic tenet is that in the civil law system, the judge serves as the main fact-finder and investigator and is expected to look to written laws for guidance when reaching a decision. Where there is no statute that directly relates to the issue presented to the court, the judge may base his determination on established customs. The "precedent" found in common law jurisdictions does not occur in this system.

Compare "Common Law."
Compare "Equity."

Compare "Ethics."
See also "Statutory Law."

For a more in-depth focus, see "Chapter 2: Ethics and the Law."

CLOSING OF MUSEUMS

When a museum finds it is time to move into the next phase of its organizational lifecycle, a number of important considerations must occur to ensure the museum is meeting its legal and ethical obligations to its staff and volunteers, members, community, collection, and oversight institutions. This is true whether the museum is merging with another existing institution or closing its doors entirely.

Throughout the process, the board of trustees will exert oversight of the museum and the windup process, as their fiduciary duties to the museum will not cease until the entire process is finalized. The fiduciary duties of loyalty, care, and obedience will continue to apply to all trustee actions, requiring that they continue to hold the interests of the museum above their own interests. This also requires that the trustees dissolve the museum in a manner consistent with the founding documents, mission, applicable state and local laws, and IRS regulations.[101]

Museums that have obtained nonprofit status will be subject to their state's nonprofit corporation law, which will govern the process of dissolution. In many jurisdictions, this will require a mandatory vote by designated individuals, the filing of required documents with appropriate government entities (often the state attorney general), and satisfying all financial obligations, including the collection of monies owed and the satisfaction of debts. Finally, the museum will distribute its remaining assets, including the collections, in a manner that supports the museum's mission and nonprofit charitable purpose. This entire process is overseen by the attorney general, who may also require the filing of specific forms or paperwork. In some jurisdictions, the attorney general may have to approve the board's plans prior to the commencement of the winding-up process.[102] In other jurisdictions, the courts may be responsible to conduct this oversight, and the museum will be required to file paperwork, present plans for approval, or in another way subject themselves to judicial oversight.

If the museum has section 501(c)(3) status, additional responsibilities must be met at the federal level. The Internal Revenue Code requires that when a section 501(c)(3) organization undergoes a liquidation, dissolution, termination, or substantial contraction of its operations, it must inform the IRS of that termination on its final annual return (the version of the Form 990 required of the organization). The IRS will require certain supporting documents (such as the articles of dissolution or merger) and Schedule N (used to detail information about the organization's dissolution or merger).[103] This notification process will close the organization's account with the IRS.[104]

Donor restrictions on gifts, endowments, or other assets will remain in effect unless judicial approval to deviate is granted. Other issues may also impede the process, for instance if the museum holds a number of unclaimed loans or found-in-collection objects. Title to these items may need to be cleared, a potentially lengthy process. If the museum owns historic buildings, a historic preservation easement may provide a means to maintain the historic structures while transferring title to a new owner. The State Historic Preservation Office may be able to assist in this process.

The decision to close a museum can be a difficult one, impacting the volunteers and staff, the board, the members, and the community at large. Each situation is different, but once the decision is made, the board can guide the process to ensure it is done thoughtfully and with the museum's obligations upheld and the community supported. Remember that open and honest communication—with engaged stakeholders, staff, members, and the attorney general—can serve to aid the process and make it smoother for all involved.

See also "Attorney General."
See also "Board of Trustees."
See also "*Cy Pres* Doctrine."
See also "Deaccession."
See also "Disposal."
See also "Doctrine of Equitable Deviation."
See also "Fiduciary Duty."
See also "Form 990."
See also "Historic Preservation Easement."
See also "National Historic Preservation Act."
See also "Nonprofit Corporation."
See also "Section 501(c)(3)."
See also "Restricted Gift."

For more in-depth discussion of related topics, see "Chapter 3: Museum Deaccessioning and Proceeds from Disposal" and "Chapter 9: The Board of Trustees and Their Fiduciary Duty."

CODE OF ETHICS

A code of ethics is a document that outlines the core values and belief system of an organization, such as a museum or a professional body. Ethical issues arising in a museum setting may relate to, for example, community served, programs developed and presented, and objects collected. The American Alliance of Museum states that this code should ensure "that the interests of the public will be prioritized and that decisions will be made systematically rather than based on individual judgement."[105] Therefore, the code of ethics serves as a compass, guiding institutional practices and decision making.

The code of ethics should not merely require a museum adhere to legal obligations. Legal expectations governing conduct are a baseline that all museums are required to meet. Ethical standards go above and beyond this baseline, representing the best a museum can do in terms of practices, policies, and procedures. As has been so succinctly stated, "The law is not designed to make us honorable, only bearable."[106] Ethical codes raise museums above the bearable to institutions that can be trusted, can be admired, and are worthy of respect and emulation.

As with a mission statement, a museum's code of ethics is an internal document, and it should inform everything from object acquisition to programming and community engagement to deaccessions. Though it is an internal document, an argument can be made for the publication of a museum's code of ethics, as this encourages transparency and bolsters public trust. It is not, on its own, a legal document. However, the fiduciary duty of obedience requires museum trustees to be obedient to, among other things, the museum's governing documents, such as the code of ethics. Therefore, trustees who disregard the museum's ethical code or other governing documents in the pursuit of their duties may find themselves in breach of this fiduciary duty.

Compare "Articles of Incorporation."
Compare "Bylaws."
Compare "Mission Statement."
See "Duty of Obedience."
See also "Ethics."
See "Fiduciary Duty."
See "Trustee."

For a more in-depth discussion, see "Chapter 2: Ethics and the Law."

COLLECTIONS MANAGEMENT POLICY

"Collections management" refers to every activity undertaken to care for the museum's collections, including but not limited to oversight of acquisitions and accessions, documentation, inventory procedures, access policies and procedures, display, research, pest management, storage, and security. Many of these duties fall under the umbrella of the museum registrar, but input from and responsibility for can also fall under curatorial staff or others. If an activity is carried out in order to "document, care for, and develop museum collections and make them available for use,"[107] then it falls under collections care.

By extension, the collections management policy is the document, or more accurately the collection of documents, that outlines the policies that define the parameters of collections care within a particular museum. At its simplest, the collections management policy is designed to minimize any potential risks to the collection.[108] But looking at the policy overall and all the areas it should cover, the policy actually touches on many areas of care beyond mere risk management, including adherence to the institutional mission, granting authority to museum staff to carry out their duties, providing guidelines within which staff can navigate and act while upholding professional best practices, and providing a framework dictated by ethical standards and legal obligations.

Among the legal obligations impacted by the collections management policy are topics such as proper ownership (including provenance and title) and appropriate deaccessioning and disposal (for instance, adherence to donor-imposed restrictions or proper filing of tax forms when donations are disposed of within three years of donation).

Ethical obligations impacted by the collections management policy include proper documentation of collections objects and proper use of proceeds from deaccessioning.

A collections management policy is highly specific not just to the *type* of museum—art, historical, scientific, children's, etc.—but to the particular museum. The needs of one individual museum will never exactly mirror the needs of another due to differences in founding documents, mission statement, scope of collections, and countless other factors. Therefore, while another museum's policy may be referenced in determining the needs and contents of a specific museum's policy, a collections management policy should never be copied entirely for use in a different institution.

The collections management policy should be created with strict adherence to the museum's mission statement and founding documents. It should also be in compliance with any applicable laws and the current state of professional best practices as promulgated by the appropriate professional organizations. While the collections management policy is not technically a legal document, failure to have one or failure to adhere to one *could* conceivably be used as evidence a museum's board has failed to uphold its fiduciary duty.

Compare "Code of Ethics."
See also "Articles of Incorporation."
See also "Fiduciary Duty."
See also "Mission Statement."

COMMON LAW

Across the world, there are two main systems of law.[109] The common law system derives from the system developed under the English monarchy. Due to English colonialism, the common law system exists in former British colonies worldwide, including Australia, New Zealand, and Hong Kong. Additionally, most of Canada (excluding Quebec), India (excluding Goa), and the United States (excluding Louisiana) also follow the common law system. In comparison, the civil law system developed on the European continent and today can be found in a variety of forms in nations formerly colonized by European nations (such as Argentina, Brazil, South Korea, and Vietnam).[110]

In the United States, law can originate from a statute or from prior case law. The process by which law emerges from prior cases is known as precedent. Under this system, judicial opinions published by the courts are relied on in determining the outcome of future cases. The intention is that in two cases with functionally similar facts, and applying the same law, a similar and predictable outcome should result. Further, some cases carry more weight than others, depending on where they were decided within the hierarchy of the courts system. Precedent flows "down" the courts, so a decision by a state's supreme court will be binding on all lower courts in that state, but a state trial court decision would not be binding on the state's supreme court.

Compare "Civil Law."
Compare "Equity."
Compare "Ethics."
See also "Statutory Law."

For a more in-depth focus, see "Chapter 2: Ethics and the Law."

COMMON LAW PROPERTY

Under the law, there are two types of marital property: community property and common law property. Under the common law property system, property acquired by a spouse remains the individual property of that spouse unless an affirmative act is done to indicate the property is shared between the spouses. For example, if a spouse purchases a car and the title to that car is only in her name, the car will be understood to only belong to that spouse. In contrast, if the spouse were to buy a boat and put the name of both spouses on the title, the boat would belong to both parties.[111]

A spouse in a common law property state may make a gift (of money or property such as artwork) of their own property, as their spouse does not have an ownership interest in it. However, for property jointly owned by the couple, the spouse may not be able to make the gift without the consent of the co-owning spouse. Therefore, best practices would require written consent to be obtained from both spouses.

Compare "Community Property."
See also "Tenancy by the Entirety."

COMMON LAW TEST FOR WORKER CLASSIFICATION

There are two different tests to determine if a worker should be classified as an employee or as an independent contractor. These are the ABC test and the common law test.[112]

Under the common law test, the factors to consider are (1) behavior, (2) finances, and (3) relationship.[113] *Behavior* looks to what level of control the employer exerts over the worker's behavior and if the employer can direct and control the manner and means used by the worker to accomplish the tasks, for instance, when and where the work is done, the sequence followed in completing the work, the hiring of additional workers or assistants, or the purchase of necessary supplies or services.[114] A worker with independence in determining how to accomplish the job is more likely to be determined to be an independent contractor.

Finances considers the extent of control the employer has regarding the business aspects of the worker's conduct. For instance, if the employer provides necessary tools and supplies (laptop, copying facilities, office supplies), reimburses business expenses, and pays the worker a regular amount on a set schedule, it is likely the worker will be designated as an employee and not an independent contractor. Another consideration here is if the worker is free to seek out additional business opportunities outside the employer-worker relationship. If the worker is advertising their services and making themselves available to others in the relevant market, they are more likely to be classified as an independent contractor.[115]

Finally, regarding the *relationship,* if there are written contracts outlining the scope of the work and the work will cease upon completion of a specific task or set of tasks, the worker is likely to be determined to be an independent contractor. However, if the worker receives employee benefits (such as vacation pay or enrollment in a pension plan) or if the employment is ongoing with no set end date or goal, the worker is likely to be classified as an employee.[116]

See also "ABC Test for Worker Classification."

See also "Employee."
See also "Independent Contractor."
See also "Worker Classification."

For a more in-depth discussion, see "Chapter 10: Worker Classification: Distinguishing between an Employee and an Independent Contractor."

COMMUNITY PROPERTY

Under the law, there are two types of marital property: community property and common law property. Under the community property system, property owned by one spouse is communally held by the other spouse. This means that the debts of one spouse may be satisfied by the community property of the other spouse.

Due to this equal division of the marital assets, the property that is brought into the marriage during the course of the marriage, even if acquired individually by one spouse, is owned and controlled as joint property. Conversely, some types of property are still considered legally separate, such as property a spouse acquired prior to the marriage or that the spouse received individually in the form of a gift or inheritance. Community property is only recognized in a small number of states.[117]

A spouse in a community property state cannot effectuate a gift of marital property without the consent of the other spouse. If the nongifting spouse does not consent to the gift, that spouse may revoke that gift at a later date. Therefore, if a donor subject to community property wishes to make a gift, whether it is a gift of money or a gift of property such as artwork, written consent must be obtained from both spouses.

Compare "Common Law Property."
See also "Tenancy by the Entirety."

COMPLETENESS OF TITLE

See "Title."

CONDITIONAL GIFT

See "Restricted Gift."

CONFLICT OF INTEREST

When there is a conflict of two competing interests, such as the interests of a trustee and the museum, the trustee may have difficulty setting aside her personal interests and pursue the action that is in the best interests of the museum. This is a conflict of interest: the interests of the trustee and the interests of the museum. The trustee is in a position that permits her to derive a personal benefit from her official capacity. Conflicts of interest are problematic, as they make it difficult to guarantee the individual is putting the interests of the museum above her own interests.

In museums, a conflict of interest can arise at the employee level or at the board level. For example, Emily, an exhibitions manager, is married to Victor, who owns a company that builds acrylic vitrines. Emily proposes that the acrylic vitrine company become the museum's primary source without disclosing her personal involvement with Victor. This situation presents a conflict of interest, as Emily stands to personally and financially benefit from the museum doing business with Victor. Or imagine Terence, a trustee of a museum, is an avid collector of puzzle boxes. There are a number of puzzle boxes in the museum's collection. Terence pressures the museum's curator and registrar to propose some of the boxes for deaccession, knowing they will be consigned to a local auction house where he will be able to purchase them. Terence's actions constitute a conflict of interest, as he will benefit himself and his collection, to the museum's detriment, through the deaccession and disposal of the puzzle boxes.

To avoid a conflict of interest, museums should have a conflict-of-interest policy. The two most important components of any conflict-of-interest policy are: (1) a clear and unambiguous statement that any actual or potential conflict should be disclosed, and (2) a requirement that employees or trustees impacted by that conflict should be recused from the decision-making process. The policy should also address issues likely to arise in the museum setting, such as whether employees or trustees may acquire deaccessioned objects (often prohibited), how to handle acceptance of proposed donations or offers to sell from employees and trustees, and other museum-specific issues. The conflict of interest policy may be a stand-alone policy or incorporated into some other document, such as the museum's code of ethics.

If a trustee has a conflict-of-interest, failure to prevent that conflict from negatively impacting the museum may constitute a breach of the trustee's fiduciary duty, specifically the trustee's duty of loyalty to the organization, which requires the trustee place the museum's interests ahead of the trustee's own interests.

See also "Code of Ethics."
See also "Duty of Loyalty."
See also "Fiduciary Duty."
See also "Trustee."

CONSULTANT

See "Independent Contractor."

CONTRACT

A contract is a promise between parties that will be enforced by law if either party fails to perform.[118] Remedies for failure to perform vary, ranging from specific performance (a court ordering the breaching party to perform the action dictated by the contract) to monetary damages.[119] Contracts may be oral or written, and may even be inferred in whole or in part based on the conduct of the parties.[120] In order to enter a contract, each party must have the legal capacity to do so. A party will not have capacity if he is under a guardianship, is a minor,[121] is mentally ill or delayed, or is intoxicated at the time of contract creation.[122]

In order for an agreement between parties to become an enforceable contract, there must be an offer, acceptance, consideration, and mutuality. First, the *offer* is simply the offer to enter into a contract, such as an offer to sell a painting or an offer to purchase a vehicle.

Second, *acceptance* is the acceptance of an offer, such as the acceptance to purchase the painting or the acceptance to sell the vehicle.[123]

Third, *consideration* requires that there be an exchange between the parties, either of a performance or a return promise.[124] The person making the offer should have some performance or promise he seeks in exchange for the offer, something that must occur by the one who accepts the offer or sometimes by a third party to the transaction.[125]

Fourth, *mutuality* is the requirement that the parties have a so-called meeting of the minds as to the terms of the contract they are entering. The parties must have a common understanding of what they are agreeing to in order for that agreement to rise to an enforceable contract.[126]

Table 1.2. Elements of an Enforceable Contract

Element	Description
Offer	An offer must be made to enter a contract.
Acceptance	The offer must be accepted. If there is a counteroffer, the initial offer is rejected, and the counteroffer must be accepted.
Consideration	There must be an exchange of performance or promise. If there is no consideration, then a contract has not been entered. This can occur with an unenforceable gift.
Mutuality	The parties must have a shared, common understanding of the contract terms, also called a "meeting of the minds."
Capacity	While not an official element to a contract, the parties must have capacity to enter a contract. Persons under duress, intoxicated, or minors are all examples of those not considered to have the capacity to enter a contract.
Legality	Courts will not enforce an agreement to do something illegal. Agreements to purchase illegal drugs or commit a murder are unenforceable for public policy reasons.

For example, Barbara Bookseller offers to sell a book to Colleen Collector for $50. Colleen accepts the offer. Barbara delivers the book, and Colleen delivers the $50. In this example, a contract has been entered into between Barbara and Colleen: Barbara made an offer, and Colleen accepted. The delivery of the book to Colleen constitutes Barbara's performance under the contract. Colleen's payment of the $50 is her performance, and the $50 itself is the consideration. The parties also have demonstrated a meeting of the minds, in that they have demonstrated mutuality regarding the contract terms.[127]

Compare "Gift."
See also "Equity."

See also "Estoppel."
See also "Statute of Frauds."
See also "Uniform Commercial Code."

CONVENTION FOR THE PROTECTION OF CULTURAL PROPERTY IN THE EVENT OF ARMED CONFLICT

The Convention for the Protection of Cultural Property in the Event of Armed Conflict, commonly referred to as the 1954 Hague Convention (for its signatory date of 1954 at The Hague, Netherlands), is an international treaty that requires its signatories to protect cultural property in times of war. Originally drafted following the widespread damage to cultural property and cultural heritage sites during World War II (1939–1945), the 1954 Hague Convention was the first international treaty to protect cultural property in wartime. It explicitly states that "damage to cultural property belonging to any people whatsoever means damage to the cultural heritage of all mankind,"[128] meaning that damage to *any* cultural heritage site has a negative impact for humanity's collective cultural heritage.

The 1954 Hague Convention defines *cultural property* as moveable or immovable property that is of great importance to all people's cultural heritage, including property important for artistic, historic, religious, secular, or archaeological reasons.[129] Examples of moveable property would include works of art, collections of books, or archaeological objects, while examples of immovable property would include architectural sites or buildings whose main purpose is the preservation and exhibition of moveable cultural property (museums).[130]

Signatory countries are required to respect cultural property within their own borders as well as cultural property located within other signatory countries' borders.[131] Such cultural property sites may not be used in any manner likely to expose them to damage or destruction due to armed conflict, and hostile actions may not be directed against those sites.[132] However, this restriction is subject to waiver when "military necessity" requires.[133] Besides this prohibition on exposing cultural property to hostile actions, signatory countries are prohibited to undertake theft, pillage, misappropriation, or vandalism against cultural property and must prevent such acts.[134] The 1954 Hague Convention outlines further obligations of signatory countries, such as responsibilities during occupation, introduction of the Convention's protections into nations' internal military regulations, and rules regarding the transport of cultural property.

In order to further the Convention's goals, a distinct emblem was created that is used to indicate the presence of cultural property and allow it to be easily recognized.[135] This is the so-called Blue Shield.

As of August 2020, 133 countries were parties to the Convention, including the United State, which ratified it in 2009.[136]

In 1999, the 1954 Hague Convention was supplemented by the Second Protocol, which sought to improve the Convention's safeguarding of cultural property. The Second Protocol supplements the original 1954 Convention; it does not supplant it.[137] Among other changes, the Second Protocol provides guidelines for when the military necessity waiver may be invoked,[138] guidelines for when cultural property may be entitled to "enhanced protection,"[139] and criminal responsibility for certain serious actions against cultural property.[140]

The Second Protocol also established the Committee for the Protection of Cultural Property in the Event of Armed Conflict, a twelve-person group composed of individuals who represent the world's regions and cultures and who are qualified in appropriate professional fields, such as cultural heritage or international law.[141] The Committee has a variety of duties, including oversight of the new enhanced protection category.[142]

As of August 2020, eighty-three countries were parties to the Second Protocol.[143] The United States has not ratified the Second Protocol.

See also "Blue Shield International."
See also "Cultural Heritage."
See also "United Nations Educational, Scientific, and Cultural Organization."

CONVENTION ON CULTURAL PROPERTY IMPLEMENTATION ACT

Full Title: N/A
Also Known As: CPIA
Citation: 19 USC §§ 2601-13

The Convention on Cultural Property Implementation Act (CPIA) authorizes the federal government to implement Articles 7(b)(1) and 9 of the Convention on the Means of Prohibiting and Preventing the Illicit Import, Export, and Transfer of Ownership of Cultural Property.

Under the provisions of the CPIA, the president's designee is authorized to respond to a request from another State Party to enter an importation restriction agreement on stated archaeological or ethnological material.[144] The designee is advised on whether to enter the importation restriction by the Cultural Property Advisory Committee, an eleven-member committee composed of individuals representing fields impacted by the CPIA such as museums, archaeology, anthropology, and the international market in cultural heritage objects.[145]

In certain situations, emergency action may be taken to impose importation restrictions when requested by a State Party.[146] Presidential action requires consideration of the Committee's recommendations, and the emergency action may only last for only five years, subject to a three-year extension.[147]

Additional sections of CPIA concern publication of restricted objects and limitations of importation of objects that left their source country without proper documentation.[148] CPIA also addresses the importation of objects that were stolen from specific categories of locations, including museum collection objects and secular public monuments.[149]

See also "Bilateral Agreement."
See also "Convention on the Means of Prohibiting and Preventing the Illicit Import, Export, and Transfer of Ownership of Cultural Property."
See also "Cultural Heritage."
See also "Cultural Property Advisory Committee."
See also "United Nations Educational, Scientific, and Cultural Organization."

CONVENTION ON THE INTERNATIONAL RETURN OF STOLEN OR ILLEGALLY EXPORTED CULTURAL OBJECTS

In an attempt to establish common minimal laws regarding the restitution of cultural objects illegally excavated, stolen, or exported, the International Institute for the Unification of Private Law (UNIDROIT) drafted the Convention on the International Return of Stolen or Illegally Exported Cultural Objects in 1995. This 1995 UNIDROIT Convention therefore focuses on the problem of international trafficking.

It is the position of both UNIDROIT and the United Nations Educational, Scientific, and Cultural Organization (UNESCO) that the 1995 UNIDROIT Convention should be ratified by member states concurrently with the UNESCO Convention on the Means of Prohibiting and Preventing the Illicit Import, Export, and Transfer of Ownership of Cultural Property.[150]

However, as of August 2020, only fifty-eight states have signed the 1995 UNIDROIT Convention, compared to the 140 member states of the UNESCO Convention. Many of the 1995 UNIDROIT member states are so-called source countries, such as Italy, Pakistan, and Peru. The United States is not a member of the 1995 UNIDROIT Convention.

See also "Convention on the Means of Prohibiting and Preventing the Illicit Import, Export, and Transfer of Ownership of Cultural Property."
See also "International Institute for the Unification of Private Law."
See also "Restitution."

CONVENTION ON THE MEANS OF PROHIBITING AND PREVENTING THE ILLICIT IMPORT, EXPORT, AND TRANSFER OF OWNERSHIP OF CULTURAL PROPERTY

Adopted by the United Nations Educational, Scientific, and Cultural Organization (UNESCO) in 1970, the Convention is an international treaty that seeks to prevent the illicit transfer of cultural heritage, declaring that "it is incumbent upon every State to protect the cultural property existing within its territory against the dangers of theft, clandestine excavation, and illicit export."[151] Countries which become parties to the Convention are required to take action in three areas: preventive measures, restitution provisions, and participation in international cooperation. The Convention uses the term *cultural property*, which it defines as "property which, on religious or secular grounds, is specifically designated by each State as being of importance for archaeology, prehistory, history, literature, art or science" and belongs to a list of enumerated categories.[152]

In the United States, the Convention is in effect through the Convention on Cultural Property Implementation Act.[153]

It is the position of both UNESCO and the International Institute for the Unification of Private Law (UNIDROIT) that the UNESCO Convention should be ratified by member states concurrently with the UNIDROIT Convention on the International Return of Stolen or Illegally Exported Cultural Objects.[154] However, as of August 2020, only fifty-eight states have signed the 1995 UNIDROIT Convention, compared to the 140 member states of the UNESCO Convention.

See also "Convention on Cultural Property Implementation Act."
See also "Convention on the International Return of Stolen or Illegally Exported Cultural Objects."
See also "Cultural Heritage."
See also "United Nations Educational, Scientific, and Cultural Organization."

COPYRIGHT

Copyright is a form of intellectual property. Its primary purpose, as stated in the United States Constitution's Copyright Clause, is to "promote the Progress of Science and useful Arts, by securing for limited Times to Authors and Inventors the exclusive Right to their respective Writings and Discoveries."[155] In general, copyright protection exists from the moment of creation for any "original works of authorship fixed in any tangible medium of expression...."[156] The Copyright Act of 1976 lists the types of creative works eligible for copyright protection, including literary works, musical works, dramatic works, pictorial and sculptural works, and motion pictures.[157] Under current American law, no form of copyright notice is required to secure copyright protection, as copyright subsists immediately upon fixation. Further, copyright provides absolutely no protection for ideas, only works of authorship.

There are a number of exclusive rights that are protected by copyright law. These are the reproduction right, derivative works right, distribution right, public performance right, and public display right. Each of these rights are wholly separate from the physical work, meaning that it is possible to own the work and not own any of the exclusive rights under copyright. Additionally, any or all of the exclusive rights under copyright can be given or sold to a third party by the copyright owner. This process is called licensing.

The length of time copyright protection exists depends on who the original creator of the work is. For single creators who did not make the work under a work-made-for-hire relationship, copyright exists for the life of the author plus an additional seventy years. For works with two or more creators, called joint works, copyright exists for the life of the longest living creator plus seventy years. Longer terms exist for anonymous and pseudonymous works as well as for works made for hire.

Compare "Patent."
Compare "Trademark."
See also "Automatic Creation."
See also "Copyright Clause."
See also "Fair Use Doctrine."
See also "Fixation."
See also "Intellectual Property."
See also "Originality."
See also "Public Domain."

For a more in-depth discussion, see: "Chapter 4: An Overview of the Basics of Copyright Law"; "Chapter 5: Copyright Infringement and the Fair Use Doctrine"; and "Chapter 7: Intellectual Property Licensing."

COPYRIGHT CLAUSE

The Copyright Clause is a section of the United States Constitution that authorizes Congress "to promote the Progress of Science and the useful Arts, by securing for limited Times to Authors and Inventors the exclusive Right to their respective Writings and Discoveries."[158]

While this passage is often referred to as the "Copyright Clause," the section actually grants Congress the means to accomplish the goals of both copyright law (arts) and patent law (science, inventions, and discoveries). The Clause also requires that these protections be of "limited time," thereby prohibiting perpetual copyrights and patents.

The Copyright Clause does not authorize the creation of trademarks, which gives rise to some differences between copyrights and patents on the one hand and trademarks on the other. These differences include their creation and application, including the possibility of perpetual trademarks where they are used continually and properly renewed.

Compare "Trademark."
See also "Copyright."
See also "Patent."

COPYRIGHT TERM EXTENSION ACT

See "Chapter 4: An Overview of the Basics of Copyright Law."

CORPORATION

A corporation is a type of business structure where a legal entity is created separate from the owners. The corporation, therefore, can earn profits, be taxed, enter contracts, and carry legal liability separate from the owners.

Corporations may be for-profit or nonprofit. If a nonprofit corporation so wishes, it may apply for federal recognition as a tax-exempt organization. The creation of the corporation, whether as a for-profit or a nonprofit entity, is governed by the laws of the state where it incorporates.

Compare "Limited Liability Company (LLC)."
See also "Business Structures."
See also "Nonprofit Corporation."
See also "Tax-Exempt."

For a more in-depth discussion, see "Chapter 11: Understanding the Various Forms of Business Structures."

CULTURAL HERITAGE

Cultural heritage, *cultural property*, *cultural patrimony*, and other related terms have similar and overlapping meanings. However, a firm, museum-wide acceptance of each term's definition does not exist, and they are often used interchangeably.

To give some examples of the different terms and definitions of use, consider the following examples. The United Nations Educational, Scientific, and Cultural Organization defines *cultural heritage* as "the legacy of physical artefacts and intangible attributes of a group or society that are inherited from past generations, maintained in the present and bestowed for the benefit of future generations."[159] However, definitions of *cultural heritage* abound, as evidenced by the compilation of definitions prepared by International Centre for the Study of the Preservation and Restoration of Cultural Property, which provides definitions dating from the sixth century C.E. to the present day.[160]

The Convention for the Protection of Cultural Property in the Event of Armed Conflict provides a detailed definition of *cultural property*, which states, in part, that it is "movable or immovable property of great importance to the cultural heritage of every people. . . ."[161] This definition touches on the idea that cultural property may be tangible or intangible. Similarly, but in more detail, the Convention on the Means of Prohibiting and Preventing the Illicit Import, Export, and Transfer of Ownership of Cultural Property defines *cultural property* as "property which, on religious or secular grounds, is specifically designated by each State as being of importance for archaeology, prehistory, history, literature, art or science" and falls into enumerated categories.[162] The difference between these two Conventions may be due to the passage of time between them (1954 and 1970) resulting in an evolution in the term's meaning. Alternatively, or additionally, the difference could be attributed to the different focus of the two Conventions.

In its in-depth discussion of *heritage*, the International Council of Museums states that due to its etymology, "the term [heritage] and the notion that it infers have spread more widely in Romance languages since the 1930s than in the Anglo-Saxon world, which favoured the term property (goods) before adopting the term heritage in around the 1950s, while differentiating it from legacy."[163] This may give some clue as to why the terms *cultural heritage* and *cultural property* often (but not always) are used interchangeably in English.

The Native American Graves Protection and Repatriation Act defines *cultural patrimony* as "[a]n object having ongoing historical, traditional, or cultural importance . . . , rather than property owned by an individual . . . , and which, therefore, cannot be alienated, appropriated, or conveyed by any individual . . . and such object shall have been considered inalienable by such Native American group at the time the object was separated from such group."[164] With its references to property rights—"owned," "alienated," "conveyed"—this definition seems to align more closely to "cultural property," though there are also shades of "cultural heritage" present as well.

As shown by this brief discussion, these terms have a muddled relationship, and no one definition exists for any of them.[165]

CULTURAL PATRIMONY

See "Cultural Heritage."

CULTURAL PROPERTY

See "Cultural Heritage."

CULTURAL PROPERTY ADVISORY COMMITTEE

The Cultural Property Advisory Committee is an eleven-member group created under the Convention on Cultural Property Implementation Act (CPIA). Of those eleven members, two represent museums; three are experts in the fields of archaeology, anthropology, ethnology, or related disciplines; three are experts in the international sale of cultural heritage objects; and three represent the general public.[166] Committee members are appointed by the president to renewable three-year terms.[167]

The Committee has limited functions under the CPIA. These include:

1. Investigate and prepare a report providing recommendations for action in response to each State Party request for importation restrictions;[168]
2. Prepare a report providing recommendations on whether an importation restriction should be extended beyond its initial five-year term;[169]
3. Prepare a report providing recommendations in response to each State Party request for emergency action;[170] and
4. Conduct ongoing review of agreements and emergency actions, especially regarding their continued effectiveness, and providing any necessary recommendations for suspension or amendment.[171]

Reports prepared by the Committee are provided to the president's designee.

See also "Bilateral Agreement."
See also "Convention on Cultural Property Implementation Act."
See also "Convention on the Means of Prohibiting and Preventing the Illicit Import, Export, and Transfer of Ownership of Cultural Property."
See also "Cultural Heritage."

CURATION OF FEDERALLY OWNED AND ADMINISTERED ARCHAEOLOGICAL COLLECTIONS

Full Title: N/A
Also Known As: N/A
Citation: 36 CFR 79

In 1990, new federal regulations were promulgated regarding federally owned and administered archaeological collections in order to provide a minimum standard for their long-term management and care.[172] The regulations place financial responsibility for collections care on the federal agency that manages the land from where the collection was recovered.[173] The subject matter covered includes prehistoric and historic material remains, as well as their associated records, which are recovered under the authority of the Antiquities Act, the Reservoir Salvage Act, the National Historic Preservation Act,[174] or the Archaeological Resources Protection Act.[175]

The regulations cover topics such as object security and preservation;[176] funding requirements and opportunities;[177] appropriate object use, including scientific, educational, and religious uses;[178] and various aspects of collections care.[179]

See also "Antiquities Act."
See also "Archaeological Resources Protection Act."
See also "National Historic Preservation Act."

CY PRES DOCTRINE

Any legal restrictions on a donation (as compared to restrictions phrased in precatory language, which may carry a moral obligation but not a legal restriction)[180] will be enforced by the attorney general. The donee museum cannot disregard these restrictions in future actions. If a museum holds an object that is subject to a donor-imposed restriction, and the museum seeks to break from the confines of that restriction, then the museum must seek legal permission to do so.

The *cy pres* doctrine (meaning "as near as may be") is applied by courts in order to honor the donor's general charitable purpose as best as possible in light of changed circumstances. In general, courts tend toward favoring the continuation of charities. Application of the *cy pres* doctrine permits courts of equity to step in and correct a restriction when certain criteria are met. The donee, such as a museum seeking relief from a restriction, must demonstrate to the court that

1. The donor's restriction had become impossible, impractical, or illegal, and
2. The donor had a general charitable intent for the gift.[181]

This is a difficult test to meet, and a donee should not lightly attempt to do so unless all other options have been extinguished and application of the *cy pres* doctrine is the only means to accomplish an important goal.

If the court is satisfied the donee has met its burden, then the donee may suggest to the court an alternative course of action, which should conform as nearly as possible to the donor's original charitable intent.[182]

Each jurisdiction has a different approach to how the *cy pres* doctrine is applied, as well as how it is different from the similar doctrine of equitable deviation. Therefore, the laws of the specific jurisdiction should be consulted before attempting to pursue this course of action. Additionally, it must be remembered that the *cy pres* doctrine is difficult action to implement, and the donee should not pursue this course of action lightly.

Compare "Declaratory Judgment."
Compare "Doctrine of Equitable Deviation."
See also "Attorney General."
See also "Bequest."
See also "Closing of Museums."
See also "Equity."
See also "Restricted Gift."

DEACCESSION

To deaccession an object is to reverse the process of accessioning, in that the object is removed from the permanent collection with the intention that it will no longer be held by the museum for the public trust in perpetuity. The cause for the deaccession may be due to an internal decision, such as a determination the object does not fit in with the museum's mission, or due to an external decision, such as a determination by a court that the museum does not have legal title to the object and it is to be returned to the rightful owner.

Compare "Accession."
Compare "Disposal."
See also "Capitalization of Collections."
See also "Direct Care of Collections."
See also "FASB Update 2019-03."
See also "IRS Form 8282."
See also "Proceeds from Deaccessioning."
See also "Restricted Gift."

For a more in-depth discussion, see "Chapter 3: Museum Deaccessioning and Proceeds from Disposal." For a more in-depth discussion of the difference between ethical obligations and legal requirements, see "Chapter 2: Ethics and the Law."

DEALER

A dealer is an individual or company who buys and sells works of art for profit. Dealers may have a special relationship with specific artists, promoting the artist throughout the course of their career through special exhibitions, publication of catalogs, or other means. Dealers also cultivate relationships with buyers, including museums.

A number of professional associations relate to the field. These cover geographic areas and also relate to specific areas of art objects, such as prints, antiques, or photography. However, no special academic credentials or training are required to become a dealer, and membership to a professional organization is not mandatory. Therefore, a person seeking to work with a dealer must do their own research to determine if the dealer is credible and an appropriate professional to handle the transaction under consideration. The Art Dealers Association of America

(ADAA) promulgates a code of ethics to which its members are expected to adhere in addition to any applicable laws and regulations.[183]

If a museum deaccessions an object and determines to dispose of the object through sale, they may consider selling through a dealer. Such a sale may provide a level of confidentiality. It also may permit a group of objects that would possibly have been broken up if sold at auction to remain together in a unit. However, selling through a dealer may produce lower profits than selling at auction, and it is not considered as transparent of a transaction as a public auction. Whether a sale through a reputable and knowledgeable dealer is appropriate should be determined by the museum's collections management policy and code of ethics.

Compare "Auction House."
See also "Code of Ethics."
See also "Collections Management Policy."
See also "Deaccession."
See also "Disposal."

For a more in-depth discussion, see "Chapter 3: Museum Deaccessioning and Proceeds from Disposal."

DECLARATORY JUDGMENT

Any legal restrictions on a donation (as compared to restrictions phrased in precatory language, which may carry a moral obligation but not a legal restriction)[184] will be enforced by the attorney general. The donee museum cannot disregard these restrictions in future actions. If a museum holds an object that is subject to a donor-imposed restriction, and the museum seeks to break from the confines of that restriction, then the museum must seek legal permission to do so.

If a legally binding restriction exists on a museum object, including restrictions on its use, alienability, or other factor, but the proper interpretation of that restriction is unclear or open to different interpretations, the museum may seek a declaratory judgment. This is a means by which the court can resolve an uncertainty for the museum regarding the restriction, its meaning, and its application. Unlike other forms of litigation, a declaratory judgment is a preventive measure, where the museum seeks court guidance *prior* to taking action in order to avoid future litigation if the actions taken by the museum are perceived to be at odds with the donor's restrictions.

The manner by which a declaratory judgment is sought differs in each jurisdiction. Therefore, local laws and court rules must be consulted.

Compare "*Cy Pres* Doctrine."
Compare "Doctrine of Equitable Deviation."
See also "Attorney General."
See also "Bequest."
See also "Closing of Museums."
See also "Equity."
See also "Restricted Gift."

DEDUCTION

Taxpayers may be entitled to a deduction for their donations to qualified organizations. The deduction is available for donations of both cash and property. The deduction is generally computed based on the fair market value of the donated items or cash, though this may be modified in the case of *quid pro quo* donations where a substantial benefit is received in exchange for the donation.

In the case of certain types of donations, the organization is required by the Internal Revenue Service (IRS) to provide the donor with a disclosure statement. While the organization is required to provide this statement, the organization is not required to provide the donor with any advice or guidance on how the donation may affect the donor's taxes or how to best make the donation to minimize the donor's tax liability. Donors should always seek the advice of their own tax advisor to answer any such questions. "Deductions are a matter of legislative grace, and taxpayers bear the burden of proving that they are entitled to the deductions claimed."[185] Donors are solely responsible for providing the IRS with the documentation necessary to support their claimed deduction.

See also "Disclosure Statement."
See also "Donation."
See also "Fair Market Value."
See also "Qualified Organization."
See also "*Quid Pro Quo* Contribution."

DERIVATIVE WORK

The right to make a derivative work is one of the exclusive rights under copyright. As with all the exclusive rights under copyright, the right to make a derivative work is independent from ownership of the physical work and is also independent of ownership of the other exclusive rights. The author of a creative work may retain the right to derivative works to himself, or the author may give or sell the right through the process of licensing.

The derivative work right grants the right-holder the exclusive right to "prepare derivative works based upon the copyrighted work."[186] The right applies to all the subject matter categories covered by the Copyright Act. No one other than the right-holder may make any derivative works based on the original copyrighted work.

A derivative work is one that draws heavily on the artistic creation of another. Therefore, it derives from another person's copyrighted artistic creation. Examples of derivative works include translations, fictionalizations, or condensations.[187] In a museum setting, Marcel Duchamp's 1919 work *L.H.O.O.Q.*, where he added a mustache and beard onto a postcard reproduction of the *Mona Lisa*, is an example of a derivative work. Other potential examples would be if an artist were to write a short play or choreograph a dance based on an Edgar Degas painting. These examples take an existing creative work and transform it into a new piece.

Derivative works are afforded copyright protection, but in order to qualify, the new work should be transformative of the original. Copyright protection in the derivative work applies only to the adapted portions, not to the underlying work.[188] Existence of copyright in the derivative work does not affect the copyright in the underlying work.[189]

See also "Copyright."
See also "Fair Use Doctrine."
See also "Infringement."
See also "License."

DESCRIPTIVE MARK

Trademark law categorizes marks along a spectrum of distinctiveness, with marks that are considered more distinctive receiving more protection than those further down the spectrum. A mark's categorization along the spectrum determines whether it may be registered as a mark with the Patent and Trademark Office (PTO), how strong a mark the PTO will consider it to be, and whether it requires acquisition of a secondary meaning.

From most protected to least protected, marks are described as (1) arbitrary/fanciful, (2) suggestive, (3) descriptive, or (4) generic.[190] It is important to understand that a term that falls into one category for a certain product may fall into an entirely different category for another product.[191]

Descriptive marks are the least protected category on the spectrum of distinctiveness. These marks merely describe the goods identified.[192] Therefore, they are not immediately eligible for registration, as that would grant an exclusive right to use a merely descriptive term to one producer in the marketplace.

However, federal law permits registration of descriptive marks where they have "become distinctive" in the marketplace.[193] To prove this, the registration must demonstrate the mark's substantially exclusive use by the registrant and the registrant's continuous use of the mark on the goods for five years prior to the application.[194] Registration of descriptive marks is permitted solely where the mark has become closely identified with one producer's goods, acquiring "secondary meaning."[195]

Examples of descriptive marks include "Optics Outlet" for an eyewear store or "Coaster-land" for a roller-coaster amusement park. The advantage of descriptive marks is they easily convey to the consumer what goods are being marketed. However, they have the strong disadvantage that they may never acquire secondary meaning, with the result that the producer will be operating under a mark that is ineligible for federal protection.

It can be difficult to determine if a mark is suggestive or descriptive. The main distinction is that a descriptive mark merely describes the good offered, while a suggestive mark requires that little extra bit of imaginative interpretation on the part of the consumer.

Compare "Suggestive Mark."
See also "Secondary Meaning."
See also "Spectrum of Distinctiveness."
See also "Trademark."

DIRECT CARE OF COLLECTIONS

The American Alliance of Museums defines *direct care of collections* as "an investment that enhances the life, usefulness or quality of a museum's collection."[196] This definition was promulgated by AAM in order to clarify the term *direct care* as used in the AAM Code of Ethics for Museums[197] regarding the use of funds gained from the disposal of deaccessioned objects.[198]

The definition is intentionally vague so that it may be applied across the range of organizations and institutions that are members of AAM. It is designed to accommodate the needs of organizations as diverse as art museums, botanical gardens, children's museums, science and technology centers, and so on.

Direct Care of Collections Matrix

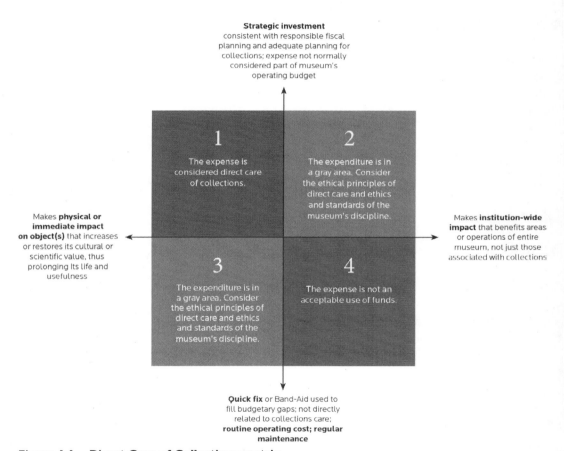

Strategic investment
consistent with responsible fiscal planning and adequate planning for collections; expense not normally considered part of museum's operating budget

1 The expense is considered direct care of collections.

2 The expenditure is in a gray area. Consider the ethical principles of direct care and ethics and standards of the museum's discipline.

Makes **physical or immediate impact on object(s)** that increases or restores its cultural or scientific value, thus prolonging its life and usefulness

Makes **institution-wide impact** that benefits areas or operations of entire museum, not just those associated with collections

3 The expenditure is in a gray area. Consider the ethical principles of direct care and ethics and standards of the museum's discipline.

4 The expense is not an acceptable use of funds.

Quick fix or Band-Aid used to fill budgetary gaps; not directly related to collections care; **routine operating cost; regular maintenance**

Figure 1.1. Direct Care of Collections matrix
Republished with permission from the American Alliance of Museums. This figure originally appeared in the AAM white paper *Direct Care of Collections: Ethics, Guidelines and Recommendations* (April 2016, updated March 2019), where it is discussed in full. Available at https://www.aam-us.org/wp-content/uploads/2018/01/Direct-Care-of-Collections_March-2019.pdf.

In order to aid organizations in determining if an activity would fall within the "direct care" definition, the AAM produced the Direct Care of Collections matrix. This tool balances the potential impact of the proposed expense (a physical impact on specific objects versus institutional-wide impact) and the overall strength of the expenditure (a strategic investment or a "quick fix"[199] to an immediate concern).[200] By plotting the proposed expense within the matrix, a user can determine if the expense would qualify as a direct care of collections, an unacceptable use of funds, or falling within one of two "gray areas." Falling within a gray area does not automatically disqualify the proposed expense, but rather indicates that further inquiry is required, for instance looking to the discipline-specific ethical code that applies to the museum or its own institutional documents such as a code of ethics or collecting plan.

See also "Capitalization of Collections."
See also "FASB Update No. 2019-03."
See also "Proceeds from Deaccessioning."

For a more in-depth discussion, see "Chapter 3: Museum Deaccessioning and Proceeds from Disposal."

DISCLOSURE STATEMENT

A disclosure statement is provided by a donee to the donor so the donor can receive the tax deduction for their donation. Organizations that fail to provide required disclosure statements face penalties from the Internal Revenue Service.[201] While organizations are required to provide disclosure statements in certain situations, organizations are *not* required or expected to provide tax advice to donors. If a donor has a question about the tax implications of a donation, the donor should be advised to contact their own independent tax advisor.

As a general rule, when a museum receives a cash donation of $250 or more, it must provide the donor with an acknowledging receipt[202] that meets the following requirements:[203]

1. Be in writing,
2. Include the amount of cash contributed by the donor,
3. Indicate whether the museum provided the donor with any goods or services that would qualify the donation as a *quid pro quo* contribution, and
4. Include a description of and good faith value for those *quid pro quo* goods and services, if applicable.

The acknowledging receipt should be provided to the donor contemporaneously to the donation but no later than by the time the donor files their tax return.[204]

There is no specific format required of the disclosure statement, but it must be in such a format that all required information is provided, including the donation amount. If a single donor makes multiple donations of $250 or more in a single tax year, the organization must provide the donor with either (1) a separate statement for each donation, or (2) a single statement listing each donation, including the date of receipt and amount, plus the total amount of donations.[205]

If the donation is noncash, the museum must again provide a disclosure statement. This should

1. Be in writing,
2. Include the name and address of the museum,
3. State the date of the donation, and
4. Describe the donated property in sufficient detail that it can be identified and understood by someone not familiar with the type of property.[206]

Also, some donations require a qualified appraisal, which the museum is not able to provide.

Also of special note are *quid pro quo* contributions, which have special reporting requirements. If a donor gives a payment over $75, and that payment constitutes a *quid pro quo* contribution, the organization is required to provide a written statement that explains to the donor that their deduction is limited to the amount of the donation in excess of the value of the goods or services received.[207] The statement must also include a good faith estimate of what the fair market value is for the goods or services received.[208] However, token benefits do not have to be reduced from the donation amount.[209] The disclosure statement may be supplied either at the time it is received by the organization or it may be included in the initial solicitation of the *quid pro quo* contribution.[210]

The guidelines provided here assume the donee museum will put the donation to a use connected to its exempt purpose. If the donation will be put to an unrelated use, there are diminished tax incentives for the donor. The donee museum should have a policy to disclose an intended unrelated use to the donor.

See also "Deduction."
See also "Donation."
See also "Exempt Purpose."
See also "Fair Market Value."
See also "Qualified Appraisal."
See also "*Quid Pro Quo* Contribution."
See also "Token Benefit."
See also "Unrelated Use."

DISPOSAL

After an object is deaccessioned, it may undergo disposal. Disposal is not a guaranteed outcome following deaccessioning, as an object could be retained by the museum in a collection other than the permanent collection. Most often, however, title to the deaccessioned object is transferred to a third party by some means, such as through sale at public auction or transfer to another museum either directly or as part of an exchange. Museum best practices and ethical codes limit what may be done with the proceeds from deaccessioning. Typically, proceeds may only be used for acquisition of new objects for the collection or, in some but not all cases, the direct care of collections.

Compare "Accession."
Compare "Acquisition."

See also "FASB Update 2019-03."
See also "Fiduciary Duty."
See also "IRS Form 8282."
See also "Proceeds from Deaccessioning."
See also "Restricted Gift."

For a more in-depth discussion, see "Chapter 3: Museum Deaccessioning and Proceeds from Disposal."

DISTRIBUTION OF ASSETS UPON DISSOLUTION

A proper manner in which assets will be distributed upon dissolution is a requirement of the organizational test, which in turn is one of four tests a nonprofit organization must satisfy if it is to receive recognition as a tax-exempt organization by the Internal Revenue Service.

The organizational test is essentially a magic word test, requiring that certain provisions be included within the organization's founding documents. Failure to have these provisions in the founding documents will result in a finding that the organization is ineligible for exemption. Bylaws are not considered founding documents for purposes of the organizational test, only articles of incorporation. The other component of the organizational test is exempt purpose.

Under the organizational test, the founding document must contain provisions addressing the distribution of the organization's assets upon dissolution. Any assets still held by the organization at the time of dissolution are required to be distributed to nonprofit organizations with a similar mission, thereby ensuring those assets are permanently dedicated to the organization's stated exempt purpose.[211]

See also "Closing of Museums."
See also "*Cy Pres* Doctrine."
See also "Doctrine of Equitable Deviation."
See also "Exempt Purpose."
See also "IRS Form 1023."
See also "Organizational Test."
See also "Tax-Exempt."

DISTRIBUTION RIGHT

The right to distribute a creative work is one of the exclusive rights under copyright. As with all the exclusive rights under copyright, the right to distribute is independent of ownership of the physical work and is also independent of ownership of the other exclusive rights. The author of a creative work may retain the distribution right to herself, or the author may give or sell the right through the process of licensing.

The distribution right grants the owner the exclusive right "to distribute copies or phonorecords of the copyrighted work to the public by sale or other transfer of ownership, or by rental, lease, or lending. . . ."[212] This exclusive right grants the right owner the ability to control the work's distribution to the public and also prevent the circulation of unauthorized copies. The right applies to all the subject matter categories covered by the Copyright Act. No one other than the right-holder may distribute the work.

This right is subject to the "first sale doctrine," which limits the exclusive right to some extent.

See also "Copyright."
See also "First Sale Doctrine."
See also "Infringement."
See also "License."

DOCTRINE OF CORPORATE OPPORTUNITY

Related to the fiduciary duty of loyalty, the doctrine of corporate opportunity dictates that when a trustee learns of a potential opportunity that the museum could be interested in pursuing, the trustee cannot use her position to privilege from that opportunity to the museum's detriment. The trustee must present the opportunity to the board and permit the board to either accept or decline the opportunity.

The doctrine of corporate opportunity ensures that trustees remain at all times loyal to the museum. Their fiduciary relationship to the museum does not permit trustees to put their own interests above that of the museum in any dealing, no matter how trivial.

Boards should adopt a conflict-of-interest policy defining what constitutes a conflict and outlining procedures to follow when a conflict arises. The conflict-of-interest policy should be regularly reviewed by all trustees, and there should be a procedure in place to ensure trustees understand that policy, such as annual review and re-adoption.

See also "Board of Trustees."
See also "Conflict of Interest."
See also "Duty of Loyalty."
See also "Fiduciary Duty."
See also "Nonprofit Corporation."
See also "Prohibition against Private Inurement."
See also "Tax-Exempt."
See also "Trustee."

DOCTRINE OF EQUITABLE DEVIATION

Any legal restrictions on a donation (as compared to restrictions phrased in precatory language, which may carry a moral obligation but not a legal restriction)[213] will be enforced by the attorney general. The donee museum cannot disregard these restrictions in future actions. If a museum holds an object that is subject to a donor-imposed restriction, and the museum seeks to break from the confines of that restriction, then the museum must seek legal permission to do so.

The doctrine of equitable deviation provides a means for a donee to deviate from donor-imposed restrictions, particularly to deviate from administrative restrictions pertaining to the method of accomplishing a purpose.[214] Unlike in a *cy pres* action, the donee must only demonstrate to the court that a method prescribed by the donor is thwarting the accomplishment of the purpose.[215] It is not necessary to show that the purpose itself is impractical or impossible.[216] Additionally, the doctrine of equitable deviation does not require that the donee demonstrate the donor had a general charitable intent, because the donor's purpose in making the restriction is not being questioned.[217]

Each jurisdiction has a different approach to how the doctrine of equitable deviation is applied, as well as how it is different from the similar *cy pres* doctrine. Therefore, the laws of the specific jurisdiction should be consulted before attempting to pursue this course of action.

Compare "*Cy Pres* Doctrine."
Compare "Declaratory Judgment."
See also "Attorney General."
See also "Bequest."
See also "Closing of Museums."
See also "Equity."
See also "Restricted Gift."

DOCTRINE OF FOREIGN EQUIVALENTS

In trademark law, the doctrine of foreign equivalents provides that foreign words are subject to the same spectrum of distinctiveness as English language words. Modern, common foreign language words are translated into their English equivalent in order to determine the mark's strength.[218] The doctrine is generally not applied to dead or obscure languages.[219]

For example, the mark "AGUA," which is Spanish for "water," would be descriptive when applied to bottled water.[220] However, "AGUA" would be arbitrary if applied to a line of women's clothing. In comparison, "AKVO," Esperanto for "water," *may* be considered suggestive when applied to a water bottle, if the trademark examiner believes Esperanto to be an obscure language.

See also "Spectrum of Distinctiveness."
See also "Trademark."

DONATION

Donations, whether from individuals, corporations, or other charitable foundations, can take the form of objects or financial support. The donation should be made to the donee voluntarily by the donor with no expectation of receiving something in return of equal value. (Donations made with the expectation of receiving something of value in return are called *quid pro quo* contributions.) Donations of objects may consist of items intended for accession into the museum collection, such as artwork, historical objects, or scientific specimens, or items intended to be used by the museum but not accessioned, such as office furniture or in kind donations of food or other materials to use in support of special events or other occasions. Financial support may take the form of donations of cash, stocks, etc.

When it comes to object donation, the donation is distinct from a loan in that title to the object transfers from the donor to the donee (the museum). While a loaned object is still the legal property of the lender and the intention is to return the object to the lender, usually and ideally after the passage of a fixed amount of time, a donation is intended to remain with the donee and the donor transfers ownership in the item to the donee. Therefore, the mere presence of an object on museum property does not constitute ownership of that object by the museum. Possession does *not* constitute ownership.

While donations appear straightforward, complications can arise when the donation takes the form of a promised gift, partial gift, or restricted gift. The terms of the donation can also be murky if it evolves out of a loan and later becomes a donation, since additional paperwork should be concluded between the lender/donor and the lendee/donee/museum.

When the donation takes the form of financial assistance, different considerations arise. Financial support may be "earmarked" for a specific purpose, such as an event or exhibition or to endow a curatorial chair. Alternatively, it may be given as general operating funds, for the museum to use and disperse as it sees fit. Restrictions on use of funds must be adhered to by the museum, so careful consideration should be given as to the appropriateness of accepting the donation in light of any donor-imposed restrictions. As with donations of physical objects, if the financial support is given in return for something from the museum, it is a *quid pro quo* contribution, and special rules apply concerning donee disclosures.

Museums that are recognized as section 501(c)(3) tax-exempt organizations by the Internal Revenue Service can accept donations, which permit the donor to take a deduction on their taxes. This is a means by which the federal government encourages support of tax-exempt organizations that conduct charitable and educational work on behalf of the public, such as museums. In order for donors to claim their deduction, they often need some form of receipt or acknowledgment of the donation from the donee/museum in the form of an acknowledging receipt. Generally, the donor is entitled to the deduction in the tax year the donation was made, which is determined as the actual date the transfer of the item takes place.

The museum should retain all documentation related to the object's donation in the object file, including paperwork indicating both the date the object came into the physical control of the museum (such as when it was provided for inspection and consideration), and a signed and dated deed of gift that should indicate both the date the museum accepted the donation and the date the donor signed over ownership.

Compare "Loans."
See also "Bequest."
See also "Deduction."
See also "Disclosure Statement."
See also "Donee."

DONEE

A donee is the recipient of a donation from a donor. A museum, in accepting a donation of objects or financial support, is the donee. When a museum is a qualified organization, the Internal Revenue Service gives it the right to accept donations for which the donor may take a deduction. This is a privilege granted to the museum, as it provides a tax incentive to donors to support the charitable and educational purposes of the museum.

Donees may be legally bound by the restrictions placed on the donation by the donor, and therefore any restrictions must be clearly stated in writing and carefully considered by the donee before the acceptance of a donation. It should be remembered that a restriction that seems merely inconvenient now may become a serious burden in the future, such as a demand that an object remain on permanent display or that certain objects must be displayed in a specific manner.

DONOR

A donor is an individual, corporation, charitable foundation, or other entity who makes a donation of goods or financial assistance to a donee, such as a museum. When making a donation to a qualified organization, the donor is entitled to certain tax benefits, often deductions.

A donor may place certain restrictions on the use of the donation. For example, funds may be required to be used for a specific purpose, such as for future acquisitions by the museum. Some donors attempt to limit how donated objects will be utilized by the museum, such as requiring objects be displayed together or never be deaccessioned by the museum. If the museum accepts these mandatory restrictions, and they are memorialized in writing at the time of the donation, then they may be legally binding on the museum.

However, should the museum later fail to adhere to the terms of the restriction, it is possible the donor will not have standing to sue to enforce the restriction. This is because enforcement of charitable organizations often rests with the state attorney general. This is based on the theory that because the donation was given for the benefit of the public, the protector of the public's interests—the attorney general—is the authority who should enforce restrictions on that donation. This is not a hard-and-fast rule, however, and courts may find a way to grant standing to the donor, especially if they are still living.[221]

See also "Attorney General."
See also "Deduction."
See also "Donation."
See also "Donee."
See also "Qualified Organization."
See also "Restricted Gift."

DROIT DE SUITE (RESALE ROYALTY)

Copyright provides a series of protections that can be viewed as economic in nature. The copyright owner has exclusive rights to utilize and transform the copyrighted work for a limited time period, and those rights provide an economic advantage to the copyright owner.

In comparison, moral rights arise from the idea that a lingering, ongoing relationship exists between the artist and her artwork that is separate from an economic interest. This ongoing relationship can be understood as arising from reputation. However, there is one moral right that does relate to economic concerns, the *droit de suite*, often translated into English as the "resale royalty."

The resale royalty, as it exists in the European Union, is intended to allow artists to share in the future economic success of their works in the marketplace.[222] Member states of the European Union are required to "provide, for the benefit of the author of an original work of art, a resale right, to be defined as an inalienable right, which cannot be waived, even in advance, to receive a royalty based on the sale price obtained for any resale of the work, subsequent to the first transfer of the work by the author."[223] This royalty is intended to level the playing field between artists and the dealers, collectors, and others who stand to potentially make a profit on the resale of artworks on which the artist may have made little if any profit. While this is clearly an economic consideration, the basis for the *driot de suite* is easily seen as relating back to the basis of moral rights, as it recognizes an ongoing relationship between the creator and her artwork that is separate from and transcends the transfer of title in the work to a third party.

In the United States, the resale royalty only existed in California.[224] The California resale royalty was waivable, unlike its European counterpart, and it applied only to artworks either sold in the state of California or by sellers who resided in the state.[225] After a series of legal challenges, the California resale royalty is essentially nonexistent, having been found to be preempted by the Copyright Act of 1976 and in violation of the Commerce Clause of the U.S. Constitution.

No federal-level legislation grants a resale royalty in America. In its report regarding the feasibility and appropriateness of a federal resale royalty, the United States Copyright Office stated that it "supports consideration of a resale royalty right as one option to address the historic imbalance in the treatment of visual artists."[226] However, the Office went on to state it was unsure that a resale royalty was the best manner to address that imbalance.

See also "Copyright."
See also "Moral Rights."

DUE DILIGENCE

The steps that an individual takes to meet a legal obligation, such as in relation to the purchase, acquisition, or sale of property, is referred to as due diligence. In a museum, due diligence may be conducted in relation to the purchase or donation of an artwork, for instance to ensure it was not illegally excavated or previously stolen. This type of research into a work's origin and ownership history is called provenance research. Such due diligence ensures the museum can acquire a good title to the object and that its acquisition is not in violation of any law.

However, due diligence can also arise in other areas. For example, due diligence should be conducted before entering a contractual arrangement, ensuring the museum is obtaining the best deal available, such as through a request-for-proposals process. Failure to conduct due diligence will not excuse a museum from the obligations of a contract, even if that contract is not in the museum's best interests.

In addition to the law, due diligence can also be understood to arise in the sphere of ethics. If a donor wishes to make a donation in exchange for a naming opportunity, the museum should conduct its due diligence to ensure the proposed name does not conflict with the museum's mission or is somehow associated with an individual or behavior that would be abhorrent to the museum or its public. While there may be no legal barrier to the naming opportunity, there may be an ethical reason not to accept the donation or permit the naming opportunity. For example, imagine that a local businessperson has recently been embroiled in a number of lawsuits related to mismanagement of the company's investment funds, but she wishes to make a financial donation in exchange for a prominent gallery being named in her honor. There may be no legal bar on entering this relationship. However, the museum may not wish to have its gallery forever associated with a name that has been tarnished in the local community. Due diligence, such as conducting research into the donor, could prevent such a scenario from having a negative impact on the museum's reputation in the community.

See also "Provenance."

DUTY OF CARE

Trustees owe three fiduciary duties to their museum: the duty of loyalty, the duty of care, and the duty of obedience.

The duty of care demands that the trustee take proper care of the museum and its assets. The duty places a burden on trustees to be reasonably informed about the museum and to exercise their own independent judgment when making decisions that pertain to the museum.

See also "Duty of Loyalty."
See also "Duty of Obedience."
See also "Fiduciary Duty."
See also "Nonprofit Corporation."
See also "Tax-Exempt."
See also "Trustee."

DUTY OF LOYALTY

Trustees owe three fiduciary duties to their museum: the duty of loyalty, the duty of care, and the duty of obedience.

The duty of loyalty demands that a trustee remain loyal to the organization and to its mission. The trustee must place the interests of the museum ahead of her own interests or the interests of any third party. When a trustee violates the duty of loyalty and places her own interests above those of the museum, she may be guilty of self-dealing. In order to avoid self-dealing, museum boards should have a conflict-of-interest policy that outlines what steps are to be taken when a trustee has a conflict in order to ensure full disclosure of the conflict and that the museum's interests are not compromised.

See also "Conflict of Interest."
See also "Doctrine of Corporate Opportunity."
See also "Duty of Care."
See also "Duty of Obedience."
See also "Fiduciary Duty."
See also "Nonprofit Corporation."
See also "Prohibition Against Private Inurement."
See also "Tax-Exempt."
See also "Trustee."

DUTY OF OBEDIENCE

Trustees owe three fiduciary duties to their museum: the duty of loyalty, the duty of care, and the duty of obedience.

The duty of obedience demands that trustees show obedience to the museum's founding documents, to its mission, and to its charitable or educational purpose that informs its tax exemption.

See also "Code of Ethics."
See also "Duty of Care."

See also "Duty of Loyalty."
See also "Fiduciary Duty."
See also "Mission Statement."
See also "Nonprofit Corporation."
See also "Tax-Exempt."
See also "Trustee."

EASEMENT

When a person has the legal right to use another's property for a specified purpose, that person has an easement. The person who owns the land is the grantor of the easement, and the person making use of the easement is the grantee. There are a number of different types of common easements. These include the "right of way," where a person is permitted to cross your property at a certain location for a certain purpose. A common example of a right of way takes place when a neighbor must cross over a portion of another's property to reach a main road.[227]

Another common form of easement is a utility easement, where a utility company needs the easement to run the utility to the property. Cable lines and power lines can connect from the street poles to the property's buildings due to this easement. Similarly, a water company may have an easement for their water pipes.

Easements are typically (but not exclusively) created by a written agreement between the originating parties. Future owners of the property may be subject to the easement, though there are exceptions.

Compare "Historic Preservation Easement."
See also "Real Property."

EMPLOYEE

As used here, an employee is understood to be a worker employed by a business or organization such as a museum. While a worker may be classified as an independent contractor if specific requirements are met, the default assumption is that workers are employees. Determining if a worker is properly classified as an independent contractor or an employee is important, as this classification has numerous ramifications, and misclassifying the worker can have consequences for the employer.

An employee is hired by the employer to perform a job in exchange for paid compensation. The employee performs the job in accordance with the employer's directions, and the work is conducted using the resources made available by the employer. For example, an employee would use an employer-provided laptop, work at an employer-provided desk, and follow guidelines developed by the employer.

Typically, an employer is responsible to withhold income taxes from wages paid to the employee.[228] In contrast, those same withholdings and payments are not made on the wages paid to an independent contractor.

Compare "Independent Contractor."
See also "ABC Test for Worker Classification."
See also "Common Law Test for Worker Classification."
See also "Worker Classification."

For a more in-depth discussion, see "Chapter 10: Worker Classification: Distinguishing between an Employee and an Independent Contractor."

EMPLOYMENT TAXES

See "Federal Insurance Contributions Act."

ENDANGERED SPECIES ACT

Full Title: Endangered Species Act of 1973
Also Known As: N/A
Citation: 16 U.S.C. § 1531-44

The Endangered Species Act was implemented to address the problem of fish, wildlife, and plants rendered extinct or depleted in the United States due to the side effects of economic growth and development without proper concern for environmental conservation.[229] This was despite the fact that America was a signatory to numerous international conservation agreements, including the Convention on International Trade in Endangered Species of Wild Fauna and Flora (CITES). Species under the Act can be classified as "endangered"[230] or "threatened."[231] The current list of species classified as endangered or threatened is available in the Code of Federal Regulations.[232]

The Endangered Species Act makes it unlawful, with limited exceptions, to import or export regulated endangered species.[233] Other prohibited acts include the possession, sale, or transport of species taken in violation of the Act, or delivering or transporting species in connection with interstate or international commercial activity.[234]

Exceptions may be available where prohibited activities are undertaken for scientific purposes or to enhance the species' survival.[235] Additionally, certain prohibited activities are not controlled by the Endangered Species Act where the specimen was legally acquired and held. The Act *does* apply to objects that contain components from endangered or threatened species. However, such objects may be exempted if they qualify as unrepaired or unmodified antiques.[236]

EQUITY

Equity differs from other categories of law in the remedies available. Civil law remedies mostly consist of monetary damages. In equity, however, the most common remedy is a judicial order to take a certain action or refrain from a certain action. Often, equitable remedies are only available when the granting of monetary damages will not be sufficient. For example, if an artwork is held by a museum and a claimant comes forward alleging the work was stolen, that claimant likely wants the work returned, not merely to be paid the monetary value of the work.

Equitable relief consists of injunctions (a court order to take or refrain from some action), declaratory relief (a declaration by the court of the parties' rights), and an accounting (a court-ordered accounting of monies owed or held by the parties).

Compare "Law."
See also "Categories of Law."
See also "*Cy Pres* Doctrine."
See also "Declaratory Judgment."
See also "Doctrine of Equitable Deviation."

ESTIMATE

When an object is consigned to an auction house for sale, the auction house will determine a low and high estimate of what it believes is the range of prices the object will sell for. These estimates are based on the appraisal the auction house prepared, which in turn is based on the fair market value. Unlike the reserve price, the estimate is public information.

See also "Appraisal (Auction House)."
See also "Fair Market Value."
See also "Guarantee."
See also "Reserve."

ESTOPPEL

When an individual has previously made a certain statement or undertaken certain conduct, they may later be prevented (estopped) from making a contrary statement or taking a contrary action. This legal principle of estoppel (or equitable estoppel) enforces a certain level of fairness into legal proceedings that may otherwise not exist. Estoppel may require that the affected party have reasonably relied on the words or actions of the other party to their own detriment.

See also "Equity."
See also "Promised Gift."

ETHICS

Ethics are the aspirational principles or value systems that govern a group's behavior. Unlike the law, which has an enforcement mechanism built in through the legal system, ethics are largely unenforceable except through the self-policing by the group that adopts the particular ethical code.

In the museum profession, various professional organizations promulgate codes of ethics that are used to disseminate and publicize the behavior the organization thinks its member-professionals and member-museums should uphold. Individual museums may also adopt codes of ethics for their own internal application.

Compare "Equity."
Compare "Law."
See also "Categories of Law."
See also "Code of Ethics."

For a more in-depth discussion, see "Chapter 2: Ethics and the Law."

EXEMPT PURPOSE

Exempt purpose is a requirement of the organizational test, which in turn is one of four tests a nonprofit organization must satisfy if it is to receive recognition as a tax-exempt organization by the Internal Revenue Service.

The organizational test is essentially a magic word test, requiring that certain provisions are found within the organization's founding documents. Failure to have these provisions in the founding documents will result in a finding that the organization is ineligible for exemption. Bylaws are not considered founding documents for purposes of the organizational test, only articles of incorporation. The other component of the organizational test is the distribution of assets upon dissolution.

Under the exempt purpose requirement, the purpose of the organization must meet the limited stated purposes available in the Internal Revenue Code (IRC). Specifically, the purpose must be one of the exempt purposes found in IRC section 501(c)(3):

1. religious,
2. charitable,
3. scientific,
4. testing for public safety,
5. literary, or
6. educational.[237]

Of these, most museums fall under the categories of charitable and/or educational. If the organization's founding documents permit activities outside of the limited list of nonexempt purposes, the organization will fail this component of the organizational test and will be deemed nonexempt by the IRS.

See also "Articles of Incorporation."
See also "Bylaws."
See also "Distribution of Assets upon Dissolution."
See also "IRS Form 1023."
See also "Nonprofit Corporation."
See also "Organizational Test."
See also "Section 501(c)(3)."
See also "Tax-Exempt."

FACTS-AND-CIRCUMSTANCES TEST

In order to determine whether a section 501(c)(3) organization qualifies as a public charity, the organization can seek to demonstrate it receives sufficient public support. If the organization is unable to meet the thirty-three and ⅓ percent support test, it may still be able to obtain or retain public charity status by meeting the facts-and-circumstances test. Under this test, the organization must inform the IRS that it is, in fact, operating as a charity (and not a private foundation) and that the organization is actively seeking to increase its public support to the 33⅓ percent threshold.[238] The IRS will then determine whether the organization can retain its public charity status.[239]

See also "Public Charity."
See also "Section 501(c)(3)."
See also "Thirty-Three and ⅓ Percent Support Test."

FAIR MARKET VALUE

The fair market value of an object is the selling price the object would receive on the open market.[240] It assumes the buyer and seller are willingly entering the transaction, both have reasonable knowledge of all relevant facts to the transaction, and neither is required to act.[241] Restrictions on the future use of the property, such as a requirement that it only be used in a certain manner or within certain limited situations, may negatively impact the fair market value.[242]

A qualified organization that must supply a fair market value to a donor is permitted by the Internal Revenue Service to use any reasonable method to estimate that value, so long as the organization exerts good faith in the selection and application of the estimation method.[243] However, some specific rules do apply regarding valuation. First, donations of cash are valued at the exact dollar amount unless the donor received something of substantial value in exchange for the cash gift, known as a *quid pro quo* contribution. Second, donations of art may be required to have a qualified appraisal prepared, and in those situations the fair market value is set by the qualified appraiser.

See also "Disclosure Statement."
See also "Donation."
See also "Qualified Appraisal."
See also "Qualified Appraiser."
See also "Qualified Organization."
See also "*Quid Pro Quo* Contribution."

FAIR USE DOCTRINE

The fair use doctrine is a limitation on the exclusive rights granted to copyright owners.[244] Fair use is an affirmative defense to copyright infringement, meaning an alleged infringement on copyright may be found to be fair if the accused infringer raises and proves the fair use defense. The Copyright Act provides that fair use purposes include, but are not limited to, "criticism, comment, news reporting, teaching . . . , scholarship, or research. . . ."[245] This is not an exhaustive list, merely illustrative.

Determination of whether a use is fair is very fact-specific, and the facts of each situation must be examined on a case-by-case basis. The factors a court will consider in order to determine if a use is fair include:

1. "the purpose and character of the use, including whether such use is of a commercial nature or is for nonprofit educational purposes";[246]
2. "the nature of the copyrighted work";[247]
3. "the amount and substantiality of the portion used in relation to the copyrighted work as a whole; and"[248]
4. "the effect of the use upon the potential market for or value of the copyrighted work."[249]

These four factors constitute a balancing test. This means the factors are considered as a whole, and no one factor, including nonprofit educational use, will guarantee a finding of fair use.[250]

See also "Copyright."
See also "Infringement."
See also "Orphaned Works (Copyright)."

For a more in-depth discussion, see "Chapter 5: Copyright Infringement and the Fair Use Doctrine."

FANCIFUL MARK

Trademark law categorizes marks along a spectrum of distinctiveness, with marks that are considered more distinctive receiving more protection than those further down the spectrum. A mark's categorization along the spectrum determines if it may be registered as a mark with the Patent and Trademark Office (PTO), how strong a mark the PTO will consider it to be, and if it requires acquisition of a secondary meaning.

From most protected to least protected, marks are described as (1) arbitrary/fanciful, (2) suggestive, (3) descriptive, or (4) generic.[251] It is important to understand that a term that falls into one category for a certain product may fall into an entirely different category for another product.[252] The highest level of protection goes to marks that are either arbitrary or fanciful. These categories apply to marks that do not describe the product in any way and are considered inherently distinctive.

A mark is fanciful when it is composed of words invented for use as a mark. The common example of a fanciful mark is "KODAK," a word invented specifically to market photography products. Other examples of fanciful marks are "EXXON," "REEBOK," or "XEROX."

Fanciful marks have the advantage of receiving strong protection under the law, but they have the disadvantage that the consumer will have no indication of what goods are being marketed without further information through advertising or other means. Fanciful marks may be registered with the PTO on their own strength.[253]

Compare "Arbitrary Mark."
See also "Spectrum of Distinctiveness."
See also "Trademark."

FASB UPDATE NO. 2019-03

The Financial Accounting Standards Board (FASB) is a private sector (nongovernmental) organization that establishes the professional standards of financial accounting. These standards govern how the financial reports of nongovernmental organizations are prepared. The Securities and Exchange Commission and the American Institute of Certified Public Accountants both recognize FASB-promulgated standards as the official authority in the proper preparation of financial reports.[254] Its official mission is "to establish and improve financial accounting and reporting standards to provide useful information to investors and other users of financial reports and educate stakeholders on how to most effectively understand and implement those standards."[255] The Board's Accounting Standards Codification provides these standards for accounting and reporting.[256]

Prior to 2019, FASB recognized the museum professional practice not to capitalize objects held in the permanent collection.[257] In acknowledgment of that professional practice, FASB did not require that a museum "recognize contributions of works of art, historical treasures, and similar assets if the donated items are added to collections"[258] when specified conditions were met. These were that the collections had to be (1) "held for public exhibition, education, or research in furtherance of public service rather than financial gain," (2) "protected, kept unencumbered, cared for, and preserved," and (3) "subject to an organizational policy [for instance, a collections management policy] that requires the proceeds from sales of collection items to be used to acquire other items for collections."[259] Notably, while FASB was seeking to keep accounting policies in alignment with museum professional practices, the last requirement under Statement No. 116 was not reflective of the profession as a whole.

In its *Code of Ethics for Museums*, the American Alliance of Museums permitted proceeds from deaccessioning to be used for acquisitions or direct care of collections.[260] Likewise, the American Association for State and Local History permits its members to use the proceeds from deaccessioning for acquisitions or the direct care of collections.[261] However, the Association of Art Museum Directors took a different approach, requiring that funds earned from deaccessioning (and income earned from those funds) could only be used for the acquisition of new collection objects.[262] The AAMD policy made no provision for direct care of collections from deaccessioning proceeds.[263] Therefore, while the third prong of the pre-2019 conditions were in alignment with the AAMD policy, it was not reflective of the best practices and ethical codes promulgated by AAM and AASLH.

In 2019, FASB issued Update No. 2019-03 to align its definition of *collections* with AAM's *Code of Ethics for Museums*. Under the new definition, FASB requires that a museum "disclose its policy for the use of proceeds from when collection items are deaccessioned. . . ."[264] Further, if the museum's policy "allows proceeds from deaccessioned collection items to be used for direct care, it should disclose its definition of the term direct care."[265] The impact of Update No. 2019-03 is that proceeds from deaccessioning may be used for both acquisition of new objects *and* direct care of existing collections without the museum being required to capitalize its collections, assuming all disclosure requirements are met. This modifies the third prong of the conditions, leaving the other two prongs intact.[266]

See also "Collections Management Policy."
See also "Deaccession."
See also "Direct Care of Collections."
See also "Disposal."
See also "Proceeds from Deaccessioning."

FEDERAL INSURANCE CONTRIBUTIONS ACT

Full title: N/A
Also known as: FICA, "Payroll Tax"
Citation: 26 U.S.C. §§ 3101 *et. seq.*

The Federal Insurance Contributions Act, sometimes called payroll taxes or employment taxes, are federal taxes paid to fund Social Security and Medicare. These funds provide benefits for retirees, persons with disabilities, and minors.

At the time of this writing,[267] employees contribute 6.2 percent of their gross wages toward the Social Security tax and 1.45 percent of their gross wages to the Medicare tax. The employer matches this amount, paying the other half of the total tax. This brings an employee's total contribution to Social Security to 12.4 percent of their gross wages and their total contribution to Medicare to 2.9 percent.

Independent contractors do not have matching contributions from the employer and are therefore responsible for 100 percent of their contributions under the Self-Employment Contributions Act (26 USC § 1401-03). In other words, employers have no mandatory payroll taxes on wages paid to independent contractors. Instead, the independent contractor is responsible to pay 15.3 percent of their net income from self-employment to cover their own contributions to Social Security and Medicare.

Tax rates, maximum earnings limits, and other issues that can impact an individual's owed taxes can vary based on the taxable year and other, personal factors. Consulting with a knowledgeable professional is recommended.

See also "ABC Test for Worker Classification."
See also "Common Law Test for Worker Classification."
See also "Employee."
See also "Independent Contractor."

For a more in-depth discussion, see "Chapter 10: Worker Classification: Distinguishing between an Employee and an Independent Contractor."

FEDERAL LAW

See "Categories of Law."

FEE SIMPLE

Under the types of ownership available for real property, the fee simple (also called fee simple absolute) is perhaps the most common. With a fee simple, the owner has the right to use and disburse the property as they see fit. In other words, the owner may sell the property, make changes and alterations, or leave it to heirs.

A fee simple interest may be owned by one person or by multiple people. When the property is owned by multiple people, they are all listed (named) on the deed as having a fee simple interest in the property. How their ownership is treated will vary, depending on if the relationship is a joint tenancy, tenancy by the entirety, or a tenancy in common.[268] These different types of tenancy illustrate that the co-owners in the real property do not have an ability to exercise absolute ownership control over the property. Instead, they share the rights of ownership with the other co-owners. That treatment will impact an owner's ability to sell or donate a property in its entirety.

Compare "Future Interest."
Compare "Life Estate."
See also "Joint Tenancy."
See also "Real Property."
See also "Tenancy by the Entirety."
See also "Tenancy in Common."

FIDUCIARY DUTY

Trustees, as fiduciaries, owe a heightened duty to the organization on whose board they serve. Fiduciary duty is a high standard of care under the law. It requires that trustees place the interests of the organization above their own interests. The fiduciary duty prohibits the trustees from profiting from their relationship to the museum. Trustees are also required to ensure that the museum's activities and properties do not stray from the museum's charitable or educational purpose, which derives from its founding documents and mission statement and in turn informs its nonprofit status and tax exemption.

The three fiduciary duties owed by a trustee to her museum are the duty of loyalty, the duty of care, and the duty of obedience.

See also "Articles of Incorporation."
See also "Duty of Care."
See also "Duty of Loyalty."
See also "Duty of Obedience."
See also "Mission Statement."
See also "Nonprofit Corporation."
See also "Tax-Exempt."
See also "Trustee."

For a more in-depth discussion, see "Chapter 9: The Board of Trustees and Their Fiduciary Duty."

FINANCIAL ACCOUNTING STANDARDS BOARD

See "FASB Update 2019-03."

FIRST AMENDMENT

See "Freedom of Speech."

FIRST SALE DOCTRINE

The first sale doctrine is a limitation of certain exclusive rights under copyright. It permits the free alienation of goods and the public display of legal copies. The first sale doctrine provides that even without ownership of copyright, the owner of a legal copy of a creative work has certain rights regarding that copy once the first sale is completed, meaning once legal ownership of the copy is transferred.

Regarding the free alienability of goods, once ownership in a particular authorized copy of the copyrighted work is transferred, the copyright owner loses all future control over that particular copy.[269] For example, once an authorized copy (meaning, legally produced and sold) of a book is sold, the copyright owner cannot prohibit the owner of the book from lending it, destroying it, or even reselling it. However, this does not give the book owner the right to make new copies of the book, as the first sale doctrine does not impact the copyright owner's other exclusive rights, including the reproduction right. This is what permits you to purchase a book, loan it to friends, sell it, or throw it away. However, you cannot photocopy or make digital scans of the book and sell those reproductions.

Additionally, the first sale doctrine permits the owner of a legal copy to publicly display that copy without the copyright owner's permission.[270] Further, the legal owner may authorize others to display that copy.[271] This display does not infringe the copyright holder's exclusive right of public display.[272] Therefore, a museum can display a legally obtained painting and loan it to another institution to display without the copyright owner's permission. However, permission (in the form of a license) is still necessary to publish a copy of the painting in an exhibition catalog.

The necessary elements that must exist for the first sale doctrine to apply are: (1) the copyright owner authorized the legally made copy; (2) the copyright owner authorized the transfer in ownership; (3) the owner of the copy is the legal owner; and (4) the owner of the copy is putting the copy to a use that solely impacts the distribution right.

There are limitations to the first sale doctrine, particularly in regard to software and phonorecords.[273] However, the limitation carves out an exception for nonprofit purposes by libraries and nonprofit educational institutions.[274] Note that this only applies to copies that were legally made. The exception does not apply to illegally made copies, even if they are made by a nonprofit educational institution.

See also "Copyright."
See also "Infringement."

FIXATION

Fixation is one of the statutory requirements to obtain copyright protection. According to the Copyright Act, protection is available to "original works of authorship fixed in any tangible medium of expression. . . ."[275] Therefore, works that are not "fixed" are not eligible for copyright.

The statute states a work is fixed "when its embodiment in a copy or phonorecord, by or under the authority of the author, is sufficiently permanent or stable to permit it to be perceived, reproduced, or otherwise communicated for a period of more than transitory duration."[276] In other words, the work must be fixed in a permanent medium wherein it may be perceived, reproduced, or communicated.

Notice that the statute does not require the work to be fixed in a manner that humans can perceive or understand. A digital artwork can be stored in the ones and zeroes of a computer hard drive. A song can be stored on a magnetic tape deck. It does not matter that a machine is necessary to interpret that stored information into visual or audio waves understandable to a human's senses.

This also means that ephemeral art that is not documented may not be entitled to copyright protection, as it is not fixed.

See also "Automatic Creation."
See also "Copyright."
See also "Originality."
See also "Works of Authorship."

FOUND-IN-COLLECTION

The term *found-in-collection* does not have a consistent definition in the museum profession, and it is often used interchangeably with the term *undocumented object*. A strong argument has been made that found-in-collection objects should be defined as undocumented objects whose status within the museum remains unclear even after all attempts have been made to reconcile them with all records, including collection object records and loan files.[277] This definition would distinguish found-in-collection objects from undocumented objects.[278]

With found-in-collection objects, there is no evidence available in museum records or elsewhere to indicate they originally entered the museum as a loan or in some other manner where title was retained by some outside party.[279] With these objects, the museum's possession of the object, for a continuous time and without claims of ownership by others, suggests that title transferred to the museum when the object arrived.[280] However, other possibilities exist, such as the object was brought in for research or authentication and not claimed by its owner.

The defining characteristic of these found-in-collection objects is that they lack documentation to indicate how they entered the museum or were added to the collection.[281] Therefore, it can be difficult for the museum to transfer ownership, such as after a deaccession.[282] The museum cannot produce evidence it holds title to the object, and therefore it cannot guarantee to a purchaser that a claim of ownership will not be brought in the future. Additional issues affecting copyright, ability to display, ability to loan, accessibility to researchers and academics, or the right to perform conservation may also exist.

Compare "Old Loans."
Compare "Undocumented Object."
See also "Temporary Custody."

FRACTIONAL GIFT

See "Partial Gift."

FREEDOM OF SPEECH

The First Amendment of the U.S. Constitution provides:

> Congress shall make no law respecting an establishment of religion, or prohibiting the free exercise thereof; or abridging the freedom of speech, or of the press; or the right of the people peaceably to assemble, and to petition the Government for a redress of grievances.[283]

Among the numerous freedoms contained in this amendment, many considered foundational to American civic society, is the freedom of speech. The freedom of speech is a protection from government limitations on speech. It does not protect repercussions in the free market or from the general public. It also does not guarantee a right to speak in private spaces. Rather, what the freedom of speech protects is that if a citizen chooses to engage in speech (whether it is an actual statement or some other form of expressive speech), the government may not impede that speech or penalize the speaker.

"Speech" as understood here covers a wide range of expression. The First Amendment protects not just spoken and written words, but also expressive conduct and symbolic expression. Artists may engage in expressive conduct in the works they create, for instance in dance, theater, or performance art. So long as the expressive conduct is communicating a message that would receive First Amendment protection, the form of the expressive conduct is largely irrelevant.[284]

The freedom of speech is not absolute. There are a number of categories of speech that are unprotected and may be subject to government regulation, including obscenity, so-called fighting words, defamation, and child pornography.[285]

See also "Obscenity."

FUNCTIONALITY DOCTRINE

Under the Lanham Act, a producer may receive federal registration for a mark that identifies the source of goods in the marketplace, so long as the mark meets statutory requirements. The federal trademark statute defines a trademark as "any word, name, symbol, or device, or any combination thereof [which is used] to identify and distinguish . . . goods. . . ."[286] This has been interpreted by the courts to be a broad statement, meaning that any mark used to distinguish goods may be used as a trademark.[287]

There is a limitation to this, however. The functionality doctrine prevents a functional component of the goods to serve as a mark. This goes to one of the purposes of trademark law, namely "to promote competition by protecting a firm's reputation. . . ."[288] If a producer could trademark a product's functional features, those features could essentially be protected by the producer's trademark monopoly forever.[289] This stifles competition and is a disadvantage to the consumer.

Imagine, for instance, a producer designs a new type of crochet hook that features a redesigned tip that results in a smoother crocheting motion, making it easier for the user to manipulate the thread or yarn. The producer could apply for a patent to protect the new design for a term of years, after which the design would become available to everyone. This encourages competition and offers the consumer a greater source of comparable goods while also granting the original producer/inventor a limited-time monopoly. If, however, the producer were permitted to obtain a trademark for the design, that trademark could be extended every ten years for as long as the design was used in the marketplace, preventing any competitors from ever adopting the improved design and limiting consumers' choices. The functionality doctrine prohibits this from occurring.

Now, instead imagine that a crochet hook producer only makes its hooks in a distinctive lime-green color. The producer is the only one in the marketplace who uses the color, the color has no functional purpose, and the color clearly identifies the crochet hooks as being manufactured by the producer. In other words, the lime-green color is utilized as a trademark in the marketplace. It is not functional, as it is not "essential to the use or purpose of the article," and it has no impact on the crochet hook's cost or quality.[290] The functionality doctrine would permit the lime-green color to be registered as a trademark.

Compare "Patent."
See also "Spectrum of Distinctiveness."
See also "Trade Dress."
See also "Trademark."

FUTURE INTEREST

There are a number of different manners by which to own real property. A future interest is, as the name suggests, an ownership right that will come into force at some future point. It is generally triggered by an event, such as the death of an identified party. It is possible that the future interest could be revoked. A future interest may be created in an instrument such as a will or trust.

For example, Octavia owns a piece of property. Octavia is a lifelong supporter of Museum and wants to leave the property to Museum. However, Octavia also wants her spouse, Simon, to be able to continue to live in the property until his own passing. Octavia could draft a will in which, upon her death, Simon gains a life estate in the property, the remainder to go to Museum upon Simon's death. In this example, Museum has a future interest in the property and will gain legal ownership of the property when Simon dies.

During Octavia's lifetime, Octavia retains the right to amend her will. Therefore, while Museum may know the will's contents, Octavia is permitted to change the terms of the will during her lifetime and may, if she so wishes, remove Museum from the will. This would mean Museum no longer has a future interest in the property. However, if Octavia keeps the provision in her will, once Octavia dies, Museum's future interest is established and cannot be amended by another party. Upon Octavia's death, Museum will gain its property interest, and that interest will be fully realized upon the death of Simon.[291]

See also "Fee Simple."
See also "Life Estate."
See also "Real Property."

GENERIC MARK

Trademark law categorizes marks along a spectrum of distinctiveness, with marks that are considered more distinctive receiving more protection than those further down the spectrum. A mark's categorization along the spectrum determines whether it may be registered as a mark with the Patent and Trademark Office (PTO), how strong a mark the PTO will consider it to be, and whether it requires acquisition of a secondary meaning.

From most protected to least protected, marks are described as (1) arbitrary/fanciful, (2) suggestive, (3) descriptive, or (4) generic.[292] It is important to understand that a term that falls into one category for a certain product may fall into an entirely different category for another product.[293]

Generic marks are those that consist of the common descriptor of the product.[294] These marks are never eligible for trademark registration or protection.[295] No amount of acquired secondary meaning, no amount of money spent on advertising, and no term of years the mark was in use will change the fact the mark is ineligible for registration and not entitled to protection. This is to prevent a producer from having a monopoly in the marketplace over the use of a generic term.[296]

A term can start out as generic (for instance, telephone or pencil) or it can become generic over time (such as escalator or aspirin). Marks that become generic lose their trademark protection.[297]

There is no advantage to using a generic term as a mark, since it merely states what the product is and gives no indication as to the source. The producer gains no consumer confidence or reputation from use of a generic mark. Additionally, the generic mark provides no protection to the producer. Producers must police their mark to ensure it does not become generic through inappropriate use by competitors, customers, or third parties.

See also "Spectrum of Distinctiveness."
See also "Trademark."

GIFT

A gift is the transfer of ownership from one to another. In order for a gift to be legally valid, three steps must occur:

1. The giver must have an *intent* to make a gift to the recipient,
2. The giver must *deliver* the gift to the recipient with an intent to pass title to the recipient, and
3. The recipient must *accept* the gift.

Without the three requirements of donative intent, delivery, and acceptance, a gift will not be legally valid.

Gifts made to charitable organizations such as museums are often referred to as donations.

Compare "Contract."
See also "Donation."
See also "Promised Gift."

GUARANTEE

When an object is consigned to an auction house for sale, the auction house may agree to pay a certain predetermined price for the object if it fails to obtain the reserve price at auction. Such an agreement ensures the object's owner that some form of profit will be achieved at auction, even if the reserve price is not met. It may also aid the object's future market value, as it will not have failed to sell previously.

See also "Auction House."
See also "Reserve."

THE HAGUE CONVENTION, 1954

See "Convention for the Protection of Cultural Property in the Event of Armed Conflict."

HEAR ACT

See "Holocaust Expropriated Art Recovery Act."

HISTORIC PRESERVATION EASEMENT

When a person has the legal right to use another's property for a specified purpose, that person has an easement. The person who owns the land is the grantor of the easement, and the person making use of the easement is the grantee.

A historic preservation easement differs from the traditional easement, in that what is given is not a right to use the property for a specified purpose. Instead, the grantee has the right to protect and preserve the historical features of the property, while the grantor retains full legal ownership of the property. Under the terms of the easement, certain modifications to the property may be prohibited, such as demolition, alteration of the façade or interiors, or additions such as a new wing, porch, or garage. The easement may also extend to other areas of the property, for instance an attached archaeological site or landscape features.

The historic preservation easement should be held by a qualified government agency or nonprofit organization. That organization should have a relevant and appropriate mission, for instance an organization dedicated to historic preservation or land conservation. The organization should also have sufficient resources to oversee and enforce the easement.

A historic preservation easement should be in writing and properly recorded. They often are designed to become a permanent part of the property's chain of title, so it should "run with the land" in perpetuity and be binding on all future owners. The easement does not impact the grantor's ability to sell the property, though it may impact the fair market value of the property.[298]

Compare "Easement."

HOLOCAUST ERA ASSETS CONFERENCE

See "Terezín Declaration on Holocaust Era Assets and Related Issues."

HOLOCAUST EXPROPRIATED ART RECOVERY ACT

Full title: Holocaust Expropriated Art Recovery Act of 2016
Also known as: HEAR Act
Citation: Pub. L. 114–308

One of the largest looting campaigns in history occurred in the years leading up to and during World War II. It has been estimated that one-fifth of all Western art was subjected to seizure or coerced sale by the Nazi forces.[299] The objects stolen were not just fine art but also included personal items such as books, household silver, religious items, and other small, portable items. When taken as a whole, the number of objects is estimated to run into the millions.[300] A number of efforts existed to identify and restitute these objects after the war, including among others the American Commission for the Protection and Salvage of Artistic and Historic Monuments in War Areas (the Roberts Commission) and the Monuments, Fine Arts, and Archives program (the Monuments Men). Despite this, hundreds of thousands of objects remain lost to this day.

A number of barriers exist for claimants in seeking the return of their property.[301] Locating the artwork can present significant challenges, even with the existence of numerous databases detailing such objects.[302] Once an object is successfully identified and located, the claimants must establish their proper ownership rights in the work. And finally, even if these first two hurdles can be overcome, claimants have to address the statute of limitations.

When a party wishes to press a legal action, the law provides a window in which that action must be pursued or it will be barred. The intent is to ensure a resolution to a harm is pursued within a reasonable amount of time.

However, in regard to Nazi-looted objects, the statute of limitations can be understood to create an unreasonable barrier to a claim. In the time period during and immediately after WWII, many claimants or their heirs feared bringing a claim or believed such efforts would be futile.[303] It was also immensely difficult to locate objects during that era, and in fact many objects and documents remained hidden well into the 1990s. "Vast stores of art and antiquities that disappeared from Germany in the aftermath of World War II were stolen by Soviet troops and remain hidden in 'secret depositories' in the Soviet Union. . . ."[304] Therefore, application of the statute of limitations in regard to Nazi-looted objects often serves to create a bar to restitution, with claims being dismissed not on the merits of the facts but due to a procedural rule.

Attempts have been made over the years to address these barriers. For example, the 1998 Washington Principles on Nazi-Confiscated Art were promulgated with the intention of supporting the restitution of these objects. However, in the United States, the issue of the statute of limitations still created a procedural barrier in some cases.[305]

The Holocaust Expropriated Art Recovery Act (HEAR Act) was drafted to "provide the victims of Holocaust-era persecution and their heirs a fair opportunity to recover works of art confiscated or misappropriated by the Nazis."[306]

The HEAR Act implements a number of significant changes intended to aid the restitution of Nazi-looted objects. It creates a uniform, nationwide statute of limitations regarding these claims. Running of the statute of limitations commences either when the claimant has actual knowledge (or enough knowledge to amount to actual knowledge) of the artwork's identity and location or of their own possessory interest in the art.[307] In other words, the statute of limitations begins to run only once the work's location is known. The statute of limitations will then last for six years.[308] The Act applies to objects taken under Nazi persecution during the period of January 1, 1933, through December 1, 1945,[309] and covers a variety of artworks, including pictures, paintings, drawings, sculptures, engravings, prints, books, musical objects, manuscripts, and others.[310]

The Act is partially retroactive, in that it applies to a limited number of preexisting claims. Specifically, civil claims and causes of action where the claimant had actual knowledge of their possessory interest but the claim had been barred by a statute of limitations, the six-year statute of limitations now commences on December 16, 2016 (the enactment date of the HEAR Act).[311] For cases pending or on appeal, the six-year statute of limitations also applies.[312] The statute of limitations extension does not apply, however, to some previously barred claims in which the claimant had knowledge of the artwork's entity and location but failed to act during a six-year period.[313] Finally, the Act has a "sunset clause," meaning the Act will cease to have any effect on January 1, 2027, except for any civil claims or causes of action still pending on that date.[314] Any claims brought on or after January 1, 2027, will be subject to the statute of limitations that exists in the applicable federal or state jurisdiction.

Speaking on the passage of the HEAR Act and its signing into law by President Obama, former Ambassador Ronald S. Lauder stated:

> The HEAR Act will end an enduring injustice for Holocaust victims and their families. For too long, governments, museums, auction houses and unscrupulous collectors allowed this egregious theft of culture and heritage to continue, imposing legal barriers like arbitrary statutes of limitations to deny families prized possessions stolen from them by the Nazis. ... This important law will help victims of Nazi looting find justice and peace. No longer will legal technicalities bar families from having their claims heard on their merits.[315]

While the HEAR Act is still relatively young and its impact not fully understood, it is possible it will have an impact on claims for the restoration of Nazi-looted art to the original owners and their surviving heirs. By addressing one of the main barriers to successful claims, the Act seeks to ensure these cases are decided on their merits and not on procedural grounds. However, a recent ase out of New York may suggest that barriers remain.

There, plaintiff Laurel Zuckerman sought to recover Pablo Picasso's rose-period painting *The Actor* from the Metropolitan Museum of Art.[316] On appeal, the Second Circuit held that the HEAR Act did not preempt the museum's laches defense. Laches is an equitable defense that bars a plaintiff from bringing an untimely claim.[317] That court stated: "While the HEAR Act revives claims that would otherwise be untimely under state-based statutes of limitations, it allows defendants to assert equitable defenses like laches."[318] This was based on the court's interpretation of the statutory language, stating, "[t]he statute explicitly sets aside 'defense[s] *at law* relating to the passage of time.' HEAR Act § 5(a). It makes no mention of defenses *at equity* [emphasis in original]."[319] On March 2, 2020, the United States Supreme Court denied Zuckerman's cert petition, declining to hear the case.[320] While the Court's declination to hear the case does not indicate the Court necessarily agreed with the Second Circuit's decision, it is possible that those holding potentially Nazi-looted works will rely on that decision going forward.[321] Alternatively, state and federal courts outside of the Second Circuit may decline to follow the *Zuckerman* decision.

See also "Laches."
See also "Statute of Limitations."
See also "Washington Principles on Nazi-Confiscated Art."

IMMUNITY FROM JUDICIAL SEIZURE

See "Arts and Artifacts Indemnity Act."

INDEPENDENT CONSULTANT

See "Independent Contractor."

INDEPENDENT CONTRACTOR

Workers employed by a business or organization such as a museum may be classified as independent contractors if specific requirements are met. Determining if a worker is properly classified as an independent contractor or an employee is important, as this classification has numerous ramifications, and misclassifying the worker can have consequences for the employer.

Typically, an employer is responsible to withhold income taxes from wages paid to the employee. The employer must also pay Social Security, Medicare, and unemployment taxes on those wages.[322] In contrast, those same withholdings and payments are not made on the wages paid to an independent contractor.

There are two different tests to determine if a worker should be classified as an employee or as an independent contractor. These are the common law test and the ABC test.[323]

If an employer classifies their workers as independent contractors when there is no reasonable basis for that classification, the employer may be liable for employment taxes.

Compare "Employee."
See also "ABC Test for Worker Classification."
See also "Common Law Test for Worker Classification."
See also "Worker Classification."

For a more in-depth discussion, see "Chapter 10: Worker Classification: Distinguishing between an Employee and an Independent Contractor."

INDEPENDENT MUSEUM PROFESSIONAL (IMP)

See "Independent Contractor."

INFRINGEMENT

Infringement occurs when one of the exclusive rights under copyright is performed without authorization by someone other than the copyright owner.[324] As recourse for infringement, the copyright owner may bring suit against the alleged infringer.[325] While registration with the United States Copyright Office is not required to obtain copyright protection,[326] registration *is* required to bring a civil lawsuit for infringement.[327]

The test to establish copyright infringement is fairly straightforward. In order to prevail, the copyright owner must establish (1) the alleged infringer had access to the work; (2) there is a substantial similarity between the works; and (3) there was an unlawful appropriation of the copyrighted work.[328]

A finding of copyright infringement can result in numerous remedies against the infringer, including temporary and final injunctions,[329] impounding and destruction of the goods,[330] monetary damages,[331] and criminal charges.[332]

See also "Automatic Creation."
See also "Copyright."
See also "Fair Use Doctrine."

For a more in-depth discussion, see "Chapter 5: Copyright Infringement and Fair Use."

INTEGRITY, RIGHT OF

The Visual Artists Rights Act (VARA) provides two moral rights. One is the right of integrity. This right grants the artist of a qualifying work of visual art the ability to prevent any *intentional* distortion, mutilation, or modification of her work that would prejudice the artist's honor or reputation.[333]

The right also allows the artist to prevent destruction of works that are of "recognized stature."[334] The Act does not define what is necessary to qualify as a work of "recognized stature." Some guidance is given by the Southern District of New York, which has adopted a test that asks (1) whether the work has "stature," meaning it is meritorious, and (2) whether that stature "is 'recognized' by art experts, other members of the artistic community, or by some cross-section of society."[335]

Intentional destruction or destruction due to gross negligence violates the right of integrity.[336] This right is easiest to consider in terms of freestanding works. Where a freestanding work of visual art is threatened with destruction, and the work is of the necessary "recognized stature," then the artist may exercise her moral right of integrity to prevent the destruction.

This right of integrity is limited in certain cases where the artwork was incorporated into a building in a manner that means its removal would constitute destruction. The "building exception"[337] provides that if the artist consented to that installation prior to June 1, 1991, or if the artist and building owner sign a document specifying the work may be distorted or destroyed upon removal, the artist has effectively waived this right.[338] Further, if the work can be removed without causing destruction or distortion, and the owner has made a diligent, good-faith effort to notify the artist and either that effort was futile or it was successful but the artist failed to remove the work within ninety days, the artist has effectively waived this right.[339]

A related issue is site-specific art, meaning art that "is conceived and created in relation to the particular conditions of a specific site."[340] This is a subset of integrated art, defined as art that "is comprised of two or more physical objects that must be presented together as the artist intended for the work to retain its meaning and integrity."[341] For site-specific art, the physical location of the artwork is one of the physical objects comprising the artwork. Under the current reading of VARA by the First Circuit, VARA does not apply to site-specific artwork.[342] However, the Seventh Circuit has called this position into question, while refraining from deciding if site-specific art is excluded from VARA.[343] For now, the status of site-specific artwork under VARA is unknown.

There are important limitations to this right. If a work's modification is due solely to the passage of time or due to the inherent nature of the materials from which it is made, this does not qualify as a distortion, mutilation, or modification in regard to the right of attribution.[344] Additionally, modification due to conservation only qualifies as a distortion, mutilation, or modification if the conservation was conducted in a manner that rises to the level of gross negligence.[345] Finally, the "public presentation" exception excludes modification due to circumstances such as lighting and placement, unless the presentation was again conducted in a manner that rises to the level of gross negligence.[346] Finally, the right of integrity does not apply to reproductions of the work.[347]

See also "Moral Rights."
See also "Visual Artists Rights Act."

INTELLECTUAL PROPERTY

The types of property rights that arise from the creative process are referred to as a whole as intellectual property. The main categories of intellectual property are copyright, patent, and trademark, along with moral rights, service marks, and trade dress. Intellectual property law provides various legal protections to the creator or owner for a (generally) limited time period.

The purpose of intellectual property is to provide exclusive rights to authors in order to encourage their creative process, which is considered beneficial to society as a whole. By providing these exclusive rights, the authors are given the opportunity to benefit from them, either financially or through elevation of their reputation, because the author is the only person permitted to exploit the creation during a certain time period.

Each category of intellectual property protects different types of creations, though there is some overlap between categories. For instance, visual art is entitled to copyright protection and may also be entitled to moral right protection. Additionally, each category of intellectual property provides different exclusive rights to the right-holder. The rights afforded by patent law are different than the rights afforded by trademark law.

A further difference between categories is how the intellectual property rights arise. Rights may vest upon completion or fixation, such as with copyright, or through a process of application and registration, as with patent and trademark.

Finally, the term of protection afforded by each category can vary considerably, from a set term of years (such as under patent law), to a term tied to the lifespan of the creator (such as moral rights and copyright), to a potentially infinite term (such as trademark).

As each category of intellectual property varies so greatly, it is important to have a firm understanding of which category applies to a particular creative endeavor.

Compare "Personal Property."
Compare "Real Property."
See also "Copyright."
See also "Moral Rights."
See also "Patent."
See also "Service Mark."
See also "Trade Dress."
See also "Trademark."

INTERNATIONAL INSTITUTE FOR THE UNIFICATION OF PRIVATE LAW

The International Institute for the Unification of Private Law (UNIDROIT)[348] is an independent intergovernmental organization that works to modernize and harmonize private and commercial law between the member states.[349] As of August 2020, UNIDROIT has sixty-three member states.[350]

See also "Convention on the International Return of Stolen or Illegally Exported Cultural Objects."
See also "Cultural Heritage."

IRS FORM 990

Organizations that have received tax-exempt recognition from the Internal Revenue Service (IRS) are required to file an annual reporting form to maintain their exemption. For section 501(c)(3) organizations, such as most museums, this annual reporting form is the IRS Form 990. There are a number of different versions of the form, and an organization will file the form required according to its budget and size.[351]

Organizations are required to file their annual reporting form with the IRS by the fifteenth day of the fifth month after the conclusion of the organization's accounting year.[352] Extensions are available, and must be timely requested of the IRS.[353] Organizations must be diligent in filing their Form 990, as repeat failure to do so will result in an automatic revocation of the organization's tax-exempt status.

Museums with annual gross receipts of $50,000 or less may file the Form 990-N, which is an electronic postcard or e-postcard. Organizations eligible to file Form 990-N may select to file Form 990-EZ or Form 990 instead. Form 990-N is a truncated form of the longer Form 990-EZ and Form 990, only requiring minimal information about the organization. The individual completing the Form 990-N on behalf of the organization must be able to provide:

1. The organization's legal name and address,
2. Any other name the organization does business under,
3. The organization's website (if they have one),
4. The name and address of the principal officer,
5. The organization's annual tax period,
6. A verification that the organization's annual gross receipts are normally $50,000 or less, and
7. A notification if the organization has terminated its activities.[354]

Much of this information should be readily available.

Mid-sized organizations with annual gross receipts less than $200,000, and total assets less than $500,000, may file the IRS Form 990-EZ, the Short Return of Organization Exempt from Income Tax.[355] While Form 990-EZ is the "short form," it still demands quite a bit of information not required for the Form 990-N, such as a breakdown of revenue[356] and expenses.[357] The organization's largest programs, measured by expense, must be listed and described. The name, title, weekly hours worked, compensation, and any additional benefits, including health benefits, must be listed for each of the organization's directors and key employees. There are also a number of questions that seek to confirm the organization is being conducted for an appropriate charitable purpose, such as information on unrelated business income or political activity. Therefore, the "short form" requires a large amount of information that may not all reside with one individual at the museum.

Finally, the standard Form 990 is a mandatory filing for organizations with gross receipts of $200,000 or more or total assets of $500,000.[358] The Form 990 collects much of the same information as the Form 990-EZ, though the standard form demands much more information and in greater detail than the shorter Form 990-EZ. As with Form 990-EZ, the Form 990 requires information that may, and likely will, not all reside with one individual at the museum.

While the annual reporting forms can be time consuming, they play an important purpose in the federal tax exemption system. As tax-exempt status is a benefit conferred by the federal government on certain organizations, the annual reporting system helps to ensure that only organizations that are fulfilling an important public and charitable purpose benefit from the tax-exempt status. They also provide a system of public inspection and oversight, as the annual reporting forms are public documents, required to be available at the organization's principal office for public inspection.[359]

See also "Articles of Incorporation."
See also "Automatic Revocation."
See also "Bylaws."
See also "Operational Test."
See also "Political Activities Test."
See also "Section 501(c)(3)."
See also "Tax-Exempt."
See also "Unrelated Business Income Tax."

For a more in-depth discussion, see "Chapter 8: Nonprofit Corporations and Tax Exemption."

IRS FORM 1023

Organizations seeking tax-exempt status as a section 501(c)(3) charitable or educational organization from the Internal Revenue Service (IRS) must complete Form 1023 and submit all required documentation.[360] Unincorporated associations, charitable trusts, and nonprofit corporations all may be eligible for tax-exempt status upon successful completion of the application process.

Some organizations can file the Form 1023-EZ, a more streamlined document. Organizations should complete the Eligibility Worksheet[361] to see if they qualify prior to completing Form 1023-EZ. Organizations ineligible to file the streamlined form can still apply using the standard Form 1023.

Upon IRS approval, the organization will receive a tax-exempt determination letter. This letter can be used by the organization as proof it is in fact a bona fide tax-exempt organization, which can be useful, for instance, in providing donors with verification that their charitable donations are tax deductible.

Compare "Nonprofit Corporation."
See also "Charitable Trust."
See also "Tax-Exempt."
See also "Unincorporated Association."

IRS FORM 8282

When a donor makes a donation to a qualified organization, that donor may be entitled to a deduction on their taxes. However, there are tax consequences for that donor if the donee museum sells, exchanges, or otherwise disposes of that donated property within three years of its acquisition.[362] Therefore, in the instance that such a disposal of donated property take place, the IRS requires the donee museum to file a Form 8282, "Donee Information Return."[363] The donee museum has 125 days from the date of disposal to file Form 8282 with the IRS, and a copy of the form must be supplied to the donor as well.[364] The donee museum may incur penalties if it is required to file Form 8282 and fails to do so.[365]

Completion of Form 8282 will require information that should be contained in the original donor paperwork and the object's file, such as the date the item was received, the date it was disposed, and how the item was used, especially if the use did or did not relate to the museum's exempt purpose. Form 8282 must be signed by an officer of the donee museum, and the signatory must include her title.

There are two instances in which a Form 8282 does not need to be filed. First, if the property is valued at $500 or less, completion of Form 8282 is not necessary.[366] Second, if the item was consumed or distributed in fulfillment of the organization's charitable purpose, Form 8282 does not need to be filed.[367] In all other instances, Form 8282 must be timely filed, and a copy must be provided to the donor.

See also "Donation."
See also "Exempt Purpose."
See also "IRS Form 8283."
See also "Unrelated Use."

IRS FORM 8283

Taxpayers who claim a total deduction in excess of $500 on their tax return must attach Form 8283, "Noncash Charitable Contributions."[368] The form requires certain information that the donor likely will have but may request from the donee museum, such as the date of the donation or the museum's address.[369] There is additional information demanded by the form that the donee museum and its staff should not supply, such as the fair market value of noncash donations.

If the taxpayer donated property with a fair market value in excess of $5,000, including art, historical items, and collectible items, then in order to obtain their deduction, the taxpayer will need an authorized official from the museum to sign Section B, Part IV of Form 8283, "Donee Acknowledgement." The person who signs on behalf of the museum must either be the official who is authorized to sign the museum's tax return or be a person authorized by that official to sign the Form 8283.[370] Specifically, the official must affirm the museum is a qualified organization and provide the date the property was received.[371] The official signature does *not* indicate the museum's acceptance of the appraisal value listed by the donor on the form.[372] Rather, the signature affirms the museum's understanding it is mandated to file IRS Form 8282 should the museum sell, exchange, or dispose of the listed donated property within three years of receipt. Additionally, the donee museum must indicate if the donated property will be put to a use unrelated to the museum's exempt purpose.[373] The donee museum must receive a copy of the completed Form 8283.[374]

See also "Deduction."
See also "Donation."
See also "Exempt Purpose."
See also "IRS Form 8282."
See also "Qualified Organization."
See also "Unrelated Use."

JOINT TENANCY

Under the types of ownership available for real property, the fee simple is perhaps the most common. When the property is owned by multiple people, that shared ownership may take the form of a joint tenancy, tenancy by the entirety, or tenancy in common.

Under the joint tenancy[375] (sometimes called a joint tenancy with right of surviviorship), the ownership rights do not survive an owner's death. When a joint tenant passes away, their ownership interest goes to the surviving joint tenants. Therefore, the last surviving joint tenant will ultimately own the property outright.

Courts generally prefer the tenancy in common relationship over the joint tenancy, so specific wording must be used in the foundational document (the deed) for a joint tenancy to be created. Additional requirements must also be strictly met for the joint tenancy to be created.[376]

A joint tenancy may be broken if the joint tenants do not maintain the joint tenancy in alignment with the strict rules that govern it. For example, Owners A and B are joint tenants in a property. Owner A sells her share to Museum. Museum and Owner B have not met the creation requirements for a joint tenancy, so the joint tenancy is broken, and Owner B and Museum now own the property as tenants in common. These issues become progressively more complicated if more joint tenants are involved and can result in a situation in which some owners are joint tenants while others are tenants in common, in turn impacting who may inherit the various shares.

Compare "Tenancy in Common."
See also "Fee Simple."
See also "Real Property."
See also "Tenancy by the Entirety."

JOINT WORK

Under copyright law, a joint work is one that was created by more than one author "with the intention that their contributions be merged into inseparable or interdependent parts of a unitary whole."[377] This is different from a collective work, which takes place when a number of separate creators contribute their own internally complete work to an assembled finished product, such as short stories collected in an anthology or essays appearing together in a periodical.[378] Instead, the contributions to a joint work are intertwined and are intended to only be perceived as a unified whole.

When a work is a joint work, its term of copyright protection is a term equal to the life of the last surviving author plus an additional seventy years.[379] As with other copyrightable works, the artistic creation must meet the requirements of copyright law, and if it does, copyright protection vests at the time of creation.[380]

See also "Copyright."

JUSTICE FOR UNCOMPENSATED SURVIVORS TODAY ACT

Full title: Justice for Uncompensated Survivors Today Act of 2017
Also known as: JUST Act
Citation: Pub. L. 115-171

See "Terezín Declaration on Holocaust Era Assets and Related Issues."

LACHES

When a party fails to assert his legal rights within a timely manner, that party's claims may be barred by laches. Essentially, the law will not assist a person who sleeps on his rights, especially when doing so will be prejudicial to his opponent. Unlike the similar statute of limitations, laches does not have a specified period of time after which a claim is barred. Instead, application of laches is fact-specific. If a party was unreasonable in delaying a claim, and the delay is prejudicial to the adverse party, laches may bar the claim, regardless of how much time has passed. This is intended to provide some fairness to the adverse party, as witnesses or evidence may become lost due to the failure of the aggrieved party to bring forth his claim, or significant monetary or other loss may result due to the failure to bring the claim in a timely manner.

For example, imagine a museum intends to build a new entrance. Due to an error, the entrance extends onto the neighboring property by a few feet. It is not enough to be noticeable to a casual observer, but it is an infringement on the neighbor's property rights nonetheless. The neighbor is aware of the actual property line's location and of the infringement on his property, but he does nothing to prevent the building of the museum's entrance. Instead, the neighbor sleeps on his rights, allowing the breaking of ground and construction of the new entrance, a project that takes over a year and costs in excess of a million dollars. After the entrance is completed, the neighbor brings suit to enforce his rights. While the statute of limitations has not passed, it is likely a court will bar the neighbor's claim through an application of laches. Had he brought a claim when he first realized the entrance extended onto his property, a great deal of effort and expense could have been saved by the museum. By waiting until construction was complete, the museum would need to demolish the entire entrance, which a court would likely find to unfairly prejudice the museum.

Laches is an equitable defense. As illustrated in the example above, some jurisdictions permit a defense of laches even if the statute of limitations has not run.

Compare "Statute of Limitations."
See also "Equity."
See also "Holocaust Expropriated Art Recovery Act," especially the discussion of *Zuckerman v. Metropolitan Museum of Art.*

LANHAM ACT

Full title: N/A
Also known as: Trademark Act of 1946
Citation: 15 U.S.C. §§ 1051 *et. seq.*

See "Trademark."

LAW

The law is the system of rules that are used to govern behavior in society. There are a number of different types of legal systems that exist, including religious-based laws (such as the canon law of various branches of Christianity or Islamic Sharia law), civil law (the system found throughout Europe and in the state of Louisiana), and common law (the Anglo-American system found in the United States and other former British colonies).

Compare "Equity."
Compare "Ethics."
See also "Categories of Law."

For a more in-depth discussion, see "Chapter 2: Ethics and the Law."

LICENSE

A license is used to transfer intellectual property rights to a person other than the rights owner. The exclusive rights protected by intellectual property law are best visualized as a bundle of sticks, where each stick represents a different right in the work. An individual can own one or many of the sticks independently, and ownership of the sticks is entirely separate from ownership of the actual creative object that gave rise to the sticks.[381]

Due to the fact that the rights are separate and distinct, each right may be licensed individually. The terms of the license can and should explicitly state what is and is not permitted under the license and any other term that is applicable and relevant to the parties.

Regardless of the rights transferred and the terms reached, note that the license must be memorialized in a written document that is signed by the owner of the rights or the owner's agent.[382]

See also "Copyright."
See also "Intellectual Property."
See also "Patent."
See also "Rights and Reproductions."
See also "Trademark."

For a more in-depth discussion, see "Chapter 7: Intellectual Property Licensing."

LIFE ESTATE

There are a number of different manners by which to own real property. The life estate gives the right to possess and use the property only during the holder's lifetime. Unlike the more common fee simple, the life estate does not permit the holder the right to use and disburse the property as they see fit, as their interest in the property expires at the time of death. Instead, they may possess the property or transfer their interest only during their lifetime.

A life estate is created in an instrument such as a deed, will, or trust. That instrument both creates the life estate and determines what will happen to the property upon the death of the life estate holder.

For example, Octavia owns a piece of property. Octavia is a lifelong supporter of Museum and wants to leave the property to Museum. However, Octavia also wants her spouse, Simon, to be able to continue to live in the property until his own passing. Octavia could draft a will in which, upon her death, Simon gains a life estate in the property, the remainder to go to Museum upon Simon's death. In this example, Museum will eventually gain full ownership of the property, but not until Simon has died.

Additionally, because Simon only has a life estate in the property, Simon cannot disburse the property in his own will. Imagine Simon would prefer the property go to University and drafts a will stating he is leaving the property to University. That provision of the will is ineffective, as Simon only has a life estate and cannot bequeath the property to University. Upon Simon's death, the property will go to Museum, not to University.[383]

See also "Fee Simple."
See also "Future Interest."
See also "Real Property."

LIMITED LIABILITY COMPANY (LLC)

A limited liability company (LLC) is a type of business structure in which the members (individuals, corporations, other LLCs, or other business entities) receive benefits of corporation and partnership business structures. This hybrid entity will protect members from personal liability while permitting income and losses to pass through without the payment of corporate taxes. LLCs exist under state law, and the laws governing them can vary widely. Most states permit an LLC to be owned by one individual, while some states prohibit this practice. Some states permit an LLC to survive a member joining or leaving, while other states require such a change to dissolve the LLC and that it be reformed with the new membership if there is not a preexisting agreement within the LLC.

Depending on state law, an LLC may be operated as a nonprofit organization. However, the Internal Revenue Service will only recognize an LLC as a tax-exempt section 501(c)(3) organization if all its members are also section 501(c)(3) organizations.[384]

Compare "Corporation."
See also "Business Structures."

For a more in-depth discussion, see "Chapter 11: Understanding the Various Forms of Business Structures."

LOANS

In terms of museum work, a loan is the temporary transfer of an object to another for (ideally) a finite period of time, for a specific purpose, and with the option to renew. Title in the work does *not* transfer, so the lender retains all ownership rights in the work.

Legally, a loan is a "bailment," where the borrowing institution is the "bailee" and the lender is the "bailor." The law imposes certain responsibilities and various duties of care on the parties, depending on which party obtains the primary benefit from the bailment. However, these responsibilities and duties only come into play if there is no express contract between the parties. An express contract, often referred to as a "loan agreement," controls the actual relationship and trumps any responsibilities and duties found at law.

While it is now a professional best practice to limit loans to a fixed duration of time, often one year with the option to renew, in the past museums would occasionally accept so-called permanent loans or loans of indefinite duration. When these loans extend for a term so long as to make it impractical or impossible to return the objects, they are often called "old loans."

Compare "Old Loans."
See also "Title."

LOCAL LAW

See "Categories of Law."

LOST PROPERTY

See "Abandoned Property."

MEDIUM OF EXPRESSION

See "Works of Authorship."

MISLAID PROPERTY

See "Abandoned Property."

MISSION STATEMENT

A mission statement is a (generally) brief statement outlining a museum's purpose in existing and operating. It may be as general as stating the museum collects and preserves a particular form of art, to being as detailed as specifying historical periods, cultures, or other limiting terms. The American Alliance of Museums lists the mission statement as one of the five "core documents" of museums, being a fundamental part of museum operations.[385]

As with a code of ethics, a museum's mission statement is an internal document, and it should inform everything from object acquisition to programming to deaccessions. While it is an internal document, as a statement that directs and inspires the organization and all it does, many museums prominently place their mission statement where the public can access it, such as in annual reports and on the museum website.

It is not, on its own, a legal document. However, the fiduciary duty of obedience requires museum trustees to be obedient to, among other things, the museum's mission. Therefore, trustees who disregard the museum's mission in the furtherance of their duties may find themselves in breach of this fiduciary duty.

Compare "Articles of Incorporation."
Compare "Bylaws."
Compare "Code of Ethics."
See "Duty of Obedience."
See "Fiduciary Duty."
See "Trustee."
See "Vision Statement."

MORAL RIGHTS

Copyright provides a series of protections that can be viewed as economic in nature. The copyright owner has exclusive rights to utilize and transform the copyrighted work for a limited time period, and those rights provide an economic advantage to the copyright owner.

In comparison, moral rights arise from the theory that a lingering, ongoing relationship exists between the artist and her artwork that is entirely separate from an economic interest. This ongoing relationship can be understood as arising from reputation. As was explained in the House Reports upon the enacting of federal law to protect moral rights:

> An artist's professional and personal identity is embodied in each work created by that artist. Each work is a part of his or her reputation. Each work is a form of personal expression (oftentimes painstakingly and earnestly recorded). It is a rebuke to the dignity of the visual artist that our copyright law allows distortion, modification and even outright permanent destruction of such efforts.[386]

An artist's developing reputation continues to impact the artwork even after its creation, and the artwork's reputation impacts that of the artist. They are bound to one another with no consideration of physical ownership nor economic interest. With this understanding of how the artwork and the artist remain tied to each other conceptually, moral rights suggest that the artist should and must maintain some control over the artwork even after its title is transferred to another.

Table 1.3. Overview of Moral Rights

Right Name	Right Description	Recognized in the United States?	Notes
Droit de suite (resale royalty)	Provides a means for an artist to receive a portion of the proceeds in future sales of the work.	Extremely limited	The only *droit de suite* in the United State was the California Resale Royalties Act.[387] However, after a series of legal challenges, that statute is now almost entirely preempted by the Copyright Act of 1976.
Protection from excessive criticism	Protection from abusive attacks on the artist personally or on the artwork.	No	The First Amendment is in contrast with this right, though there may be exceptions for defamatory statements made against an artist personally.
Right of attribution	Protects the right to claim authorship in a work created by the artist and to prevent their attribution to works that have been distorted, mutilated, or otherwise modified in a manner detrimental to the artist's honor or reputation.	Yes	Federally under the Visual Artists Rights Act 17 USC § 106A(a)(1), (2). Locally under a variety of state moral rights laws. False attribution is also protected under the Lanham Act (trademark law) Section 43(a), 15 USC § 1125(a).
Right to create	Protects the right to create or to refrain from creating.	Not as a moral right but through contract law	Contracts for personal services (such as to create an artwork) are generally not specifically enforceable. If parties enter a contract for the creation of an artwork and the artist fails to perform, they may be liable for financial damages.
Right to disclose	Protects the right to disclose (publish) a work or to not do so.	Not as a moral right but through copyright law.	Two of the exclusive rights under copyright law address the right to disclose: • 17 USC § 106(1) reproduction right • 17 USC § 106(3) distribution right
Right to withdraw	Provides a right to withdraw a work after it has been disclosed, even if ownership has been transferred. A very limited right even in countries with expansive moral rights protection.	No	17 USC § 109(c) permits the owner of a lawfully made copy to publicly display that copy.

Right Name	Right Description	Recognized in the United States?	Notes
Right of integrity	Prevents the intentional distortion, mutilation, or other modification of the artwork in a manner prejudicial to the artist's reputation.	Yes	Federally under the Visual Artists Rights Act 17 USC § 106A(a)(3)(A). Site-specific artwork may not receive full protection, though this is not entirely settled. Locally under a variety of state moral rights laws. Possibly under the Lanham Act (trademark law) Section 43(a), 15 USC § 1125(a).[388]
	Prevent the destruction of artworks that have "recognized stature."	Yes	Federally under the Visual Artists Rights Act 17 USC § 106A(a)(3)(B). "Recognized stature" is not defined in the Act, but in *Carter v. Helmsley-Spear, Inc.*,[389] the Southern District of New York adopted a two-tiered definition: "(1) that the visual art in question has 'stature,' *i.e.* is viewed as meritorious, and (2) that this stature is 'recognized' by art experts, other members of the artistic community, or by some cross-section of society." This approach was adopted in the "5Pointz" case in 2018.[390] Locally under a variety of state moral rights laws.

In addition to VARA, a number of states have passed moral rights legislation, with California passing the first in 1979.[391] VARA does not fully preempt these state laws.[392] However, the extent of preemption for any particular state law may not be known, especially if there has not been a legal challenge to establish the existence or extent of any preemption.

There are a number of moral rights that exist in the various countries that recognize them. Some moral rights are also recognized by the Berne Convention for the Protection of Literary and Artistic Works, an international copyright agreement. In the United States, the only federally recognized moral rights are the rights of attribution and integrity. Both are contained within the Visual Artists Rights Act.

Compare "Copyright."
See also "Attribution, Right of."
See also "Berne Convention for the Protection of Literary and Artistic Works."
See also "*Droit de Suite* (Resale Royalty)."
See also "Integrity, Right of."
See also "Visual Artists Rights Act."

MORALITY CLAUSE

See "Termination Clause."

MUSEUM CLOSURE

See "Closing of Museums."

NAMING RIGHTS

Organizations seeking financial support may consider offering naming rights to donors in exchange for their donations. Essentially, the organization will agree to name a specific facility, collection, endowment, etc., in honor of the donor. These naming rights are often negotiated and are highly specific to the interests of the particular donor, so the terms of these can vary from donation to donation and from donor to donor.

Despite this specificity and personalization, organizations seeking to pursue donations in exchange of naming rights should keep some parameters in mind. A selection of factors to consider include: Does the organization wish to place a monetary threshold amount that must be met before naming rights will even be considered? Does the organization want to standardize how these types of donations will be recognized, for instance on a plaque, in annual reports, on the website, etc.? What would the process be to amend or change the name in the future if the donor desires?

There are also some limitations an organization may wish to place on naming rights in terms of duration. First, an organization may want to retain some flexibility in its ability to seek similar financial support in the future. For instance, if a new museum wing is named after a donor in perpetuity, that may limit the museum from seeking future donations in support of that wing should a need arise—even if it is decades later. By including a sunset clause, the organization retains the ability to accept future gifts without being limited by the acceptance of the original donation.

Second, the organization should consider the inclusion of a termination clause. This would permit the removal of the donor's name should an issue arise in the future in which the organization would not want to be associated with the donor's name.

One good approach to naming rights is to have an organizational policy outlining what the internal policies and expectations are in regard to these types of donations.[393] This policy may be a stand-alone policy or incorporated into a comprehensive gift acceptance policy.

See also "Charitable Gift."
See also "Donor."
See also "Donation."
See also "Sunset Clause."
See also "Termination Clause."

NATIONAL HISTORIC LANDMARKS PROGRAM

See "National Historic Preservation Act."

NATIONAL HISTORIC PRESERVATION ACT

Full Title: National Historic Preservation Act of 1966
Also Known As: N/A
Citation: 16 U.S.C. § 470 *et. seq.*

Based on the belief that "the preservation of this irreplaceable heritage is in the public interest so that its vital legacy of cultural, educational, aesthetic, inspirational, economic, and energy benefits will be maintained and enriched for future generations of Americans,"[394] the National Historic Preservation Act (NHPA) preserves America's historical and archaeological sites. Under the NHPA, historic preservation occurs at all levels of government, from local to federal, and across public and private institutions and individuals.[395]

The NHPA established the National Register of Historic Places, the State Historic Preservation Officers, and the National Historic Landmarks program, as well as the Advisory Council on Historic Preservation and the Section 106 review process.

National Register of Historic Places

Citation: 54 U.S.C. §§ 302101 – 302108.

Overseen and maintained by the National Park Service, the National Register of Historic Places (NRHP) is the federal government's official list of historic or archaeologically significant places deemed worthy of preservation.[396] Generally, the NRHP is "composed of districts, sites, buildings, structures, and objects significant in American history, architecture, archeology, engineering, and culture."[397] The National Park Service promulgates criteria for evaluation of proposed additions to the list.[398] Properties must meet age requirements and have significance, such as archaeological or historic significance, to be considered for inclusion. Preservation organizations, historical societies, property owners, and other groups may nominate a site and should contact their State Historic Preservation Officer to do so.[399]

Properties and sites included on the NRHP are eligible for federal preservation grants, federal investment tax credits, and other preservation incentives.[400] Inclusion on the NRHP does not automatically invoke any local historic district zoning, and public access is not mandated for listed properties.

State Historic Preservation Programs

Citation: 54 U.S.C. §§ 302301 – 302304.

Under the NHPA, the State Historic Preservation Officers (SHPOs) administer each State Historic Preservation Program.[401] The SHPO cooperates with government agencies (federal, state, and local), private organizations, and individuals to produce a comprehensive, statewide survey of the historic properties located in the state.[402] This would include any museum that holds or maintains a historic property. The SHPO also identifies and nominates eligible historic properties to the National Register while administering the National Register applications.[403] Other duties and responsibilities include administration of the state's assistance for historic preservation, preparation and implementation of a statewide historic preservation plan, and assistance in the evaluation of rehabilitation project proposals that may be eligible for federal assistance.[404] The SHPO also appoints members to the state's historic preservation review board, which is the body responsible, among other duties, to review National Register nominations and provide guidance to the SHPO in the carrying out of his or her duties.[405] Every state, territory, and the District of Columbia has its own appointed SHPO.[406]

National Historic Landmarks Program

Citation: 36 CFR Part 65.

Administered by the National Park Service, the National Historic Landmarks (NHL) program designates nationally significant historic places that are considered exceptionally valuable in illustrating or interpreting American heritage.[407] Compared with the National Register of Historic Places, which lists over 90,000 properties in its database,[408] the NHL program lists just over 2,500 historic places as of June 2015.[409] NHL historic places are of national importance, as compared to NRHP sites, which may have importance on the local, state, or national level. Additionally, while NRHP sites may have a good level of historic integrity, the standard for the NHL program has a higher criteria, demanding they possess a high level of historic integrity.[410]

The NHL program is administered by regional offices, which can be contacted directly.[411] Nomination of a site to the program can be initiated by a SHPO, Tribal Historic Preservation Officer, Federal Preservation Officer, private owner, or any interested member of the general public. The National Park Service has provided a guide to determine if a potential site meets the NHL criteria.[412]

Advisory Council on Historic Preservation

Citation: 54 U.S.C. §§ 304101 – 304112.

The Advisory Council on Historic Preservation (ACHP) is an independent federal agency established under the NHPA. Its mission statement, as adopted by the ACHP membership, is to "promote[] the preservation, enhancement, and sustainable use of our nation's diverse historic resources, and [to] advise[] the President and the Congress on national historic preservation policy."[413] The ACHP provides policy advice to the president and Congress regarding federal agencies' responsibilities in the arena of historic preservation.

The ACHP has twenty-three members, including a presidentially appointed chairperson, the architect of the Capitol, the secretary of agriculture, one presidentially appointed governor, one presidentially appointed mayor, the president of the SHPO National Conference, the chairperson of the National Trust, one presidentially appointed member of an Indian tribe or Native Hawaiian organization, and other presidential appointees representing appropriate disciplines, such as history and archaeology, and the general public.[414]

In its advisory capacity, the ACHP encourages public interest and participation in historic preservation, makes recommendations on the impact of tax policies on historic preservation, and provides advice to state and local governments when drafting legislation that relates to historic preservation.[415] The ACHP also oversees the NHPA's Section 106 review process (see below).

Protection of Historic Properties

Also Known As: Section 106 Review
Citation: 36 CFR Part 800.

To encourage preservation, the NHPA mandates that federal agencies consider the effect of their actions on historic properties.[416] The Section 106 review is intended to "accommodate historic preservation concerns with the needs of Federal undertakings through consultation among the agency official and other parties with an interest in the effects of the undertaking on historic properties,"[417] thereby balancing the needs of the federal agency with the goal of historic preservation. Section 106 review does not guarantee that historic preservation will occur,[418] but it does guarantee that the value of historic preservation is given due consideration by a federal agency before proceeding with a project.

In order for Section 106 review to apply, two thresholds must first be met. First, there must be a federal action or federally licensed action, including but not limited to the awarding of a grant or permit. Second, the action must potentially have an effect on properties listed on the NRHP or eligible for such listing. When these two preliminary criteria are met, Section 106 review is triggered.

The ACHP's regulations on Section 106 review, titled "Protection of Historic Properties,"[419] is a valuable resource for parties engaging in the review process. The ACHP also publishes numerous pamphlets and documents to aid the Section 106 review process.[420]

See also "Curation of Federally Owned and Administered Archaeological Collections."

NATIONAL REGISTER OF HISTORIC PLACES

See "National Historic Preservation Act."

NATIONAL STOLEN ART FILE

Maintained by the Federal Bureau of Investigation, the National Stolen Art File (NSAF) is a computerized index that lists stolen art objects and cultural heritage objects as reported by American and international law enforcement agencies.[421] In order to be included in the NSAF, a number of criteria must be met:

- The object must be uniquely identifiable;
- The object must have historical or artistic significance;
- The object must be valued at least $2,000 or be associated with a major crime; and
- The request for inclusion must come from a law enforcement agency and be accompanied by a physical description, photograph if available, and police records or other information relevant to the investigation.[422]

A searchable database of stolen objects listed on the NSAF is available on the Federal Bureau of Investigation website. Public access is granted by the FBI Field Offices (for domestic requests) and the FBI Legal Attaché offices (for international requests).

Compare "Nazi-Era Provenance Internet Portal."
See also "Object ID."
See also "Provenance."

NATIVE AMERICAN GRAVES PROTECTION AND REPATRIATION ACT

Full Title: N/A
Also Known As: NAGPRA
Citation: 25 U.S.C. §§ 3001 – 3013

Enacted in 1990, the Native American Graves Protection and Repatriation Act (NAGPRA) requires federal agencies and public and private institutions, including museums, that receive federal funding to repatriate (return) certain Native American cultural items to the appropriate lineal descendants and culturally affiliated Indian tribes and Native Hawaiian organizations.[423]

NAGPRA required federal agencies and institutions to be compliant, due to their acceptance of federal funding, to conduct inventories of the human remains and associated funerary objects in their collections and prepare summaries of those objects, identifying their geographical and cultural affiliations.[424] Those inventories were used to facilitate the notification to Indian tribes and Native Hawaiian organizations of the presence of those culturally affiliated human remains and associated funerary objects, as well as such objects whose cultural affiliation could not be determined.[425] Those human remains were then repatriated to the known lineal descendant or to the appropriate Indian tribe or Native Hawaiian organization, when requested.[426]

Museums or federal agencies that remain noncompliant with NAGPRA's inventory and summaries requirements may be subject to a civil penalty.[427] In order to bring institutions and federal agencies into compliance and meet the important goals of NAGPRA, the National Park Service urges those in noncompliance to contact the National NAGPRA Program staff.[428]

Under the terms of NAGPRA, any Native American human remains and associated funerary objects that are excavated or discovered on federal or tribal lands after November 16, 1990, are the property of the lineal descendants, with additional provisions made for when the lineal descendants cannot be determined.[429] If the excavation or discovery does not take place on federal or tribal lands, NAGPRA provisions regarding ownership will not apply. However, other cultural preservation laws may apply.[430] Further, repatriation may be required for objects that are in the possession of federal agencies or museums even if they were obtained prior to November 16, 1990.[431]

The Secretary of the Interior administers a number of grants to assist with various aspects of NAGPRA compliance, including consultation, documentation, and repatriation.[432]

See also "Curation of Federally Owned and Administered Archaeological Collections."
See also "Provenance."
See also "Restitution."

NAZI-ERA PROVENANCE INTERNET PORTAL

Maintained by the American Alliance of Museums, the Nazi-Era Provenance Internet Portal (NEPIP) is a registry of objects held in American museum collections that were present in Continental Europe during the period of Nazi looting (1933–1945).[433] The Portal makes publicly available provenance information on these objects in a searchable database. Museum participation is completely voluntary; however, participation is strongly recommended by the American Alliance of Museums, the Association of Art Museum Directors, and the Presidential Advisory Commission on Holocaust Assets in the United States.[434] As of June 2015, over 29,000 objects from 179 participating museums were listed in the NEPIP.[435] Additionally, the Portal maintains a list of American museums that hold in their permanent collections European fine art objects that do not qualify for inclusion in the Portal.[436]

Museums are encouraged to participate in the Portal if they hold any objects that meet the following criteria:

1. Were created prior to 1946 and acquired after 1932 (during the Nazi era), *or*
2. Changed ownership between 1932 and 1946, *and*
3. Were or reasonably may have been in Continental Europe between 1932 and 1946.[437]

Participation may require additional effort and resources on the part of the museum, as provenance research can be difficult, time-consuming, and expensive, but doing so demonstrates the museum's commitment to the highest ethical standards.[438]

Compare "National Stolen Art File."
See also "Ethics."
See also "Provenance."

NEPOTISM

The practice of showing preference in the workplace to persons with whom you share a close, personal relationship rather than basing preference on relevant experience and qualifications is known as nepotism. While historically the term related specifically to family members, today it can be understood in relation to both family members and close friends.[439]

For example, if an executive director were to hire her child for a position at her museum for which the child is unqualified, and the relationship between the individuals was not disclosed, that could be an example of nepotism. However, if the child was, in fact, qualified for the position, the hiring would not necessarily be an example of nepotism, though it could potentially be considered a conflict of interest on the part of the ED. Other factors to consider may be the amount paid to the child, the benefits package offered, or whether the child is not subject to the same requirements or expectations as other employees.

Nepotism is not necessarily illegal, depending on the workplace and the specific circumstances. In the private sector, the hiring of family members and friends is largely understood to be legal.[440] As long as the hiring preferences are not conducted in a manner that also discriminates a protected class, there may be little recourse.

In the public sector, government employment practices are regulated by state laws that are designed to prevent actual conflicts of interest or the appearance of such conflicts. As each state has its own laws, they vary considerably and may regulate different types of relationships, have different penalties for violation, or impact different types of hiring managers. Therefore, consultation with a specific jurisdiction's law is necessary to determine if the hiring is in violation.[441]

Even where nepotism is not illegal, there can be ethical ramifications for a museum that should be considered. A museum that hires based on personal relationship rather than qualifications or expertise may be doing a disservice to its members and the community it serves. For this reason, these hiring practices should be included in the organization's conflict-of-interest policy.

Compare "Self-Dealing."
See also "Conflict of Interest."

NONDISTRIBUTION CONSTRAINT

For nonprofit corporations, the nondistribution constraint limits what the corporation may do with its profits. Specifically, the constraint requires that any profits generated by the nonprofit corporation after the payment of all expenses (such as salaries and debts) must be retained by the corporation and used to further the corporation's nonprofit purpose.

The nondistribution constraint is a fundamental difference between nonprofit corporations and traditional for-profit corporations, where revenues retained after the payment of expenses are generally expected to be paid out to shareholders in the form of dividends.

See also "Nonprofit Corporation."
See also "Tax-Exempt."

NONPROFIT CORPORATION

A nonprofit corporation is an incorporated organization that is organized and operated in a manner in which all profits generated by the corporation are reinvested in the corporation's nonprofit purpose. This differs from a for-profit corporation, where profits are paid out to the owners or shareholders.

A nonprofit corporation is regulated by state law, and it must satisfy those laws both to properly incorporate and to be recognized by the state as a nonprofit. A nonprofit corporation is not automatically a tax-exempt organization under federal law, and the nonprofit must meet federal requirements to obtain exempt status.

Nonprofit corporations are subject to oversight by the state's attorney general, whose powers arise under applicable state law, often the state's nonprofit corporation statute.

Compare "Charitable Trust."
Compare "Tax-Exempt."
Compare "Unincorporated Association."
See also "Articles of Incorporataion."
See also "Attorney General."
See also "Bylaws."
See also "IRS Form 1023."
See also "Nondistribution Constraint."
See also "Third Sector."

For a more in-depth discussion, see "Chapter 8: Nonprofit Corporations and Tax Exemption."

OBJECT ID

Object ID is an international standard developed through a collaboration of the museum community, law enforcement and customs agencies, and others. Its primary purpose is to develop a standard means to describe artistic and archaeological objects and other cultural heritage items, which in turn makes identification of such objects easier within the museum community as well as by insurance companies, the art trade, and law enforcement agencies.

Currently, the Object ID project is administered by the International Council of Museums. The Object ID Checklist, with instructions on how to properly apply the standards to an object, and useful publications related to the standards as well as issues of object documentation, illicit trade, and other related topics, are available on the Object ID website.[442] The Object ID standard identifies nine categories of descriptive information necessary to properly identify an object (type of object, materials and techniques, measurement, inscriptions and markings, title, subject, date or period, and maker).[443] The standard also lists four steps to properly obtain and record this information (taking photographs of the object, collecting the information on the nine categories, writing a short description, and keeping the resulting documentation in a secure location).[444]

OBSCENITY

Occasionally, an exhibition may be proposed that seeks to challenge the community and museum's public in new ways of thinking about or perceiving their world. Such exhibitions may contain materials that some on the museum staff or in the community find questionable, offensive, or possibly even obscene. It can be difficult to decide whether such materials should be displayed. The final decision must come down to the museum's mission and whether the materials individually, or the exhibition as a whole, furthers that mission. However, a discussion of what qualifies as "obscene" in the legal sense may assist that determination.

The First Amendment of the United States Constitution protects the freedom of speech.[445] However, there are some forms of speech that are excepted from this protection. One of these exceptions is obscenity, which the Supreme Court has held may be regulated without infringement of the First Amendment.[446]

Obscenity is defined as "material which deals with sex in a manner appealing to prurient[447] interest."[448] The concern is that such materials may be disseminated in a manner that creates a "significant danger of offending the sensibilities of unwilling recipients or of exposure to juveniles."[449] In order to determine what materials may be regulated by the government, the Supreme Court has established a test.

The Miller test, named for the case in which it was first formulated, has three requirements. It requires that for a work to be legally obscene and therefore not eligible for First Amendment protection, the court must look to whether

1. the average person, applying contemporary community standards, would find that the work, taken as a whole, appeals to the prurient interest;
2. the work depicts or describes, in a patently offensive way, sexual conduct specifically defined by the applicable state law; and
3. the work, taken as a whole, lacks serious literary, artistic, political, or scientific value.[450]

If all three prongs are satisfied, the speech is obscene and may be subjected to government regulation. If the test is not entirely satisfied, regulation is inappropriate. "At a minimum, prurient, patently offensive depiction or description of sexual conduct must have serious literary, artistic, political, or scientific value to merit First Amendment protection."[451] Whether the offensive depictions have the necessary merit is a question the courts leave to the jury.[452]

The third prong is, perhaps, the hardest to satisfy, as it looks to a national standard of what may be deemed lacking in regard to literary, artistic, political, or scientific value. The Court recognized that there is no national standard of what is offensive or obscene. What is acceptable in New York City or Los Angeles may be shocking in Cleveland or Denver. Therefore, the determination as to whether material appeals to the "prurient interest" is based on the community standard, not a hypothetical nationwide standard.[453] In applying the Miller test, the jury will be instructed to apply a standard that represents "the average person, applying contemporary community standards" to determine if material is, in fact, obscene.[454]

Clearly, application of the Miller test is a fact-based inquiry, so no bright-line rule exists. However, by being engaged with the community and adhering to the museum's mission, it should be possible to determine whether a proposed object or exhibit will merely be challenging or cross the line to obscenity within a particular community.

See also "Freedom of Speech."
See also "Public Forum."

OLD LOANS

In terms of museum work, a loan is the temporary transfer of an object to another for (ideally) a finite period of time, for a specified purpose, and possibly with the option to renew. Title in the work does *not* transfer, so the lender retains all ownership rights in the work. While it is now a professional best practice to limit loans to a fixed duration of time, often one year with the option to renew, in the past museums would occasionally accept so-called permanent loans or loans of indefinite duration.

When these loans extend for a term so long as to make it impractical or impossible to return the objects, they are often called "old loans." Old loans can also arise when a loan of finite duration ends but the lender fails to reclaim the object.

Old loans present a problematic situation for the lendee museum, as it finds itself with custody of an object to which it does not have legal title. The museum bears the burden of care, including storage costs, security, insurance, and employee resources.[455] However, the museum reaps none of the benefits of a loan, as it may not have the ability or permission to display outside the scope of the initial loan agreement, to make the object available to researchers, to reproduce images of the object outside the scope of the original license (if applicable), or to loan the object to other institutions.

Legally, a loan, including an old loan, is a "bailment," where the borrowing institution is the "bailee" and the lender is the "bailor." The law imposes certain responsibilities and various duties of care on the parties, depending on which party obtains the primary benefit from the bailment. However, these responsibilities and duties only come into play if there is no express contract between the parties. An express contract, often referred to as a "loan agreement," controls the actual relationship and trumps any responsibilities and duties found at law. Regardless of whether the lendor-lendee relationship is controlled by bailment laws or a loan agreement, the responsibilities of the museum extend until the object is returned to its owner, meaning the museum has an indefinite responsibility to care for the object if the lender does not claim the loaned object.[456]

Unfortunately, there is no easy or quick process to legally resolve old loans and claim title to an object left under museum control. As of September 2020, almost all states have passed old loan legislation, which can provide steps for the museum to assert title over these objects, though some of those statutes only apply to certain types of museums.[457] Each state law takes a different approach and has different requirements that must be met by a museum seeking to assert title over its old loans, but they all provide a means by which a museum may terminate the original lender's ownership rights and gain title to the old loan.[458]

In the absence of a state law, common law may provide guidance on how to settle the old loan and assert title.[459] Under this approach, the museum must often make some type of good faith effort to notify the lender that title in the old loan will be claimed by the museum (undergo conversion).[460] What qualifies as a good faith effort varies from one state to another, but may include the mailing of a letter to the lender's last known address, possibly by certified mail, publication in a local newspaper, or some other means.[461] Additionally, it is possible that the statute of limitations may block a claim of ownership by the original lender, though this is in no way guaranteed.[462]

Compare "Found-in-Collection."
Compare "Loans."
Compare "Undocumented Object."
See also "Abandoned Property."
See also "Categories of Law."
See also "Orphaned Works (Collections Management)."
See also "Statute of Limitations."
See also "Title."

OPERATIONAL TEST

The operational test is one of four tests a nonprofit organization must satisfy if it is to receive recognition as a tax-exempt organization by the Internal Revenue Service. The test requires that the nonprofit organization conduct its activities in a manner that is primarily for an exempt purpose.[463] Unlike the organizational test, the operational test seeks to examine the actual activities of the organization, not merely what the organization states as its purpose in its founding documents.

Compare "Organizational Test."
See also "Political Activities Test."
See also "Private Inurement Test."
See also "Tax-Exempt."

For a more in-depth discussion, see "Chapter 8: Nonprofit Corporations and Tax Exemption."

ORGANIZATIONAL TEST

The organizational test is one of four tests a nonprofit organization must satisfy if it is to receive recognition as a tax-exempt organization by the Internal Revenue Service. It is essentially a "magic word" test, requiring that certain provisions be contained within the organization's founding documents. Failure to have these provisions in the founding documents will result in a finding that the organization is ineligible for exemption. Bylaws are not considered founding documents for purposes of the organizational test, only articles of incorporation.

The two components of the organizational test are the exempt purpose requirement and the distribution of assets upon dissolution requirement.

See also "Articles of Incorporation."
See also "Bylaws."

See also "Distribution of Assets upon Dissolution."
See also "Exempt Purpose."
See also "Operational Test."
See also "Political Activities Test."
See also "Private Inurement Test."
See also "Tax-Exempt."

For a more in-depth discussion, see "Chapter 8: Nonprofit Corporations and Tax Exemption."

ORIGINALITY

Under the Copyright Act, copyright provides legal protection to "original works of authorship fixed in any tangible medium of expression...."[464] Therefore, originality is a basic requirement for copyright protection to arise in a work.

A common misunderstanding of the statute's originality requirement is that originality equates to novelty. This is incorrect. The statute does not have any requirement that a work be novel in subject matter nor in presentation. If an artist creates a painting by laying the canvas on the floor and dripping paint onto it, that painting is entitled to copyright protection, even though the subject and the process are not by any means *novel*. What matters is that the work is *original*, meaning the artist's own artistic expression. The work was independently conceived by the artist and therefore satisfies the statute's requirements.

See also "Automatic Creation."
See also "Copyright."
See also "Fixation."
See also "Infringement."
See also "Works of Authorship."

ORPHANED WORKS (COLLECTIONS MANAGEMENT)

Orphaned works, in the realm of collections management, may refer to one of two scenarios. First, orphaned works may refer to works or objects that have been abandoned by their owners. For instance, a work that was brought in on temporary custody in consideration of a loan or acquisition and the owner fails to return to retrieve the object may be considered an orphaned work. Similarly, an old loan concerning which the legal owner can no longer be reached may be referred to as an orphaned work.

Second, accessioned objects that have no curatorial support may be referred to as orphaned works. For example, if a museum has a collection of lace doilies that do not properly conform to the museum's mission and are not assigned to a particular internal collection or curator, it may be referred to as an orphaned work.

For either use of the term, the museum retains legal obligations to the objects, and therefore they must be treated with the same level of care as any other object in the museum's custody.

Compare "Orphaned Works (Copyright)."
See also "Abandoned Property."
See also "Collections Management Policy."
See also "Old Loans."
See also "Temporary Custody."

ORPHANED WORKS (COPYRIGHT)

Copyright law gives a length of protection that outlasts the life of the original author. Additionally, there is no longer a requirement that works be registered or feature a copyright notice to obtain copyright protection. Therefore, it is possible that a work will be entitled to copyright protection, but there is little or no way to find the original author or the author's heir to obtain a license to use the work. When the owner of the copyright rights in a work are unknown and unknowable, it is called an orphaned work.

The United States Copyright Office has been examining the problem of orphaned works under U.S. copyright law, and in June 2015 it released a report that makes a series of recommendations based on current case law and overseas examples. Included in those recommendations is a proposed "safe harbor" for certain eligible users, including museums, that allows for noncommercial and educational uses of orphaned works.[465] However, at the time of writing, there has been no legislative action on the report. This means that use of orphaned works leaves open the possibility of liability, as technically their use constitutes an infringement.

Compare "Orphaned Works (Collections Management)."
See also "Copyright."
See also "Fair Use."
See also "Infringement."

PARTIAL GIFT

A partial gift occurs when a donor donates only a portion of her entire ownership rights in the donated property, with the intention that the remaining portion will be donated to the donee at some later date. The donated property itself may be a single object or multiple objects. The "partiality" refers to the ownership rights in the property itself. A donor may have positive tax consequences for extending donations over a number of tax years, which is what often gives rise to this type of donation.

For example, a donor approaches a museum with the intention of donating a painting. However, the donor wishes to donate only a one-quarter interest in the painting, with the remaining three-quarters to be donated over a course of years. In addition to owning one-quarter of the painting, the museum also will have the right to physically possess the painting for one-quarter of each year. This constitutes a partial gift to the museum.[466]

The IRS has strict rules concerning when a partial gift may give rise to a deduction for the taxpayer donor. The museum should not provide advice in this regard. Instead, the donor should consult with her tax professional. Any eventualities that may arise over the course of the donation should be fully considered, and the manner in which those eventualities will be addressed should be memorialized in writing at the time of the initial transfer.[467]

If the donor does not complete the partial gift within certain time frames, or if the donee museum does not take substantial physical possession of the object, then the donor may be required by the Internal Revenue Service to recapture the deduction that was received.

See also "Donation."
See also "Recapture of Deduction."

PARTNERSHIP (GENERAL)[468]

A partnership is a type of for-profit business structure in which two or more parties (individuals or businesses) agree to carry on a trade or business together. In this formation, each partner contributes to the business, and in exchange, each partner receives a share in the business' losses and profits. Each partner carries unlimited personal liability for the partnership's debts.

A partnership is automatically created at the time the parties agree to do business together and to share the partnership's profits and losses. The partnership is governed by state law, so the specific laws and regulations pertaining to partnerships will vary depending on the home jurisdiction. Depending on the laws of the state, the partnership may be required to file an annual informational return.

Compare "Unincorporated Association."
See also "Business Structures."

For a more in-depth discussion, see "Chapter 11: Understanding the Various Forms of Business Structures."

PATENT

Patent law is a form of intellectual property that protects the rights of inventors in their work. Authority to create a system of patents derives from the United States Constitution, which grants Congress the right "to promote the Progress of Science and the useful Arts, by securing for limited Times to Authors and Inventors the exclusive Right to their respective Writings and Discoveries."[469]

Patents are available to a person who "invents or discovers any new and useful process, machine, manufacture, or composition of matter, or any new and useful improvement thereof. . . ."[470] Eligibility for a patent requires the invention to be both novel[471] and nonobvious.[472]

Similar to trademark, and unlike copyright, patents require an application process, wherein they are subjected to examination by an examiner who will determine whether the patent may be issued.[473] Because they arise from the Copyright Clause, patents are subject to term limits, after which the patent holder's rights expire.

Compare "Copyright."
Compare "Moral Rights."
Compare "Trademark."
See also "Copyright Clause."
See also "Intellectual Property."

PAYROLL TAXES

See "Federal Insurance Contributions Act."

PERMANENT LOAN

See "Loans" and "Old Loans."

PERSONAL PROPERTY

Personal property is the category of property that is moveable. Examples of personal property are jewelry, artwork, and motor vehicles. A more encompassing definition would be property that is not real estate.

Compare "Intellectual Property."
Compare "Real Property."
See "Title."

POLITICAL ACTIVITIES TEST

The political activities test is one of four tests a nonprofit organization must satisfy if it is to receive recognition as a tax-exempt organization by the Internal Revenue Service. It examines whether the organization is involved in any of three regulated activities: direct lobbying, indirect or grassroots lobbying, and electioneering. Direct lobbying and indirect lobbying are permitted by the political activities test so long as the lobbying activities are kept to an insubstantial degree. Electioneering, however, is expressly forbidden to tax-exempt organizations by the Code.

The political activities test is reflective of both the organizational test and the operational test, as it looks both to the organization's founding documents and its actual activities to determine whether prohibited activities are either expressly permitted or actually undertaken by the organization. An organization that fails the political activities test will not be granted tax-exempt status.

See also "Operational Test."
See also "Organizational Test."
See also "Private Inurement Test."
See also "Tax-Exempt."

For a more in-depth discussion, see "Chapter 8: Nonprofit Corporations and Tax Exemption."

PRAGUE HOLOCAUST ERA ASSETS CONFERENCE

See "Terezín Declaration on Holocaust Era Assets and Related Issues."

PREEMPTION

See "Statutory Law."

PRIVATE FOUNDATION

Tax-exempt organizations can be organized as private foundations or public charities. One distinguishing factor between private foundations and public charities is how they acquire their initial and ongoing monetary support.

At inception, private foundations receive the majority of their assets from one benefactor (also referred to as the founder). This benefactor may be a for-profit corporation, a solitary philanthropist, or other private entity or individual. In addition, this donor may maintain their connection to the private foundation, though this ongoing involvement is not required. The donor is permitted significant control over the future direction of the foundation, establishing what type of charitable work the foundation will pursue during its life cycle. Examples of this include a donor establishing a foundation to be a grant-making organization to support charitable causes, to establish and operate its own charitable organization (such as a museum or school), or to provide direct support to a charitable cause or organization.

The money received from that initial major donor is invested, and the income of that investment is used to support an educational or charitable purpose under section 501(c)(3). The Internal Revenue Code does not directly define private foundations. Instead the Code lists the types of section 501(c)(3) organizations that are *not* private foundations, including so-called traditional public charities;[474] "gross-receipts" organizations, which can include museums that charge admission fees;[475] "supporting" organizations;[476] and finally, organizations that test for public safety.[477]

Regarding ongoing financial support, an organization is classified as a private foundation if it does not receive enough of its financial support from either governmental sources or from direct support by the general public.[478] Because private foundations tend to be controlled by a small number of closely related people, such as family members, and derive their financial support from limited sources or investment income, they receive much less public scrutiny than public charities. They also have a mandatory minimum distribution requirement that they must meet annually or face tax consequences.

See also "Facts-and-Circumstances Test."
See also "Thirty-Three and ⅓ Percent Support Test."
See also "Public Charity."
See also "Section 501(c)(3)."
See also "Tax-Exempt."

For a more in-depth discussion, see "Chapter 8: Nonprofit Corporations and Tax Exemption."

PRIVATE INUREMENT TEST

The private inurement test is one of four tests a nonprofit organization must satisfy if it is to receive recognition as a tax-exempt organization by the Internal Revenue Service. This test requires that the organization function in a manner that is primarily beneficial to the public and not to individuals or groups closely related to the organization.[479]

See also "Operational Test."
See also "Organizational Test."
See also "Political Activities Test."
See also "Tax-Exempt."

For a more in-depth discussion, see "Chapter 8: Nonprofit Corporations and Tax Exemption."

PROCEDURAL LAW

See "Categories of Law."

PROCEEDS FROM DEACCESSIONING

Once a museum makes the decision to deaccession an object from the collection and to dispose of it in a manner that will generate profit, it must decide what to do with that profit. In the museum profession, the most accepted manner to use those proceeds is to dedicate them to the acquisition of new collection objects. This specific use for deaccession proceeds is promulgated by the two largest American museum professional organizations, the American Alliance of

Museums[480] and the Association of Art Museum Directors,[481] as well as many smaller regional, local, or category-specific museum organizations.[482]

Legally, there are few impediments to using deaccession proceeds for purposes other than acquisition of new collection objects.[483] However, when a museum board seeks to capitalize its collection in order to rectify serious financial distress, fund building projects, or otherwise use the collection to fund operating costs, it is possible the board has breached its fiduciary duty to the museum by failing to properly oversee the museum's finances or for seeking to profit from a collection that is held in the public trust. This, in turn, may give rise to intervention from the attorney general. Additionally, use of deaccessioning proceeds may result in censure by any professional organizations of which the museum is a member, due to breach of that organization's ethical codes.

See also "Attorney General."
See also "Code of Ethics."
See also "Deaccession."
See also "Direct Care of Collections."
See also "Disposal."
See also "Ethics."
See also "FASB Update 2019-03."
See also "Fiduciary Duty."

For a more in-depth discussion, see "Chapter 3: Museum Deaccessioning and Proceeds from Disposal."

PROHIBITION AGAINST PRIVATE INUREMENT

Related to the fiduciary duty of loyalty, the prohibition against private inurement requires that a trustee not use her position to receive any funds in a manner that would inappropriately benefit the trustee. While a trustee may receive reasonable compensation, an excessive amount of compensation or other unreasonable means of benefiting at the expense of the museum will result in a breach of this prohibition and the fiduciary duty of loyalty.

See also "Doctrine of Corporate Opportunity."
See also "Duty of Loyalty."
See also "Fiduciary Duty."
See also "Nonprofit Corporation."
See also "Tax-Exempt."
See also "Trustee."

For a more in-depth discussion, see "Chapter 9: The Board of Trustees and Their Fiduciary Duty."

PROMISED GIFT

A promised gift is, simply, a promise to make a gift to another at some future time. To be legally enforceable, a gift requires donative intent, delivery, and acceptance, and without the satisfaction of these three elements, a gift is merely a promise with no legal backing.

A promised gift is not the same as a contract, which requires an offer, acceptance, consideration, and mutuality.[484] For example, Barbara Bookseller offers to sell a book to Colleen Collector for $50. Colleen accepts the offer. Barbara delivers the book, and Colleen delivers the $50. The $50 is the consideration in this example, which is a contract between the parties. In comparison, Barbara Bookseller offers to donate a book worth $50 to City Museum. City Museum accepts the generous offer. However, Barbara fails to deliver the book. City Museum made no performance or return promise in exchange for the book, so there was no consideration. Therefore, this example shows merely a promised gift, not a contract, and the promised gift would not be enforced against Barbara.[485]

However, there are some exceptions to the unenforceability of a promised gift. First, if the intended recipient can show the promise was, in fact, a valid contract, then the promise will be enforceable. This may invoke the statute of frauds, which dictates mandatory requirements for certain types of contracts.

Second, if the intended recipient relied on the promise to its own detriment, then a court *may* enforce the promised gift. For example, Daniel Donor promises to donate a specific painting to City Museum so long as City Museum renovates a certain gallery space and renames the gallery in Donor's honor. The donation would be a major addition to City Museum's collection, and the museum is pleased to accept Donor's terms. City Museum takes on the gallery renovation, installing new HVAC systems and security measures. Donor attends the planning meetings for the new space, and he personally approves the new gallery name. Donor also attends the press conference announcing the reopening of the gallery, along with giving numerous interviews discussing the planned donation and the installation of the work in the new gallery space.[486] If Donor then reneges on his promise and fails to deliver the promised painting, it is possible a court would find that City Museum has detrimentally relied on Donor's promise and the promised gift will be enforced against Donor.[487]

Compare "Contract."
See also "Donation."
See also "Equity."
See also "Estoppel."
See also "Gift."
See also "Statute of Frauds."

PROTECTION OF HISTORIC PROPERTIES

See "National Historic Preservation Act."

PROVENANCE

Provenance is an object's history of ownership.[488] Provenance includes any transfer in ownership and, in the case of archaeological objects, the source location and conditions of discovery. An object's provenance may be incomplete, as artworks are not required to have specific documentation generated when a sale occurs, as compared to other types of personal property such as an automobile, where an owner would receive a copy of the vehicle's title. An artwork can be legally sold without any document memorializing the sale.

For museums and other collecting institutions, provenance can be helpful for a variety of reasons. Provenance can provide information about an object's cultural importance and its place in an artist's oeuvre, and it can help to ensure the museum holds proper title to the object.[489] To this last point, it is important to remember that ignorance as to an object's legal status—for instance, the failure to discover an object was stolen—does not insulate a museum from potential legal repercussions.

An object's provenance is what demonstrates that a "good" title can be transferred from the seller/donor to the buyer/donee. "Provenance research supports a museum's mandate to ensure that all collections in its custody are lawfully held and rightfully owned; in turn this kind of responsible stewardship helps to maintain a high level of public trust."[490] Therefore, provenance research and documentation touches on a museum's legal and ethical obligations. For these reasons, provenance research should be conducted on all objects prior to acquisition and accessioning, and also on any collections objects for which such research has not already been completed.

See also "Due Diligence."
See also "National Stolen Art File."
See also "Nazi-Era Provenance Internet Portal."
See also "Personal Property."
See also "Title."

PSEUDONYMOUS WORK

Under copyright law, a pseudonymous work is any work where "the author is identified under a fictitious name."[491] Identification of the author's legal name is not a requirement for copyright protection, and these works are entitled to the same level of protection as any other work.

When a creation is a pseudonymous work, it is entitled to copyright protection for a term of 95 years from the date of its first publication, or a term of 120 years from when it was created, whichever term ends first.[492] However, if the author or authors of the pseudonymous work are at any point identified in registration records filed with the Copyright Office, then the term will be the standard term for single-creator or joint works as applicable.[493] As with other copyrightable works, the artistic creation must meet the requirements of copyright law and, if it does, copyright protection vests at the time of creation.[494]

See also "Copyright."

PUBLIC CHARITY

Tax-exempt organizations can be organized as private foundations or public charities. One distinguishing factor between private foundations and public charities is how they acquire their ongoing monetary support.

A public charity may be founded in a similar manner to a private foundation, receiving the majority of its initial assets from one benefactor (also referred to as the founder). A public charity may also be founded by a larger number of people coming together to start the organization together and each contributing assets or soliciting donations.

All section 501(c)(3) organizations are presumed to be private foundations. In order to qualify as a public charity, the organization must request (and qualify for) a ruling to determine it is a public charity. Among the categories of organizations that can be classified as a public charity are publicly supported organizations. These are organizations that receive a substantial amount of their ongoing financial support from either governmental sources or from direct support by the general public.[495] The "public" in "public charity" can be understood to refer to the organization receiving funding from the community in support of the organization's work. In other words, a public charity has a diverse source of funding and diverse leadership (rather than the closely related leadership of a private foundation).

To determine whether an organization qualifies as a public charity, the IRS applies one of the two public charity support tests: the "thirty-three and ⅓ percent support test" or the "facts-and-circumstances test." Both tests look to the organization's public support over a period of years.

See also "Facts-and-Circumstances Test."
See also "Private Foundation."
See also "Section 501(c)(3)."
See also "Tax-Exempt."
See also "Thirty-Three and ⅓ Percent Support Test."

For a more in-depth discussion, see "Chapter 8: Nonprofit Corporations and Tax Exemption."

PUBLIC CHARITY SUPPORT TEST

See either the "Facts-and-Circumstances Test" or the "Thirty-Three and ⅓ Percent Support Test."

PUBLIC DISPLAY RIGHT

The right to publicly display a work is one of the exclusive rights under copyright. As with all the exclusive rights under copyright, the right to publicly display a work is independent of ownership of the physical work and is also independent of ownership of the other exclusive rights. The author of a creative work may retain the right to herself, or the author may give or sell the right through the process of licensing.

The public display right grants the right-holder the exclusive right to "perform the copyrighted work publicly."[496] The right applies to "literary, musical, dramatic, and choreographic works, pantomimes, and motion pictures and other audiovisual works."[497] This statutory definition applies to pictorial, graphical, and sculptural works, and also stills from motion pictures. No one other than the right-holder may publicly display the work.

The Copyright Act defines *public* as a place that is "open to the public or . . . any place where a substantial number of persons outside of a normal circle of a family and its social acquaintances is gathered. . . ."[498] This public display includes whether the display is made "by means of any device or process, whether the members of the public capable of receiving the . . . display receive it in the same place or in separate places and at the same time or at different times."[499]

The Copyright Act defines *display* as "to show a copy of [the work], either directly or by means of a film, slide, television image, or any other device or process or, in the case of a motion picture or other audiovisual work, to show individual images nonsequentially."[500] To publicly display the work without the right-owner's permission constitutes copyright infringement.

Despite these protections, there is an important limitation to this right. The Copyright Act provides that an owner of a lawfully created copy of the work may publicly display that copy without the copyright owner's permission.[501] Additionally, the owner of the legal copy may authorize another to do the same.[502] However, this "first sale doctrine" does not impact the copyright owner's reproduction right. For instance, if an individual purchases a painting, that individual may display that painting to the public. However, the painting owner does not have the right to make copies of the painting and display them.

For museums, this means that even if the museum holds no copyright interests in a collection object, it may still display it in the museum's galleries. Further, a museum may authorize another to display the work, such as during an inter-museum loan. The museum also may be authorized to display works on loan from other museums or private collectors, again without the copyright owner's permission. The creative author or copyright holder cannot prevent the public display of a lawful copy.

See also "Copyright."
See also "First Sale Doctrine."
See also "Infringement."
See also "License."

PUBLIC DOMAIN

When copyrightable works no longer have copyright protection, they are referred to as belonging in the "public domain." This means that any use, by any individual, is legal and does not constitute copyright infringement. Public domain works may be reproduced, performed, distributed, and displayed free of any license, as there are no rights to infringe. Further, derivative works, such as adaptations or parodies, may be freely created.

Copyrightable works may fall into the public domain due to a failure to comply with copyright law formalities, such as the pre–1976 Act notice requirements. An author may choose to forfeit his or her copyright protection, such as computer programmers who choose to release their software of all intellectual property constraints or authors who release their works under the "CC0 No Rights Reserved" license available through Creative Commons.[503] Due to the duration limits placed on copyright by the Copyright Act and the United States Constitution's Copyright Clause, all copyrightable works will eventually fall into the public domain merely due to the passage of time. Works that were created prior to the existence of copyright are in the public domain. Finally, works authored by the United States Government are not entitled to copyright protection and are all in the public domain.[504]

Works that are in the public domain are often subject to free and widespread use and adaptation. Popular examples include the works of William Shakespeare, Leonardo da Vinci's *Mona Lisa*, and the 1960 film version of *The Little Shop of Horrors*.

Compare "First Sale Doctrine."
See also "Copyright."
See also "Copyright Clause."
See also "Infringement."

For a more in-depth discussion, see "Chapter 4: An Overview of the Basics of Copyright Law," especially the section "Special Consideration: The Copyright Term Extension Act and Public Domain Day."

PUBLIC FORUM

When presenting artwork that may be offensive to some of the viewing public, a balancing act must be employed. On the one hand, you have the right of the artist to express herself. This right is protected from governmental censorship by the First Amendment's freedom of speech provision. However, you also have the rights of the viewing public not to be exposed to the artwork against their will. If the viewers are a captive audience, meaning they have no option but to be exposed to the artwork, then the two interested parties' interests fall out of balance and a problem arises for the artist, the viewers, and the exhibiting institution.

There is an important distinction here. The First Amendment's protection of the freedom of speech applies to *governmental* censorship. Therefore, the party doing the censoring must be a state actor, such as a public school, for the First Amendment protection to apply. A state museum may be a state actor in the meaning of the Amendment, but a private museum would not.[505]

Balance can be restored between the rights of the speaker and the public listeners by content-neutral "time, place, and manner" restrictions. This means that the regulations cannot restrict the material based on the content of the material.[506] Additionally, the regulations cannot force the artist to alter how or what she expresses in the artwork. If the restriction is content neutral, is narrowly tailored, serves a legitimate governmental interest, and leaves open alternative channels of communication, then it may be acceptable under the requirements of the Constitution.[507]

See also "Freedom of Speech."
See also "Obscenity."

PUBLIC PERFORMANCE RIGHT

The right to publicly perform a work is one of the exclusive rights under copyright. As with all exclusive rights granted under copyright, the right to publicly perform a work is independent of ownership of the physical work and is also independent of ownership of the other exclusive rights. The author of a creative work may retain the right to herself, or the author may give or sell the right through the process of licensing.

Regarding literary, musical, dramatic, and choreographic works, as well as pantomimes, motion pictures, and audiovisual works, the public performance right grants the right-holder the exclusive right to "to perform the copyrighted work publicly."[508] Where the work is a sound recording, the public performance right grants the right-holder the exclusive right to "perform the copyrighted work publicly by means of a digital audio transmission."[509] No one other than the right-holder may publicly perform the work.

The Copyright Act defines *public* as a place that is "open to the public or . . . any place where a substantial number of persons outside of a normal circle of a family and its social acquaintances is gathered. . . ."[510] This public display includes whether the display is made "by means of any device or process, whether the members of the public capable of receiving the . . . display receive it in the same place or in separate places and at the same time or at different times."[511]

The Copyright Act defines the *performance* of a work as "to recite, render, play, dance, or act it, either directly or by means of any device or process."[512] To publicly perform the work without the right owner's permission constitutes copyright infringement.

There is a limited exemption to the public performance right where the copyrighted work is performed in face-to-face educational instruction by nonprofit educational institutions.[513]

See also "Copyright."
See also "First Sale Doctrine."
See also "Infringement."
See also "License."

QUALIFIED APPRAISAL

A qualified appraisal is one that meets certain criteria in order to be accepted by the Internal Revenue Service (IRS) in support of a donor's claimed deduction in association with a donation to a qualified organization. This qualified appraisal must:[514]

1. Be prepared, signed, and dated by a qualified appraiser who applied generally accepted standards in making the appraisal,[515]
2. Meet all IRS-promulgated requirements,
3. Not be prepared earlier than sixty days before the date of the donation,[516]
4. Not be prepared in exchange for a prohibited appraisal fee,[517] and
5. Include all required information.[518]

If these requirements are met, the qualified appraisal will likely be accepted by the IRS to support the deduction. It should be remembered, however, that the IRS will not accept any appraisal without question.[519]

The donor is solely responsible for obtaining a qualified appraisal when necessary. The donee museum should not be involved in this process, and the museum and its employees are not qualified appraisers according to the IRS. If the museum would like to assist the donor in obtaining a qualified appraisal, it may choose to provide the names of a selection (three or more) of professional appraisers or the contact information for an appropriate appraiser professional organization or accreditation organization.

Compare "Appraisal (Donation)."
See also "Deduction."
See also "Donation."
See also "Fair Market Value."
See also "Qualified Appraiser."
See also "Restricted Gift."

QUALIFIED APPRAISER

In order to receive a deduction for a donation to a qualified organization, a donor must submit a qualified appraisal. One of the requirements for a qualified appraisal is that it be prepared by a qualified appraiser.

In order to be a qualified appraiser, an individual must meet a number of requirements. She must:

1. Hold herself out to be an appraiser or perform appraisals regularly;[520]
2. Be qualified to appraise the type of property being appraised;[521]
3. Not be an excluded person, including but not limited to the donor, any person who was party to the donor's acquisition of the item (such as an agent or gallery owner) unless the item is donated within two months of the donor's acquisition and the donation's appraised value does not exceed the donor's purchase price, and the donee museum or any of its employees;[522]
4. Any person who has knowledge that would cause a reasonable person to expect the appraiser to provide a falsely inflated value;[523]
5. Understand the consequences of making an intentionally false or fraudulent appraisal;[524] and
6. Not have been prohibited from practicing before the Internal Revenue Service (IRS) at any time during the three-year period ending on the appraisal date.[525]

The donor is solely responsible for obtaining a qualified appraisal. The donee museum should not be involved in this process, and the museum and its employees are not qualified appraisers to give a qualified appraisal. If the museum would like to assist the donor in obtaining a qualified appraisal, it may choose to provide the names of a selection (three or more) of professional appraisers or the contact information for an appropriate appraiser professional organization or accreditation organization.

Even if all these requirements are met, the IRS will not accept the provided appraisal without question.[526] Also, the IRS does not recognize the members of any one appraiser organization as being uniquely or without question qualified to provide qualified appraisals for deduction purposes.[527] The appraisal provided by a qualified appraiser will not be binding on the Service.[528]

See also "Deduction."
See also "Donation."
See also "Fair Market Value."
See also "Qualified Appraisal."

QUALIFIED CONSERVATION CONTRIBUTION

A qualified conservation contribution is a special class of donation. It is a donation of a qualified real property interest that is given to a qualified organization for the express purpose that it be used for conservation.[529] The organization in receipt of the qualified conservation contribution must be committed to protect the donation's conservation purposes and must have the appropriate resources to enforce any restrictions related to that conservation.[530] Therefore, to qualify as a qualified conservation contribution, it must:

1. Consist of a qualified real property interest, and
2. Be made to a qualified organization[531]
3. With the exclusive purpose of conservation.[532]

Records related to the donation must indicate the real property's fair market value both before and after the donation.[533] Also included must be an explanation of the conservation purpose that is furthered by means of the donation.[534]

Examples of a qualified conservation contribution include the preservation of open space such as farmland for the public's scenic enjoyment or the preservation of a certified historic structure.[535]

Compare "Donation."
See also "Real Property."

QUALIFIED FUND-RAISING CAMPAIGN

In relation to a *quid pro quo* contribution, a qualified fund-raising campaign is one that is intended by the qualified organization to attract donations.[536] The qualified organization is responsible to determine the fair market value of any goods or services offered as incentives for the donations.[537] When it is not possible to place an exact value on the goods or services, a reasonable estimate is acceptable.[538] Once the fair market value is determined, the organization can use it to calculate by how much the donation exceeds the fair market value, providing the amount of the donation that is eligible for a deduction.

[Amount of Donation] – [Fair Market Value of Benefits] = [Deductible Amount]

This deductible amount must be included in all solicitations and other documents issued in relation to the donation, such as on receipts or tickets.[539]

However, if only insubstantial benefits are offered, such as token items or many common membership benefits, then the full amount of the *quid pro quo* contribution will be eligible for a deduction.[540] This information should be conveyed to the donors in the fund-raising materials.

See also "Disclosure Statement."
See also "Donation."
See also "Fair Market Value."
See also "*Quid Pro Quo* Contribution."
See also "Token Benefit."

QUALIFIED ORGANIZATION

The Internal Revenue Service permits donations to qualified organizations to be deducted from the donor's taxes, providing an incentive for donations to these organizations. To be classified as a qualified organization, it must be a recognized tax exempt organization that has an appropriate purpose, such as being charitable or educational in nature.[541] The IRS specifically lists "nonprofit educational organizations, including . . . museums" as an example of a qualified organization.[542]

See also "Deduction."
See also "Donation."
See also "Nonprofit Corporation."
See also "Section 501(c)(3)."
See also "Tax-Exempt."

For a more in-depth discussion, see "Chapter 8: Nonprofit Corporations and Tax Exemption."

QUALITY OF TITLE

See "Title."

QUID PRO QUO CONTRIBUTION

Donations made to a qualified organization in exchange for goods or services from that organization are known as *quid pro quo* contributions.[543] Unlike other donations in which no benefits are received by the donor, *quid pro quo* contributions result in a charitable deduction limited to the amount of the donation that is in excess of the value of the benefit.[544]

[Amount of Donation] – [Fair Market Value of Benefits] = [Deductible Amount]

These types of donations are common in the museum setting. For example, a donor may make a cash donation to a museum, and in return, the donor receives a tote bag with the museum's logo or the right to attend special members-only events such as exhibition openings.[545] These are *quid pro quo* contributions, and museums must comply with special disclosure statement requirements for these donations. The intent of these special disclosure statements is to ensure the organization is properly and accurately informing donors of what portion of their donation is deductible for income tax purposes.[546]

A disclosure statement is required for any *quid pro quo* contribution over $75.[547] The qualified organization has two opportunities to disclose the information to the donor: either at the time of the solicitation, or upon receipt of the *quid pro quo* contribution.[548] While the Internal Revenue Service (IRS) does not provide a model format for these disclosures, the Service does require that the disclosure be in writing and be presented in such a manner that the donor is likely to be aware of the disclosure.[549] The disclosure must indicate the fair market value of the goods or services exchanged for the donation.[550]

When the organization is determining the fair market value of the goods or services, it must be noted that the value of those goods or services may be deemed insubstantial by the IRS. When the goods or services merely qualify as a token benefit, the full amount of the donation may be deductible.[551]

See also "Disclosure Statement."
See also "Donation."
See also "Fair Market Value."
See also "Qualified Fund-Raising Campaign."
See also "Token Benefit."

REAL PROPERTY

Real property is the category of property commonly referred to as "real estate." It is unmovable or fixed. Both land and the fixed buildings on that land constitute real property. There are a number of different manners by which real property may be owned, determined by the rights the owner has in the property and how that ownership is split between co-owners.

Table 1.4. Overview of the Different Types of Ownership Available in Real (Immovable) Property

Type of ownership		Term for owners	Right of survivorship?	Right to sell, bequeath, etc.?
Fee simple		If one person, sole owner	N/A	If sole owner, yes. If owned by multiple persons, see below.
Owned by multiple persons	Joint tenancy	Joint tenants	Yes. Upon death, ownership passes to surviving joint tenants.	Yes, but only the seller's ownership interest. Selling breaks the joint tenancy.
	Tenancy by the entirety	Spouse	Yes. Upon death, ownership passes to surviving spouse.	No, not without the consent of the other spouse.
	Tenancy in common	Co-tenants	No. Upon death, ownership passes to the deceased's heirs or persons named in their will.	Yes, but only the seller's ownership interest.
Marital property	Common law property	Spouse	For individually owned property, no. Upon death, separately owned property is distributed according to the will or per probate. For jointly owned marital property, it is distributed depending on if the couple owns the property as joint tenants, tenancy by the entirety, or as tenancy in common (see above).	Yes, unless an affirmative act was done at the time of acquisition to indicate the property ownership is shared between the spouses.
	Community property	Spouse	For individually owned property, no. Upon death, separately owned property is distributed according to the will or per probate. For jointly owned marital property, yes. Upon death, ownership passes to surviving spouse.	No, property owned by one spouse is communally held by the other spouse. (50/50 split.)
Life estate		Holder	No. Upon death of the holder, ownership passes in whatever manner defined in the instrument that created the life estate.	The holder may permit another to possess or use the property during their own lifetime, but may not transfer interest in the property beyond their lifetime.

These are all governed by state law, and not all forms of ownership are available in all jurisdictions. Further, local rules may interpret the specifics for the different types of ownership in different ways. Be sure to consult local law for availability and applicability.

The most common form of ownership is the fee simple, but that simple ownership may be complicated when the fee (vested, inheritable, possessory interest in the land) is co-owned by multiple people. In those circumstances, the type of ownership will impact who may inherit the portions and what happens when one or more co-owners sell their portions.

Compare "Future Interest."
Compare "Intellectual Property."
Compare "Life Estate."
Compare "Personal Property."
See also "Joint Tenancy."
See also "Qualified Conservation Contribution."
See also "Tenancy by the Entirety."
See also "Tenancy in Common."
See also "Title."

RECAPTURE OF DEDUCTION

When a donor makes a partial gift[552] to a qualified organization and either fails to complete that donation in its entirety within certain time frames or the donee museum fails to take significant physical possession of the object, the donor may be required to recapture the deduction that was given on her taxes.

First, if a partial gift of tangible personal property was made after August 17, 2006, and the donor did not donate the remainder of the property to the original donee (or to another qualified organization if the original donee no longer existed) either within ten years of the original donation or before the donor's death, the *donor* must recapture the deduction by including it in her income.[553]

Second, if a partial gift was made and the donee museum failed to take substantial physical possession of the object and use the object in a manner related to its exempt purpose either within ten years of the original donation or before the donor's death, the *donor* must recapture the deduction by including it in her income.[554]

The donee museum should not provide tax advice to donors regarding the tax consequences of recapture. However, the donee museum *may* decide, from a donor relations standpoint, to encourage the donor to adhere to the donation schedule so that the donation will be completed before recapture is mandated and also to make the object available to the museum for proper use.

See also "Donation."
See also "Exempt Purpose."
See also "Partial Gift."
See also "Unrelated Use."

REPATRIATION

See "Restitution."

REPRODUCTION RIGHT

The right to make a reproduction of a copyrighted work is one of the exclusive rights under copyright. As with all the exclusive rights under copyright, the right to make a reproduction is independent of ownership of the physical work and is also independent of ownership of the other exclusive rights. The author of a creative work may retain the right to himself or herself, or the author may give or sell the right through the process of licensing.

The reproduction right grants the right-holder the exclusive right to "reproduce the copyrighted work in copies or phonorecords."[555] The right applies to all the subject matter categories covered by the Copyright Act. No one other than the right-holder may make any copies of the work. For example, to reproduce a painting on a T-shirt without the right-holder's authorization is an infringement of the reproduction right. Similarly, photocopying a book or making a copy of a music CD constitute infringement of this right.

An infringement may occur even when only a portion of the work is reproduced without authorization. There is no bright-line rule that dictates how much may be copied before infringement occurs. Rather, the test is if a "substantial and material" portion was copied.[556] Therefore, reproduction on a T-shirt of the central figure in a painting may be found to infringe the reproduction right, as may photocopying a chapter out of a book. The determination of what constitutes substantial and material is a fact-based question, and the facts and circumstances of the particular case will determine what is and is not infringement.

See also "Copyright."
See also "Fair Use Doctrine."
See also "Infringement."
See also "License."

RESALE ROYALTY

See "*Droit de Suite* (Resale Royalty)."

RESERVE

When an object is sold at auction, the seller may elect to have a reserve price, which is a price the object must reach or it will not be sold. The reserve is generally set at or below the low estimate as prepared by the auction house. For instance, if the auction house sets the low estimate for an object at $100,000, the reserve can be $100,000 or less. A reserve should not be set above the low estimate, as this would require the object to sell for more than the auction house thinks it is likely to fetch at auction. Unlike the high and low estimates, which are public information, the reserve price amount is confidential between the seller and the auction house.

See also "Auction House."
See also "Estimate."

RESTITUTION

In the realm of cultural property, restitution refers to the return of objects to their proper owner, cultural group, or other claimant. Restitution may be the result of a legal action, such as arising from a suit or a properly made claim under the Native American Graves Protection and Repatriation Act (in which it is referred to as "repatriation"), or to fulfill an ethical obligation, such as the voluntary return of an object without resorting to the legal system.

Other terms with similar, though not necessarily identical, meanings include *return*, *repatriation*, or *recovery*.

See also "Provenance."

RESTRICTED GIFT

Restricted gift is a term applied to donations that have a donor-imposed restriction on their use, alienability, display, or other aspect. A donation that prohibits an item to ever be deaccessioned and sold is an example of a restricted gift. A donation requiring a set of objects only be displayed together as a group is another example of a restricted gift.

A donor may request a restriction that would make current or future care and use of the object difficult, and those future developments can be hard to anticipate or plan for. Therefore, it is a generally accepted best practice to try to have all donations be restriction-free. However, the decision regarding whether a particular restriction is agreeable to the donee museum is fact specific and personal to the particular institution. Even if a museum has a policy not to accept restricted gifts, that policy must permit deviation when necessary. If such deviation will further the museum's mission and interest, and appropriate consideration is given to the impact of the restriction on future use and care, then it may be possible to accept the donation despite the donor's restrictions.

A restricted gift that comes as a bequest can be a more difficult decision, since the donor is deceased and discussion or compromise over the restriction cannot occur. Any restriction accompanying the bequest must be honored if the museum chooses to accept the bequest, though it is possible the donor's heirs or executor will agree to a certain interpretation of the donor's restriction. If such an agreement is made, it should be memorialized and included in the object file.

Any legal restrictions on a gift (as compared to restrictions phrased in precatory language, which may carry an ethical obligation but not a legal restriction)[557] will be enforced by the attorney general. The donee museum cannot disregard these restrictions in future actions. If a museum holds an object that is subject to a donor-imposed restriction, and the museum seeks to break from the confines of that restriction, then the museum must seek legal permission to do so, often in the form of a declaratory judgment, through a *cy pres* action, or through application of the doctrine of equitable deviation.

See also "Attorney General."
See also "Bequest."
See also "*Cy Pres* Doctrine."

See also "Declaratory Judgment."
See also "Doctrine of Equitable Deviation."
See also "Donation."
See also "Equity."

RIGHTS AND REPRODUCTIONS

There are a number of exclusive rights protected by copyright law. These rights are best visualized as a bundle of sticks, where each stick represents a different right in the work. An individual can own one or many of the sticks independently, and ownership of the sticks is entirely separate from ownership of the actual creative object that gave rise to the sticks.[558] Among these rights are the reproduction right, which grants the right-holder the exclusive right to "reproduce the copyrighted work in copies or phonorecords."[559] The right applies to all the subject matter categories covered by the Copyright Act. No one other than the right-holder may make any copies of the work.

The reproduction right, like the other rights, or "sticks," may be given or sold to a third party by the copyright owner. This process is called licensing. To manage the licensing of the works in its collections, museums may have a "Rights and Reproductions" (R&R) department. This department often falls under the jurisdiction of the registrar, archivist, or curator, though other arrangements exist. The R&R department is responsible for ensuring that reproductions of collection objects are carried out according to the department's established guidelines and that proper credit is given to the institution for any reproductions.

Remember that copyright protections exist separately from the physical object, and ownership of an object does not ensure ownership of the underlying copyright rights. A museum cannot grant permissions greater than what the museum actually owns. Proper record keeping will ensure the R&R department knows what rights are held in the works and what rights it may grant to others.

See also "Copyright."
See also "License."

SECONDARY MEANING

Trademark law categorizes marks along a spectrum of distinctiveness. One of the categories on that spectrum is descriptive marks, which merely describe the goods identified.[560] Marks that merely describe the goods are not immediately available for registration with the Patent and Trademark Office, since a merely descriptive mark fails to meet one of the main requirements of trademark, namely to identify the source of goods in the marketplace.

However, a descriptive mark may be permitted to be registered if it can be demonstrated that it has "become distinctive" of the goods in the marketplace and therefore has acquired a "secondary meaning."[561] The registrant must demonstrate that the mark meets statutory requirements and is closely identified with one producer's goods.[562]

Marks that are composed merely of a surname also require acquisition of a secondary meaning prior to registration.[563] The test to prove secondary meaning is identical to that for descriptive marks.[564]

Descriptive marks can be difficult to distinguish from suggestive marks. The distinction is that a descriptive mark merely describes the good offered, while a suggestive mark requires that little extra bit of imaginative interpretation on the part of the consumer.

See also "Descriptive Mark."
See also "Spectrum of Distinctiveness."
See also "Trademark."

SECTION 106 REVIEW

See "National Historic Preservation Act."

SECTION 501(C)(3)

Under the Internal Revenue Code, section 501(c)(3) organizations are those that are exempt from taxation.[565] To qualify as a section 501(c)(3) organization, it must fit within this definition:

> Corporations, and any community chest, fund, or foundation, organized and operated exclusively for religious, charitable, scientific, testing for public safety, literary, or educational purposes, . . . no part of the net earnings of which inures to the benefit of any private shareholder or individual, no substantial part of the activities of which is carrying on propaganda, or otherwise attempting, to influence legislation . . . , and which does not participate in, or intervene in (including the publishing or distributing of statements), any political campaign on behalf of (or in opposition to) any candidate for public office.[566]

Museums are generally recognized as being charitable or educational organizations under the Code, and this categorization of museums is explicitly stated in the Treasury Regulations.[567] The Internal Revenue Service and Congress recognize the public benefit that museums bring to society as a whole through their promotion of art appreciation and educational programs.[568]

An important distinction to be aware of is that section 501(c)(3) tax-exempt status is not the same as nonprofit status. Nonprofit categorization is controlled by state law, and section 501(c)(3) status is a federal recognition. Therefore, an organization could be a nonprofit on the state level but not have federal section 501(c)(3) status, either because it is ineligible for some reason or simply because it has not completed the required application process through the IRS.

Organizations that seek to obtain and maintain tax-exempt status must follow the application and annual reporting guidelines set forth by the IRS. Those guidelines dictate what types of activities the organization may participate in, and they also have requirements regarding how the organization is organized and operated.

Compare "Nonprofit Corporation."
See also "Automatic Revocation."
See also "Categories of Law."
See also "IRS Form 990."
See also "IRS Form 1023."
See also "Tax-Exempt."

For a more in-depth discussion, see "Chapter 8: Nonprofit Corporations and Tax Exemption."

SELF-DEALING

The practice of an individual acting on behalf of their own interests rather than the interests of the nonprofit organization such as a museum is self-dealing. When self-dealing is done by an employee, it may be a violation of the organization's conflict-of-interest policy if such a policy exists and it applies to the employee. However, when self-dealing is done by a trustee who owes a fiduciary duty to the museum, that self-dealing may qualify as a breach of the trustee's fiduciary duty.

Compare "Nepotism."
See also "Conflict of Interest."
See also "Duty of Loyalty."
See also "Fiduciary Duty."
See also "Trustee."

For a more in-depth discussion, see "Chapter 9: The Board of Trustees and Their Fiduciary Duty."

SELF-EMPLOYMENT CONTRIBUTIONS ACT

See "Federal Insurance Contributions Act."

SERVICE MARK

A service mark is any mark or symbol (word, phrase, image, sound, etc.) that is used by a provider of services to convey to the consumer the source of those services and to distinguish the services from those of competitors. The service mark must identify specific services that are offered on their own, not as an additional component to the provider's main business. Service marks can be protected without federal registration (indicated by use of the "SM" symbol), but greater protection is given to marks that have been registered with the federal Patent and Trademark Office (indicated by use of the "R" symbol, which should never be used for unregistered marks).

Compare "Trademark."

For a more in-depth discussion, see "Chapter 6: An Introduction to Trademarks."

SOLE PROPRIETORSHIP

A sole proprietorship is a type of for-profit business structure in which a person owns a business on their own, without partners or investors. All income and losses related to the business are reported on the individual's personal income taxes. Sole proprietorships are created automatically when an individual begins to conduct business activities, even if the individual does not register with their state as a business.

As there is no legal distinction between the individual and the business, the individual carries full legal responsibility for the sole proprietorship. This means the individual is personally liable for the debts and responsibilities of the business.

Sole proprietorships are not eligible for tax-exempt recognition.

Compare "Nonprofit Corporation."
See also "Business Structures."
See also "Tax-Exempt."

For a more in-depth discussion, see "Chapter 11: Understanding the Various Forms of Business Structures."

SPECIALIST CONFERENCE: 20 YEARS OF THE WASHINGTON PRINCIPLES: ROADMAP TO THE FUTURE

See "Washington Principles on Nazi-Confiscated Art."

SPECTRUM OF DISTINCTIVENESS

Under trademark law, a mark's ability to function as such is determined by where it falls on the so-called spectrum of distinctiveness. A mark's categorization along the spectrum determines whether it may be registered as a mark with the Patent and Trademark Office (PTO), how strong a mark the PTO will consider it to be, and whether it requires the acquisition of a secondary meaning.

From most protected to least protected, marks are described as (1) arbitrary/fanciful, (2) suggestive, (3) descriptive, or (4) generic.[569] It is important to understand that a term that falls into one category for a certain product may fall into an entirely different category for another product.[570] For example, the mark "Apple" is classified as arbitrary when applied to computers, but it would be considered generic if applied to apple juice. It is the interaction between the mark and the goods that determines the mark's categorization on the spectrum.

See also "Arbitrary Mark."
See also "Descriptive Mark."
See also "Doctrine of Foreign Equivalents."
See also "Fanciful Mark."
See also "Generic Mark."
See also "Secondary Meaning."
See also "Suggestive Mark."
See also "Trademark."

STATE HISTORIC PRESERVATION OFFICERS

See "National Historic Preservation Act."

STATE HISTORIC PRESERVATION PROGRAM

See "National Historic Preservation Act."

STATE LAW

See "Categories of Law."

STATE PARTY

See "Convention on Cultural Property Implementation Act."

STATUTE OF FRAUDS

A statute of frauds is a statute that forbids the enforcement of certain types of contracts unless they are written down or an exception applies that would permit the contract to be enforced despite the missing writing.[571] In America, each state has adopted its own version of the statute of frauds, and therefore it is necessary to consult the state law of the specific jurisdiction to determine the exact categories and exceptions that may apply to a particular situation. However, there are some generalities that can be discussed.

Subject to local law, the common types of contracts that are subject to the statute of frauds that may be applicable to a museum, its employees, or its trustees, are:

1. A contract to perform the duty of executor or administration,[572]
2. A contract related to the sale of an interest in land,[573]

3. A contract that will not be fulfilled within one year from the contract's creation,[574] and
4. A contract for a sale of goods for $500 or more.[575]

When entering this type of contract, the local or state law should be consulted to ensure any requirements for the writing are met so the underlying contract will be enforceable.

See also "Categories of Law."
See also "Contract."

STATUTE OF LIMITATIONS

When an aggrieved party wishes to press a legal action, the law provides a window of time during which that action must be pursued or it will be barred. This statute of limitations, literally a limitation of the time a particular type of claim may be brought as defined by statute, is intended to ensure a resolution is pursued within a reasonable amount of time while also ensuring that actions are brought while access to witnesses and evidence is still reasonably possible.

The cause of action is what determines what the statute of limitations will be. For instance, a suit alleging breach of contract will have a different limitation than a suit alleging personal injury. Further, certain causes of action have no statute of limitations in some jurisdictions, such as murder or sexual assault. The statute of limitations depends on the jurisdiction, so local law must be consulted.

While a statute of limitations typically begins to run when the cause of action accrues (for instance, when a contract is breached or when a theft occurs), there are various fact scenarios in which the statute of limitations will be "tolled," meaning the running of the statute of limitations is delayed despite the triggering cause of action. For example, if the parties are engaged in a good faith effort to resolve a breach of contract, the statute of limitations will often be tolled during the course of those negotiations, which permits the parties to engage in those negotiations without the threat of losing the right to bring suit should the negotiations fail.

Compare "Laches."
See also "Categories of Law."
See also "Holocaust Expropriated Art Recovery Act."

STATUTORY LAW

Statutory law is the law that derives from statutes, which are passed by a legislature and signed by a governmental officer. In America, on the state level, a bill would be passed by a vote in both chambers of the legislature and then signed by the governor.[576] On the federal level, the bill would be voted on by both chambers of Congress and signed by the president.

If a state or local law conflicts with a federal law, the federal law will generally prevail, unless the federal law in some way oversteps its proscribed boundaries. However, some federal laws leave space for state and local governments to operate in the same legal arena. In this situation, the state or local law is understood not to be "preempted" by the federal law.

Compare "Civil Law."
Compare "Common Law."
Compare "Equity."
Compare "Ethics."
See also "Categories of Law."

For a more in-depth focus, see "Chapter 2: Ethics and the Law."

SUBSTANTIVE LAW

See "Categories of Law."

SUGGESTIVE MARK

Trademark law categorizes marks along a spectrum of distinctiveness, with marks that are considered more distinctive receiving more protection than those further down the spectrum. A mark's categorization along the spectrum determines whether it may be registered as a mark with the Patent and Trademark Office (PTO), how strong a mark the PTO will consider it to be, and whether it requires acquisition of a secondary meaning.

From most protected to least protected, marks are described as (1) arbitrary/fanciful, (2) suggestive, (3) descriptive, or (4) generic.[577] It is important to understand that a term that falls into one category for a certain product may fall into an entirely different category for another product.[578]

Suggestive marks fall in the middle of the spectrum, being less distinctive than arbitrary and fanciful marks, and therefore receiving less protection under the law, but being more distinctive than descriptive marks. A mark is suggestive if it takes a little work on the part of the consumer to make the mental connection between the mark and the product it represents. If the mark requires that the consumer use his imagination to understand the nature of the goods identified, it is a suggestive mark.[579] The "Greyhound" mark used for buses is an example of a suggestive mark.

It can be difficult to determine if a mark is suggestive or descriptive. The main distinction is that a descriptive mark merely describes the good offered, while a suggestive mark requires that little extra bit of imaginative interpretation on the part of the consumer.

Suggestive marks may be registered with the PTO on their own strength.[580] They have the advantage of often conveying to the consumer the type of good offered with a little mental effort on the consumer's part, but they have the disadvantage of receiving a narrower scope of protection under trademark law than some other categories.

Compare "Descriptive Mark."
See also "Spectrum of Distinctiveness."
See also "Trademark."

SUNSET CLAUSE

Organizations seeking financial support of their mission may consider offering naming rights to donors in exchange for those donations. While these naming opportunities can provide strong financial support for an organization with the right donor, they can also cause issues when grated in perpetuity. When indefinite rights are granted in exchange for a onetime donation—even a substantial donation—the organization loses the flexibility to seek similar financial support in the future. A right granted in perpetuity will be just that—a name forever associated with a wing, collection, or endowment. While this is not necessarily a bad thing, some organizations may prefer to limit these rights.

A sunset clause sets a limit to the time the naming rights will persist. Instead of naming a new wing after a substantial donor forever, the organization will be able to revisit the name and seek further donations—with the potential of a new name—after a certain period of time passes. Such a sunset clause would be negotiated with the donor and expressly stated in all relevant paperwork, including the final gift acknowledgment.

Organizations can consider a sunset clause of a few decades or other time frame, so long as it makes sense in relation to the size of the donation received and is agreed upon by all parties. The organization can also consider including in the sunset clause a provision offering a right of first refusal to the original donor when the time comes to seek a new donor for the naming opportunity.

See also "Donation."
See also "Donor."
See also "Naming Rights."
See also "Termination Clause."

TAX-EXEMPT

Tax-exempt status is a benefit the Internal Revenue Service (IRS) grants to certain organizations in recognition of the service they perform for society. As such, it is regulated by federal law. Additionally, because tax-exempt status is a privilege and not a right, the IRS has strict requirements that must be met regarding how the organization is organized and operated to obtain exempt status, and there are ongoing reporting requirements that must be met if exemption is to be retained. The application process starts with the filing of IRS Form 1023. Ongoing reporting is accomplished through filing of IRS Form 990, and repeat failure to do so will result in automatic revocation of the organization's tax-exempt status.

The term *tax-exempt* is a bit of a misnomer, as tax-exempt organizations do still pay a variety of taxes. For instance, if the organization has employees, then payroll taxes will still be owed, despite the organization's tax-exempt status. Additionally, if the organization generates profits from activities that are unrelated to its exempt purpose, it may owe tax on those profits, referred to as unrelated business income tax or UBIT.

Compare "Nonprofit Corporation."
See also "Automatic Revocation."

See also "Federal Insurance Contributions Act."
See also "IRS Form 990."
See also "IRS Form 1023."
See also "Operational Test."
See also "Organizational Test."
See also "Political Activities Test."
See also "Private Inurement Test."
See also "Unrelated Business Income Tax."

For a more in-depth discussion, see "Chapter 8: Nonprofit Corporations and Tax Exemption."

TEMPORARY CUSTODY

Objects held in the temporary custody of a museum are those that are on site at the museum and are not owned or accessioned by the museum. Objects held in temporary custody are the responsibility of the museum and must be properly protected and cared for during the duration of their time on premises. The museum has no ownership rights in such objects, as title has not transferred, and they should be promptly returned to their rightful owner once the purpose of their custody concludes. Reasons an object may enter a museum on temporary custody include examination in contemplation of a loan or for research purposes.

Compare "Accession."
Compare "Acquisition."
Compare "Loans."
Compare "Old Loans."
See also "Orphaned Works (Collections Management)."

TENANCY BY THE ENTIRETY

Under the types of ownership available in real property, the fee simple is perhaps the most common. When the property is owned by multiple people, that shared ownership may take the form of a joint tenancy, tenancy by the entirety, or tenancy in common.

The tenancy by the entirety[581] is a fairly archaic system of property ownership that can only exist between spouses. It is most closely aligned to the joint tenancy, in that there is a right of survivorship. This means that when one of the spouses passes away, the surviving spouse automatically takes over that ownership interest.

However, unlike in the joint tenancy, the tenancy by the entirety does not permit the tenancy to be broken up by one spouse acting on their own. For example, Spouse A and Spouse B own property as tenants by the entirety. Spouse A wants to sell his share in the property to Museum without Spouse B's permission. Any attempt at the sale will be invalid, and the property will remain with Spouse A and Spouse B.

See also "Common Law Property."
See also "Community Property."
See also "Fee Simple."
See also "Joint Tenancy."
See also "Real Property."
See also "Tenancy in Common."

TENANCY IN COMMON

Under the types of ownership available for real property, the fee simple is perhaps the most common. When the property is owned by multiple people, that shared ownership may take the form of a joint tenancy, tenancy by the entirety, or tenancy in common.

Under the tenancy in common,[582] the owners (called co-tenants) each have a full and equal right to occupy or use the property. There is no limit to the number of co-tenants, and their ownership does not have to be proportional. Three co-tenants may own the property in equal shares (33.3 percent each). Alternatively, the property's ownership may be split any number of other ways, for instance 50/25/25 or 50/30/20. However, even if the ownership is not split proportionally, each co-tenant has the right to use (occupy) the entire property.

A co-tenant may transfer their co-tenancy to a third party, meaning they can sell their interest to a buyer or leave it to an heir in a will. That new co-tenant will step into the shoes of the transferor, assuming the rights and obligations of the co-tenancy. A co-tenant cannot transfer (by sale or otherwise) the ownership rights of the other co-tenants. Further, a co-tenant cannot block the transfer of ownership by a fellow co-tenant. A co-tenant may "buy out" their fellow co-tenants, increasing their proportion of the total ownership amount or obtaining the entire property for themselves.

For example, Owners A and B are tenants in common in a property and each have a 50 percent ownership interest in the property. Owner A wishes to sell to Museum. Owner A may only sell her interest, and Museum will then become a co-tenant in the property with Owner B.

See also "Fee Simple."
See also "Joint Tenancy."
See also "Real Property."
See also "Tenancy by the Entirety."

TEREZÍN DECLARATION ON HOLOCAUST
ERA ASSETS AND RELATED ISSUES

Just over a decade following the adoption of the Washington Principles in 1998, an international meeting took place at Terezín,[583] Prague, Czech Republic, for the Holocaust Era Assets Conference.[584] At the conclusion of the conference, the attendees adopted the Terezín Declaration on Holocaust Era Assets and Related Issues. As with the Washington Principles, the Terezín Declaration is nonbinding on the forty-seven signatory nations.[585] The primary focus is on immovable (real) property, that which was both privately and communally owned, but issues related to Jewish cemeteries and burial sites, Nazi-looted objects, and Judaica are also addressed. Issues related to archives, education and research, and details on future actions, both general and specific, are also included.

These best practices were designed "to bring a measure of justice to Holocaust (Shoah) survivors as well as other victims of these persecutions, and their heirs."[586] Included are a number of recommendations focused on restitution when possible and monetary compensation when not, a minimization of administrative costs, and a means to address heirless and unclaimed property. Of special note is the recommendation that nations provide assistance to Holocaust survivors (such as special pensions, special funds, or social security benefits to nonresidents) through the creative leveraging of heirless property and related assets.[587]

Following up on the Terezín Declaration, in 2018 the United States Congress passed the Justice for Uncompensated Survivors Today Act (JUST Act of 2017).[588] The Act required the secretary of state to produce a report to assess the progress nations had made in implementing the provisions of the Terezín Declaration.[589] The JUST Act Report[590] consists of forty-six reports (one for each signatory nation, excluding the United States[591]), each with a historical overview and a summary of the country's laws and policies regarding the various types of properties addressed in the Terezín Declaration.[592] The Report's Executive Summary also includes an overview of how American museums and the country as a whole have responded to Nazi loot restitutions.[593]

See also "Washington Principles on Nazi-Confiscated Art."

TERMINATION CLAUSE

Organizations seeking financial support of their mission may consider offering naming rights to donors in exchange for those donations. While these naming opportunities can provide strong financial support for an organization with the right donor, they can also cause issues when situations change. There may come a time when the organization no longer wishes to be publicly associated with the donor, or the donor may fail to meet the terms they agreed to under the original donation. In these situations, a termination clause permits the organization to terminate the naming rights of the donor.

While an organization may find the inclusion of a termination clause distasteful or assuming the worst at the start of a relationship, it can help to ensure the organization's public reputation remains strong should unforeseen issues arise with the donor at some point. The inclusion of a "morality" clause can give the organization a means to revoke the rights and rename the object should the donor suffer a significant negative change to their reputation.[594]

Additionally, a termination clause ensures the organization can retreat from the agreement should the donor fail to meet their own obligations. For instance, if a donor agrees to make a series of donations over a number of years and does not honor those promised gifts, a termination clause is one possible mechanism for the organization to retreat from the naming rights for failure to comply.

See also "Charitable Gift."
See also "Donation."
See also "Donor."
See also "Sunset Clause."

THIRD SECTOR

The *third sector* is a term used to identify social service activities conducted by organizations that are neither private business nor governmental entities. Nonprofit corporations such as museums fall within the third sector.

See also "Nonprofit Corporation."

THIRTY-THREE AND ⅓ PERCENT SUPPORT TEST

In order to determine if a section 501(c)(3) organization qualifies as a public charity, the organization can seek to demonstrate it meets the thirty-three and ⅓ percent support test. Under this test, the organization must receive one-third (or 33.3 percent) of its total donations from public donors, and these donors must give less than 2 percent of the organization's overall income. There are a number of exceptions regarding government support and other sources of income. There are a number of subcategories for section 501(c)(3) organizations, including so-called traditional public charities;[595] "gross-receipts" organizations, which can include museums that charge admission fees;[596] "supporting" organizations;[597] and finally, organizations that test for public safety.[598] Using the Form 990 Schedule A, the IRS determines whether or not the organization receives enough public support to qualify as a public charity.[599] An organization that does not meet the requirements of the thirty-three and ⅓ percent support test may look to the facts-and-circumstances test to obtain public charity status.

See also "Facts-and-Circumstances Test."
See also "Public Charity."
See also "Section 501(c)(3)."

THUMBNAIL

Thumbnails are small images often used in online image searches, as well as in software databases and other uses, to provide an image that relates to the search term entered. Some museums display thumbnail images on their websites for users who are searching the online catalog. Additionally, search engines such as Google often display thumbnails alongside text searches or as part of their image search feature.

The creation of a thumbnail necessarily requires the reproduction of an entire image, though generally at a much-reduced size. While this is technically an infringement of copyright holders' rights, this infringement has been found to be a fair use.[600] However, fair use is a very fact-specific determination, and there is no guarantee that any particular use will be found to be a fair use by the courts.

See also "Copyright."
See also "Fair Use."
See also "Infringement (Copyright)."
See also "Reproduction Right."

TIME, PLACE, MANNER RESTRICTIONS

See "Public Forum."

TITLE

Within the realm of property law, "title" refers to the legal right to possess property indefinitely and exert the rights in that property. It may be best understood as "ownership" of the property. The rights associated with ownership can be thought of as a bundle of sticks, and it is possible to own some or all the sticks. The rights that exist in a property depend on the type of property it is, such as real, personal, or intellectual. Traditionally, personal property ownership rights include, among others, the rights of exclusive possession, exclusive use, conveyance, and alienation. For example, a museum that owns the title to a deck of playing cards owns the right to exclusive possession—the museum is not compelled to share ownership of the cards with a third party. The sticks in the bundles for real property and intellectual property vary from these personal property rights.

In acquiring title, however, restrictions on the ways and means an owner may utilize or dispose of the property may be imposed. For example, ownership of the playing cards does not guarantee ownership in the copyrights related to those cards. Transfer of copyright interest needs to be accomplished through a separate conveyance. Additionally, the means of acquisition may impact the ownership rights. If the playing cards were donated, and the donor imposed a restriction prohibiting the museum to ever deaccession and dispose of the cards, the museum will still have title (ownership) of the cards while not having the right of alienation. Donor restrictions will generally be upheld by the courts, and museums seeking relief from donor restrictions must do so either through a renegotiation with the donor, if possible, or through legal remedies.

These additional interests and restrictions on the use of the object relate to the "completeness" of the title. To ensure complete title is conveyed to the museum, regardless of the means of acquisition, it is important to fully examine what rights are being transferred.

Imagine potential donor Patrice inherits her grandmother's diamond ring. In the grandmother's will, the ring passed to Patrice, but at the time of Patrice's death, the ring will pass to Cathy. Therefore, under the terms of the grandmother's will, Patrice does not have the right to leave the ring to someone in her own will, as her ownership interest in the ring ceases upon her death. Assuming the will and the provision related to the ring meet legal requirements,[601] Patrice may only transfer possession of the ring to the museum for the length of her own lifetime; therefore possession serves more as a long-term loan than an actual donation. If the museum attempts to retain ownership of the ring after Patrice's death, it possibly does so in violation of Cathy's ownership rights in the ring.

In addition to the completeness of title, another consideration is the title's "quality." It is also important to ensure the transferor (whether by donation, sale, etc.) is the actual owner of the property. A person who does not hold title in property cannot effectively transfer title to a third party.[602] For example, imagine that the donor who gifted the playing cards to the museum was not, in fact, the legal owner of the cards. Perhaps the donor stole them or purchased them from a thief. Even if the donor had no way of knowing the cards were stolen, he still did not have title in the cards, as a thief cannot acquire good title to personal property in America. Therefore, the donor was not able to pass title in the cards to the museum. In this situation, the museum has not acquired "good" title in the playing cards, and the proper owner may at some point present herself and claim the cards as her property. Research into the object's provenance history prior to acquisition would hopefully reveal such a defect of title.

Finally, remember that possession does not equate to title ownership. If a museum finds an object in its collection and does not have documentation to demonstrate title ownership in the object, the museum should not automatically assume it has title in the object.

See also "Acquisition."
See also "Donation."
See also "Found-in-Collection."
See also "Future Interest."
See also "Intellectual Property."
See also "Personal Property."
See also "Provenance."
See also "Real Property."
See also "Restricted Gift."
See also "Undocumented Object."
See also "Voidable."
See also "Warranty of Title."

TOKEN BENEFIT

Donations made to a qualified organization in exchange for goods or services from that organization are known as *quid pro quo* contributions.[603] Unlike other donations in which no benefits are received by the donor, *quid pro quo* contributions result in a charitable deduction limited to the amount of the donation that is in excess of the value of the benefit.[604]

The Internal Revenue Service provides guidelines as to when benefits will qualify as insubstantial.[605] These guidelines include when the donor makes a payment of $75 or less and only receives annual membership benefits in return (such as free or discounted admission or parking).[606] When the goods or services received qualify as insubstantial, the entire donation will be entitled to a deduction. In the disclosure statement, the organization can inform the donor that the donation is fully deductible.

Worth special mention is newsletters, which will be treated as though they have neither a fair market value nor a cost so long as the newsletter's primary purpose is to communicate to members any upcoming organization events and activities.[607] However, this treatment will not apply if the newsletter is also available to nonmembers who either pay a subscription to obtain the newsletter or who can purchase it on newsstands.[608]

Two other exceptions exist. The first is for intangible religious benefits, such as admission to a religious ceremony, which will not be applied against the donation.[609] The second is regarding unreimbursed expenses, such as where an individual pays out of pocket to perform her donative services.[610]

See also "Deduction."
See also "Disclosure Statement."
See also "Donation."
See also "Qualified Fund-Raising Campaign."
See also "*Quid Pro Quo* Contribution."

TOLL

See "Statute of Limitations."

TORT

A tort is an act or omission that causes an injury or harm in another. The injury can be the invasion of any legal right. The harm is a loss suffered by the victim. Courts will impose a liability for a tort.

There are three general categories of torts. An intentional tort is caused by an intentional act, such as purposely injuring someone. A negligent tort is caused by a negligent action, for instance failing to heed safety warnings. And finally, strict liability torts are those that occur due to the manufacturing and selling of defective consumer products. While torts can cause bodily harm, they are not criminal actions as they are private wrongs.

Potential torts can occur in many museum settings. For example, a visitor could suffer a slip-and-fall injury due to a freshly mopped but unmarked floor or a failure to clear snow and ice from entrance steps. Remedies that can occur in response to a tort are monetary (compensatory or punitive) or injunctive relief (which compels a party to perform or refrain from some action).

TRADE DRESS

Trade dress is a subcategory of trademark law that deals with the packaging and design of products. While a trademark is a sign, symbol, or other mark placed on a product to indicate the source of goods, trade dress is the total packaging of a product.[611] As a category of trademark, trade dress is entitled to the same legal protections and can be registered, with the limitation that the trade dress cannot be functional.[612]

For an example of the distinction between trademark and trade dress, the familiar McDonald's logo is a trademark, but the distinctive Happy Meal box, including its color scheme and shape, is trade dress.

Compare "Trademark."

For a more in-depth discussion, see "Chapter 6: An Introduction to Trademarks."

TRADEMARK

Trademark is a form of intellectual property where the purpose is to assist the consumer in distinguishing products and identifying the source of goods in the marketplace. A trademark is any mark or symbol (word, phrase, image, sound, etc.) used by a seller of goods to convey to the consumer the source of those goods and to distinguish the goods from those of competitors. Trademarks can be more than just a mere logo. For instance, a fragrance applied to sewing thread and embroidery yarn has been used as a trademark.[613] A nonfunctional color has also been used as a trademark.[614]

Trademarks can be protected without federal registration (indicated by use of the "TM" symbol), but greater protection is given to marks that have been registered with the federal Patent and Trademark Office (indicated by use of the "R" symbol, which should never be used for unregistered marks).

Unlike copyrights, trademarks are subject to an application process to obtain federal protection, during which the mark is reviewed by an examiner. This process ensures that any new marks do not infringe on existing marks, which would lead to consumer confusion. Examination also ensures marks are not issued that would grant an unfavorable monopoly to any one producer over a generic or descriptive phrase for goods. To ensure this, marks are examined through the lens of the so-called spectrum of distinctiveness.

Trademarks are registered for ten years. If the mark is still being used in the marketplace to identify the source of goods, they can continue to be renewed for additional terms of ten years each. Therefore, the producer has a monopoly on the use of the mark in the marketplace for as long as the producer continues to use the mark and meets statutory registration requirements. The oldest American trademark still in use was registered on May 27, 1884.[615]

Compare "Copyright."
Compare "Service Mark."
Compare "Trade Dress."

See also "Intellectual Property."
See also "Spectrum of Distinctiveness.

For a more in-depth discussion, see "Chapter 6: An Introduction to Trademarks."

TRUST

A trust is created when assets are placed with an entity to be held and used for the benefit of certain persons or entities (beneficiaries). A trust may be founded by one or more persons (called the trustors, grantors, or settlors), and those persons outline the trust's parameters and how it is intended to function in a document called a declaration.

During the lifetime of the trust, its investment profits may be distributed to the beneficiaries.[616] The trust may distribute all its remaining assets at a future date, either to the beneficiaries or to some other named entity, such as a charitable organization.

A trust may be made by the settlors during their lifetime, in which case they may elect to manage the trust themselves or have a named third party oversee the trust's management. Alternatively, a settlor may create the trust in their will as a way to manage the assets being left to the beneficiaries.

There is a large variety of trusts available, depending on the terms of the trust, how it was created, whether it may be amended or revoked, and other factors.

See also "Charitable Trust."
See also "Trustee."

TRUSTEE

A trustee—also called an officer, director, or some other term—is a member of the board that oversees the operations of a corporation or trust, such as a museum. Trustees are often selected for board membership due to their professional skills, their connections in the community, their passion for the organization's mission, or another similar and relevant reason.

Trustees should receive an orientation to the organization and the board and be well briefed on all board activities, including any committees, expectations, board policies and procedures, and other information applicable to the institution. The term they serve on the board, and whether they may serve multiple consecutive terms, will be dictated in the organization's controlling documents, typically the bylaws or the articles of incorporation.

Trustees have a legal obligation to uphold the organization and place its interests above their own personal interests. This is called the fiduciary duty, and it is a serious responsibility of every trustee to uphold their fiduciary duty in all matters. Failure to do so can put the individual trustee, the board, and the organization at risk.

See also "Articles of Incorporation."
See also "Attorney General."

See also "Board of Trustees."
See also "Bylaws."
See also "Charitable Trust."
See also "Conflict of Interest."
See also "Fiduciary Duty."
See also "Nonprofit Corporation."

For a more in-depth discussion, see "Chapter 9: The Board of Trustees and Their Fiduciary Duty."

UBIT

See "Unrelated Business Income Tax."

UNCLAIMED LOAN

See "Old Loans."

UNDOCUMENTED OBJECT

The term *undocumented object* does not have a consistent definition in the museum profession, and it is often used interchangeably with the term *found-in-collection*. A strong argument has been made that undocumented objects should be defined as objects that are similar to objects held in the collection and are located in appropriate collections storage areas, but they are lacking object numbers, object files, or any identifying characteristics that would permit them to be associated with museum documentation.[617]

When faced with an undocumented object, museum staff should attempt to connect the object with its correct identifying accession number and object file. If, after attempts at reconciliation, the object remains unidentified, it may be properly classified as found-in-collection. This application would distinguish undocumented objects from found-in-collection objects, which still may not be connected to museum records or loan documents even after all attempts to do so have been completed.[618]

Compare "Found-in-Collection."
Compare "Old Loans."

UNESCO

See "United Nations Educational, Scientific, and Cultural Organization."

UNIDROIT

See "International Institute for the Unification of Private Law."

UNIFORM COMMERCIAL CODE

In an effort to harmonize the law relating to the sale of goods across state lines, the Uniform Commercial Code (UCC) is a uniform act that addresses commercial transactions such as sales, leases, and other topics.[619] As a uniform act, the UCC is not law. However, sections have been adopted in whole or in part by all fifty states.[620]

UNINCORPORATED ASSOCIATIONS

An unincorporated association is one that is formed by individuals to meet some shared goal. Unlike a corporation or charitable trust, the unincorporated association has no legal existence separate from the individuals that comprise it. Because the unincorporated association has no separate legal existence, the individual members can potentially be held personally liable for the unincorporated association's debts or legal obligations. It also means that unless there is state legislation providing otherwise, the unincorporated association cannot own property in its own name, nor can it enter contracts in its own name.

In order for the unincorporated association to be recognized as a nonprofit, it must comply with all the rules governing nonprofit corporations, including the reinvestment of income back into the nonprofit purpose. An unincorporated association that meets federal requirements may also qualify as a tax-exempt organization.[621]

While forming an unincorporated association is relatively easy compared to the requirements of founding a nonprofit corporation, the risks involved mean it is not an ideal structure for organizations such as museums. Despite the ease of formation and the eligibility for tax-exempt status, unincorporated associations do have drawbacks. These have to do with the exposure to potential personal liability and the limited ability to raise funds through grants, donations, or lines of credit.

Compare "Charitable Trust."
Compare "Nonprofit Corporation."
Compare "Partnership (General)."
See also "Business Structures."
See also "Nondistribution Constraint."
See also "Nonprofit Corporation."
See also "Tax-Exempt."

For a more in-depth discussion, see "Chapter 11: Understanding the Various Forms of Business Structures."

UNITED NATIONS EDUCATIONAL, SCIENTIFIC, AND CULTURAL ORGANIZATION

The United Nations Educational, Scientific, and Cultural Organization, commonly referred to as UNESCO, was created in 1945 to aid in the creation and maintenance of peace in the wake of two world wars.[622] Among its many works, UNESCO promotes intercultural understanding, including protection of the world's cultural heritage and supporting cultural diversity.[623] As of August 2020, it had 193 Member States and eleven Associated Members.[624]

UNESCO promulgates numerous conventions and recommendations that may be of interest to museums. All its conventions and recommendations are available on the UNESCO website.[625] Note that the United States is not a signatory to all UNESCO conventions.

See also "Convention on the Means of Prohibiting and Preventing the Illicit Import, Export, and Transfer of Ownership of Cultural Property."

UNRELATED BUSINESS INCOME TAX

For organizations that have received recognition as tax-exempt from the Internal Revenue Service (IRS), any income-generating activities that do not relate to the organization's exempt purpose may be subject to the unrelated business income tax (UBIT). The requirements for income to be classified as unrelated business income are that the income arises from a (1) regularly carried on (2) trade or business that is (3) not substantially related to the organization's exempt purpose.[626] The trade or business may involve the sale of goods or the performance of services.[627]

Remember that for tax-exempt organizations, income generated from activities substantially related to the organization's charitable and exempt purpose are exempt from federal taxation.[628] However, when an exempt organization conducts income-generating activities that are unrelated to that exempt purpose, the IIRS will tax those revenues.[629] Further, if the unrelated trade or business becomes too large a portion of the organization's activities, then those unrelated activities can jeopardize the organization's continued exempt status due to the operational test for exemption. In applying the operational test, it does not matter that the organization as a whole is operated for charitable and exempt purposes, and such activities by the organization will not reclassify an otherwise unrelated trade or business as exempt.[630]

See also "Operational Test."
See also "Tax-Exempt."

UNRELATED USE

When a donor makes a donation to a qualified organization such as a museum, that donor may expect to take advantage of the deduction that may be available to her. These deductions serve as an incentive the federal government provides as a means of supporting and encouraging such donations. The extent of that deduction is regulated in part by whether the donation will be put to a use related to the qualified organization's exempt purpose.

A use is unrelated to the museum's exempt purpose when it is "unrelated to the purpose or function constituting the basis of the charitable organization's exemption under section 501 of the Internal Revenue Code,"[631] which would be the museum's section 501(c)(3) exempt status.

For example, consider a donor who makes a donation of a painting depicting a local businessman, painted in a style popular in the region fifty years before. The museum displays the painting to the public in its galleries, using it in interpretive programs for students. This use is related to the museum's educational and charitable purposes. However, if the museum instead sells the painting and uses the sale proceeds to further its educational programs, the museum has put the painting to an unrelated use.[632]

While a donor may be entitled to a positive tax deduction when making a donation that will be put to an unrelated use, that deduction will likely be much less favorable.[633] The museum should not provide any tax advice to potential donors related to the tax consequences of a donation. However, the museum should honestly inform the potential donor if the donation will be put to an unrelated use. This open dialogue with the potential donor ensures that the donor is not misled regarding the tax consequences of the donation, which in turn promotes a positive and hopefully long-term relationship with that donor.

See also "Deduction."
See also "Donation."
See also "Exempt Purpose."
See also "Qualified Organization."
See also "Section 501(c)(3)."

VISION STATEMENT

A vision statement is a companion statement that some nonprofit organizations have created in addition to their mission statement. To understand the distinction, it helps to start with the mission statement. For many museums, the mission statement outlines the organization's purpose in existing and operating. In a sense, it is a practical statement, describing who the museum is and what it does.

In contrast, the vision statement is more aspirational, seeking to describe the condition of the museum's community if the museum were to successfully achieve its most visionary aspirations. It conveys what impact the organization would have on the world if it achieved all its goals.

Used together, the mission and vision statements can inspire and motivate internal stakeholders, such as staff, volunteers, and board members, while also inspiring the larger community, including visitors, members, funders, and collaborators. Unlike the mission statement, the AAM does not classify the vision statement as a core document for museums.[634]

See also "Mission Statement."

VISUAL ART

Under the Visual Artists Rights Act (VARA), only works that meet the statutory definition of "work of visual art" are entitled to moral rights protections. This definition is significantly more limited than what is entitled to copyright protection, excluding copyright protectable creations such as posters, sound records, and motion pictures.

It is easiest to think of the visual art definition under VARA as consisting of a positive definition *and* a negative definition. For the positive definition, included works are:[635]

1. Paintings, drawings, prints, and sculptures that are either a single copy or in an edition limited to two hundred or fewer copies, each signed and numbered by the artist; *or*
2. Sculptures that are cast, carved, or sculpted in a run of two hundred or fewer, each signed and numbered by the artist; *or*
3. Still photographs created for the purpose of being exhibited, which are either a single copy or in an edition limited to two hundred or fewer copies, each signed and numbered by the artist.

A work must fit into this positive definition to obtain VARA protection. Clearly this list is very limited, and it excludes many of the original, fixed works in tangible mediums of expression that are entitled to copyright protection.

Further, the work must not fit into the negative definition. VARA works must *not* be:

1. "Any poster, map, globe, chart, technical drawing, diagram, model, applied art, motion picture or other audiovisual work, book, magazine, newspaper, periodical, data base, electronic information service, electronic publication, or similar publication";[636] *nor*
2. "any merchandising item or advertising, promotional, descriptive, covering, or packaging material or container."[637]

If a work fits the positive definition *and* the negative definition, it is not entitled to VARA protection. For example, a print created in a run of one hundred, each signed and consecutively numbered by the artist and intended to advertise a music concert, fits the negative definition of advertising and would not be entitled to VARA protection, despite its fitting into the positive definition.

Finally, VARA protection is not available to works made for hire.[638] Also, the work must otherwise be eligible for copyright protection.[639] Therefore, the work must meet the requirements of copyright.

Compare "Works of Authorship."
See also "Copyright."
See also "Visual Artists Rights Act."

VISUAL ARTISTS RIGHTS ACT

Full Title: Visual Artists Rights Act of 1990
Also Known As: VARA
Citation: 17 U.S.C. § 106A

The Visual Artists Rights Act of 1990 was included within the Copyright Act to bring that statute and American law into compliance with the Berne Convention for the Protection of Literary and Artistic Works, an international copyright agreement that had been signed by the United States in 1989. Berne mandated the recognition of moral rights, which were not at the time acknowledged under American law. VARA introduced moral rights to the American legal landscape and extended newly recognized moral rights to certain works.

Under VARA, the moral rights of attribution and integrity are extended to works of visual art as defined by the Act. Another common moral right, *droit de suite*, or the "resale right," is not recognized by VARA.

While VARA is enshrined within the larger Copyright Act,[640] there are significant differences between VARA's moral rights protections and the protections afforded under copyright. First, unlike copyright's "bundle of sticks," moral rights under VARA may not be transferred, so it is not possible to license or in other manner transfer these rights to a third party.[641] Therefore, only the actual artist may exercise the VARA rights.[642] For a museum, this means that while a museum may license copyright rights from the copyright owner, it cannot license the artist's moral rights.

Second, VARA only extends protections to works of visual art, which is defined by the statute and is significantly more limited in scope than the types of creations that enjoy copyright protection. This means that not all works entitled to copyright are also entitled to VARA's moral rights. A museum must recognize which works in its collection are subject to moral rights and which are not.

Third, unlike with copyright, VARA protection generally only lasts for the lifetime of the artist.[643] If the work is a joint work, VARA rights last for the lifetime of the last surviving artist.[644] An important but limited exception is in the case of works that were created prior to June 1, 1991, but whose title was not transferred until after that date. For these works, VARA's rights last for the length of the copyright in the work.[645] For example, consider an artist who creates a painting in 1987 and keeps it in her studio, never transferring title through sale or gift. In 2012, she decides to gift it to a local art museum, which gladly accepts the donation. The artist then passes away in 2014. Under this hypothetical, the artist's moral rights continue for seventy years after her death, because as of VARA's effective date of June 1, 1991, the title to the artwork had not been transferred. The museum must respect those moral rights for the length of copyright protection.

There are also a number of similarities between VARA rights and copyright protection. Like a copyright owner who chooses to release her work into the public domain, artists may waive their VARA rights.[646] Such a waiver must be in writing and signed by the artist in order to be effective.[647] Also, as with copyright, VARA rights are separate and distinct from ownership in the artwork that gave rise to the moral rights.[648] Simple ownership of the artwork has no bearing on ownership or waiver of the moral rights. The VARA rights are also separate from the copyright "bundle of sticks," so transfer of any or all copyright protection also has no impact on an artist's moral rights.[649]

Compare "Copyright."
See also "Attribution, Right of."
See also "Berne Convention for the Protection of Literary and Artistic Works."
See also "*Droit de Suite* (Resale Royalty)."
See also "Integrity, Right of."
See also "Moral Rights."
See also "Visual Art."

VOIDABLE

A contract, title, or other transaction that is voidable is one that is not void from the outset or otherwise unenforceable, but that may electively become void and unenforceable. This occurs when one party has the ability to annul or affirm that contract.

For example, contracts entered into by minors are often voidable, with the minor able to exit the contract. If a minor (generally under the age of eighteen, though the age of maturity varies by state) attempts to donate an object to a museum, the museum should know that the donation may be voidable by the minor or, possibly, by her parent or guardian. A mutual mistake of fact could also give rise to a voidable contract, for instance if the donor and the museum both mistakenly believe a vase is an authentic antique when, in fact, it is a contemporary fake. If, upon examination, the museum determines the vase is a fake, the donation may potentially be voidable.

Whether a contract, title, or transaction is voidable is a fact-specific determination. It is always best to attempt to properly enter a valid contract with all eventualities considered and addressed, rather than to enter a contract relying on it being voidable if the facts and circumstances do not work out in the manner hoped. Additionally, failure to read or understand a contract does not make it voidable.

See also "Contract."
See also "Title."
See also "Warranty of Title."

WARRANTY OF TITLE

Warranty of title is often implied, meaning it does not appear in the actual written contract (which would be an express warranty). It implies that the seller actually has the right to sell the object. A seller would not have that right if, for example, the object was stolen, as a thief (in America) cannot pass good title. Therefore, even if the seller is not the thief, if the object was stolen at any point, good title cannot pass. Or a seller cannot sell an object if it already had been given or sold to someone else. For instance, if Owen gives his set of dishes to his daughter, he cannot then consign the dishes to an auction house to sell. Owen is no longer the owner of the dishes—his daughter is—and therefore Owen would be breaching the warranty of title if he attempts to sell the dishes.

See also "Acquisition."
See also "Provenance."
See also "Title."
See also "Uniform Commercial Code."

WASHINGTON PRINCIPLES ON NAZI-CONFISCATED ART

In late 1998, a group of forty-four government representatives and thirteen nongovernmental organizations (including museums and auction houses) convened in Washington, D.C., to hold the Washington Conference on Holocaust Era Assets.[650] The stated intention was to address the issue of Nazi-looted artworks and objects.

The result of that conference were eleven nonbinding principles. The prefix to these principles states:

> In developing a consensus on non-binding principles to assist in resolving issues relating to Nazi-confiscated art, the Conference recognizes that among participating nations there are differing legal systems and that countries act within the context of their own laws.[651]

The intention of the principles was to promote the identification and restitution of objects confiscated by the Nazis before and during World War II, to make archives and records open and accessible to researchers to facilitate that process, and to encourage the pre–WWII owners of the works and their heirs to come forward and make claims. The principles also encourage nations to develop alternative dispute resolution processes to resolve any ownership issues, specifically: "Nations are encouraged to develop national processes to implement these principles, particularly as they relate to alternative dispute resolution mechanisms for resolving ownership issues."[652]

Speaking at the conclusion of the conference, Stuart E. Eizenstat, then-U.S. Under Secretary of State for Economic, Business, and Agricultural Affairs, stated in his closing remarks:

> [W]e established a goal to complete by the end of this century the unfinished business of the middle of the century: the completion of the historical record on Holocaust-era assets and the provision of some measure of justice—however belated—to the victims and survivors of that unparalleled tragedy. Now with the conclusion of this conference approaching, we have made great strides toward achieving that historic goal.[653]

The Washington Principles do not have the force of law. While a nation may cosign them, there is no enforcement mechanism to require a nation to uphold them.[654]

In 2018, on the twentieth anniversary of the Washington Principles, a conference was held in Berlin, Germany.[655] At the conclusion of the conference, museums, libraries, and archives were encouraged to "actively live up to their responsibility for the further and continuous application of the Washington Principles"[656] and to create permanent employee positions for provenance research. Also included were recommendations for greater digitization of collections, easier access to those through databases and websites, and the development of best practices.[657]

In the twenty years since the adoption of the nonbinding Washington Principles, only five countries have established dedicated panels to issue recommendations and encourage alternative dispute resolution practices in relation to disputed artworks.[658]

See also "Terezín Declaration on Holocaust Era Assets and Related Issues."

For a more in-depth discussion, see "Chapter 2: Ethics and the Law."

WORK MADE FOR HIRE

A work made for hire is one in which the work was either created by an employee for their employer within the scope of the employment or a work that was commissioned.[659] In either scenario, the copyright is owned by the employer or the person who commissioned the work from the author.[660] This is an exception to the general rule of copyright ownership, where ownership vests in the author(s) of the work upon fixation.[661] The parties may reach a different agreement regarding copyright ownership in a written and signed document.[662]

Regarding employees, ownership only vests with the employer where the work was created by an employee within the scope of the employment. This means that if an art teacher creates a sculpture on her own time, with her own materials, in her own studio, entirely separate from her employment with the school, she retains copyright in the completed sculpture.

If the parties have not been clear in defining their work relationship, it may not be obvious if the creator is an employee or an independent contractor. The Supreme Court has held that in making this determination for works made for hire, "Congress intended the terms such as 'employee,' 'employer,' and 'scope of employment' to be understood in light of [the general common law of] agency law . . . rather than the law of any particular state. . . ."[663] Therefore, courts look to agency law to determine that relationship through the application of the so-called Reid test.[664] Under this test, the court considers a variety of factors—such as whether the hiring party could control how the work was produced, who provided the necessary tools, whether the hiring party had the right to assign additional projects, and the tax treatment of the hired party—to determine whether the relationship was that of an employer and employee.[665]

In addition to works made by the employee within the scope of employment, certain works that are specially ordered or commissioned are considered works made for hire. These are works for use:

1. "as a contribution to a creative work,
2. "as a part of a motion picture or other audiovisual work,
3. "as a translation,
4. "as a supplementary work,
5. "as a compilation,

6. "as an instructional text,
7. "as a test,
8. "as answer material for a test, or
9. "as an atlas."[666]

If the commissioned work fits into one of these categories *and* the parties entered a signed written instrument agreeing the work was a work made for hire, then the hiring party owns the copyright in the work.[667]

Works made for hire have a copyright term of ninety-five years from first publication or 120 years from creation, whichever expires first.[668] Termination of transfers and licenses does not apply to works made for hire.[669]

See also "Contract."
See also "Copyright."
See also "License."

WORKER CLASSIFICATION

Classification of workers refers to properly identifying workers as independent contractors or as employees. This classification can have numerous ramifications for both the employer and the worker, as the worker's classification impacts the worker's access to rights and protections, such as the minimum wage and employer contributions to plans such as Social Security. It is important to understand that the worker's classification is not determined by the language used between the parties, but rather by the facts and circumstances of the employer-worker relationship. The more control an employer exerts over a worker, the more likely that worker will be legally classified as an employee regardless of what term the parties use in their own interactions or written documents.

See also "ABC Test for Worker Classification."
See also "Common Law Test for Worker Classification."
See also "Employee."
See also "Independent Contractor."

For a more in-depth discussion, see "Chapter 10: Worker Classification: Distinguishing between an Employee and an Independent Contractor."

WORKS OF AUTHORSHIP

Under the Copyright Act, legal protection exists for "original works of authorship fixed in any tangible medium of expression. . . ."[670] The term *works of authorship* is intentionally vague and expansive, allowing new tangible mediums of expression to fall within the Copyright Act as they are invented. Therefore, to qualify for copyright protection, the work must be a "work of authorship" in the broadest sense of the term.

The Act defines this to mean certain types of authorship, specifically:

1. "Literary works;
2. "Musical works, including any accompanying words;
3. "Dramatic works, including any accompanying music;
4. "Pantomimes and choreographic works;
5. "Pictorial, graphic, and sculptural works;
6. "Motion pictures and other audiovisual works;
7. "Sound recordings; and
8. "Architectural works."[671]

Additionally, the statute explicitly states that copyright protection does not exist for "any idea, procedure, process, system, method of operation, concept, principal, or discovery, regardless of the form in which it is described, explained, illustrated, or embodied in such work."[672] For these categories of creation, it is impossible to secure copyright protection, regardless of its originality.

See also "Automatic Creation."
See also "Copyright."
See also "Fixation."
See also "Originality."

NOTES

1. Wex Law Dictionary, Legal Information Institute at Cornell University Law School, "Abandoned Property," https://www.law.cornell.edu/wex/abandoned_property.

2. Ibid.

3. For abandoned property laws that apply to museums, see the list compiled by The Society of American Archivists, "Abandoned Property Project," https://www2.archivists.org/groups/acquisitions-appraisal-section/abandoned-property-project.

4. At the time of writing, the common law test was used by the IRS, the District of Columbia, and eighteen states. The ABC test (or some variation of it) was used by the Department of Labor and thirty-three states, with the state of California adopting the ABC test following the state's Supreme Court decision in *Dynamex Operations West, Inc. v. Superior Court of Los Angeles*, 4 Cal. 5th 903 (2018). Effective January 1, 2020, California Assembly Bill 5 codified the *Dynamex* ABC test and expanded its reach to all wage and hour Labor Code violations in the state. Since the passage of AB5, lawsuits have been filed challenging the law as unconstitutional. These lawsuits are still pending at the time of writing. Additionally, representatives from the music industry have successfully negotiated relief for musicians, songwriters, and others in that industry who were adversely impacted by AB-5, allowing workers in the professional music industry to follow a different test for worker classification in regard to live performances and studio recordings. Aswad, Jem. (2020, April 17). "Musicians to Be Exempt from California's 'Gig' Economy Assembly Bill 5." *Variety*. https://variety.com/2020/music/news/california-gig-economy-assembly-bill-5-ab5-musicians-1234583320/.

A new piece of legislation has been introduced to address the impact of AB-5 on the creative sector by, among other things, providing clarification on the "fine artist exemption." At the time of this writing, Assembly Bill 1850 had been referred to the California State Senate Standing Committee on Labor, Public Employment and Retirement.

As this is an expanding and fluctuating area of law, be sure to consult with an attorney to determine the current status of the law in your organization's state. Also note that because of the two tests being applied in different states and by different agencies, it is possible for a worker to be classified as an independent contractor by the IRS and an employee on the state level, which can impact such things as unemployment benefits.

5. Your state may use a different name for the ABC test, and the test may arise from statutory or case law. Consult a local attorney to determine the exact name and wording of your state's test.

6. This language is taken from *Dynamex*, 4 Cal. 5th at 916-17. Language in your state may vary.

7. John E. Simmons and Toni M. Kiser, "Acquisitions and Accessioning," in *Museum Registration Methods* [6th], eds. John E. Simmons and Toni M. Kiser (New York: Rowman & Littlefield, 2020), 42.

8. Ibid. "All accessioned objects are acquired, but not all acquisitions are meant to be accessioned." Ibid.

9. Ibid.

10. John E. Simmons, *Things Great and Small: Collections Management Policies* [2nd] (New York: Rowman & Littlefield), 46.

11. Ibid., 47.

12. But see Simmons, who states, "[a]quisition does not mean that a transfer of ownership has taken place." Ibid., 46.

13. 17 U.S.C. § 101, "anonymous work."

14. Ibid. § 302(c).

15. Ibid.

16. Ibid. § 302(a).

17. 16 U.S.C. § 431.

18. National Trust for Historic Preservation (n.d.), "Antiquities Act," at https://savingplaces.org/antiquities-act#.X00z-ot7nIU, and National Trust of Historic Preservation (2017, December 6), "Broad Coalition Sues to Stop Trump Administration's Unlawful Dismemberment of the Bears Ears National Monument," at https://savingplaces.org/press-center/media-resources/broad-coalition-sues-to-stop-trump-administrations-unlawful-dismemberment-of-the-bears-ears-national-monument#.X00zQot7nIU.

19. President Trump's 2017 proclamation reduced Bears Ears by approximately 85 percent, resulting in two small, noncontiguous monuments. In response, a number of lawsuits were filed, challenging the action as unlawful under, among other causes of action, the Antiquities Act. The plaintiffs in the lawsuits represent Native American tribes, nonprofit organizations, environmental groups, and others. The cases were consolidated in January 2018, and on November 7, 2019, the plaintiffs filed their amended complaint, *Hopi Tribe v. Trump*, No. 1:17-cv-02590-TSC (*amended compl. filed* D.D.C. Nov. 8, 2019). The parties have since filed cross motions for summary judgment, with pleadings in support of those motions submitted as of June 9, 2020. At the time of writing, the court's decision on those motions has not been issued. The plaintiffs argue that the president does not have the authority under the Antiquities Act to reduce a national monument.

20. 16 U.S.C. § 432.

21. Ibid.

22. A list of monuments created under the Antiquities Act is available from the National Parks Conservation Association at https://www.npca.org/resources/2658-monuments-protected-under-the-antiquities-act.

23. Merriam-Webster Dictionary, available at http://www.merriam-webster.com/dictionary/appraisal.

24. *Abercrombie & Fitch Co. v. Hunting World, Inc.*, 537 F.2d 4, 9 (2d Cir. 1976).

25. Ibid.

26. Ibid., 11.

27. 16 U.S.C. § 470aa(b).

28. Ibid. § 470bb(3).

29. Ibid. § 470bb(4).

30. Ibid. § 470bb(1).

31. Ibid. § 470bb(1).

32. Ibid.

33. Ibid. § 470cc and 36 C.F.R. Part 296.

34. 16 U.S.C. § 470dd and 36 C.F.R. Part 79.

35. Marie C. Malaro and Ildiko Pogány DeAngelis, *A Legal Primer on Managing Museum Collections* [3rd] (Washington, DC: Smithsonian Books), 356.

36. National Endowment for the Arts, "Arts and Artifacts Indemnity Program: International Indemnity," http://arts.gov/artistic-fields/museums/arts-and-artifacts-indemnity-program-international-indemnity.

37. Ibid.

38. Ibid.

39. Ibid.

40. A full list of ineligible objects is available at http://arts.gov/artistic-fields/museums/arts-and-artifacts-indemnity-program-international-indemnity.

41. Ibid.

42. Ibid.

43. Ibid.

44. See ibid. for the current instructions and deadline.

45. National Endowment for the Arts, "Arts and Artifacts Indemnity Program: Domestic Indemnity," http://arts.gov/artistic-fields/museums/arts-and-artifacts-indemnity-program-domestic-indemnity.

46. Ibid.

47. While this conversation uses the word *state*, the attorney general has the same authority in U.S. commonwealths and territories.

48. Jason R. Goldstein, "Note, Deaccession: Not Such a Dirty Word," *Cardozo Arts and Entertainment Law Journal* 15 (1997): 214.

49. George Gleason Bogert, "Proposed Legislation Regarding State Supervision of Charities," *Michigan Law Review* 52 (1954): 633–34.

50. Luis Kutner and Henry H. Koven, "Charitable Trust Legislation in the Several States," *Northwestern University Law Review* 61 (1966): 411.

51. Jennifer L. White, "When It's OK to Sell the Monet: A Trustee-Fiduciary-Duty Framework for Analyzing the Deaccessioning of Art to Meet Museum Operating Expenses," *Michigan Law Review* 94 (1996): 1045. There are some situations in which a donor or individual may have standing to sue, which falls outside the scope of this discussion.

52. See, for instance, New York State Office of the Attorney General, "Charities: Guides & Publications," available at http://www.charitiesnys.com/guides_advice_new.jsp.

53. The National Association of Attorney Generals maintains a list of all current AGs with their contact information at https://www.naag.org/naag/attorneys-general/whos-my-ag.php.

54. 17 U.S.C. § 106A(a)(1)(A).

55. Ibid. § 106A(a)(1)(B).

56. Ibid. § 106A(c)(3).

57. Ibid. § 106A(a)(2).

58. Marcel Duchamp, *L.H.O.O.Q.*, 1913.

59. 17 U.S.C. § 113(d)(1).

60. Ibid. § 113(d)(2). The Act provides the specific procedural steps that must be followed by the building owner to effect a diligent and good faith attempt to notify the artist.

61. Ibid. §102(a).

62. Ibid. § 401(a).

63. Ibid. § 411(a). Until recently, there had been a circuit split (federal courts were not in agreement) as to when an infringement action could actually be brought. In some federal circuits, an action could commence once the application had been made, including the associated deposit and payment of the application fee. This was the so-called application approach. However, other federal circuits stated the application alone was not sufficient and an infringement action could only commence once the registration had actually been issued. This was the so-called registration approach. As registrations can take months after application to be issued, this created a fairly significant difference in when an action could be brought to the courts depending on the location of the parties. However in 2019, the Supreme Court heard a case that settled the matter between the circuits, officially establishing that "registration occurs, and a copyright claimant may commence an infringement suit, when the Copyright Office registers a copyright." *Fourth Estate Public Benefit Corp. v. Wall-Street .com*, 586 U.S. ___ (2019). Further: "The registration approach, we conclude, reflects the only satisfactory reading of §411(a)'s text." Ibid.

64. 17 U.S.C. § 412.

65. Department of the Treasury, Internal Revenue Service, "Publication 557: Tax-Exempt Status for Your Organization" (revised January 2020): 12.

66. Ibid., 11.

67. Ibid., 12.

68. Ibid.

69. Ibid.

70. "The works mentioned in this Article shall enjoy protection in all countries of the Union. This protection shall operate for the benefit of the author and his successors in title." Berne Convention for the Protection of Literary and Artistic Works art. 2(6), Sept. 9, 1886, 1161 U.N.T.S. 3.

71. World Intellectual Property Organization, "Contracting Parties: Berne Convention (Total Contracting Parties: 168)," http://www.wipo.int/treaties/en/ShowResults.jsp?lang=en&treaty_id=15.

72. Ibid.

73. Berne Convention art. 2(1).

74. Ibid., art. 2(3).

75. Ibid., art. 5(2).

76. Copyright Act of 1909, Pub. L. 60-349 § 10 (repealed by the Copyright Act of 1976).

77. Ibid. § 11.

78. Ibid. § 19.

79. Berne Convention art. 6*bis*.

80. Berne requires that "the author shall have the right to claim authorship of the work [right of attribution] and to object to any distortion, mutilation or other modification of, or other derogatory action in relation to, the said work, which would be prejudicial to his honor or reputation [right of integrity]." Berne Convention art. 6*bis*(1). The *droit de suite*, however, is only available in signatory countries in which legislation permits the right. Ibid., art. 14*ter*(2).

81. Convention on Cultural Property Implementation Act, 19 U.S.C. § 2602(a)(1). Before this importation restriction can be instituted, it must first be determined that the State Party's cultural patrimony is in jeopardy from pillaging, the State Party has taken measures to protect that cultural patrimony, less drastic remedies are unavailable, and the importation restrictions would deter pillaging. Ibid.

82. Ibid. § 2602(a)(2).

83. Ibid. § 2602(b).

84. Ibid. §§ 2605(b) and (f)(1). The current list of committee members is available at https://eca.state.gov/cultural-heritage-center/cultural-property-advisory-committee/committee-members.

85. Ibid. § 2605(f)(2).

86. Available at https://eca.state.gov/cultural-heritage-center/cultural-property-advisory-committee/current-import-restrictions.

87. Blue Shield International, "About Us: Who We Are," https://theblueshield.org/about-us/what-is-blue-shield/.

88. Convention for the Protection of Cultural Property in the Event of Armed Conflict, First Protocol, ch. V, art. 16.

89. Blue Shield International, "Why the Blue Shield Is Needed," https://theblueshield.org/why-we-do-it/why-blue-shield-is-needed/.

90. Blue Shield International, "Training," https://theblueshield.org/what-we-do/training/.

91. Blue Shield International, "Blue Shield National Committee Activities," https://theblueshield.org/what-we-do/the-national-committees/.

92. Some exceptions exist, such as with some restricted gifts or other scenarios outside the scope of this discussion.

93. Incorporation is governed by state law. Consult local law to determine what documents must be filed with the state in your particular jurisdiction.

94. Bank accounts, real estate, vehicles, etc. Only such things that can be sold or used as security for debts qualify as assets.

95. "Museum financial accounting systems do not always meet conventional standards of completeness for like sized firms . . . but because of the centrality of collecting, conservation, and duties to donors of objects, all museums maintain meticulous non-financial records of the objects in their collection. . . . In one sense, then, museums are completely accountable for their principal asset, the collection. . . ." Michael O'Hare. (2005). *Capitalizing Art Museum Collections: Awkward for Museums but Good for Art and Society.* Association for Public Policy Analysis and Management Research Conference, Washington, D.C., November 2005, at 5.

96. American Association for State and Local History. (2020). *Valuing History Collections*. Nashville, TN: Author. Retrieved from http://download.aaslh.org/AASLH+Valuing+History+Collections+Position+Paper+-May+2020.pdf. This position paper replaces the 2003 paper, *The Capitalization of Collections: Ethics Position Paper #1*, and was prepared by the AASLH Standards & Ethics Committee in response to the 2019 Financial Accounting Standards Board (FASB) Accounting Standards Update No. 2019-03. FASB had updated that organization's definition of "collections." See also AASLH. (2018). *Statement of Standards and Ethics*. At page 2: "Historical resources shall not be capitalized or treated as financial assets." Retrieved from http://download .aaslh.org/AASLH+Statement+of+Standards+and+Ethics+-+Revised+2018.pdf. See dictionary entry "FASB Update No. 2019-03" for more information. For transparency, be aware the author of this text participated in the writing of the *Valuing History Collections* paper.

97. Association of Art Museum Directors. (2011). *Professional Practices in Art Museums*. New York: Author. Retrieved from https://aamd.org/sites/default/files/document/2011ProfessionalPracitiesinArtMuseums.pdf. At page 11: "To present fairly the museum's financial position, collections should not be capitalized." At page 20: "Member museums should not capitalize or collateralize collections or recognize as revenue the value of donated works." These guidelines were published prior to the 2019 Financial Accounting Standards Board (FASB) Accounting Standards Update No. 2019-03, which updated that organization's definition of "collections." See FASB Update No. 2019-03 for more information.

98. At the time of this writing, the American Alliance of Museums appears to agree with AASLH and AAMD regarding capitalization of collections. In their Code of Ethics for Museums, the AAM states that "collections in its custody are lawfully held, protected, secure, *unencumbered*, cared for and preserved" [emphasis added]. AAM. (1993, revised 2000). Code of Ethics for Museums. https://www.aam-us.org/programs/ethics-standards-and-professional-practices/code-of-ethics-for-museums/. No other statement from the AAM addressed capitalization practices, and on the "capitalization of collections" page of their "financial stability resources" website, AAM provides links to outside sources, but no direct guidance.

99. This is a very simplified discussion. Many countries use a mixture of the common and civil law systems.

100. The legal system of a country may also be influenced by other factors outside the scope of this discussion, such as religious law or the prevailing economic or political system.

101. Portions of this section are drawn from an early draft of the author's contribution to the AASLH position paper "What's Next? A Guide to Museum Transitions and Closures." [forthcoming].

102. The National Association of Attorneys General website maintains a list of all Attorneys General, with links to their websites, at https://www.naag.org/naag/attorneys-general/whos-my-ag.php.

103. Information about Schedule N can be found at https://www.irs.gov/forms-pubs/about-schedule-n-form-990.

104. Your state AG may require certified copies of some or all of the IRS paperwork.

105. American Alliance of Museums, "Alliance Reference Guide: Developing an Institutional Code of Ethics," 2018, 1.

106. Marie C. Malaro, *Museum Governance: Mission, Ethics, Policy* (Washington, D.C.: Smithsonian Institution Press, 1994), 17.

107. John E. Simmons, "Collections Management Policies," in *Museum Registration Methods* [6th], 30.

108. Ibid.

109. This is a very simplified discussion. Many countries use a mixture of the common and civil law systems.

110. The legal system of a country may also be influenced by other factors outside the scope of this discussion, such as religious law or the prevailing economic or political system.

111. The majority of U.S. states are common law property states. At the time of writing, forty-one were common law property states.

112. At the time of writing, the common law test was used by the IRS, the District of Columbia, and eighteen states. The ABC test (or some variation of it) was used by the Department of Labor and thirty-three states, with the state of California changing to the ABC Test following the state's Supreme Court decision in *Dynamex*, 4 Cal. 5th 903 (2018). Effective January 1, 2020, California Assembly Bill 5 codified the *Dynamex* ABC test and expanded its reach to all wage and hour Labor Code violations in the state. See note 4 for more information on AB-5 and its current status at the time of writing.

113. The IRS used to apply what was known as the "20-factor test" to determine if a worker should be classified as an employee. That test looked at a variety of factors to determine who (the employer or the worker) had control over each factor's activity. Factors considered included how much company-provided training the

worker was required to undergo, the level of continuity in the employer-worker relationship, the requirement for the worker to work on site, methods of payment, and payment of travel and business expenses. The twenty factors were not necessarily evenly weighed: Depending on the worker's occupation and other relevant context, some factors were weighed more heavily than others in the final determination. The IRS no longer uses the 20-factor test and instead uses the common law test discussed here.

114. Internal Revenue Service, Department of the Treasury. (2019, December 23). Publication 15-A: Employer's Supplemental Tax Guide, p. 7. Washington, D.C.: Author.

115. Ibid. at 8.

116. Ibid.

117. At the time of writing, only nine states operate under the regulations of community property rules. These are: Arizona, California, Idaho, Louisiana, Nevada, New Mexico, Texas, Washington, and Wisconsin. Additionally, Alaska permits a married couple to "opt in" to a community property system. Some of the states have domicile requirements, and the specifics for each jurisdiction can be complicated for the unwary. The Internal Revenue Service maintains a chart that compares the differences between the community property laws in each of these states. Department of the Treasury, Internal Revenue Services. (Reviewed 2017, September 10.) Internal Revenue Manual Part 25, chapter 18.8, section 1. Basic Principles of Community Property Law. Exhibit 25.18.1-1, "Comparison of State Law Differences in Community Property." https://www.irs.gov/irm/part25/irm_25-018-001#idm140332604123232.

118. Restatement (2d) of Contracts § 1.

119. Ibid. § 1, comment e.

120. Ibid. § 4. Though contracts, as a general rule, are enforceable when made orally, the statute of frauds requires certain types of contracts to be in writing or they will not be enforced at law.

121. Individuals called an infant in legal texts are commonly understood by laypersons to be a minor, not merely an individual in their infancy of one year old or younger. In most states, this age is set by statute to eighteen years old, but this may vary depending on the jurisdiction.

122. Ibid. § 12(2).

123. Offer and acceptance are generally straightforward, though complications can arise, such as if an offer is rescinded or if an acceptance attempts to change the terms of the offer. Other complications, such as when offer revocation and acceptance cross in the mail, are also possible. These situations are outside the scope of this text.

124. Ibid. § 71(1).

125. Ibid. § 71(4).

126. Ibid. § 17.

127. This example is drawn from ibid. § 71, comment b, illustrations 1d and 2.

128. Convention for the Protection of Cultural Property in the Event of Armed Conflict, First Protocol, Preamble, May 14, 1954, 249 U.N.T.S. 240.

129. For the full definition of *cultural property* under the 1954 Hague Convention, see ibid., ch. I, art. 1.

130. Ibid., ch. I, art. 1(a).

131. Ibid., ch. I, art. 4(1).

132. Ibid., ch. I, art. 4(1).

133. Ibid., ch. I, art. 4(2).

134. Ibid., ch. I, art. 4(3).

135. Ibid., ch. V, art. 16.

136. United Nations Educational, Scientific and Cultural Organization, "Convention for the Protection of Cultural Property in the Event of Armed Conflict with Regulations for the Execution of the Convention. The Hague, 14 May 1954," https://pax.unesco.org/la/convention.asp?KO=13637&language=E&order=alpha.

137. Convention for the Protection of Cultural Property in the Event of Armed Conflict, Second Protocol, ch. 1, art. 2, Mar. 26, 1999, 2253 U.N.T.S. 172.

138. Ibid., ch. 1, art. 6.

139. Ibid., ch. 3.

140. Ibid., ch. 4.

141. Ibid., ch. 6, art. 24.

142. Ibid., ch. 6, art. 27.

143. United Nations Educational, Scientific and Cultural Organization, "Second Protocol to the Hague Convention of 1954 for the Protection of Cultural Property in the Event of Armed Conflict. The Hague, 26 March 1999," http://www.unesco.org/eri/la/convention.asp?KO=15207&language=E&order=alpha.

144. 19 U.S.C. § 2602(a)(1). Before this importation restriction can be instituted, it must first be determined that the State Party's cultural patrimony is in jeopardy from pillaging, the State Party has taken measures to protect that cultural patrimony, less drastic remedies are unavailable, and the importation restrictions would deter pillaging.

145. Ibid. §§ 2605(b) and (f)(1). The current list of committee members is available at https://eca.state.gov/cultural-heritage-center/cultural-property-advisory-committee/committee-members.

146. Ibid. § 2603(a).

147. Ibid. § 2603(c). The Committee's recommendations must be received within ninety days to be considered. Ibid. § 2603(c)(2). The Committee may also make recommendations concerning the extension of emergency actions beyond the original five-year period, so long as those recommendations are again received within ninety days. Ibid. § 2603(c)(3).

148. For more information on the statutory requirement of the publication of restricted objects, see ibid. § 2604.

149. 19 U.S.C. § 2607.

150. United Nations Educational, Scientific and Cultural Organization, "UNESCO and UNIDROIT—Cooperation in the Fight Against Illicit Traffic in Cultural Property," June 24, 2005, 1, http://unesdoc.unesco.org/images/0013/001399/139969E.pdf.

151. Convention on the Means of Prohibiting and Preventing the Illicit Import, Export, and Transfer of Ownership of Cultural Property, Preamble, Nov. 11, 1970, 823 U.N.T.S. 231.

152. Ibid., art. 1.

153. At the time of writing, 140 countries are listed as State Parties by UNESCO, http://www.unesco.org/eri/la/convention.asp?KO=13039&language=E&order=alpha.

154. "UNESCO and UNIDROIT—Cooperation in the Fight Against Illicit Traffic in Cultural Property," 1.

155. U.S. Const. art. 1, § 8, cl. 8.

156. 17 U.S.C. § 102(a).

157. 17 U.S.C. § 102(a).

158. U.S. Const. Art. I, § 8, Cl. 8.

159. United Nations Educational, Scientific and Cultural Organization, "Permanent Delegation of Nigeria to UNESCO," https://nigeria-del-unesco.org/intangible-cultural-heritage/.

160. J. Jokilhto, comp., International Centre for the Study of the Preservation and Restoration of Cultural Property Working Group "Heritage and Society," *Definitions of Cultural Heritage: References to Documents in History*, 1990, revised Jan. 15, 2005. http://cif.icomos.org/pdf_docs/Documents%20on%20line/Heritage%20definitions.pdf.

161. Convention for the Protection of Cultural Property in the Event of Armed Conflict, First Protocol, ch. I, art. 1(a).

162. Convention on the Means of Prohibiting and Preventing the Illicit Import, Export, and Transfer of Ownership of Cultural Property, art. 1.

163. André Desvallées and François Mairesse, eds., *Key Concepts of Museology*, trans. Suzanne Nash (International Council of Museums, 2010), 39, citation omitted.

164. 25 U.S.C. § 3001(3)(D).

165. For more information on this topic, see Yahaya Ahmad, "The Scope and Definitions of Cultural Heritage: From Tangible to Intangible," *International Journal of Heritage Studies* 12 (May 2006): 292, which examines the broadening of the definition of *heritage* and the issue that there has been no standardization of terminology on an international level.

166. 19 U.S.C. § 2605(b)(1). The current Committee members can be found at the United States Department of State, Bureau of Educational and Cultural Affairs, Cultural Heritage Center, "Cultural Property Advisory Committee," http://eca.state.gov/cultural-heritage-center/cultural-property-protection/process-and-purpose/cultural-property-advisory.

167. 19 U.S.C. § 2605(b)(3)(A). The current list of committee members is available at https://eca.state.gov/cultural-heritage-center/cultural-property-advisory-committee/committee-members.

168. Ibid. § 2605(f)(1).

169. Ibid. § 2605(f)(2).

170. Ibid. § 2605(f)(3).

171. Ibid. § 2605(g).

172. National Park Service, "Archaeology Program: Curation of Federally Owned and Administered Archaeological Collections (36 C.F.R. 79)," http://www.nps.gov/archeology/tools/laws/36C.F.R.79.htm.

173. Ibid.

174. Specifically, objects recovered under 16 US.C. § 470h-2.

175. 36 C.F.R. Part 79.1.

176. Ibid. Part 79.6.

177. Ibid. Part 79.7.

178. Ibid. Part 79.10.

179. Ibid. Part 79.11, and Appendixes.

180. Precatory language is language that expresses a wish or suggestion but does not have the legal force of a restriction. For instance, compare a donor's desire that a museum display two statuettes together with a donor's mandated restriction that they must be displayed together at all times.

181. Malaro and Pogány DeAngelis, *A Legal Primer* [3rd], 159.

182. Ibid.

183. Art Dealers Association of America, "Code of Ethics and Professional Practices," https://www.art-dealers.org/about/code-of-ethics-and-professional-practices.

184. Precatory language is that which expresses a wish or suggestion but does not have the legal force of a restriction. For instance, compare a donor's desire that a museum display two statuettes together with a donor's mandated restriction that they must be displayed together at all times.

185. *Towell v. Comm'r*, T.C. Summary Opinion 2010-141 (2010). This case may not be treated as precedent for future litigation.

186. 17 U.S.C. § 106(2).

187. Ibid. § 101, "derivative work."

188. Ibid. § 103(b).

189. Ibid.

190. *Abercrombie*, 537 F.2d at 10.

191. Ibid.

192. Ibid.

193. 15 U.S.C. § 1052(f).

194. *Abercrombie*, 537 F.2d at 10.

195. *Carter–Wallace, Inc. v. Procter & Gamble Co.*, 434 F.2d 794, 800 (9th Cir. 1970).

196. American Alliance of Museums. (2016, April). *Direct Care of Collections: Ethics, Guidelines and Recommendations* [White paper]. Washington, D.C.: Author, at 7. Retrieved from https://www.aam-us.org/wp-content/uploads/2018/01/direct-care-of-collections-ethics-guidelines-and-recommendations-pdf.pdf. AASLH adopts this definition verbatim in their 2018 revision of their *Statement of Standards and Ethics*. See endnote 2. Retrieved from http://download.aaslh.org/AASLH+Statement+of+Standards+and+Ethics+-+Revised+2018.pdf.

197. Available at https://www.aam-us.org/programs/ethics-standards-and-professional-practices/code-of-ethics-for-museums/.

198. Specifically, the AAM Code of Ethics states, "Proceeds from the sale of nonliving collections are to be used consistent with the established standards of the museum's discipline, but in no event shall they be used for anything other than acquisition or direct care of collections." However, the Code of Ethics does not define *direct care*, giving rise to the need for an exploration of the term in the AAM *Direct Care of Collections* white paper.

199. AAM, *Direct Care of Collections* at 10.

200. See AAM, *Direct Care of Collections*, for a full explanation of the use and application of the matrix.

201. IRS Pub. 557, 16. As of this writing, an organization that fails to make required disclosures for *quid pro quo* contributions of more than $75 face a penalty of $10 per donation, limited to a $5,000 penalty for each fund-raising event or mailing. If the organization can show its failure to disclose was due to reasonable cause, the penalty may be avoided. Ibid.

202. Throughout this discussion, "acknowledging receipt" will be used to describe a disclosure statement that does not memorialize a *quid pro quo* contribution, meaning a donation where no donor-received benefit must be disclosed by the donee museum.

203. Department of the Treasury, Internal Revenue Service, "Publication 526: Charitable Contributions" (2019), 20. These requirements were accurate at the time of writing. Consult current requirements to ensure compliance.

204. Ibid.

205. Ibid.

206. Donors may need to provide additional documents and information, depending on the amount of the deduction they claim on their tax forms. Deductions over $500 will require the donor to submit IRS Form 8283. That form requires an acknowledgment from the museum, which will need to provide their taxpayer identification number and signature from an authorized individual who is authorized to sign on behalf of the museum. The museum will also have to disclose whether they intend to use the donated property in a manner unrelated to its tax-exempt purpose.

207. IRS Pub. 557, 16. For example, if Betty Ball pays $100 for a ticket to attend the annual fund-raising event of City Museum, which is a qualified organization, and the fair market value of the ticket is only $30, Ball may deduct the difference, $70. Ibid.

208. Ibid., 16.

209. IRS Pub. 526, 4.

210. IRS Pub. 557, 16.

211. IRS Pub. 557, 25.

212. 17 U.S.C. § 106(3).

213. Precatory language is that which expresses a wish or suggestion but does not have the legal force of a restriction. For instance, compare a donor's desire that a museum display two statuettes together with a donor's mandated restriction that they must be displayed together at all times.

214. Malaro and Pogány DeAngelis, *A Legal Primer* [3rd], 160.

215. Ibid.

216. Ibid.

217. Ibid.

218. United States Patent and Trademark Office, "Trademark Manual of Examining Protocol" (October 2018) § 1210.10

219. Ibid.

220. *In re Bayer Aktiengesellschaft*, Trademark Trial and Appeal Board, 2005 TTAB LEXIS 521 (2005), finding that a mark of "Aspirina," Spanish for "aspirin," was merely descriptive when applied to analgesics (painkillers).

221. Malaro and Pogány DeAngelis, *A Legal Primer* [3rd], 28.

222. "On the Resale Right for the Benefit of the Author of an Original Work of Art," Council Directive 2001/84/EC, preamble paras. 2 and 3, 2001 *Official Journal of the European Communities* (L 272) 32.

223. Ibid., ch. 1, art. 1, para. 1.

224. C.A. Civ. Code § 986.

225. Ibid. § 986(a).

226. United States Copyright Office, Office of the Register of Copyrights, "Resale Royalties: An Updated Analysis" (2013), 66.

227. This may be called an easement by necessity. If the particular purpose of the easement is necessary and used openly and continuously over a period of time (as long as twenty years in some jurisdictions), it may be called a prescriptive easement.

228. Internal Revenue Service, Department of the Treasury. (2017, July 20). FS-2017-09: Understanding Employee vs. Contractor Classification. Retrieved from https://www.irs.gov/. Section 501(c)(3) organizations, while exempt from federal income tax under 26 USC 501(a), are still required to pay both Social Security and Medicare taxes unless one of two exempting situations applies: The organization pays the employee less than $100 in the calendar year or the organization fits certain criteria related to churches and church-controlled organizations that have filed required IRS forms. Internal Revenue Service, Department of the Treasury, Publication 15-A.

229. 16 U.S.C. § 1531(a)(1), (2).

230. "[A]ny species which is in danger of extinction throughout all or a significant portion of its range other than a species of the Class Insecta determined by the Secretary to constitute a pest whose protection under the provisions of this chapter would present an overwhelming and overriding risk to man." Ibid. § 1532(6).

231. "[A]ny species which is likely to become an endangered species within the foreseeable future throughout all or a significant portion of its range." Ibid. § 1532(20).

232. 50 C.F.R. Part 17.

233. 16 U.S.C. § 1538(a)(1), (2).

234. Ibid. § 1538(a)(1)(D), (E).

235. Ibid. § 1539(a)(1)(A). Specimens imported or exported for scientific purposes or to enhance the species' survival must travel through designated ports. Additionally, permits must be acquired. There are different permits available, depending on the purpose of the use. Information is promulgated by the U.S. Fish and Wildlife Service at http://www.fws.gov/ENDANGERED/permits/index.html.

236. To qualify, the object must be over one hundred years old, not have be repaired or modified with any part of any threatened or endangered species on or after December 28, 1973, and enter the United States through a statutorily designated port. 16 U.S.C. § 1539(h). Documentation requirements apply and must be submitted if the object is to be permitted entry by the customs officer. Museums seeking to transport regulated objects should consult legal counsel.

237. IRC § 501(c)(3).

238. This is done on Form 990 Schedule A.

239. Instructions for Schedule A of the Form 990 or Form 990-EZ can be found at https://www.irs.gov/pub/irs-pdf/i990sa.pdf.

240. Department of the Treasury, Internal Revenue Service, "Publication 561: Determining the Value of Donated Property" (revised Feb. 2020): 2.

241. Ibid.

242. Ibid.

243. IRS Pub. 557, 16.

244. 17 U.S.C. § 107.

245. Ibid.

246. Ibid.

247. Ibid.

248. Ibid.

249. Ibid.

250. *Campbell v. Acuff-Rose Music, Inc.*, 501 U.S. 569, 577 and 584 (1994).

251. *Abercrombie*, 537 F.2d at 9.

252. Ibid.

253. Ibid., 11.

254. Financial Accounting Standards Board, "Facts," https://www.fasb.org/facts/,

255. Financial Accounting Standards Board. "About the FASB [updated July 1, 2020]." www.fasb.org/cs/ContentServer?c=Page&pagename=FASB%2FPage%2FSectionPage&cid=1176154526495.

256. Ibid.

257. Financial Accounting Standards Board, "Statement of Financial Accounting Standards No. 116: Accounting for Contributions Received and Contributions Made" (Norwalk, CT: Financial Accounting Foundation, 1993), ¶ 125.

> Collections, as used in this Statement, generally are held by museums, botanical gardens, libraries, aquariums, arboretums, historic sites, planetariums, zoos, art galleries, nature, science and technology centers, and similar educational, research, and public service organizations that have those divisions; however, the definition is not limited to those entities nor does it apply to all items held by those entities.

Ibid., ¶ 128. Organizations which hold objects such as art works and historic objects but do not have an educational mission are not exempted from the requirement to capitalize. Ibid., ¶ 135.

258. Ibid., ¶ 11.

259. Ibid., ¶ 11.

260. "Proceeds from the sale of nonliving collections are to be used consistent with the established standards of the museum's discipline, but in no event shall they be used for anything other than acquisition or direct care of collections." American Alliance of Museums, AAM Code of Ethics for Museums.

261. American Association for State and Local History. (2018). *Statement of Standards and Ethics.* http://download.aaslh.org/AASLH+Statement+of+Standards+and+Ethics+-+Revised+2018.pdf.

262. Association of Art Museum Directors. (2010, June 9, amended October 2015). AAMD Policy on Deaccessioning. https://aamd.org/sites/default/files/document/AAMD%20Policy%20on%20Deaccessioning%20website_0.pdf.

263. In April 2020, in direct response to the ongoing COVID-19 pandemic, AAMD made a temporary change to its policy regarding the use of funds from deaccessioning. Through April 10, 2022, AAMD has issued a moratorium on censuring or sanctioning members for using funds from deaccessioning for the direct care of collections. This is a temporary response to the global pandemic and does not constitute a permanent change to AAMD's policies or professional best practices. Further, while AAMD will temporarily refrain from censoring or sanctioning members for using deaccessioning proceeds to provide direct care for collections, that does not mean an attorney general or other oversight authority may not bring a legal challenge to such actions, as the ethical standards maintained by AAMD do not control legal obligations that may impact a museum in their particular jurisdiction. More can be read about the AAMD's temporary moratorium in the "Press Release: AAMD Board of Trustees Approves Resolution to Provide Additional Financial Flexibility to Art Museums During Pandemic Crisis." (2020, April 15). https://aamd.org/for-the-media/press-release/aamd-board-of-trustees-approves-resolution-to-provide-additional.

264. Financial Accounting Standards Board. (n.d.) *Accounting Standards Update 2019-03: Not-For-Profit Entities (Topic 958): Updating the Definition of Collections.* fasb.org/cs/ContentServer?c=FASBContent_C&cid=1176172408217&d=&pagename=FASB%2FFASBContent_C%2FCompletedProjectPage.

265. Ibid.

266. For an in-depth discussion of the FASB update, see American Association for State and Local History position paper *Valuing History Collections.*

267. On August 8, 2020, President Donald Trump issued a Memorandum to the Secretary of the Treasury titled "Deferring Payroll Tax Obligations in Light of the Ongoing Covid-19 Disaster," wherein he instructs the Secretary to use his 26 U.S.C. § 7508A authority to defer the withholding, deposit, and payment of FICA employee contributions from September 1, 2020, through December 31, 2020. As this is a deferment of the payroll tax, employees will have to repay the monies during the first quarter of 2021 unless future actions are taken to make the deferments more permanent. There are specific limitations to this, including income thresholds. (Employees who earn less than $4,000 before taxes during any biweekly pay period, coming to those salaried employees who earn $104,000 or less per year.) At the time of writing, the exact impact of this memo and how it will be implemented is not fully understood. The memo is available on the White House website at https://www.whitehouse.gov/presidential-actions/memorandum-deferring-payroll-tax-obligations-light-ongoing-covid-19-disaster/. Some preliminary guidance on the deferral has been published by the IRS in Notice 2020-65, available at https://www.irs.gov/pub/irs-drop/n-20-65.pdf.

268. These provide just a general overview of the types of tenancies available in real property. Your jurisdiction may recognize others or treat the tenancies slightly differently than can be covered in an overview here.

269. 17 U.S.C. § 109(a).

270. Ibid. § 109(c).

271. Ibid.

272. Ibid.

273. Ibid. § 109(b)(1)(A).

274. Ibid.

275. Ibid. §102(a).

276. Ibid. § 101, "fixed."

277. Rebecca Buck [edited and updated by John E. Simmons and Toni M. Kiser], "Found-in-Collection," in *Museum Registration Methods* [6th], 126. Buck provides a comprehensive list of possible sources for undocumented objects, including gifts, abandoned objects, exhibition props, unclaimed or old loans, and others. See Table 3J.1, page 126.

278. Ibid at 126.

279. Malaro and Pogány DeAngelis, *A Legal Primer* [3rd], 391.

280. Ibid.

281. Ibid.

282. The Association of Registrars and Collections Specialists maintains a living document that lists legislation relevant to old loans and found-in-collection objects. See "Museum Property Acts and Abandoned Loan Legislation" at http://www.arcsinfo.org/content/documents/arcsmuseumpropertyandoldloanlegislation-june2018.pdf.

283. U.S. Const. First Amend.

284. For instance, consider the numerous cases that have focused on desecration of the American flag. *Texas v. Johnson*, 491 U.S. 397 (1989), *United States v. Eichman*, 496 U.S. 310 (1990), and others.

285. *New York v. Ferber*, 458 U.S. 747 (1982), extended to possession in *Osborne v. Ohio*, 495 U.S. 103 (1990). Regulations on child pornography may not be so overbroad as to impact protected speech, as the Supreme Court found to have occurred with some provisions of the Child Pornography Prevention Act of 1996. See *Ashcroft v. Free Speech Coalition*, 535 U.S. 234 (2002), finding that a provision of that Act covered

> materials beyond the categories recognized in *Ferber* and *Miller*, and the reasons the Government offers in support of limiting the freedom of speech have no justification in our precedents or in the law of the First Amendment. The provision abridges the freedom to engage in a substantial amount of lawful speech. For this reason, it is overbroad and unconstitutional.

Ibid. at 256.

286. 15 U.S.C. § 1127.

287. *Qualitex Co. v. Jacobson Products Co., Inc.*, 514 U.S. 159, 162 (1995).

288. Ibid., 164.

289. Ibid. If the producer has actually invented the functional feature, that feature is best protected by patent law, which gives the producer/inventor a term-limited monopoly. See also "Patent."

290. Ibid., 165, citation omitted.

291. Obviously, interpretation of testamentary documents can be quite complex, and local laws or precedent may impact the outcome in any particular situation. This example is provided only to give insight and the results in an actual situation may differ from what is described here. Future interests are incredibly complex areas of property law, and consultation with a knowledgeable attorney is recommended if necessary.

292. *Abercrombie*, 537 F.2d at 9.

293. Ibid.

294. Ibid.

295. Ibid.

296. Ibid.

297. 15 U.S.C. § 1127.

298. For more information on historic public easements, including requirements, tax benefits, and what constitutes a qualified property or organization, see Charles Fischer (2010), *Easements to Protect Historic Properties: A Useful Historic Preservation Tool with Potential Tax Benefits*. Washington, D.C.: National Park Service, Technical Preservation Services. https://www.nps.gov/tps/tax-incentives/taxdocs/easements-historic-properties.pdf.

299. Howard N. Spiegler (2001). "Recovering Nazi-Looted Art: Report from the Front Lines." *Connecticut Journal of International Law, 16*(2), 297–312 at 298.

300. Ibid. This is only the briefest of overviews of the extensive Nazi looting program, which could never be adequately covered here. For more information, see Hector Feliciano (1997). *The Lost Museum*. New York: Harper Collins; Lynn Nicholas (1994). *The Rape of Europa*. London: Macmillan Publishers; Anne-Marie O'Connor (2012). *The Lady in Gold: The Extraordinary Tale of Gustav Klimt's Masterpiece, Portrait of Adele Bloch-Bauer*, New York: Alfred A. Knopf; and others.

301. For a more in-depth examination of these barriers to reclamation, see Spiegler. "Recovering Nazi-Looted Art."

302. See, for instance, the AAM-managed Nazi-Era Provenance Internet Portal at http://www.nepip.org/, the Holocaust Claims Processing Office maintained by New York State at https://www.dfs.ny.gov/consumers/holocaust_claims, the Object Database at https://www.lootedart.com/, or the database maintained by the Monuments Men Foundation at https://www.monumentsmenfoundation.org/.

303. Spiegler "Recovering Nazi-Looted Art," at 305.

304. William H. Honan (1991, March 30). "Soviets Reported to Hide Looted Art." *The New York Times.* https://www.nytimes.com/1991/03/30/arts/soviets-reported-to-hide-looted-art.html.

305. Consider, for instance, the case involving three works by painter George Grosz held by the Museum of Modern Art, NYC. Grosz's son and daughter-in-law alleged that after Grosz fled Germany, the Third Reich named him an "enemy of the state" and rendered him "stateless," revoking his citizenship and confiscating his German assets. *Grosz v. Museum of Modern Art*, 772 F.Supp.2d 473, 476 (S.D.N.Y. 2010), citing First Am. Compl., May 28, 2009, ¶¶ 3, 45–46, 124. Grosz saw the painting displayed at MoMA in 1953:

> At that time, Grosz wrote to his brother-in-law: "Modern Museum exhibits a painting stolen from me (I am powerless against that) they bought it from someone, who stole it." (Compl. ¶ 105.) In a second letter dated January 9, 1953, Grosz wrote: "Modern Museum bought a painting that was stolen from me . . . (one cannot do anything) old affair." (*Id.*)

Grosz, 772 F.Supp.2d at 481. Ultimately, the court held that the three-year statute of limitations had run and therefore the museum's motion to dismiss the complaint on procedural grounds was granted. *Grosz*, 772 F.Supp.2d at 490.

306. Holocaust Expropriated Art Recovery Act of 2016, Pub. L. No. 114-308, 130 Stat. 1524 (2016). In the Congressional findings it is stated:

> Victims of Nazi persecution and their heirs have taken legal action in the United States to recover Nazi-confiscated art. These lawsuits face significant procedural obstacles partly due to State statutes of limitations, which typically bar claims within some limited number of years from either the date of the loss or the date that the claim should have been discovered. In some cases, this means that the claims expired before World War II even ended. (See, e.g., *Detroit Institute of Arts v. Ullin*, No. 06–10333, 2007 WL 1016996 [E.D. Mich. Mar. 31, 2007].) The unique and horrific circumstances of World War II and the Holocaust make statutes of limitations especially burdensome to the victims and their heirs. Those seeking recovery of Nazi-confiscated art must painstakingly piece together their cases from a fragmentary historical record ravaged by persecution, war, and genocide. This costly process often cannot be done within the time constraints imposed by existing law.

Ibid. at § 2(6).

307. Ibid. at § 5(a).

308. Ibid. at § 5(a).

309. Ibid. at § 4(3).

310. Ibid. at § 4(2).

311. Ibid. at § 5(c).

312. Ibid. at § 5(d)(1).

313. Ibid. at § 5(e).

314. Ibid. at § 5(g).

315. Ambassador Lauder is the chairman of both the Commission for Art Recovery and the World Jewish Restitution Organization. Quote from Commission for Art Recovery, "HEAR Act Signed into Law," http://www.commartrecovery.org/hear-act.

316. *Zuckerman v. Metropolitan Museum of Art*, 928 F.3d 186 (2d Cir. 2019).

317. See "Laches" for more information on how this defense is different from the statute of limitations issue addressed in the HEAR Act.

318. *Zuckerman*, 928 F.3d at 196.

319. Ibid.

320. *Zuckerman v. Metropolitan Museum of Art*, 140 S.Ct. 1269 (2020), *cert. denied* (U.S. March 2, 2020) (No. 19-942).

321. For a fuller discussion, see Mary-Christine Sungaila, William Feldman, and Marco A. Pulido. (2020, March 11). "Holocaust-Era Art and Property Recovery Claims after 'Zuckerman,'" *The Recorder*, https://www.law.com/therecorder/2020/03/11/holocaust-era-art-and-property-recovery-claims-after-zuckerman/.

322. Internal Revenue Service, Department of the Treasury, Fact Sheet-2017-09. Section 501(c)(3) organizations, while exempt from federal income tax under 26 USC 501(a), are still required to pay both Social Security and Medicare taxes unless one of two exempting situations applies: The organization pays the employee less than $100 in the calendar year or the organization fits certain criteria related to churches and church-controlled organizations that have filed required IRS forms. Internal Revenue Service, Department of the Treasury, Publication 15-A.

323. At the time of writing, the common law rules were used by the IRS, the District of Columbia, and eighteen states. The ABC test (or some variation of it) was used by the Department of Labor and thirty-three states, with the state of California changing to the ABC Test following the state's Supreme Court decision in *Dynamex*, 4 Cal. 5th 903 (2018). Effective January 1, 2020, California Assembly Bill 5 codified the *Dynamex* ABC test and expanded the reach to all wage and hour Labor Code violations in the state. See note 4 for more information on AB-5 and its current status at the time of writing.

324. 17 U.S.C. § 501(a).

325. Ibid. § 501(b).

326. United States Copyright Office, "Circular 1: Copyright Basics" 2012, 3.

327. 17 U.S.C. § 411(a). See Chapter 5: "Copyright and the Fair Use Doctrine" for an in-depth discussion on when an infringement action may be brought.

328. *Wallace Computer Systems, Inc. v. Adams Business Forms, Inc.*, 837 F.Supp. 1413, 1416 (N.D. Ill. 1993).

329. 17 U.S.C. at § 502.

330. Ibid. §§ 503(a), (b).

331. Ibid. § 504.

332. Ibid. § 505.

333. Ibid. § 106A(a)(3)(A).

334. Ibid. § 106A(a)(3)(B).

335. *Carter v. Helmsley-Spear, Inc.*, 861 F. Supp 303, 325 (S.D.N.Y. 1994), *aff'd in part, vacated in part, rev'd in part*, 71 F.3d 77 (2nd Cir. 1995). The *Carter* approach was adopted in the so-called 5Pointz Case, in which it was used to determine the "recognized stature" of the forty-five graffiti works destroyed at that location to make way for a high-rise construction project. *Cohen v. G&M Realty L.P.*, Case No. 13-CV-05612(FB)(RLM) (E.D.N.Y. Jun. 13, 2018), at 20, *aff'd Castillo v. G&M Realty L.P.*, 18-498-cv (L) (2d Cir. 2020). The plaintiffs were awarded $6.75 million in damages, sending shockwaves through the art world and signifying a significant win under VARA. On July 20, 2020, the estate of the defendant filed a petition for a writ of certiorari with the Supreme Court of the United States. Among other arguments, they argue VARA's "recognized stature" provision is unconstitutionally vague. At the time of writing, the Supreme Court has not granted the cert.

336. 17 U.S.C. § 106A(a)(3)(B).

337. *Kelley v. Chicago Park Dist.*, 635 F.3d 290, 299 (7th Cir. 2011).

338. 17 U.S.C. § 113(d)(1).

339. Ibid. § 113(d)(2). The Act provides the specific procedural steps that must be followed by the building owner to effect a diligent and good faith attempt to notify the artist.

340. *Serra v. United States Gen. Servs. Admin.*, 847 F.2d 1045, 1047 (2d Cir. 1988), quoting sculptor Richard Serra.

341. *Phillips v. Pembroke Real Estate*, 459 F. 3d 128, 129 (1st Cir. 2006).

342. Ibid., 143, "VARA does not apply to site-specific art at all."

343. *Kelley*, 635 F.3d at 306-7.

344. 17 U.S.C. § 106A(c)(1).

345. Ibid. § 106A(c)(2).

346. Ibid.

347. Ibid. § 106A(c)(3).

348. Acronym is from the French, *Institut international pour l'unification du droit privé*.

349. International Institute for the Unification of Private Law (UNIDROIT), "History and Overview," http://www.unidroit.org/about-unidroit/overview.

350. Ibid.

351. The information provided here regarding the different IRS Form 990 versions is correct at the time of writing. Current IRS regulations or legal counsel should be consulted before determining the correct form for your organization.

352. IRS Pub. 557 at 11. For an organization whose accounting period coincides with the calendar year, this places the due date at May 15th.

353. For more information on extensions, see "Chapter 8: Nonprofit Corporations and Tax Exemption."

354. IRS Pub. 557 at 11.

355. The information provided here regarding the different IRS Form 990 versions is correct at the time of writing. Current IRS regulations or legal counsel should be consulted before determining the correct form for your organization. Organizations eligible to file to Form 990-EZ may choose to instead file the standard Form 990.

356. Revenue that needs to be itemized includes income from programs, membership dues, investment income, and fund-raising events.

357. Expenses that need to be itemized include salaries, member benefits, and facilities costs.

358. The information provided here regarding the different IRS Form 990 versions is correct at the time of writing. Current IRS regulations or legal counsel should be consulted before determining the correct form for your organization. Organizations eligible to file to Form 990-EZ may choose to instead file the Form 990.

359. IRC § 6104 requires organizations to make available their current year's Form 990 plus the two previous years. Additionally, the organization's exemption application and all associated documents must be available. These forms are to be available at the organization's principal office and any district office that has employees who work a minimum of 120 hours per week. Organizations must comply with requests for photocopies of these documents, though the organization may charge a reasonable photocopy fee plus the actual cost to mail the documents. On-site inspections of these documents may not be burdened with a fee.

360. Some organizations do not have to file IRS Form 1023. These include religious organizations (churches, mosques, synagogues, temples), some organizations officially affiliated with those religious organizations, and organizations who normally have gross receipts below $5,000.

361. Available within the Form 1023-EZ instructions. The most recent version (revised January 2018) is available at https://www.irs.gov/pub/irs-pdf/i1023ez.pdf.

362. IRS Pub. 557, 15.

363. Ibid.

364. Ibid.

365. Ibid.

366. Ibid.

367. Ibid.

368. The $500 threshold was accurate at the time of writing. Consult current law.

369. See Department of the Treasury, Internal Revenue Service, "Form 8283: Noncash Charitable Contributions" (rev'd Nov. 2019).

370. IRS Pub. 557, 16.

371. IRS Form 8283, sec. B, part IV.

372. IRS Pub. 557, 16.

373. "The signature [on Form 8283] doesn't represent concurrence in the appraisal value of the contributed property." IRS Form 8283, B part IV.

374. IRS Pub. 557, 16.

375. The specifics of how this tenancy works in your jurisdiction may vary from the general overview provided here. Be sure to check with local law or competent legal counsel prior to making any decisions. Joint tenancies are generally disfavored by the courts; they prefer that property be owned as a tenancy in common.

376. These are the "four unities," having to do with the joint tenants' rights regarding (1) time, (2) title, (3) interest, and (4) possession. Each joint tenant must (1) take their share at the exact same time, (2) acquire their ownership in the same instrument (deed, will, etc.), (3) have an exactly equal interest in the ownership (including a same proportional share), and (4) have a right to possess the entire property.

377. 17 U.S.C. § 101, "joint work."

378. Ibid., "collective work."

379. Ibid. § 302(b).

380. Ibid. § 302(a).

381. Ibid. § 202.

382. Trademark: 15 U.S.C. § 1060(a)(3). Copyright: 17 U.S.C. § 204(a). Slightly different rules apply to patents: 35 U.S.C. § 261.

383. Obviously, interpretation of testamentary documents can be quite complex, and local laws or precedent may impact the outcome in any particular situation. These examples are provided only to give insight, and the results in an actual-fact situation may differ from what is described here.

384. Other regulations apply for an LLC to receive tax-exempt recognition from the Internal Revenue Service. Consulting an attorney is recommended.

385. American Alliance of Museums, "Core Documents," http://www.aam-us.org/resources/assessment-programs/core-documents/documents. The other four core documents are: the institutional code of ethics, the strategic plan, the disaster preparedness and emergency response plan, and the collections management policy.

386. House of Representatives Report No. 101-514, at 15 (1990), cited in *Martin v. City of Indianapolis*, 192 F.3d 608, 611 (1999).

387. Cal. Civ. Code § 986.

388. See *Gilliam v. American Broadcasting Companies*, 538 F.2d 14 (2d Cir. 1976), in which the television network aired significantly edited episodes of Monty Python comedy shows. The court found that ABC had mutilated the works and misrepresented the plaintiffs as the creators of those mutilated works. *Gilliam*, 538 F.2d at 24-25. "[T]he edited version broadcast by ABC impaired the integrity of appellants' work and represented to the public as the product of appellants what was actually a mere caricature of their talents. We believe that a valid cause of action for such distortion exists. . . ." (Ibid. at 25.)

389. 861 F. Supp 303 (S.D.N.Y. 1994).

390. *Cohen v. G&M Realty L.P.*, Case No. 13-CV-05612(FB)(RLM) (E.D.N.Y. Jun. 13, 2018), at 20, *aff'd Castillo v. G&M Realty L.P.*, 18-498-cv (L) (2d Cir. 2020).

391. California Art Preservation Act, Cal. Civ. Code § 987.

392. 17 U.S.C. § 301(f)(2): "Nothing in paragraph (1) annuls or limits any rights or remedies under the common law or statutes of any State with respect to (B) activities violating legal or equitable rights that are not equivalent to any of the rights conferred by section 106A with respect to works of visual art; or (C) activities violating legal or equitable rights which extend beyond the life of the author."

393. A benefit of adopting a naming rights policy or an overall gift acceptance policy is that the organization can draft the policies to ensure they are in compliance with the Donor Bill of Rights, created by the Association of Fundraising Professionals along with the Association for Healthcare Philanthropy and the Giving Institute. The list of rights available to donors includes to "be assured their gifts will be used for the purposes for which they were given" (para.IV) and to "receive appropriate acknowledgement and recognition" (para.V). The entire document can be found online at https://afpglobal.org/donor-bill-rights.

394. 16 U.S.C. § 470(b)(4).

395. National Park Service, Archaeology Program, "National Historic Preservation Act (NHPA)," http://www.nps.gov/archeology/tools/Laws/NHPA.htm.

396. National Park Service, "National Register of Historic Places," http://www.nps.gov/nr/. More information on the NRHP may be found at 54 U.S.C. § 302101-108.

397. 54 U.S.C. § 302101.

398. Available at https://www.nps.gov/subjects/nationalregister/publications.htm.

399. A list of all State Historic Preservation Officers is available online through the National Park Service at https://www.nps.gov/subjects/nationalregister/state-historic-preservation-offices.htm. For more information on the State Historic Preservation Officers, see the following section.

400. National Park Service, National Register of Historic Places, "What Is the National Register of Historic Places?" https://www.nps.gov/subjects/nationalregister/what-is-the-national-register.htm.

401. 54 U.S.C. § 302303(a).

402. Ibid. § 302303(b)(1).

403. Ibid. § 302303(b)(2).

404. For the full list of SHPO duties, see ibid. § 302303.

405. Ibid. § 300318.

406. National Conference of State Historic Preservation Officers, "What Is a State Historic Preservation Officer (SHPO)?" http://www.ncshpo.org/whatisashpo.shtml.

407. National Park Service, "National Historic Landmarks Program," http://www.nps.gov/nhl/.

408. National Park Service, "National Register of Historic Places Program: Research," http://www.nps.gov/nr/research/index.htm.

409. NPS, "National Historic Landmarks Program."

410. National Park Service, National Historic Landmarks "Frequently Asked Questions: How Are National Historic Landmarks Different from Other Historic Properties in the National Register of Historic Places?" https://www.nps.gov/subjects/nationalhistoriclandmarks/faqs.htm.

411. The regional offices are listed, with contact information, on the National Park Service website at https://www.nps.gov/subjects/nationalhistoriclandmarks/contactus.htm.

412. National Park Service, "Determining the Eligibility of a Property for National Historic Landmark Designation," https://www.nps.gov/subjects/nationalhistoriclandmarks/eligibility.htm.

413. Advisory Council on Historic Preservation, "About the ACHP," https://www.achp.gov/about.

414. 54 U.S.C. § 304101(a). The current membership, including their qualifications and biographies, may be found at Advisory Council on Historic Preservation, "Council Members," https://www.achp.gov/about/council-members.

415. For a full list of ACHP duties, see 54 U.S.C. § 304102(a).

416. 36 C.F.R. Part 800.1(a).

417. Ibid.

418. "Section 106 review encourages, but does not mandate, preservation. Sometimes there is no way for a needed project to proceed without harming historic properties." Advisory Council on Historic Preservation, *Protecting Historic Properties: A Citizen's Guide to Section 106 Review* (Washington, D.C.: Advisory Council on Historic Preservation), 4.

419. 36 C.F.R. Part 800.

420. Available at Advisory Council on Historic Preservation, "Working with Section 106," https://www.achp.gov/protecting-historic-properties.

421. Federal Bureau of Investigation, "National Stolen Art File (NSAF)," https://www.fbi.gov/investigate/violent-crime/art-theft/national-stolen-art-file.

422. Federal Bureau of Investigations, "Protecting Your Treasures: Advice from Our Art Theft Expert," https://archives.fbi.gov/archives/news/stories/2006/july/protecting-your-treasures-advice-from-our-art-theft-expert.

423. The Smithsonian Institution is exempted from compliance with NAGPRA. Instead, the Smithsonian Institution's repatriation program is governed by the National Museum of the American Indian Act of 1989, 20 U.S.C. § 80q.

424. 25 U.S.C. § 3003(a).

425. Ibid. § 3003(d).

426. Ibid. § 3005(a).

427. Ibid. § 3007(a).

428. National NAGPRA Program, National Park Service, 1849 C Street NW, Mail Stop 7360, Washington, D.C. 20240. Phone: (202) 354-2201. E-mail form available at https://www.nps.gov/orgs/1335/contactus.htm.

429. 25 U.S.C. § 3002(a).

430. The National Conference of State Historic Preservation Officers is a valuable resource if a museum is not certain if any cultural preservation laws have been triggered by excavation activity, including unintentional discoveries. Their directory of State Historic Preservation Officers can be found at https://www.nps.gov/subjects/nationalregister/state-historic-preservation-offices.htm. For more information on State Historic Preservation Officers, see the "National Historic Preservation Act" dictionary entry.

431. See 25 U.S.C. § 3005.

NAGPRA Regulations are subdivided into two distinct subparts that separately address repatriation and ownership. Subpart B concerns the disposition of Native American items discovered or excavated, either inadvertently or intentionally, on federal lands after November 16, 1990. 43 C.F.R. §§ 10.3(a) & 10.4(a) (1995). Subpart C addresses repatriation of Native American objects in possession of federal agencies and museums. 43 C.F.R. §§ 10.8—10.10 (1995). Regulations concerning repatriation do not contain a limiting date . . .

Pueblo of San Ildefonso v. Ridlon, 103 F. 3d 936 (10th Cir. 1996).

432. For more information on these grants, visit National Park Service, "Grant Opportunities," https://www.nps.gov/subjects/nagpra/grant-opportunities.htm.

433. Nazi-Era Provenance Internet Portal, "The Nazi-Era Provenance Internet Portal Project," http://www.nepip.org/.

434. American Alliance of Museums, "Recommended Procedures for Providing Information to the Public about Objects Transferred in Europe during the Nazi Era" (Washington, D.C.: American Alliance of Museums, 2013) 1. https://www.aam-us.org/wp-content/uploads/2018/01/nepip-recommended-procedures.pdf.

435. NEPIP, http://www.nepip.org/.

436. Nazi-Era Provenance Internet Portal, "Museums Holding No Relevant Objects," http://www.nepip.org/public/info/nocov.cfm?menu_type=&menu_type=info.

437. Nazi-Era Provenance Internet Portal, "Who Should Participate?" http://www.nepip.org/public/museuminfo/participate.cfm?menu_type=museuminfo.

438. Addressing this ethical component, the American Alliance of Museums has stated:

> Researching the Nazi-era provenance of objects and providing provenance information to the public is [consistent] with the fundamental mission of museums to document and publish their collections. . . . By participating in the Portal, museums demonstrate that they are committed to the open and responsible stewardship of the objects under their care. In so doing, they show themselves to be worthy of the high public trust we as a community are privileged to enjoy.

Ibid.

439. "Nep-" comes from *nepote*, which is a seventeenth-century spelling of *nipote*, Italian for "nephew." The term originated in relation to Pope Sixtus IV (served 1471–1484), who granted many official favors to family members, most especially his nephews. "Nepotism," *Merriam-Webster Online*. https://www.merriam-webster.com/dictionary/nepotism.

440. There are some specific legal requirements in certain situations, such as in publicly held companies, which are designed to protect shareholders. That discussion is outside the scope or application of this discussion.

441. The National Conference of State Legislatures maintains a chart outlining the limitations on nepotism in state legislatures, some of which also apply to other types of government employees. Available at https://www.ncsl.org/research/ethics/50-state-table-nepotism-restrictions.aspx. Additionally, at the federal level, there are rules against nepotism in the federal civil service (5 U.S.C. § 2302(b)(7)) and regulations regarding the ethical conduct of federal employees (5 C.F.R. § 2635.502.).

442. https://icom.museum/en/resources/standards-guidelines/objectid/.

443. Ibid.

444. Ibid.

445. "Congress shall make no law . . . abridging the freedom of speech. . . ." U.S. Const. amend. 1. Note the First Amendment is in regard to federal government action regarding the abridgement of free speech. The Fourteenth Amendment extends this prohibition to the states.

446. *Miller v. California*, 413 U.S. 15, 20 (1973).

447. "[Adj.] 1. having, inclined to have, or characterized by lascivious or lustful thoughts, desires, etc. 2. Causing lasciviousness or lust. 3. Having a restless desire or longing." https://www.dictionary.com/browse/prurient?s=t.

448. *Miller*, 18 n.2, citing *Roth v. United States*, 354 U.S. 476, 487 (1957).

449. *Miller*, 413 U.S. at 18–19.

450. Ibid., 24, citations omitted. The requirement for "serious literary, artistic, political, or scientific value" requirement is also known as the LAPS test or the SLAPS test.

451. Ibid., 26.

452. Ibid.

453. Ibid., 30–34.

454. Ibid., 33.

455. Ildiko Pogány DeAngelis [updated and edited by John E. Simmons and Toni M. Kiser], "Old Loans and Museum Property Laws," in *Museum Registration Methods* [6th], 106.

456. Ibid. "[T]he passage of time will not alter this legal relationship."

457. The Association of Registrars and Collections Specialists maintains a living document that lists legislation relevant to old loans and found-in-collection objects. See "Museum Property Acts and Abandoned Loan Legislation" at http://www.arcsinfo.org/content/documents/arcsmuseumpropertyandoldloanlegislationjune2018

.pdf. At the time of writing, only the District of Columbia, Hawaii, Idaho, Maryland, and West Virginia had no relevant legislation.

458. Pogány DeAngelis, "Old Loans and Museum Property Laws," 109.

459. The common law approach for converting an old loan varies by jurisdiction. A detailed overview is provided in ibid., 106–9.

460. Ibid.

461. Ibid.

462. Ibid. The Association of Registrars and Collections Specialists held an informative session on old loans titled "Old Loans: Out of Sight, Out of Mind." It provided practical advice and guidance on how to deal with these objects. A written overview can be found at their website at http://www.arcsinfo.org/content/documents/old_loans__out_of_sight_out_of_mind__report.pdf.

463. *Spanish American Cultural Assoc. of Bergenfield v. Comm'r*, T.C. Memo 1994-510, *11 (1994), citations omitted.

464. 17 U.S.C. § 102(a).

465. United States Copyright Office, "Orphan Works and Mass Digitization: A Report of the Register of Copyrights," June 2015, 64–65.

466. This example is drawn from IRS Pub. 526, 9. The legal term is a fractional gift in tangible property, but in the museum field the more commonly used term is *partial gift*.

467. Malaro and Pogány DeAngelis, *A Legal Primer* [3rd], 410–11.

468. Only general partnerships are discussed in full in this text. For a more in-depth discussion, see "Chapter 11: Understanding the Various Forms of Business Structures," specifically note 10.

469. U.S. Const. art. I, § 8, cl. 8.

470. 35 U.S.C. § 101.

471. Ibid. § 102.

472. Ibid. § 103.

473. Ibid. § 111 *et. seq.*

474. 26 U.S.C. § 509(a)(1).

475. 26 U.S.C. § 509(a)(2): The organization must receive more than one-third of its financial support from "gifts, grants, contributions, or membership fees" or the gross receipts from activities such as admission fees or the sale of goods or services, provided these activities do not qualify as unrelated business income but rather is related to the organization's exempt purpose. Additionally, there is a limit regarding their organization's support from gross investment income and net unrelated business income: These sources cannot be more than one-third of their overall support.

476. 26 U.S.C. § 509(a)(3). These are organized and operated "exclusively for the benefit of, to perform the functions of, or to carry out the purposes of one or more specified organizations" that themselves qualify as a traditional public charity or gross receipts organization. The relationship between the supporting organization and the supported organization must be formalized in some manner so that the supported organization is supervising the supporting organization. The supporting organization can be understood as subservient to the supported organization. The type of relationship between the supported and supporting organization will determine the supporting organization's type. This analysis is fact specific—speak with a knowledgeable professional for assistance. Generally, the supporting organization runs programs that benefit the supported organization, or it turns over its income to the supported organization.

477. 26 U.S.C. § 509(a)(4).

478. Treas. Reg. § 1.170A-9(f)(1): "An organization is [publicly supported] if it . . . normally receives a substantial part of its support from a government unit . . . or from direct or indirect contributions from the general public. . . ." This is determined by either the "thirty-three and ⅓ percent support test" or the "facts and circumstances" test. See those dictionary entries for more information.

479. Treas. Reg. § 1.501(c)(3)-1(d)(1)(ii).

480. "[D]isposal of collections through sale, trade or research activities is solely for the advancement of the museum's mission. Proceeds from the sale of nonliving collections are to be used consistent with the established standards of the museum's discipline, but in no event shall they be used for anything other than acquisition or direct care of collections." American Alliance of Museums, "Code of Ethics for Museums," adopted 1991, amended 2000. https://www.aam-us.org/programs/ethics-standards-and-professional-practices/code-of-ethics-for-museums/.

481. "Funds received from the disposal of a deaccessioned work shall not be used for operations or capital expenses. Such funds, including any earnings and appreciation thereon, may be used only for the acquisition of works in a manner consistent with the museum's policy on the use of restricted acquisition funds." "AAMD Policy on Deaccessioning," 4, adopted June 9, 2010, amended October 2015. https://aamd.org/sites/default/files/document/AAMD%20Policy%20on%20Deaccessioning%20website_0.pdf.

482. See, for example, American Association for State and Local History, *Statement of Standards and Ethics*; and College Art Association, "Statement Concerning the Deaccession of Works of Art," https://www.college-art.org/standards-and-guidelines/guidelines/sales.

483. Malaro and Pogány DeAngelis, *A Legal Primer* [3rd], 265–66.

484. Consideration is the performance or return promise of the person accepting the contract. Rstmt. 2nd Contracts § 71. For instance, consideration is the promise to pay for an item that is offered for sale.

485. This example is drawn from Restatement (2nd) Contracts § 71, comment b, illustrations 1 and 2.

486. The Restatement (2nd) of Contracts defines promissory estoppel as "A promise which the promisor should reasonably expect to induce action . . . on the part of the promisee . . . and which does induce such action . . . is binding if injustice can be avoided only by enforcement of the promise. The remedy granted for breach may be limited as justice requires." Ibid. § 90. For more examples, see the illustrations provided in ibid. § 90, comment a, b, and f.

487. This example is given for illustrative purposes only. Promissory estoppel is a highly fact-specific legal doctrine, and it should not be assumed that any certain circumstance will give rise to an enforceable gift. Consult legal counsel. Additionally, it must be noted that while a museum may find itself in a position where it would likely prevail in litigation against a donor who failed to make a promised donation, such litigation would surely have a negative impact on the donor-donee relationship the museum enjoys with that potential donor and could possibly have a chilling effect on the willingness of others to donate to the museum. The museum must weigh all possible consequences, including consequences that would occur outside the sphere of litigation, in deciding what to do when a donor fails to deliver a promised gift.

488. Karen Daly, "Provenance Research in Museum Collections: An Overview," in *Museum Registration Methods* [6th], 68.

489. For example, provenance research can indicate a work was potentially looted by the Nazis or was illegally excavated.

490. Daly, 62.

491. 17 U.S.C. § 101, "pseudonymous work."

492. Ibid. § 302(c).

493. Ibid.

494. Ibid. § 302(a).

495. Treas. Reg. § 1.170A-9(f)(1): "An organization is [publicly supported] if it . . . normally receives a substantial part of its support from a government unit . . . or from direct or indirect contributions from the general public. . . ." This is determined by either the "thirty-three and ⅓ percent support test" or the "facts and circumstances" test. See those dictionary entries for more information.

496. 17 U.S.C. § 106(5).

497. Ibid.

498. Ibid. § 101, "publicly."

499. Ibid.

500. Ibid. § 101, "display."

501. Ibid. § 109(c).

502. Ibid.

503. Creative Commons, "CC0: 'No Rights Reserved,'" https://creativecommons.org/share-your-work/public-domain/cc0.

CC0 enables scientists, educators, artists and other creators and owners of copyright or database-protected content to waive those interests in their works and thereby place them as completely as possible in the public domain, so that others may freely build upon, enhance and reuse the works for any purposes without restriction under copyright or database law.

Ibid.

504. 17 U.S.C. § 105.

505. The protections afforded through the First Amendment are extended to the States by the Fourteenth Amendment.

506. "In order to secure the First Amendment's guarantee of freedom of speech and to prevent distortions of 'the market-place of ideas,' . . . governments generally are prohibited from discriminating among viewpoints on issues within the realm of protected speech." *Perry Education Assocn. v. Perry Local Educators' Assocn.*, 460 U.S. 37, 70–71 (1983), citation removed.

507. *Ward v. Rock Against Racism*, 491 U.S. 781, 798–99 (1989). For example, in a case in which an administrator and faculty member at a public college displayed in the main gathering space for the school a number of works depicting nude female forms that were considered misogynistic and racist to some viewers, and the school ordered the works removed but offered alternative locations in the building for their display, no First Amendment violation was found.

> When we consider that the expression in this case was not political, that it was regulated rather than suppressed, that the plaintiff is not only a faculty member but an administrator, that good alternative sites may have been available to him, and that in short he is claiming a First Amendment right to exhibit sexually explicit and racially offensive art work in what amounts to the busiest corridor in a college that employs him in a responsible administrative as well as academic position, we are driven to conclude that the defendants did not infringe the plaintiff's First Amendment rights merely by ordering him to move the art to another room in the same building.

Piarowski v. Illinois Community College, 759 F.2d 625, 632 (7th Cir. 1985).

508. 17 U.S.C. § 106(4).

509. Ibid. § 106(6).

510. Ibid. § 101, "publicly."

511. Ibid.

512. Ibid. § 101, "perform."

513. Ibid. § 110(a).

514. The following bullets are from IRS Pub. 561, 9.

515. IRS Regs. § 1.170A-13(c)(3)(i)(B).

516. Ibid. § 1.170A-13(c)(3)(i)(A).

517. In general, the fee may not be set at a percentage of the appraised value, either in part or in whole. Ibid. § 1.170A-13(c)(6)(i).

518. In general, see ibid 1.170A-13, "Recordkeeping and return requirements for deduction for charitable contributions."

519. IRS Pub. 561, 10.

520. IRS Regs. § 1.170A-13(c)(5)(i)(A).

521. Ibid. § 1.170A-13(c)(5)(i)(B).

522. Ibid. § 1.170A-13(c)(5)(iv). If the donor is not taking the deduction, the excluded person is the taxpayer who will claim the deduction. IRS Pub. 561, 10.

523. Ibid., 11

524. IRS Regs. § 1.170A-13(c)(5)(i)(D).

525. IRS Pub. 561, 11.

526. Ibid.

527. Ibid.

528. Ibid., 8.

529. IRS Pub. 526, 9.

530. Ibid.

531. A qualified organization, for this type of donation, is defined as:
   1. "A government unit,"
   2. "A publicly supported charity, or"
   3. "An organization controlled by, and operated for the exclusive benefit of, a governmental unit or a publicly supported charity."

Ibid.

532. IRC § 170(h)(1).

533. IRS Pub. 526, 22.

534. Ibid.

535. 26 U.S.C. § 170(h)(4)(A).

536. Rev. Proc. 90-12, 1990-1 C.B. 471, § 3.02.

537. Ibid.

538. Ibid.

539. Ibid.

540. Ibid.

541. IRS Pub. 526, 2.

542. Ibid.

543. IRS Pub. 557, 16.

544. IRS Pub. 526, 3.

545. These examples suggest that there is a donative intent, which is required for a *quid pro quo* contribution. Otherwise, there was no donation, just a regular transaction. To illustrate the distinction, consider the example of a donation for which the donor receives a tote bag with the museum's logo. Assuming the donor made the donation in connection with a qualified fund-raising campaign, and the donor made the donation in order to support the museum, then a disclosure statement may be required, considering all factors involved. However, if the same individual were to walk into the museum's gift shop and purchase a tote bag featuring the museum's logo, there would be no donative intent. While the price paid by that individual for the tote bag would exceed the amount paid by the museum to stock its inventory, that difference constitutes profit to the museum and not a donation by the individual. The donor had no donative intent to make a donation, and no disclosure statement would be necessary. Department of the Treasury, Internal Revenue Service, "Publication 1771: Charitable Contributions: Substantiation and Disclosure Requirements," (Rev'd March 2016), 6. "For the excess amount to qualify, you must pay it with the intent to make a charitable contribution." IRS Pub. 526, 3.

546. Rev. Proc. 90-12, § 2.01.

547. IRS Pub. 557, 16. The monetary threshold refers to the actual donation amount, not the amount entitled to a deduction. Therefore, if a donor makes a donation of $100, and $30 represents the fair market value of the benefit received, the donor is entitled to a deduction of $70. A disclosure statement is required from the organization because the donation is in excess of $75, even though the deductible amount is only $70.

548. IRS Pub. 1771, 11.

549. Ibid., 4 and 11. Regarding the manner of presentation, the Service provides that "a disclosure in small print within a larger document might not meet this requirement." Ibid., 11.

550. IRS Pub. 557, 16.

551. Rev. Proc. 90-12, § 2.05.

552. The legal term is a fractional gift in tangible property, but in the museum field the more commonly used term is *partial gift*.

553. IRS Pub. 526, 9.

554. Ibid.

555. 17 U.S.C. § 106(1).

556. For example, the Supreme Court held that the copying and publishing of just a few sentences from a memoir was a substantial infringement, because the copied passages went to "the heart of the book." *Harper & Row v. Nation Enterprises*, 471 U.S. 539, 565 (1985).

557. Precatory language is that which expresses a wish or suggestion but does not have the legal force of a restriction. For instance, compare a donor's desire that a museum display two statuettes together with a donor's mandated restriction that they must be displayed together at all times.

558. 17 U.S.C. § 202.

559. Ibid. § 106(1).

560. 15 U.S.C. § 1052(e)(1).

561. Ibid. § 1052(f).

562. *Carter-Wallace*, 434 F.2d at, 800.

563. 15 U.S.C. § 1052(e)(4).

564. Ibid. § 1052(f).

565. Internal Revenue Code § 501(a).

566. Ibid. § 501(c).

567. Treas. Reg. § 1.501(c)(3)-1(d)(3)(ii) Example 4.

568. "It has long been the position of the Internal Revenue Service that so-called 'cultural' type organizations may be exempt from Federal income tax as educational or charitable." *Rev. Rul. 64-175*, 1964-1 C.B. 185, *3 (1964).

569. *Abercrombie*, 537 F.2d at 9.

570. Ibid.

571. Restatement (2d) of Contracts § 110(1).

572. Ibid. § 110(1)(a).

573. Ibid. § 110(1)(d).

574. Ibid. § 110(1)(e).

575. Uniform Commercial Code § 2-201(1).

576. This is a very simplified explanation. In practice, bills at both the state and federal level go through a committee vetting process, are debated at various stages, and often must go through a conference committee if the bills passed in the two legislative chambers have any differences. Additionally, the specifics can differ in the various state legislatures.

577. *Abercrombie*, 537 F.2d at 9.

578. Ibid.

579. Ibid., 11.

580. Ibid.

581. The specifics of how this tenancy works in a jurisdiction may vary from the general overview provided here. Be sure to check with local law or competent legal counsel prior to making any decisions. At the time of writing, tenancy by the entirety exists in about half the states and the District of Columbia. The type of property that may be subject to tenancy by the entirety (only real property or all forms of property) varies from state to state.

582. The specifics of how this tenancy works in a jurisdiction may vary from the general overview provided here. Be sure to check with local law or competent legal counsel prior to making any decisions.

583. Location of the Theresienstadt concentration camp during World War II.

584. The conference took place June 26–30, 2009.

585. "We encourage states to consider these and other alternative national actions, and we further encourage them to find ways to address survivors' needs." Terezín Declaration (2009, June 30), at 3. https://wjro.org .il/cms/assets/uploads/2019/06/terezin_declaration.pdf.

586. World Jewish Restitution Organization (WJRO). (n.d.). "Guidelines and Best Practices for Restitution." https://wjro.org.il/our-work/international-declarations-resolutions/guidelines-and-best-practices/.

587. Terezín Declaration (2009, June 30), at 3.

588. Publ. L. 115-171, signed by President Donald Trump on May 9, 2018. Pub.L. 115-171.

589. Ibid. at § 2(b). "Not later than 18 months after the date of the enactment of this Act, the Secretary of State shall submit a report to the appropriate congressional committees that assesses and describes the nature and extent of national laws and enforceable policies of covered countries regarding the identification and the return of or restitution for wrongfully seized or transferred Holocaust era assets consistent with, and evaluated with respect to, the goals and objectives of the 2009 Holocaust Era Assets Conference. . . ."

590. Released July 29, 2020. Available on the U.S. Department of State website at https://www.state.gov/ release-of-the-just-act-report/.

591. The JUST Act did not mandate a review of American laws and policies.

592. The JUST Act Report at 4.

593. The Report is not favorable toward U.S. museums:

> After a promising start on provenance research, art restitution, and the creation of a portal to facilitate claims, American museums later began asserting affirmative defenses to block restitution of looted artwork, in contravention of the Washington Principles on Nazi-Confiscated Art and the Terezin principles. This led Congress in 2016 to enact the HEAR Act (Holocaust Expropriated Art Recovery Act). American museums also trail behind some of their European counterparts, such as Germany, Austria, and the Netherlands, in conducting art provenance research. One factor

contributing to this difference is that most U.S. museums are not government-run (in contrast to most museums in Europe), and many of their directors have not made provenance research a priority. The use of antiquated software in some cases also complicates the identification of potential Nazi-looted art by claimants.

The JUST Act Report at 5.

594. For example, in 1997 Seton Hall University (South Orange, New Jersey) named a new academic building and the rotunda of the university library after alumnus Dennis Kozlowski in recognition of his long-time financial support of the university. Kozlowski was later accused of stealing hundreds of millions of dollars from the manufacturing company Tyco, where he had served as CEO. After being found guilty in June 2005, Kozlowski requested his name be removed from the university buildings in order to protect the school's reputation (2005, August 18). "College Strips of Kozlowski Name: Seton Hall University Says the Former Tyco Chief Asked to Have His Name Removed." *CNN Money*. Retrieved from https://money.cnn.com/2005/08/18/news/newsmakers/kozlowski_seton/. While Kozlowski voluntarily had his name removed, depending on the original donation agreement, he might have been able to retain the naming rights, leaving the university with the option to be publicly associated with an alumnus convicted of criminal behavior or enter legal proceedings to force a name change.

595. 26 U.S.C. § 509(a)(1).

596. 26 U.S.C. § 509(a)(2).

597. 26 U.S.C. § 509(a)(3).

598. 26 U.S.C. § 509(a)(4).

599. Instructions for Schedule A of the Form 990 or Form 990-EZ can be found at https://www.irs.gov/pub/irs-pdf/i990sa.pdf.

600. *Kelly v. Arriba Soft Corp.*, 280 F.3d 934 (9th Cir. 2002) withdrawn and refiled at 336 F.3d 811 (9th Cir. 2003).

601. This is a fairly large assumption, as many factors outside the scope of this discussion could impact the legality of a will and any provisions therein.

602. See Malaro and Pogány DeAngelis, *A Legal Primer on Managing Museum Collections* [3rd], especially their discussion of title and acquisition of objects in chapter 4.

603. IRS Pub. 557, 16.

604. Ibid.

605. Rev. Proc. 90-12, § 3.08. "[D]epending on the facts of each case, benefits received in connection with contributions may be 'insubstantial' even if they do not meet these guidelines." Ibid.

606. IRS Pub. 526, 4. The $75 amount and other information is accurate at the time of writing and may be adjusted by the IRS for future tax years.

607. Rev. Proc. 90-12, § 3.04.

608. Ibid.

609. IRS Pub. 526, 20.

610. Where the donor expends $250 or more out of pocket in a single donation, the organization must provide a written acknowledgment of the donation. The acknowledgment must include a description of the donor's services to the organization, a statement as to if goods or services were provided in exchange for the donation, a description and good faith estimate of those goods or services, and, if applicable, a statement that the goods or services were intangible religious benefits. Ibid., 14.

611. Trademark Manual of Examining Protocol § 1202.02, "Registration of Trade Dress."

612. Ibid. § 1202.02(a)(iii)(A).

613. *In re Celia Clarke*, Trademark Trial and Appeal Board, 17 U.S.P.Q.2D (BNA) 1238 (1990).

614. *Qualitex*, 514 U.S. 159.

615. U.S. Trademark Reg. No. 11210, filed Apr. 7, 1884, reg. issued May 24, 1884, Samson Rope Technologies, Inc., Ferndale, WA.

616. Some trusts also allow a portion of the principal (or corpus) to also be distributed.

617. Buck, "Found-in-Collection," in *Museum Registration Methods* [6th], 126.

618. Ibid.

619. The American Law Institute, "Uniform Commercial Code," https://www.ali.org/publications/show/uniform-commercial-code/.

620. The Legal Information Institute provides an online locator that provides links to state statutes that correspond to the Uniform Commercial Code. It is available at the Legal Information Institute, Cornell University College of Law, "Uniform Commercial Code Locator," https://www.law.cornell.edu/uniform/ucc#a2.

621. Unincorporated associations who wish to apply for 501(c)(3) tax-exempt status will most likely have to generate documents they would not already have, for instance articles of association. Any documents created in contemplation of tax-exempt recognition should be drafted to comply with Internal Revenue Service requirements.

622. United Nations Educational, Scientific and Cultural Organization, "Introducing UNESCO," http://en.unesco.org/about-us/introducing-unesco.

623. Ibid.

624. United Nations Educational, Scientific and Cultural Organization, "Member States," http://en.unesco.org/countries/member-states.

625. Visit http://portal.unesco.org/en/ev.php-URL_ID=13649&URL_DO=DO_TOPIC&URL_SECTION=-471.html.

626. IRS Pub. 557, 12.

627. IRC § 513(c).

628. Ibid.

629. There are certain exemptions, such as when the trade or business is conducted by volunteers or if the trade or business is conducted primarily for the convenience of the organization's members or employees. See ibid. § 513(a). Consult legal counsel or a trained financial advisor to ascertain if a trade or business will be subject to the unrelated business income tax. As with other trades or businesses, the IRC permits the deduction of expenses in generating those profits. Ibid. § 162.

630. Ibid. § 513(c).

631. IRS Regs. § 1.170-A-4(b)(3)(i).

632. This example is based on the example found in ibid. § 1.170-A-4(b)(3)(i).

633. Malaro and Pogány DeAngelis, *A Legal Primer* [3rd], 408.

634. American Alliance of Museums, "Core Documents," https://www.aam-us.org/programs/ethics-standards-and-professional-practices/core-documents/. Per the AAM, the five core documents are the mission statement, institutional code of ethics, strategic institutional plan, disaster preparedness and emergency response plan, and the collections management policy.

635. 17 U.S.C. § 101, "visual art."

636. Ibid.

637. Ibid.

638. Ibid.

639. Ibid.

640. Ibid. § 106A.

641. Ibid. § 106A(e)(1).

642. Ibid. § 106A(b). If the work is a joint work, then the artists collectively are co-owners of the moral rights.

643. Ibid. § 106A(d)(1). As with copyright, VARA rights expire on December 31 of the calendar year they are set to terminate. Ibid. § 106A(d)(4).

644. Ibid. § 106A(d)(3).

645. Ibid. § 106A(d)(2).

646. Ibid. § 106A(e)(1). In the case of joint works, waiver by one creator also waives the rights of the other creators. Ibid. The other creators do not have to give their consent for this waiver to take effect.

647. Ibid.

648. Ibid. § 106A(e)(2).

649. Ibid.

650. The conference was co-hosted by the United States Department of State and the United States Holocaust Memorial Museum. It took place November 30–December 3, 1998. Proceedings from the conference are available from the Central Registry of Information on Looted Cultural Property 1933–1945, which itself was established to satisfy Principle VI: "Efforts should be made to establish a central registry of [information regarding art that is found to have been confiscated by the Nazis and not subsequently restituted]." Access conference proceedings at https://www.lootedart.com/MG8D5622483.

651. The principles in their entirety are hosted online by the U.S. Department of State at https://www.state.gov/washington-conference-principles-on-nazi-confiscated-art/.

652. Washington Conference Principles on Nazi-Confiscated Art, No. 11.

653. Eizenstat, Stuart E. (1998, December 3). Concluding statement, Washington Conference on Holocaust-Era Assets, Washington, D.C. https://www.lootedart.com/web_images/pdf2014/12-3-98-%20Eizenstat%20--%20Concluding%20statement,%20Washington%20Conference%20on%20Holocaust-Era%20Assets.pdf.

654. In 1939, Lilly Cassirer sold Camille Pissarro's 1892 painting *Rue St. Honoré, Afternoon, Rain Effect* to a Nazi under duress. The heirs to Cassirer have long sought the return of the painting from the Thyssen-Bornemisza Collection (TBC) Museum in Madrid, Spain. On August 17, 2020, the Ninth Circuit Court of Appeals affirmed a lower court's judgment to allow the museum to keep the painting. *Cassirer v. Thyssen-Bornemisza Collection Found.* No. 19-55616 (9th Cir. Aug. 17, 2020). In an extensive footnote, the court stated:

> In 1998, forty-four countries, including the Kingdom of Spain, agreed to several non-binding principles set forth in the Washington Principles on Nazi-Confiscated Art. . . . The district court noted that Spain and TBC's refusal to return the Painting to the Cassirers is inconsistent with Spain's moral commitments under the Washington Principles. . . . It is perhaps unfortunate that a country and a government can preen as moralistic in its declarations, yet not be bound by those declarations. But that is the state of the law. . . . We agree with the district court that we cannot order compliance with the Washington Principles. . . .

Cassirer, No. 19-55616 at fn. 3. At the time of writing, no further action has been taken in the case, though it is possible the Cassirers may seek an appeal. For an in-depth explanation of the case and history of the painting, see O'Donnell, Nicholas. (2020, August 18). "Moralistic Preening and Broken Commitments under the Washington Principles: Ninth Circuit Chastises Spain for Keeping Nazi-looted Pissarro but Rules Painting Will Not Return to Cassirer Family." Art Law Report. https://blog.sullivanlaw.com/artlawreport/moralistic-preening-and-broken-commitments-under-the-washington-principles-ninth-circuit-chastises-spain-for-keeping-nazi-looted-pissarro-but-rules-1597770460850?utm_campaign=Art&utm_medium=email&_hsmi=93457992&_hsenc=p2ANqtz-86-Vd8HJs7f5JUpS6Fu0O6go-EFBbALSdcqFW73RjHmjeKaGCMZ398MtFqy3W20f0NCX4y530Z93dw6-1LpTtS0HVXzQ&utm_content=93457992&utm_source=hs_email.

655. Specialist Conference: 20 Years Washington Principles: Roadmap for the Future, held by the German Lost Art Foundation in cooperation with the the Kulturstiftung der Länder and the Stiftung Preußischer Kulturbesitz and sponsored by the Federal Commissioner for Culture and Media, November 26–29, 2018, Berlin, Germany. Conference presentations, documentation, and program can be accessed from the German Lost Art Foundation Conference at https://www.kulturgutverluste.de/Content/01_Stiftung/EN/Event-review/2018/2018-11-26_Specialist-Conference-20-Years-Washington-Principles-Roadmap-for-the-Future.html.

656. German Lost Art Foundation, Results of the Specialist Conference, https://www.kulturgutverluste.de/Content/02_Aktuelles/EN/Press-releases/2018/2018-11-29_PressRelease_Results20YearsWP.pdf;jsessionid=8DE06095564C9F3B6260CA3448EF22E8.m7?__blob=publicationFile&v=4.

657. Ibid.

658. These are Austria, France, Germany, the Netherlands, and the United Kingdom. Hickley, Catherine (2018, November 26). "Washington Principles: The Restitution of Nazi-Looted Art Is Still a Work in Progress, 20 Years On." *The Art Newspaper.* https://www.theartnewspaper.com/news/restitution-of-nazi-looted-art-a-work-in-progress.

659. 17 U.S.C. § 101, "work made for hire."

660. Ibid. § 201(b).

661. Ibid. § 201(a).

662. Ibid. § 201(b).

663. *Community for Creative Non-Violence v. Reid*, 490 U.S. 730, 740 (1989), citation omitted.

664. Ibid.

665. This is a nonexhaustive list of factors the court will consider when applying the *Reid* test.

666. United States Copyright Office, "Circular 30: Works Made for Hire" (rev'd Sept. 2017), 2.

667. Ibid., 2.

668. 17 U.S.C. § 302(c).
669. Ibid. § 203(a).
670. Ibid. § 102(a).
671. Ibid.
672. Ibid. § 102(b).

CHAPTER 2

ETHICS AND THE LAW

At times it can be easy to confuse or conflate ethics and the law, as they often overlap both in topics addressed and in application. However, they are not the same, and the distinction should be remembered whenever a discussion involving either ethics or the law is undertaken.

The legal system sets a different standard for conduct than it does for ethics. In general, the law is intended "to require conduct that allows us to live in society without undue harassment."[1] It permits us to live our lives and interact with others in a manner that leaves us mostly unmolested and unharmed. Seen in this light, the law sets a fairly low bar for conduct. In comparison, ethics "sets forth conduct that a profession considers essential in order to uphold the integrity of the profession."[2] This is a higher hurdle, demanding behavior that is above and beyond what is required by the law. The law sets the base requirements for behavior, while ethics describes an aspirational ideal.

In the museum setting, ethics and the law interact in a variety of areas. For example, consider museum deaccessioning and disposal. So long as there is nothing to prevent deaccessioning from a legal standpoint, such as a donor restriction or a statute that impacts the museum's ability to deaccession an object, the process of deaccessioning is legal, as is disposal through a variety of mechanisms, including sale. Once an item is sold, again barring any specific legal limitation, the museum is largely free to do what it wishes with the earnings.[3] However, museum professional organizations have ethics codes that limit otherwise-legal deaccessioning, disposal, and use of disposal proceeds. The ethics codes impose additional requirements and restrictions that are lacking from the legal arena.[4]

As an illustration, imagine Midwest Museum owns a 1920s cityscape painting by a well-known artist from upstate New York. The painting has been in the museum collection since it was purchased from a dealer thirty years ago using unrestricted acquisition funds, and it has been prominently displayed in the galleries, as well as included in numerous exhibitions, both at the museum and on loan to other institutions. However, the museum has recently revisited its mission, and the museum is being refocused on contemporary and modern art from the local metropolitan region. As the work of a New York artist who never lived or worked in the museum's midwestern region, the painting does not fit into this new mission. The museum's trustees, with input from the curator and registrar, decide to deaccession the painting. They sell it at public auction, receiving negative commentary in the press and from the local community, who protest the sale of a beloved artwork. The trustees use the proceeds from the auction to conduct some much-needed and overdue building projects in the museum's out-of-date storage areas, updating the HVAC systems and addressing some pest management concerns.

From a legal standpoint, the museum and its trustees *may* have met their legal requirements regarding the deaccession. The museum's mission had evolved to a point where the painting no longer fits in the museum's collection. Based on the evolved mission, retention of the painting in the collection does not appear to be in furtherance of the museum's educational purpose. The painting was purchased using unrestricted funds, so there were no donor restrictions to prevent the deaccession. The use of the sale proceeds may also be fine from a legal standpoint, as the proceeds belong to the museum and can be utilized as they see fit.

However, from an ethical standpoint, problems may arise. Most museum professional organizations promulgate ethical codes that require that proceeds from deaccessioning be used solely for the acquisition of new collection objects or direct care of the collection.[5] Therefore, the use of the proceeds in this illustration for collections care and building maintenance and not for the acquisition of new collection objects *may* give rise to ethical repercussions for the museum, despite its sound legal footing.

The interplay of legal and ethical responsibilities exists throughout the museum setting, not just in object deaccessioning and disposal. What audiences the museum caters to and issues are related to community engagement, the museum's physical accessibility, whether to accept corporate sponsorship or accept a donation from a specific category of donors, collecting goals, object interpretation, exhibit signage and languages utilized, and diversity in staffing and governance are just a sampling of areas where application of the law and professional ethics may result in a different standard of practice. For some of these, such as physical access, it could almost be argued that the legal requirements are in line with the ethical standards. But this is not the norm, and generally the law sets a relatively low bar while the profession's ethical codes may set higher expectations.

Besides the different standards, another contrast between legal and ethical obligations is the repercussions for failure to comply. When a law is broken, there can be a variety of repercussions depending on the law. If a museum attempts to deaccession an object, the attorney general may step in to prevent the deaccession, especially (but by no means limited to) if the deaccession is in violation of a donor restriction, if it represents a breach of fiduciary duty, or if there is some other limitation on the museum's abilities to act. If a copyright is infringed, there can be civil liabilities, including statutory fines or even criminal liabilities, depending on the extent of the infringement. If a museum attempts to import an object in violation of customs regulations, the object may be seized or destroyed.

When an ethical standard is breached, there is no legal repercussion. Instead, the museum may be subject to sanctions from the museum profession. The American Alliance of Museums ("AAM") and the Association of Art Museum Directors ("AAMD") have in the past taken actions against member-museums that have failed to meet the ethical standards promulgated by these groups. For example, in 2014 the AAM revoked the Delaware Art Museum's accredited status when that museum deaccessioned works and used the proceeds from disposal for purposes other than acquisition or direct care of collections.[6]

However, while everyone is subject to the law, ethical obligations only apply to those who adopt them. If a museum is not a member of AAM, than AAM has little influence over that museum. While a professional organization can ask its members to suspend loans to or collaborations with a museum that is not upholding the organization's ethical standards, as AAMD did to the Delaware Art Museum in the wake of the deaccession discussed above,[7] there is little else a professional organization can do.[8] While the legal standard is lower, the ability to enforce the legal standard through civil and criminal liability provides that lower standard with a degree of clout unattainable by ethical codes.[9] When reviewing codes of ethics, this lack of enforcement must be borne in mind.[10]

As demonstrated in these examples, when museums voluntarily adopt and adhere to ethical codes, they are agreeing to abide by a higher standard than the law. This self-regulation is a hallmark of the profession and a reason museums enjoy such a high level of trust within their served communities.[11] Due to the lower legal standard it is possible to engage in actions that are perfectly legal but ethically questionable.[12] However, few laws directly address the day-to-day issues faced in museums. It is unlikely a museum will have an applicable statute it can look to if it is faced with a question regarding collections care or donor relations. In these situations, the ethical codes provide more definitive guidance for the real-world issues that typically arise within the profession.[13] Breaching legal requirements may result in civil or criminal liability. Enforcement of ethical codes is more nuanced and requires "a consistent and voluntary commitment from a sizeable portion of the profession" if it is to happen at all.[14]

A final consideration regarding ethics is the so-called *New York Times* rule. While this rule has numerous variations, the simplest way it is expressed is this: One should only undertake behavior one would feel comfortable seeing reported on the front page of the *New York Times* (or your local newspaper). If a museum is considering a course of action that is legal, but the museum would not feel comfortable having the action reported on the cover of the local newspaper, then that is a "red flag" the action may be in some manner ethically inappropriate. This is ethics "from the gut," but that gut reaction may act as an early warning system before institutional or professional codes of ethics are even consulted.

Museums are public trusts and their collections are held, preserved, interpreted, researched, and exhibited for the public good. If the museum is to retain its position of authority and respect within the community, it must conduct itself in a manner that is above reproach. If an action would likely be attacked or ridiculed by the local community and the public served, and the museum cannot justify the action through reference to internal or external established guidelines or professional best practices, then the museum should take the time to carefully examine that action, the motivation behind adopting it, and whether an alternate course would serve the institution's needs while meeting its ethical obligations.[15]

NOTES

1. Marie C. Malaro, *Museum Governance: Mission, Ethics, Policy* (Washington, D.C.: Smithsonian Institution Press, 1994), 17.

2. Ibid.

3. This assumes the proposed use is in alignment with the jurisdiction's nonprofit laws and applicable tax-exempt laws and regulations.

4. These examples are crafted to draw a distinction between ethics and morals. While those terms are used interchangeably in some circles—and were conflated in the first edition of this book—for clarity, it seems best to distinguish the two for this conversation. What is being discussed here is professional ethics, not the personal guiding principles that can be better understood as morals and can derive from a person's upbringing, community membership, religious or spiritual belief system, or other set of highly personal guiding principles.

5. For an overview of this, see Malaro and Pogány DeAngelis, *A Legal Primer*, 263–64. For an in-depth discussion, see "Chapter 3: Museum Deaccessioning and the Proceeds from Disposal."

6. American Alliance of Museums, "Statement on the Deaccessioning by the Delaware Art Museum and the Action Taken by the AAM Accreditation Commission."

7. Association of Art Museum Directors, "Association of Art Museum Directors Sanctions Delaware Art Museum," in its *Professional Practices in Art Museums*, the AAMD states that:

> In the event an AAMD member or museum violates one or more of the provisions of this policy, the member may be subject to censure, suspension, and /or expulsion; and the museum may be subject to censure and /or sanctions . . . includ[ing], without limitation, suspension of loans and shared exhibitions between the sanctioned museum and museums of which the AAMD members are directors.

The Association of Art Museum Directors, *Professional Practices in Art Museums*, June 2009, 25.

8. In 2018, facing a series of monetary issues, the Berkshire Museum put up thirteen works at auction. Eleven sold for a total amount of just over $15 million. The sale was protested by local groups, and AAMD had attempted to offer alternative methods of raising monies. In response to the sale, AAMD sanctioned the museum, stating that the museum's intention to use the funds to address budgetary shortfalls was "in opposition to AAMD's policy that such funds must be used only to support acquisitions of art." Press Release: AAMD Statement on Sanction of Berkshire Museum and La Salle University Art Museum, May 25, 2018. Per the terms of the sanctions, AAMD's members were to "refrain from lending or borrowing works of art to . . . the Berkshire Museum . . . , and to also refrain from collaborating with [the museum] on exhibitions." Ibid. AAMD essentially attempted to cut off the Berkshire from its professional peers. However, sanctions as a deterrent are unproven as seen by the professional community's response to the Berkshire. "Within months of the imposition of sanctions against the Berkshire Museum, an AAMD member museum ignored the sanction and requested a loan for an upcoming exhibition." Marc S. Gold and Stefanie S. Jandl, "Why the Association of Art Museum Directors's [*sic*] Move on Deaccessioning Matters So Much" (18 May 2020), *The Art Newspaper*. The museum also received an unrestricted gift of $1 million in art from a private donor and had one of their most lucrative years in raising cash donations. Ibid. Asked about the impact of the sanctions, Berkshire president Ethan S. Klepetar stated, "It doesn't really matter. They make absolutely no difference to the Berkshire Museum." Ibid.

9. Malaro, *Museum Governance*, 17. "Quite frequently codes of ethics have no enforcement mechanism. They depend on self-education, self-motivation, and peer pressure for their promulgation." Ibid. Organizations in which members are invited to join (such as the Association of Art Museum Directors) or that have an accreditation program (such as the American Alliance of Museums) may be able to enforce their ethical codes by revoking membership or accreditation for noncompliance.

10. This lack of enforcement means that while professional codes are widely promulgated, there is limited remedy when a museum does not follow the codes (generally, removal from the membership ranks of the professional organization that promulgated the code). In contrast, institutional codes of ethics can only be enforced against the institution by itself. This means that institutional codes of ethics tend to represent what the institution considers the lofty aims the institution should strive for, but it has even less enforcement options than professional codes.

> A code of ethics sets forth conduct deemed necessary by a profession to uphold the integrity of the profession. It sets a higher standard because it is based on principles of personal accountability and service to others. A code of ethics, however, frequently has no enforcement power. It is effective only if there is personal commitment and informed peer pressure.

Marie C. Malaro, "Deaccessioning: The American Perspective," in *A Deaccession Reader*, ed. Stephen E. Weil (Washington, D.C.: American Association of Museums, 1997), 40.

11. "The American public considers museums the most trustworthy source of information in America, rated higher than local papers, nonprofit researchers, the U.S. government, and academic researchers." American Alliance of Museums. (n.d.) Museum Facts & Data. www.aam-us.org.

12. "If a profession does not police itself [via ethical codes], the law allows the profession to sink quite low before liability is imposed." Malaro, *Museum Governance*, 17.

13. Ibid., 18.

14. Ibid., 17.

15. Museums struggling with making a decision in regard to an ethical issue may consider applying the "Framework for Approaching Ethical Problems" in Sally Yerkovich's *A Practical Guide to Museum Ethics* (Rowman & Littlefield, 2016).

MUSEUM DEACCESSIONING AND PROCEEDS FROM DISPOSAL

As part of a strong collections management program, many museums utilize deaccessioning to maintain the strength and quality of the collection. Deaccessioning can be useful in keeping the collection in alignment with the museum's mission and collecting goals, while also culling objects that have outlived their useful life or in some manner no longer are fit for museum preservation, research, education, or exhibition purposes.

DEACCESSIONING AND DISPOSAL

While often conflated in discussions around the topic, deaccessioning should be understood as a different process than disposal. While deaccessioning is the process of removing an object from the permanent collection, disposal is a separate, though often related, process by which the museum relinquishes ownership rights (title) to the object. This means that an object can be deaccessioned but not disposed by the museum.

For example, Historic House Museum has a large number of Depression-era handkerchiefs that were acquired as part of a bulk donation forty years ago. Many are deteriorating, and they have limited or no provenance other than belonging to the grandmother of the original donor. Following an inventory project, the curator and director agree the handkerchiefs are not in alignment with the collections. They complete the process of deaccessioning a dozen of the handkerchiefs in compliance with the museum's collection management policy. The deaccessioned handkerchiefs are added to the museum's handling collection, where they are used as tactile objects for school groups. In this example, the handkerchiefs were removed from the permanent collection—they were deaccessioned—but they were not disposed of, as the museum retained ownership. While it is likely they will eventually be disposed of, especially since the deterioration process will now accelerate due to handling by the public, disposal was not the automatic step following deaccession.

A BRIEF OVERVIEW OF ACCESSIONING

To deaccession an object is to reverse the process of accessioning.[1] It involves the removal of the object from the permanent collection with the intention that it will no longer be held by the museum for the public trust in perpetuity. An understanding of the accessioning process is vital to any discussion about deaccessioning, as "the best control a museum has over deaccessioning is a good accessions policy."[2] Accessioning as discussed here is the process by which objects enter the museum collection.[3] It can be understood as a two-step process: (1) The object is acquired by the museum; and (2) the object is recorded or processed into the permanent collection.

The acquisition can occur by a number of means, including as a donation or bequest, purchase, trade, or any other manner by which the title of the object is legally transferred to the museum. All objects accessioned into the collection must first be acquired by the museum, but not all items acquired will necessarily be accessioned. For instance, office furniture, display vitrines, and shipping crates are acquired by museums for use in their day-to-day operations, but none of these objects would or should necessarily be accessioned into the permanent collection.

A museum's accession policies outline the procedures by which an object is processed (accessioned) into the permanent collection. They ensure that the process of acquiring new collections objects is conducted in a judicious manner, furthers the museum's mission, ensures compliance with the collections management plans and goals, and brings in objects that can be used and cared for.[4] Due to potential tax liabilities, objects the museum intends to deaccession or sell for profit (for instance at a fund-raising auction) should not be accessioned.[5] Accessioning objects into the permanent collection is a long-term allocation of the institution's resources,[6] including staff, facilities, and finances.[7] Therefore, the collecting plan's goals and the decision to accession must be carefully considered, requiring that the acquisition and accessioning of the object will not adversely impact the museum's ability to care for other objects or in some other way impact the museum's ability to carry out its mission.[8]

DEACCESSIONING: LEGAL AND ETHICAL CONSIDERATIONS

There are many reasons why a museum may decide to deaccession an object. The impetus for the choice may be due to an internal decision, such as a determination that the object does not fit in with the museum's mission or has deteriorated beyond repair. Alternatively, it may be due to an external decision, such as a determination by a court that the museum does not hold legal title and the object is to be returned to the rightful owner.

In a 2011 limited survey of professional and institutional codes of ethics and collections management policies, the most commonly acceptable reason to deaccession was when the object was inconsistent with institutional mission or collecting goals.[9] Closely following this was when the object was deemed a duplicate or redundant object and when the museum was unable to provide necessary and appropriate care. Other acceptable reasons included when holding the object was in violation of law, the deaccession was intended to refine or improve the collection, the object's authenticity or attribution was questioned, and when restoration was impractical. Receiving little support in the reviewed policies was when the object was considered to be of poor quality and when the deaccession was being done to generate funds for the acquisition of superior works.[10]

A decision to deaccession an object may have legal and ethical components. For instance, if the object entered the collection through a gift or bequest, there may be donor restrictions that would create a legal impossibility to deaccession the object. If the donor included restrictions, such as a requirement that the object never be deaccessioned, the museum is bound by that restriction and may not deaccession the object without the granting of donor or judicial leave to do so. Additionally, if the museum's articles of incorporation or other founding documents prohibit objects from being deaccessioned, the museum is legally prohibited from doing so. Even if the museum does have the legal authority to deaccession, some museums feel they should notify the donor (or donor's heir or next of kin, if the donor is deceased) prior to conducting the deaccession. Without a specific legal impetus requiring this, such notification is purely an ethical matter, and there are strong arguments for and against the practice.[11]

The deaccessioning process should follow a written deaccessioning policy, which may live within the larger collections management policy or be a stand-alone document. Either way, the deaccessioning policy should state the criteria for deaccessioning to precede, list acceptable reasons to deaccession, set up a review and approval procedure,[12] and indicate when, if ever, outside opinions or appraisals are necessary. The policy should also indicate what level of authority is needed to approve the deaccession, that is, which museum professional standards indicate should be at least at the level needed to approve an accession, if not higher.[13] A well-drafted deaccession policy clearly states the criteria to be considered when determining whether an object will be deaccessioned. Finally, the deaccession policy will list the appropriate methods of disposal, detailing what the preferred methods are and how a method should be selected.

Even if there is no limitation on a museum's legal right to deaccession, it may still find itself facing challenges if it attempts to deaccession collection objects. Many members of the general public, and some in the museum profession, believe that deaccessioning is inherently unethical and goes against the purpose of museums. While this view is not upheld by the museum profession as a whole, this does mean that deaccessioning can be a lightning rod for controversy if not done well. Open and honest communication, adherence with professional best practices and the museum's internal policies (including its code of ethics), and transparency of the process will all aid the museum in conducting a successful deaccession.[14]

When legal oversight of a deaccession does occur, it generally comes in the shoes of the state's attorney general. The attorney general is the top law enforcement agent of the state.[15] The attorney general has a variety of responsibilities, including oversight of nonprofit organizations such as museums. While museums serve the general public, that public does not generally have standing to sue to enforce the museum's legal obligations. That responsibility falls to the attorney general. On the other hand, ethical oversight can come from professional organizations, most commonly AAM and AAMD. These organizations can rescind institutional membership and sanction the museum in a variety of ways.

DISPOSAL OF DEACCESSIONED OBJECTS AND PROCEEDS FROM DEACCESSIONING

Besides the issue of deaccessioning itself, complications and controversies can arise from the manner in which the deaccessioned objects are disposed of and how the proceeds from deaccessioning are used by the museum. If it is determined a deaccessioned object will be disposed of, there are a number of options available to the museum. Again, disposal is not a guaranteed outcome following deaccessioning, as discussed above. Most often, however, title to the deaccessioned object is transferred to a third party by some means, such as through sale at public auction or transfer to another museum either directly or as part of an exchange. Objects may also be destroyed, such as if a work is dangerous (think live bullets or unstable chemicals) or if it is a forgery that the museum is concerned will reenter the market purporting to be an authentic work. When the deaccession was involuntary on the part of the museum, such as the repatriation of cultural property or the return of stolen or Nazi-looted artworks, the disposal will often be a return to the country or community of origin or to the proper owner(s).

While there are many options for disposal, there are certain means of disposal that are generally looked down upon in the museum profession. For instance, selling deaccessioned objects in the museum gift shop or transferring them to museum staff or trustees is unacceptable.[16] In the case of museum trustees, acceptance of deaccessioned objects would be a breach of that trustee's fiduciary duty to the museum. Private sales are also looked poorly upon, as there is a lack of transparency in such transactions.

Once a museum makes the decision to deaccession an object from the collection and to dispose of it in a manner that will generate profit, it must decide what to do with that profit. Legally, there are few impediments to using deaccession proceeds for a wide variety of purposes, including operating expenses.[17] However, when a museum board seeks to liquidate its collection in order to rectify serious financial distress, fund building projects, or otherwise use the collection to fund operating costs, it is possible the board has breached its fiduciary duty to the museum by failing to properly oversee the museum's finances or for seeking to profit from a collection that is held in the public trust. This, in turn, may give rise to intervention from the attorney general. Finally, use of deaccessioning proceeds for reasons other than acquisition or direct care may result in censure by any professional organizations of which the museum is a member, due to breach of that organization's ethical codes.

Ethically, these considerations are more complicated. In the museum profession, the most accepted manner to use those proceeds is to dedicate them to the acquisition of new collection objects. This specific use for deaccession proceeds is promulgated by the American Alliance of Museums,[18] the Association of Art Museum Directors,[19] and the American Association for State and Local History,[20] as well as many smaller regional, local, or category-specific museum organizations.[21] The AAM and AASLH also provide that proceeds from deaccessioning may be used for the direct care of collections.[22]

Defining "Direct Care of Collections"

Since 1993, AAM has permitted the use of proceeds from deaccessioning for the direct care of collections.[23] Specifically, the AAM provides the following guidance: "[D]isposal of collections through sale, trade or research activities is solely for the advancement of the museum's mission."[24] Further: "Proceeds from the sale of nonliving collections . . . in no event shall . . . be used for anything other than acquisition or direct care of collections."[25] AASLH provides similar guidance: "Funds from the sale of collections may be used for the acquisition of collections, or the direct care or preservation of existing collections."[26] Despite the acceptance of direct care by AAM and AASLH, the term was not defined until April 2016 with the publication of an AAM white paper that provides guidelines for museum staff and their governing authorities on how to define "direct care" for their institution.[27]

As established in that white paper, the AAM now defines *direct care of collections* as "an investment that enhances the life, usefulness or quality of a museum's collection."[28] The definition is intentionally nebulous so that it may be applied across the range of organizations and institutions that are members of the AAM. It is designed to accommodate the needs of organizations as diverse as art museums, botanical gardens, children's museums, science and technology centers, and so on. In order to aid organizations in determining if an activity would fall within the "direct care" definition, the AAM produced the Direct Care of Collections matrix.[29] This tool balances the potential impact of the proposed expense (a physical impact on specific objects versus institutional-wide impact) and the overall strength of the expenditure (a strategic investment or a "quick fix"[30] to an immediate concern).[31] By plotting the proposed expense within the matrix, a user can determine if the expense would qualify as a direct care of collections, an unacceptable use of funds, or falling within one of two "gray areas." Falling within a gray area does not automatically disqualify the proposed expense, but rather indicates that further inquiry is required, for instance looking to the discipline-specific ethical code that applies to the museum or its own institutional documents, such as a code of ethics or collecting plan.

In 2019, the Financial Accounting Standards Board (FASB) issued Update No. 2019-03 to align its definition of *collections* with the AAM's Code of Ethics for Museums. FASB is a private sector (nongovernmental) organization that establishes the professional standards of financial accounting. Their standards govern how the financial reports of nongovernmental organizations are prepared.

Prior to 2019, FASB had already established a system wherein museums did not have to capitalize their collections if they met certain requirements. The first two prongs of that definition were the collections had to be (1) "held for public exhibition, education, or research in furtherance of public service rather than financial gain"[32] and (2) "protected, kept unencumbered, cared for, and preserved."[33] As of 2019, the third prong has been replaced to state that the collections are "subject to an organizational policy that requires the use of proceeds from items that are sold to be used for the *acquisitions of new collection items*, the *direct care* of existing collections, or *both* [emphasis added]."[34] Further, if the organization does permit acquisitions, direct care, or both, they must disclose that policy and also disclose their definition of "direct care."[35] The impact of Update No. 2019-03 is that proceeds from deaccessioning may be used for both acquisition of new objects and direct care of existing collections without the museum being required to capitalize its collections, assuming all disclosure requirements are met. This brings FASB's policies into alignment with museum professional practices as promulgated by the AAM and the AASLH.[36]

SUMMARY

Deaccessioning is an aspect of collections management and care that is accepted in the museum profession, though it is not without possible pitfalls for the museum that does not approach it in a manner that is mission-forward, or when the museum is not open and transparent about the process. Disposal, a potential follow-up procedure to deaccessioning, is another area in which a museum may find itself facing inquiry or criticism. For the museum that successfully navigates these processes, it will hopefully find themselves with a stronger, more focused collection that it can care for ethically and professionally. However, even at that stage, the question will remain as to what to do with the proceeds from deaccessioning if the objects were sold. Here, the profession is split in regard to the appropriate use of proceeds, with the AAM and the AASLH permitting both the acquisition of new objects and the direct care of collections, and the AAMD only permitting acquisition with those realized funds. Museums are advised to look to the appropriate professional code of ethics, as well as their own ethical codes, collections management policies, and other appropriate internal documents. Throughout the process, it is important to remember that while museum ethics rule much of the decisions, legal factors come into play as well. Legal restrictions on deaccessioning may exist for a particular object, collection, or institution, and oversight of that deaccessioning or the museum as a whole may come in the form of the state's attorney general and museum professional organizations. However with proper forethought, clear policies and procedures, and sufficient oversight, a museum should be able to navigate the waters of deaccessioning successfully.

NOTES

1. Portions of this chapter are adapted from the author's article "All in a Day's Work: How Museums May Approach Deaccessioning as a Necessary Collections Management Tool," *DePaul Journal of Art, Technology and Intellectual Property* 22 (2011) (published as Heather Hope Stephens). While the author did look to that work in preparation of this chapter, many sections have been significantly rearranged or updated.

2. John E. Simmons (2018.) *Things Great and Small: Collections Management Policies* [2nd ed.]. (New York: Rowman & Littlefield, 2018), at 61.

3. *Accession* may also refer to the actual process of recording the object's information as part of the overall accessioning process. In that sense, "accession" is the steps that are taken when an object is added to the permanent collection, for instance taking photographs and measurements, assessing the object's condition, assigning and affixing an accession number, creating an object file, etc.

4. Title passes to the museum through the process of acquisition, for instance through purchase or donation, so accessioning is not mandatory for objects to become the property of the museum. As a general rule, objects that the museum does not intend to keep in perpetuity in the permanent collection and to hold in the public trust are not accessioned. For a more in-depth discussion, see Simmons, *Things Great and Small*, chapter 6, and *Museum Registration Methods* (6th) at 30–35.

5. Because of these potential adverse effects to donors who take deductions for donations that the museum does not intend to put to a related use, museums should be clear and transparent about their intentions.

6. Malaro, *Museum Governance*, at 44.

7. There are numerous financial costs associated with the acquisition of an object, including the purchase price, curation costs, documentation, conservation, and storage. (Gail Dexter Lord, *Forward Planning and the Cost of Collecting 2*, available at https://www.lord.ca/Media/Artcl_ForwardPlanningCostofCollecting-GL.pdf.) While nonprofessionals may assume that storage of collections objects is a minor part of a museum's budget, the fact is that storage of an object does not simply involve the physical space of the object; museum storage facilities are expensive spaces that require adequate security, proper atmospheric controls, and complex

design elements to permit efficient access to a large variety of objects. (Malaro and Pogány DeAngelis, *Legal Primer* [3rd], at 249–50.) A 1989 study found that 66 percent of museums' operating budgets were related to collections care. (Lord, at 1.) Direct care of the collections cost 38 percent of the budget. *Id.* In 1983, American museums were paying an average of $50 per year per object for proper storage and preservation. Introduction to *A Deaccession Reader*, at 3. "The museum can benefit from an analysis of the ongoing costs associated with collecting and maintaining collections, including not only the cost to acquire—e.g., purchase cost, transportation and insurance, initial conservation—but also long term costs such as cataloging, storage, conservation, photography, and inventory control." Morris, at 101.

8. One way to ensure compliance with collecting goals and museum mission is by requiring an appropriate authorization process. Accession policies and/or collections management policies should specify who may authorize an accession. Some accession policies indicate different levels of authority needed depending on the type of object proposed for accession, for instance based on the object's monetary value.

9. Stephens, "All in a Day's Work," at 156. In that article, the reviewed codes of ethics and collections management policies were from: the American Alliance of Museums, the Association of Art Museum Directors, the Museum of Modern Art, the Metropolitan Museum of Art, the Guggenheim, and the Newark Museum.

10. Ibid.

11. A museum may wish to notify a donor (or their heirs) of the deaccession in order to maintain a positive relationship with that donor. By notifying the donor, the museum may hope to frame the narrative around the decision in a manner that would be difficult or impossible if the donor found out about the deaccession from some other source, such as the museum's website or a news article. A donor who learns of a deaccession from a third party may question whether they want to support the museum in the future, either by donations of objects or through other supports, such as museum membership, gala attendance, or financial contributions. However, by notifying the donor, the museum may be opening themselves up to a demand for return of the object. By donating the object, the donor has relinquished all ownership interests in the object (barring a restriction in the original donation paperwork, which may demand a return upon deaccession or for the museum to donate the deaccessioned object to some third party such as a different nonprofit or historical society). Another consideration is that the donor may have received a tax benefit for the original donation. If the donor did receive such a benefit, and the museum later deaccessions and returns the object, the donor gets the best of both worlds—the past tax benefit plus the present possession of the object.

12. While the process of deaccessioning can be used to cull and improve the collections overall, it does raise questions. One obvious concern may be that there was some error in accessioning the object, suggesting the object should not have been accessioned into the permanent collection. These concerns demonstrate some potential issues associated with deaccessioning, highlighting why a high level of authority should be required. Again, a good accession policy will limit the need for future deaccessioning.

13. Simmons, *Things Great and Small* (2nd), at 64. Museum professional standards also dictate that the museum retain indefinitely the deaccession records for the object. Malaro and Pogány DeAngelis, *Legal Primer* (3rd), at 228. By not permitting staff to acquisition and accession objects without oversight, the museum can ensure that objects unrelated to the mission or inappropriate in some other way do not enter the collection. Likewise, a high level of authority encourages the ramifications of a potential deaccession, including donor relations and the reaction of the public, be considered by not only staff members but also the director and the trustees.

14. This conflict of opinions regarding deaccessioning can be described as two competing views on the fundamental purpose of museums. One the one hand, museums can be understood to serve the purpose of preserving collections in perpetuity, where the objects accessioned into collections are held for both the benefit of the present community and future generations. From this point of view, to deaccession an object is to deny future generations the benefits of the object, be those benefits aesthetic, historical, cultural, or scientific.

On the other hand, a convincing argument can be made that thoughtful deaccessioning goes to the very heart of collections care. From this perspective, deaccessioning is seen as a means of removing objects that are inappropriate to the collection, thereby freeing up museum resources (collections space, storage costs, staff resources, etc.) for objects more befitting the collections. See, for instance: "Deaccessioning is a legitimate part of the formation and care of collections and, if practiced, should be done in order to refine and improve the quality and appropriateness of the collections, the better to serve the museum's mission." Association of Art Museum Directors, "AAMD Policy on Deaccessioning," June 9, 2010, amended Oct. 2015, at 4.

These two perspectives give light to the fact that deaccessioning can be highly controversial, and museums have found themselves in the center of negative press, professional sanctions, and legal challenges when deaccessioning has been conducted without proper understanding of legal obligations, ethical guidelines, proper transparency, and public engagement.

15. Or the federal government, when referring to the U.S. Attorney General. The term *state* is used here, but attorneys general also operate, with the same oversight capacity, in commonwealths and territories.

16. See Simmons, *Things Great and Small* (2nd), at 71. For further reading, see Association of Art Museum Directors, "AAMD Policy on Deaccessioning."

17. But see Malaro and Pogány DeAngelis, *Legal Primer* (3rd), at 265–69, providing an overview of some recent legal issues that arose from the use of deaccessioning proceeds outside of the acquisition of new collections objects or the direct care of collections. If a museum is considering using deaccession proceeds for operating funds or other uses outside the limited scope provided in the ethical codes, there is a possibility of legal intervention. This is very fact-specific, but the examples of museums that have found themselves subject to attorney general oversight or lawsuits is extensive and should perhaps serve as a warning for museums considering such a route.

18. "[D]isposal of collections through sale, trade or research activities is solely for the advancement of the museum's mission." American Alliance of Museums, "Code of Ethics for Museums," adopted 1991, amended 2000, www.aam-us.org/resources/ethics-standards-and-best-practices/code-of-ethics. "Proceeds from the sale of nonliving collections . . . in no event shall . . . be used for anything other than acquisition or direct care of collections." Ibid.

19. "Funds received from the disposal of a deaccessioned work shall not be used for operations or capital expenses." "AAMD Policy on Deaccessioning," at 4. "Such funds, including any earnings and appreciation thereon, may be used only for the acquisition of works in a manner consistent with the museum's policy on the use of restricted acquisition funds." Ibid.

20. American Association for State and Local History, "AASLH Statement of Standards and Ethics (revised 2018)," at 2. http://download.aaslh.org/AASLH+Statement+of+Standards+and+Ethics+-+Revised +2018.pdf.

21. See, for example, the College Art Association, "Statement Concerning the Deaccession of Works of Art" (adopted November 3, 1973, reaffirmed June 17, 1991, revised October 27, 2013), www.collegeart.org/guidelines/sales.

22. AAMD does not permit deaccessioning proceeds to be used for the direct care of collections. In April 2020, the AAMD promulgated a resolution in response to the COVID-19 global pandemic and its substantial impact on the museum field, wherein they announced a temporary moratorium on censuring or sanctioning museums that "use the proceeds from deaccessioned art to pay for expenses associated with direct care of collections." AAMD (15 April 2020), "Press Release: Association of Art Museum Directors' Board of Trustees Approves Resolution to Provide Additional Financial Flexibility to Art Museums During Pandemic Crisis." Through April 10, 2022, the AAMD will not censure or sanction members for using funds from deaccessioning for the direct care of collections. The announcement also addressed uses of restricted endowments, trusts, and donations outside the scope of this discussion. This is a temporary response to the global pandemic and does not constitute a permanent change to the AAMD's policies or professional best practices. While the impact of the AAMD resolution is unclear at the time of writing, what it essentially does is to temporarily permit member art museums to use proceeds from deaccessioning for the direct care of collections in addition to the already permitted acquisition of new works, procedures already permitted by the AAM and the AASLH. While this so-called financial flexibility is intended to be short-lived, it will be interesting to see how this shift by the AAMD is used by its members and whether the AAMD can successfully revert to their more stringent guidelines after two years of permitting direct care, as has become common in other areas of the profession.

Further, while the AAMD will temporarily refrain from censoring or sanctioning members for using deaccessioning proceeds to provide direct care for collections, that does not mean an attorney general or other oversight authority may not bring a legal challenge to such actions, as the ethical standards maintained by the AAMD do not control legal obligations that may impact a museum in their particular jurisdiction. The AAMD press release can be found at https://aamd.org/for-the-media/press-release/ aamd-board-of-trustees-approves-resolution-to-provide-additional.

23. For an excellent overview of how "direct care of collections" came to be added to the document, see the white paper: American Alliance of Museums, "Direct Care of Collections: Ethics, Guidelines, and

Recommendations." (The white paper was revised in March 2019 in response to the Financial Accounting Standard Board's updated "definition of collections," which aligned the Board's guidelines with the AAM's Code of Ethics for Museums regarding the use of proceeds from deaccessioning. The white paper was otherwise unchanged.) Compare the approach of the AAM and the AASLH with that of the Association of Art Museum Directors: "Funds received from the disposal of a deaccessioned work shall not be used for operations or capital expenses." Association of Art Museum Directors, "AAMD Policy on Deaccessioning." "Such funds, including any earnings and appreciation thereon, may be used only for the acquisition of works in a manner consistent with the museum's policy on the use of restricted acquisition funds." Ibid. Direct care is not a permitted use of proceeds from disposal under the AAMD's standard policies. But see note 22 above regarding a temporary moratorium on AAMD's censuring of member museums in response to COVID-19.

24. American Alliance of Museums, "Code of Ethics for Museums."

25. Ibid.

26. American Association for State and Local History, "AASLH Statement of Standards and Ethics (revised 2018)," 2.

27. AAM, "Direct Care of Collections: Ethics, Guidelines, and Recommendations."

28. American Alliance of Museums. (2016, April). *Direct Care of Collections: Ethics, Guidelines and Recommendations* [White paper]. Washington, D.C.: Author, at 7. Retrieved from https://www.aam-us.org/wp-content/uploads/2018/01/direct-care-of-collections-ethics-guidelines-and-recommendations-pdf.pdf. AASLH adopts this definition verbatim in their 2018 revision of their *Statement of Standards and Ethics*.

29. See the Direct Care of Collections matrix, reprinted as table 1.2 in the "Direct Care of Collections" dictionary entry.

30. AAM, *Direct Care of Collections*, at 10.

31. See AAM, *Direct Care of Collections*, for a full explanation of the use and application of the matrix.

32. Financial Accounting Standard Board (2019, March), "Update No. 2019-03: Updating the Definition of *Collections*," at 3. https://www.fasb.org/jsp/FASB/Document_C/DocumentPage?cid=1176172375318&acceptedDisclaimer=true.

33. Ibid.

34. Ibid.

35. Ibid., at 5.

36. For an in-depth discussion of the FASB update and the capitalization of collections in general, see the May 2020 AASLH position paper *Valuing History Collections,* available at http://download.aaslh.org/AASLH+Valuing+History+Collections+Position+Paper+May+2020.pdf. This replaced the AASLH's previous paper, "Capitalization of Collections," and was prepared by members of the AASLH Standards and Ethics Committee in response to the FASB Update No. 2019-03.

CHAPTER 4

AN OVERVIEW OF THE BASICS OF COPYRIGHT LAW

Copyright is a form of intellectual property intended to "promote the Progress of Science and useful Arts, by securing for limited Times to Authors and Inventors the exclusive Right to their respective Writings and Discoveries."[1]

The easiest way to think about these rights is as a bundle of sticks, where each stick is a specific protection or right. The sticks in the bundle may be retained by the work's author, or they may be given or sold to someone else by the owner/author. This means that an individual may own one stick but not the others. Additionally, an individual may control the right to exercise the rights of a specific stick without actually owning the actual creative object itself (this is called licensing).

It is important to understand that the bundle of sticks exists completely separately from the actual physical object. A museum (or any person or institution) may own a physical object, such as a painting, but not own any of the sticks associated with that object. Just because you own the copyrighted object does not mean you own any of the sticks, nor do you necessarily have the right to exercise the rights of any of the sticks. For a museum, this may mean that the institution owns an artwork but it cannot gain any economic advantage from that object.

For example, say a museum owns a charcoal drawing created by a popular visual artist, Agatha, active in the mid- to late 1900s. Agatha Artist's drawing is the centerpiece of a new exhibit. The museum plans to prominently display the work. Additionally, the museum wishes to reproduce the drawing on messenger bags to be sold in the museum's shop. There are also plans to have the museum's current artist-in-residence undertake a series of paintings that will be response pieces to the drawing, reinterpreting it in new styles and directions for the contemporary audience. As will be seen below, the museum may be unable to execute most of these plans without proper copyright clearances.

There are four considerations that arise in any discussion of copyright: (1) subject matter, (2) the exclusive rights protected, (3) ownership of those rights, and (4) duration of protection.

1. SUBJECT MATTER OF COPYRIGHT

In any discussion of copyright, the first consideration is if the work at issue falls within the subject matter of copyright. The Copyright Act of 1976, which is the current federal copyright law and was implemented on January 1, 1978, provides guidance on what is and is not eligible for copyright protection. In order to qualify, the item must be an **original** work that has been **fixed** into a **tangible medium of expression**.[2] This can be broken down into various components.

A common misunderstanding is that the requirement of originality is synonymous with novelty. Originality is not the same as novelty under the Copyright Act. For instance, an artist's painting *Still Life with Fruit* would qualify for copyright protection, even though thousands of such still-life paintings have been created over the centuries. It does not matter that the artist's chosen subject is not *novel*, only that it is the artist's *original* artistic expression. This also means that if the artist's still life was painted in a classroom with twenty other art students, all the paintings depicting the same arrangement of fruit, each and every painting would be entitled to copyright protection. Each art student's painting would be an original artistic expression, even if they are all based on the same arrangement of fruit.

In addition to originality, it is required that the work be fixed into a tangible medium of expression. Copyright protection does not exist for ideas or concepts.[3] Because an idea or concept is not fixed, it cannot receive the protections afforded by copyright. The Copyright Act enumerates a list of works that are entitled to copyright protection, including literary, musical, and dramatic works, works of visual art ("pictorial, graphic, and sculptural works"), audiovisual works, sound recordings, and architecture.[4] All of these can be "fixed," such as on a canvas, in a novel, or through a digital file. Note that the work does not need to be fixed into a medium that is perceivable by a human. The ridges on a vinyl record cannot be perceived as music by the unassisted human ear, but the fixation still qualifies under copyright laws.

In the Agatha Artist hypothetical, the artwork falls within the subject matter of copyright, as it is a work of visual art, it meets the originality standard, and it is properly fixed into a tangible medium of expression. Therefore, the hypothetical drawing is entitled to copyright protection.

2. EXCLUSIVE RIGHTS DEFINED

Once it is determined that a work is eligible for copyright protection, the second consideration is what protections are afforded by copyright. Again, remember that the various exclusive rights are best conceptualized as a bundle of sticks, with each stick representing a different right or protection. Ownership of the individual sticks in the bundle is separate from ownership of the physical object that gave rise to copyright protections.

The sticks in the bundle confer specific, exclusive rights. These rights are:

1. The right to reproduce (make copies of) the work,[5]
2. The right to make derivative works (adaptations),[6]
3. The right to distribute copies to the public (by sale, rental, lease, lending, etc.),[7]
4. The right to perform the work in public (as applicable, such as with musical or dramatic works),[8] and
5. The right to publicly display the work.[9]

As a general rule, unless you own the right to do any of these activities with the copyrighted work, doing so constitutes copyright infringement.

Table 4.1. Rights Protected by Copyright Law

Right Protected by Copyright	Statutory Source	Examples of Infringement	Notes
Reproduction Right The right to reproduce (make copies of) the work.	17 U.S.C. § 106(1)	Creating an unauthorized reproduction of an artwork, such as on a postcard or in a calendar. To make unauthorized copies of music, such as copying CDs of an opera.	
Derivative Works Right The right to make derivative works (adaptations).	17 U.S.C. § 106(2)	To make an unauthorized motion picture based on a play. To make a translation of a novel into a foreign language without permission. To add a mustache and beard onto a postcard reproduction of a famous painting (see Marcel Duchamp's L.H.O.O.Q. [1919], also known as *The Mona Lisa with a Mustache*.)	
Distribution Right The right to distribute copies to the public (by sale, rental, lease, lending, etc.).	17 U.S.C. § 106(3)	To sell unauthorized objects depicting the work, such as T-shirts depicting an artwork.	Subject to the "first sale doctrine," permitting the legal purchaser of a copyrighted work to dispose of that copy as they wish (i.e., they can sell, loan, etc., the copy purchased) without permission of the copyright holder. 17 U.S.C. § 109(a).
Public Performance Right The right to perform the work in public (as applicable, such as with musical or dramatic works).	17 U.S.C. § 106(4) And 17 U.S.C. § 106(6)	To legally rent a motion picture and then screen it to the public.	
Public Display Right The right to publicly display the work.	17 U.S.C. § 106(5)	To capture "stills" from a television show and display them to the public.	After the work is legally sold, the work's owner has the right to publicly display the work without the copyright owner's permission, and may authorize others to do the same. 17 U.S.C. § 109(c).

However, an exception of importance to museums does exist. The copyright owner's exclusive right to publicly display the work is limited by the Act when the object is lawfully sold. This is the "first sale doctrine." Under this exception, the legal owner of the work has the right to publicly display the work without the copyright owner's permission.[10] Additionally, the legal owner of the work may authorize another to display the work. For museums, this means that even without the copyright owner's permission, the museum may publicly display the works in its collection and may authorize institutions to which the work is loaned to do the same.

The museum's planned activities for the Agatha Artist drawing all touch on copyright. Regardless of copyright ownership, the museum may display the drawing without the copyright holder's permission thanks to the first sale doctrine, because the museum in our hypothetical is the legal owner of a lawfully made copy.

Problems arise, however, regarding the plans to make and sell messenger bags featuring reproductions of the drawing, as this would infringe on the copyright holder's exclusive reproduction right. The plans for the artist-in-residence to create response pieces may infringe upon the copyright holder's exclusive right to make derivative works. If the museum does not own the copyrights in the work and has not negotiated a license, these activities would be an infringement. Further, the circumstances of this infringement would be unlikely to permit a finding of fair use. (See "Chapter 5: Copyright Infringement and the Fair Use Doctrine.")

3. OWNERSHIP OF EXCLUSIVE RIGHTS

Of course, it is not enough to understand what rights are protected by copyright. The third consideration is determining who owns the copyright. The answer to this is determined by the circumstances of the work's creation and also by when it was created, and thus there are multiple lines of reasoning.

For works created after 1978, the implementation date of the current Copyright Act, the answer tends to be more straightforward. For the majority of works, copyright exists from the time of creation, and it is owned by the creator.[11] In other words, once the artist lays aside her brush, the painting is complete, copyright protection exists for it, and the artist is the owner of that copyright. No special registration with the United States Copyright Office is required, nor is it required to place a copyright notice (the © symbol with appended information) on the work.

If the work is created by two or more people ("joint work"), then they are co-owners of the copyright.[12] If the work was created by an employee in the course of her employment ("work made for hire"), then the employer owns the copyright.[13] As more people are involved in the creative process, the more likely it is that copyright ownership may become contested, and outlining everyone's expectations and ownership in a written contract is recommended.

In our Agatha Artist hypothetical, ownership of the copyright would have belonged to Artist herself, as she was the original author. Copyright's various "sticks" of rights are separate from ownership in the underlying physical work, so the museum does not necessarily own the copyright, even though it owns the drawing. Therefore, the museum's plans surrounding the exhibition, selling the messenger bags and creating derivative response pieces, would infringe upon that copyright. However, the museum may be able to move forward with its plans by licensing the necessary rights from the copyright holder. (See "Chapter 7: Intellectual Property Licensing.")

4. DURATION OF COPYRIGHT PROTECTION

The final consideration is the duration of copyright protection, which is linked to who the copyright owner is. The U.S. Constitution's Copyright Clause, with which we started this discussion, specifically states that copyright protection is to exist for a limited time. Under current law, for works created by a single author and not a work made for hire, that limited time is the life of the author plus an additional seventy years.[14] For joint works, copyright exists for life plus seventy years after the death of the last surviving author.[15] For works made for hire, copyright exists for 95 years from first publication or 120 years from the time of creation, whichever term expires first.[16] The work-made-for-hire term also applies to anonymous and pseudonymous works.[17] Because copyright protections subsist beyond the lifetime of the original author, those interests may be passed by will or inheritance. Whatever the duration of copyright protection, copyright terminates on December 31 of the calendar year.[18]

When a work's term of copyright protection expires, it falls into the public domain. Works in the public domain may be freely used by anyone without fear of infringement and without needing to negotiate licensing arrangements for use. This permits the creation of new derivative works and furthers the Constitution's Copyright Clause's stated purpose to "promote the Progress of Science and useful Arts."[19]

Table 4.2. Duration of Protection under the 1976 Copyright Act

Copyright Act of 1976 (for works created on or after January 1, 1978)

Type of Artistic Work	Copyright Duration
Single creator	Life of the author + 70 years
Joint work	Life of last surviving author + 70 years
Anonymous work	95 years from first publication OR 120 years from creation, whichever expires first
Pseudonymous work	95 years from first publication OR 120 years from creation, whichever expires first
Work made for hire	95 years from first publication OR 120 years from creation, whichever expires first
Published between 1978 and March 1, 1989, without copyright notice and not registered within five years	In the public domain
Published between 1978 and March 1, 1989, without copyright notice but registered within five years	Standard duration for type of work (single author, joint work, work made for hire)

The duration terms provided here are correct as of the time of writing and may have since been amended. Consult current law or legal counsel.

In the Agatha Artist hypothetical, assuming the drawing was created late enough in her career to fall under the 1976 Act, Artist's copyright in the work would last until seventy years after her death. This means that if Artist died in 1990, her copyrights would not expire until 2060. The museum would have to contact the current copyright holder to obtain the proper licenses.

SPECIAL CONSIDERATION: COPYRIGHTABLE WORKS THAT PREDATE THE 1976 COPYRIGHT ACT

Complicating the issue of copyright is the law as it existed prior to the current Copyright Act. For works created before 1978, a different system applied. Under the 1909 Copyright Act, a work had to meet a number of requirements for copyright protection to initially exist and then to continue. Because the previous Act had a complicated scheme of requirements, it can be difficult to determine if a pre-1978 work has copyright protection and who is the copyright owner. Further, the current 1976 Act did not affect those copyrights (for the most part), so an overview of the prior law is necessary.

Copyright Creation, Ownership, and Extension under the 1909 Copyright Act

The first two considerations, copyright subject matter and copyright protections, are largely unchanged under the 1909 Act. Therefore, this discussion begins with the third consideration, determining who owns the copyright. However, prior to determining who the copyright owner is, it must first be established if copyright even exists.

Copyright protection could only be obtained by publishing the work with proper notice affixed[20] or by registering the unpublished work with the U.S. Copyright Office.[21] The copyright notice consisted of the word "Copyright," the abbreviation "Copr.," or the "©" symbol, accompanied by the creator's name and the year of publication.[22] An exception for artworks, drawings, photographs, and prints permitted an abbreviated notice consisting of the "©" symbol along with the artist's initials, monogram, or symbol.[23] The publication year could be omitted on those works. "Publication" was understood to occur when the work was held out to the public for sale or publicly distributed.[24] However, "publication" could be more difficult to determine for works that exist in a single copy. Failure to comply with notice or registration requirements resulted in the work falling into the public domain.

Returning to our Agatha Artist hypothetical, it was originally established that Artist was active throughout the mid- and late 1900s and she passed away in 1990. This means that much of Artist's career occurred under the 1909 Act. As with many artworks held in museum collections, Artist's earlier works would be held to the more complicated copyright scheme that existed under that earlier statute. The specific details of the work, including proper copyright notice and publication history, would have to be researched to determine whether the work was entitled to copyright protection.

Copyright Duration under the 1909 Copyright Act

The fourth consideration, term of copyright protection, was also more complicated under the pre-1978 law. Under the 1909 Act, copyright was initially granted for a twenty-eight-year term.[25] A second twenty-eight-year term could be obtained by applying for a renewal and extension with the Copyright Office within one year prior to the expiration date.[26] Failure to apply for a renewal resulted in the work entering the public domain at the expiration of the first twenty-eight-year term.[27]

However, if the work was unpublished and unregistered as of January 1, 1978, the implementation date of the 1976 Act, then the work is subject to current duration terms.[28] These extension terms can be quite complicated and are determined by if and when the work was eventually published.

Returning to our hypothetical Agatha Artist drawing, the work's specific history would have to be researched to determine whether it was still protected by copyright. It is possible that even if the work was at one time protected by copyright, that term has since expired, and it would be in the public domain. However, it is also possible the work is entitled to the current copyright protection duration if it was unpublished and unregistered as of January 1, 1978. Copyright term duration is fact-specific to the particular work, and the museum would have to conduct proper research to ensure it is complying with the law.

SPECIAL CONSIDERATION: THE COPYRIGHT TERM EXTENSION ACT AND PUBLIC DOMAIN DAY

In 1988, the United States officially became a signatory of the Berne Convention for the Protection of Literary and Artistic Works, an international agreement administered by the World Intellectual Property Organization, with the passage of the Berne Convention Implementation Act. The United States had avoided joining Berne (which had existed since 1887), as it had a number of requirements that conflicted with American copyright law at the time. Among these, Berne had required since 1971 that copyright terms last, at minimum, for the life of the author plus fifty years.[29]

When originally passed, the 1976 Copyright Act granted copyright terms for a single author of the length of the author's lifetime plus fifty years, meeting Berne's minimum requirement. However, in 1993 the European Union adopted the Copyright Duration Directive 93/98/EEC. This Directive harmonized the copyright terms across EU member states, ensuring that authors in all EU countries would enjoy the same copyright protections. Significantly, the term adopted was life of the author plus seventy years.[30]

Following the adoption of the EU Directive, authors in the United States lobbied for an extension of copyright ownership under American law so they would enjoy the same protections as their European counterparts. This was eventually accomplished by the passage of the Copyright Term Extension Act (CTEA), which extended existing copyright terms to those in effect today, including the life of the author plus seventy years for single authors.

The CTEA also made a change to the term of works covered under the prior copyright law. In effect, the CTEA extended the term of works that were then under copyright so they would not enter the public domain until January 1, 2019, at the earliest. The retroactive application of the CTEA to preexisting works still under protection had the result that all works published in or before 1922 had entered the public domain by January 1998. However, works that would have entered the public domain on or after January 1999 received a twenty-year extension to their term.[31]

As a result, there was a freeze on published works in the United States automatically entering the public domain from 1999 to 2018. That freeze finally ended on January 1, 2019. That date was the first so-called public domain day in the United States in twenty years. On that date, copyrighted works originally published in 1923 entered the public domain, allowing them to be reused, reimagined, remixed, or reproduced by anyone for any reason without needing to secure permission from a copyright holder. This was the first time since 1998 that a mass number of works entered the public domain and represented the first of the now-annual "public domain days" as new works enter the public domain each year on New Year's Day.

CONCLUSION

While certain aspects of copyright law have been simplified under the 1976 Act, the copyright system in America is complicated due to the fact that many works, including works held in museum collections, fall under the earlier 1909 Act. For this reason, museums are well-advised to seek legal guidance or other professional expertise if there is any doubt as to the copyright status of a particular work. Some concerns about potential copyright infringement may be alleviated by the opening of new works to the public domain starting annually on January 1, 2019. Going forward, published works previously protected by the term extensions of the Copyright Term Extension Act will enter the public domain each year, giving free access to works that were previously bound by copyright protections. Museums must remember that ownership of a work does not guarantee ownership of the copyright. However, by keeping careful records and being well-informed about copyright, museum staff can ensure they are using their collection to its fullest potential while also respecting the rights of the creator-artists.

NOTES

1. This is the "Copyright Clause" found in Article I of the United States Constitution. U.S. Const. art. 1, § 8, cl. 8.
2. 17 U.S.C. § 102(a).
3. Ibid. § 102 (b).
4. Ibid.
5. Ibid. § 106(1).
6. Ibid. § 106(2).
7. Ibid. § 106(3).
8. Ibid. §§ 106(4), (6).
9. Ibid. § 106(5).
10. "[T]he owner of a particular copy lawfully made under this title, or any person authorized by such owner, is entitled, without the authority of the copyright owner, to display that copy publicly, either directly or by the projection of no more than one image at a time, to viewers present at the place where the copy is located." Ibid. § 109(c). See also the amicus brief filed with the Supreme Court by the AAMD and a number of major art museums:

> Most U.S. art museums have permanent collections that were acquired through purchases, gifts, and bequests, and on which they draw for exhibitions to the public. Museums also present special exhibitions, largely made up of works not in their collections, through loans from private collectors, galleries, and other institutions. For all these activities museums depend on the protections afforded by Section 109. Section 109(c) provides that the owners of a particular copy "lawfully made under

this title" is entitled to display that copy publicly without the copyright owner's permission. Section 109(a) similarly allows museums to buy, borrow, loan, and sell such "lawfully made" artworks.

Brief for the Association of Art Museum Directors, et al., as Amici Curiae Supporting Petitioner, *Kirtsaeng v. John Wiley & Sons, Inc.*, 568 U.S. 519 (2013) (No. 11-697), at 2.

11. Ibid. § 201(a).
12. Ibid. § 201(a).
13. Ibid. § 201(b).
14. Ibid. § 302(a). To be more precise, the original 1976 Act granted a copyright term for the life of the author for fifty years. This term was extended in 1998 by the Copyright Term Extension Act (CTEA). The CTEA has been nicknamed the Mickey Mouse Protection Act, as the law effectively kept the character Mickey Mouse out of the public domain. The terms given for copyright protection here and elsewhere take into the account the CTEA and reflect the current length of copyright terms.
15. Ibid. § 302(b).
16. Ibid. § 302(c).
17. Ibid.
18. Ibid. § 305.
19. U.S. Const. art. 1, § 8, cl. 8.
20. Copyright Act of 1909 § 10.
21. Ibid. § 11.
22. Ibid. § 19.
23. Ibid.
24. Ibid. § 26.
25. Ibid. § 24.
26. Ibid.
27. Ibid.
28. 17 U.S.C. § 301(a).
29. Berne Convention for the Protection of Literary and Artistic Works art.7(1).
30. The Council of the European Communities (1993, November 24). Council Directive 93/98/EEC of 29 October 1993 Harmonizing the Term of Protection of Copyright and Certain Related Rights. Art. 11.

> Whereas in order to establish a high level of protection which at the same time meets the require-ments of the internal market and the need to establish a legal environment conducive to the har-monious development of literary and artistic creation in the Community, the term of protection for copyright should be harmonized at 70 years after the death of the author or 70 years after the work is lawfully made available to the public. . . .

Ibid. The Directive takes a number of other actions related to copyright that are outside the scope of this discussion. The Directive was later amended and ultimately repealed in 2006 to be replaced by an updated harmonizing directive.

31. This is what gave rise to the CTEA's nickname, the "Mickey Mouse Protection Act," as the copy-right for Mickey Mouse was extended under the CTEA to at least 2024. The character Mickey Mouse was created in 1928 and appeared in the animated short *Steamboat Willie* that year. Only that early version of the character will enter the public domain in 1928. For an in-depth analysis of this, see Jesse Kirkland (December 4, 2019). In 2024, Mickey Mouse will finally enter the public domain—sort of. *The Blog of the NYU Journal of Intellectual Property and Entertainment Law.* https://blog.jipel.law.nyu.edu/2019/12/in-2024-mickey-mouse-will-finally-enter-the-public-domain-sort-of/#_ftn4.

The constitutionality of the CTEA was upheld by the Supreme Court in *Eldred v. Ashcroft*, 537 U.S. 186 (2003).

CHAPTER 5

COPYRIGHT INFRINGEMENT AND THE FAIR USE DOCTRINE

As discussed previously (see chapter 4), there are certain rights that are retained by the copyright owner to the exclusion of all others. These are:

1. The right to reproduce (make copies of) the work,[1]
2. The right to make derivative works (adaptations),[2]
3. The right to distribute copies to the public (by sale, rental, lease, lending, etc.),[3]
4. The right to perform the work in public (as applicable, such as with musical or dramatic works),[4] and
5. The right to publicly display the work.[5]

When an individual violates these exclusive rights, they are infringing on the copyright.[6]

For this discussion, let's revisit and expand upon the hypothetical introduced in chapter 4. City Museum owns a charcoal drawing created by a popular visual artist, Agatha Artist. Here, we will state that the drawing was completed in 1990, just a few months before Artist's death. Per the terms of her will, upon Artist's death there was created the Agatha Artist Foundation (AAF), which owns Artist's copyrights, as well as a large number of her works, and publishes Artist's *catalogue raisonné*. Over the years, the AAF has entered a number of profitable endeavors intended to popularize Artist and her works, for instance producing consumer goods featuring her artworks.

City Museum is including the drawing as the centerpiece of a new exhibit and prominently displaying the work. In addition, the museum has reproduced the drawing on messenger bags to be sold in the museum's shop. The museum's current artist-in-residence, Parker Painter, has created a series of paintings in response to the drawing, being inspired by Artist's work and reinterpreting it in new styles and directions for the contemporary audience. These responsive works are displayed in the exhibit as well. Neither City Museum nor Parker Painter communicated with the AAF prior to producing the messenger bags or creating the responsive pieces.

UNDERSTANDING COPYRIGHT INFRINGEMENT

When a copyright owner believes their work has been infringed, they may bring suit against the alleged infringer. The test to establish copyright infringement is fairly straightforward. In order to prevail, the copyright owner must establish (1) the alleged infringer had access to the work, (2) there is a substantial similarity between the works, and (3) there was an unlawful appropriation of the copyrighted work.[7] The "substantial similarity" condition requires that there be a "likeness between [the works] great enough to give rise to an inference that the [alleged infringer] took ideas from the [copyright owner's] work."[8] This substantial similarity, coupled with access to the copyrighted work and unlawful appropriation, establishes infringement.

In our hypothetical, Agatha Artist's copyrights are still in force. She passed away in 1990, and copyright in the work lasts seventy years past her death, or until 2060. Under the copyright laws in effect in 1990, copyright vested in the drawing at creation with no formality or deposit requirements.[9] City Museum has apparently exerted a right held by the AAF in the creation of the messenger bags, because the bags carry a reproduction of the drawing and the AAF holds Artist's copyrights. The elements of copyright infringement also appear to be satisfied under the hypothetical in regard to the messenger bags: (1) as the owner, City Museum has access to the drawing; (2) there is substantial similarity between the works, as the bags carry an exact replica of the drawing; and (3) the appropriation of the drawing was done without the AAF's permission and was thus unlawful. Based on the facts in the hypothetical, it does appear that City Museum has committed copyright infringement.

The facts in regard to Parker Painter's works are a little more complicated. In evaluating the elements of copyright infringement: (1) Painter is in residence at City Museum and has access to the drawing; (2) it is unclear what level of similarity exists between the paintings and Artist's drawings, as they appear to be inspired by but not replicas of the drawing; and (3) the appropriation, if it was an appropriation, would have been completed without the AAF's permission. Here, without knowing more about the paintings themselves and what Painter means by "inspired," it is not fully clear that an infringement has occurred.

Legal Remedies for Copyright Infringement

Remedies for copyright infringement include temporary and final injunctions to prevent or restrain infringement,[10] impounding and destruction of the infringing articles,[11] actual or statutory monetary damages,[12] or criminal charges in the case of willful infringement under certain circumstances.[13]

If the AAF wished to pursue a copyright infringement action against City Museum and/or Parker Painter, the AAF would first have to establish that the copyright had been registered. While registration with the U.S. Copyright Office is no longer required to obtain copyright protection, registration *is* required prior to pursuing a civil infringement action.[14] Once prior registration is confirmed (or application made and registration received), the copyright holder could pursue an infringement action against City Museum and/or Parker Painter.

THE FAIR USE DOCTRINE

The Copyright Act provides various limitations on a copyright owner's exclusive rights.[15] One of the most important limitations for museums is the fair use doctrine, which initially grew out of case law but is now codified in the Copyright Act.[16] Understand, fair use is an affirmative defense to copyright infringement. This means that just because an infringing use is claimed to be conducted under the auspices of fair use does not mean the infringer cannot or will not be subject to a cease-and-desist notice or legal action. It also does not mean a lawsuit will be thrown out by the courts once it is filed. Rather, it places the burden on the alleged infringer to prove that even though an infringement occurred, such infringement was, in fact, fair use and therefore protected under the Copyright Act. For good or bad, reliance on fair use can still result in litigation, with all the associated monetary and personal costs that go into defending a suit.

This is not to detract from the importance of fair use in our copyright system. Copyright protection is enshrined in our Constitution's Copyright Clause, with its stated purpose therein to "promote the Progress of Science and useful Arts, by securing for limited Times to Authors and Inventors the exclusive Right to their respective Writings and Discoveries."[17] This is a noble purpose, and fair use "permits [and requires] courts to avoid rigid application of the copyright statute when, on occasion, it would stifle the very creativity which [copyright] is designed to foster."[18] In other words, the fair use doctrine permits the courts to balance the constitutionally protected rights of authors with the equally protected rights of the public to comment on those authors' works.

The Four Fair Use Factors

The Copyright Act provides examples of when fair use may apply. The examples in the statute are not exhaustive, merely illustrative, and the examples to likely pertain to museums include "criticism, comment, . . . teaching, . . . scholarship, or research. . . ."[19] The statute also provides the four factors that courts consider in determining if a use qualifies as fair. These are:

1. "the purpose and character of the use, including whether such use is of a commercial nature or is for nonprofit educational purposes";[20]
2. "the nature of the copyrighted work";[21]
3. "the amount and substantiality of the portion used in relation to the copyrighted work as a whole; and"[22]
4. "the effect of the use upon the potential market for or value of the copyrighted work."[23]

These four factors are considered together as a whole, and one factor will not outweigh the others to find that fair use exists. As a result, any determination of fair use requires a specific analysis of the facts at hand in each individual case.[24] This also means that the mere fact that a use is a nonprofit, educational one does not in any way guarantee that the use will be found to be fair use under application of the test.[25] For example, under the first factor, even if it is a museum or another nonprofit, educational institution that is raising the fair use defense, the other three factors will still be considered and balanced.

Regarding the second factor, the nature of the work, the court will consider, for instance, whether the copyrighted work is fiction or nonfiction. Also considered is whether the work is published or unpublished. The fact that a work is unpublished does not prevent an infringement from being found to be fair use,[26] but it is something the courts will carefully consider.[27]

The "amount and substantiality" of the amount used, the third fair use factor, is perhaps the factor that is most dependent on the individual facts of the case. There is a case in which the copying of an entire television program was considered fair.[28] Conversely, there is a case in which copying and publishing just a few short sentences from a memoir was considered substantial, because the passages copied went to "the heart of the book."[29] Clearly, it is not enough to rely on taking less than a certain percentage or other bright-line rules when it comes to the amount and substantiality factor.

Finally, note that the fourth factor goes to the *potential* market, not the actual market. Just because the copyright owner is not currently exploiting the work does not mean this factor finds in favor of fair use. The copyright owner could decide to exploit the work in the future, and the impact of the infringement will therefore be considered.

Returning to our hypothetical, application of the four fair use factors to the messenger bags does not appear to support City Museum. First, while the museum is a nonprofit institution, the purpose of the use is commercial. The messenger bags were created for sale in the museum store. Second, the nature of the drawing itself is a creative work. Third, City Museum reproduced the drawing in its entirety. Fourth and finally, while we do not have enough facts here to analyze the effect of the messenger bags on the potential market, the fact that the AAF exists and has monetized other works by Agatha Artist does suggest there is a potential future market for or value to the work that has been impacted by City Museum's actions.

As above, with the analysis of the potential infringement action against Parker Painter, the analysis here regarding fair use is more complicated. First, the purpose of the use here appears to be commentary and possibly noncommercial. Second, again, the nature of the drawing is that it is a creative work. Third, it is unclear what is the amount and substantiality of the portion used by Painter. Based on the facts, it appears Painter was inspired by Artist's drawing but did not replicate it. Analysis by the court, likely with the assistance of expert testimony, would be necessary to determine this factor. And finally, we again do not have enough information in the hypothetical to analyze the impact of the paintings on the potential future market for or value of the drawing. Therefore, additional facts and much analysis are necessary to determine whether there would be a finding of fair use. This highlights the fact-specific nature of fair use, as minor changes to the hypothetical could drastically change the outcome.

Copyright Infringement and Statutory Damages

As discussed above, when an infringement of copyright occurs, the Copyright Act provides for a variety of available damages, including statutory damages. Statutory damages are different from actual damages, in that statutory damages are based on what is permitted in the language of the statute and not based on the actual harm suffered by the copyright owner. The amount of statutory damages depends on the facts of the case, and the statute raises and lowers the permitted amount of statutory damages depending on whether the infringement was or was not willful or if the infringer "was not aware and had no reason to believe" the acts conducted constituted copyright infringement.[30]

The statute also provides that in the case of a finding of fair use, the court shall not impose statutory damages if certain requirements are met by the infringing party. The scenario that most applies to museums is when the infringer was the employee or agent of a qualifying nonprofit educational institution and was working within the scope of that employment when she infringed upon the copyright by making reproductions.[31] In such a scenario, a finding of fair use should prevent the awarding of statutory damages to the copyright owner despite the infringement.

In our hypothetical, if City Museum was found to have infringed on the drawing with the production of the messenger bags and there was no finding of fair use, they could be subject to monetary and nonmonetary damages. This means not just paying of monies to the AAF, but also the bags could be seized and destroyed. If Parker Painter was found to have infringed upon the drawing and there was no finding of fair use, the same remedies could be sought against Painter. As City Museum commissioned the works, it could be liable for some part of those monetary damages as well.

CONCLUSION

Fair use protects the public's access to copyrighted works, permitting a robust culture of comment, criticism, and education. However, the fair use doctrine does not completely erase the protections afforded to copyright owners—our culture's artistic creators—in favor of public comment and dialogue. Rather, fair use is a means to balance two important but competing interests. Museums should carefully consider the use with which they are using a copyrighted work and determine in a thoughtful and honest manner whether the proposed use is truly fair, furthering the interests of commentary, criticism, and education. Such use is beneficial to the museum's audience and the public at large, but uses that are not fair and are merely infringing and place the museum in a position of exploiting our society's artistic creators, whom the museum should instead be uplifting and supporting.

NOTES

1. 17 U.S.C. § 106(1).
2. Ibid. § 106(2).
3. Ibid. § 106(3).
4. Ibid. §§ 106(4), (6).
5. Ibid. § 106(5). Regarding the public display of works, 17 U.S.C. 109(c) provides a provision that permits the public display of lawfully made copies without the permission of the copyright owner. This is discussed in more depth in chapter 4.
6. Ibid. § 501.
7. *Wallace Computer Systems*, 837 F.Supp. at 1416.
8. Ibid.
9. See chapter 4 in general, and table 4.2 specifically regarding copyright creation and terms.
10. 17 U.S.C. at § 502.

11. Ibid. §§ 503(a), (b).

12. Ibid. § 504.

13. Ibid. § 505.

14. Ibid. § 411. Until recently, there had been a circuit split (federal courts were not in agreement) as to when an infringement action could actually be brought. In some federal circuits, an action could commence once the application had been made, including the associated deposit and payment of the application fee. This was the so-called application approach. However, other federal circuits stated the application alone was not sufficient and an infringement action could only commence once the registration had actually been issued. This was the so-called registration approach. As registrations can take months after application to be issued, this created a fairly significant difference in when an action could be brought to the courts depending on the location of the parties. However, in 2019 the Supreme Court heard a case that settled the matter between the circuits, officially establishing that "registration occurs, and a copyright claimant may commence an infringement suit, when the Copyright Office registers a copyright." *Fourth Estate Public Benefit Corp. v. Wall-Street .com*, 586 U.S. ___ (2019). Further: "The registration approach, we conclude, reflects the only satisfactory reading of §411(a)'s text." Ibid.

15. See 17 U.S.C. §§ 107–118.

16. Ibid. § 107.

17. U.S. Const. art. 1, § 8, cl. 8.

18. *Campbell*, 501 U.S. at 577, citation omitted.

19. 17 U.S.C. § 107.

20. Ibid.

21. Ibid.

22. Ibid.

23. Ibid.

24. "The task is not to be simplified with bright-line rules, for the statute, like the doctrine it recognized, calls for case-by-case analysis." *Campbell*, 501 U.S. at 577.

25. "[T]he mere fact that a use is educational and not for profit does not insulate it from a finding of infringement, any more than the commercial character of a use bars a funding of fairness." Ibid., 584.

26. 17 U.S.C. § 107.

27. "[A]ll the rights protected by copyright, including the right of first publication, are subject to fair use. . . . Under ordinary circumstances, . . . the author's right to control the first public appearance of his undisseminated expression will outweigh a claim of fair use. . . . [T]he Court gives special weight to the fact that the copied work is unpublished when considering the second factor, the nature of the copyrighted work." *Salinger v. Random House, Inc.*, 811 F.2d 90, 95-96 (2d Cir. 1987).

28. For instance, see *Sony Corp. of America v. Universal City Studios, Inc.*, 464 U.S. 417 (1984), where the copying of entire television programs using Betamax and other VCRs by individuals so they could watch the programs at their own leisure ("time-shifting") was found to be fair use.

29. *Harper & Row*, 471 U.S. at 565.

30. 17 U.S.C. §§ 504(c)(1), (2).

31. Ibid.

CHAPTER 6

AN INTRODUCTION TO TRADEMARKS

Trademark is a form of intellectual property where the purpose is to assist the consumer in distinguishing the source of goods. The symbol used as a trademark may be a word, phrase, image, sound, or any other indicator as permitted by the very wide definition found in the Lanham Act,[1] which is the federal statute that governs trademark law. The ultimate purpose is to distinguish sellers for the benefit of the consumer, and therefore the question in comparing marks is whether the newly proposed mark will create consumer confusion as to source. The benefit to the consumer is that her shopping costs are reduced, in that she can rely on the trademark to ensure the product will be made by the same producer as other goods carrying the mark and therefore meet the same quality expectations.[2] While the intended beneficiary of trademark law is the consumer, the producer also benefits from use of the mark. It is because of trademark law that the producer can ensure she will be the one to reap any benefits from the mark, such as financial gain or increased reputation, as competitors and imitators are barred from using the mark.[3]

For museums, trademark law can provide a means for the museum to protect its public image. A museum's name, logo, exhibition titles, event names, and overall branding can be used in the marketplace to distinguish the museum from other institutions. A museum's name and logo, when presented in the marketplace through goods, on letterhead, in advertising, and other means, carries with it the institutional reputation. The public comes to associate the goods or services produced by the museum with its name and logo, making effective logos readily identifiable to the public, sometimes even without the accompanying name. Think of the Museum of Modern Art "MoMA" textual logo or the Smithsonian Institution's sunburst logo. These are just as familiar as the Nike "swoosh" or the Starbucks twin-tailed "Siren," with no identifying text necessary to convey to the public what producer is represented by the logo.

Trademark law allows the museum to protect that reputation and goodwill by prohibiting others to use the museum's mark. It also allows the public to identify that a good is provided by the museum and not a competitor. For example, imagine an art museum opens in New York City. It adopts the name "New York Metropolitan Museum" and produces exhibitions, provides lectures and symposium, and begins to acquire a stellar collection of contemporary and modern art. This museum would likely cause significant consumer confusion, as its name and activities closely mirror those of the preexisting Metropolitan Museum of Art. The public may be confused as to which institution is the city's beloved "Met." However, trademark law would prevent this scenario, as the upstart "New York Metropolitan Museum" would likely be found to be infringing on the trademark of the "Metropolitan Museum of Art."[4]

Trademark provides various levels of protection, and the producer must meet certain criteria to maintain that protection. Because a producer can operate in the marketplace indefinitely, trademark law does not limit how long a trademark can be protected for. This is an important distinction from copyright, where protections last for a limited time before the copyrighted work falls into the public domain and can be exploited by any person for any reason. So long as a producer continues to use the mark in the marketplace to identify the source of goods, trademark protection can essentially last forever, assuming all requirements are met as outlined below.

LEVELS OF TRADEMARK PROTECTION

Trademarks can be protected at common law, under state law, or under federal law. These different levels of protection each have advantages and disadvantages, and a producer should consider which level of protection is most beneficial for the particular product and their needs. In general, the higher the level of protection, the more financial costs are associated with gaining the protection, generally through filing fees, and the more procedural requirements there are to maintain the protection. The lower levels of protection are comparatively cheaper to obtain, but less protection is afforded, both in scope and geographic coverage.

Common Law Trademark Protection

Common law provides that a mark will be protected if it is used in the market to identify goods that originate from a single source and if the mark is used to distinguish the goods from those of competitors. So long as this test is met, the trademark will provide protection to the producer as soon as its use in the market begins, even though the mark has not been registered. And since the mark is not registered, the producer saves the monetary investment of applying for registration with a state agency or the United States Patent and Trademark Office (USPTO).

The limitation to this common law protection is that the mark cannot be "generic" or "descriptive" of the goods offered under the mark (see below). Where two identical or confusingly similar marks are used in the marketplace, the producer's rights are governed by priority of use. The senior user (the producer who entered the marketplace first) has greater common law rights to the mark than the junior user (the producer who entered the marketplace subsequently).

State Trademark Protection

Besides relying on common law protection, a producer may seek state registration of the mark. While a number of states offer registration of marks that are used in commerce within that state, the state registration tends to not offer the same level of protection as federal registration. However, state registration is often a shorter process and a more financially economical option compared with the federal registration process. State protection only provides rights in the state where the mark is registered. If a producer seeks nationwide protection, then the producer must file for federal protection.

Federal Trademark Protection

The greatest level of protection afforded to trademarks is provided by federal registration through the USPTO. There are two options for federal registration, the Principal Register and the Supplemental Register. To qualify for the Principal Register, the proposed mark must already be actively used in commerce, and the mark must meet statutory registration requirements.[5] If the mark is "capable of distinguishing applicant's good or services" but it does not meet the requirements of the Principal Register, it may be eligible for the Supplemental Register.[6]

Table 6.1.   Trademark Renewal Deadlines and Forms

Form to File	When to File	Grace Period	Consequence of Failure to File
Principal Register			
Declaration of Use (Section 8 Declaration)	Between fifth and sixth year following registration AND with every Section 9 Renewal filing	Six months, with additional fee owed	Cancellation of Mark
Renewal Application (Section 9 Renewal)	Between ninth and tenth year following registration AND Before the end of each successive ten-year period following registration	Six months, with additional fee owed	Cancellation of Mark
Declaration of Incontestability (Section 15 Declaration) *optional	Within one year after a five-year period of continuous use in commerce.	N/A	N/A
Supplemental Register			
Declaration of Use or Excusable Non-Use (Section 71 Affidavit)	Between fifth and sixth year following registration AND Between ninth and tenth year following registration AND Before the end of each successive ten-year period following registration	6 months, with additional fee owed	Cancellation of Mark

The trademark renewal information provided here is correct as of the time of writing and may have since been amended. Consult current law or legal counsel. Only one mark may be filed in an application, so additional marks will require their own applications and associated filing fees. Further, each class of goods and/or services contained in the application must be accompanied by their own application fee.

By obtaining a federal registration on the Principal Register, a producer can prevent any subsequent use of a confusingly similar mark that is adopted after the producer's registration filing date anywhere in the United States where the producer currently uses the mark or has immediate intention to use the mark. The federal registration acts as presumptive evidence that the mark's registration is valid and that the registrant owns the mark.[7] Federal registration on the Principal Register lasts for ten years and can be renewed indefinitely, so long as the mark continues to meet registration requirements.[8]

THE SPECTRUM OF DISTINCTIVENESS

A mark's ability to function as such, and thus its ability to be registered at the state or federal level or to provide common law protection, depends on where it falls on the so-called spectrum of distinctiveness. From most protected to least protected, marks are understood as (1) arbitrary/fanciful, (2) suggestive, (3) descriptive, or (4) generic.[9] It is important to understand that a mark that falls into one category of the spectrum for a certain product may fall into an entirely different category for another product.[10]

Highest Protection: Arbitrary and Fanciful Marks

The highest level of protection goes to marks that are either arbitrary or fanciful. These categories apply to marks that do not describe the product in any way. They are considered inherently distinctive and therefore are awarded the highest level of legal protection. A mark is arbitrary when its English language meaning is entirely unrelated to the product it identifies. Perhaps the most common example of an arbitrary mark is "APPLE," used to identify computers. A fanciful mark is one composed of words invented for use as a mark. A common example of a fanciful mark is "KODAK," a word invented specifically to market photography products.

Intermediate Protection: Suggestive Marks

The next category along the spectrum of distinctiveness is suggestive, and like arbitrary and fanciful marks, suggestive marks are able to be registered with the USPTO on their own strength.[11] Suggestive marks are entitled to this protection because the Lanham Act and USPTO consider them to be inherently distinctive. However, because they are not considered to be as distinctive as fanciful and arbitrary marks, suggestive marks receive a narrower level of legal protection. A mark is suggestive if it takes a little work on the part of the consumer to make the mental connection between the mark and the goods and/or services. If the mark requires that the consumer use his imagination to understand the nature of the goods identified, it is a suggestive mark.[12]

Weakest Protection: Descriptive Marks and Secondary Meaning

Moving along the spectrum of distinctiveness, marks categorized as descriptive are those that, as the name suggests, merely describe the goods identified.[13] Such marks are not eligible for immediate registration, because allowing registration would grant an exclusive right to use a term to one sole producer in the marketplace, even though that term merely describes the goods offered. Imagine, for instance, if a producer could trademark "MODERN ART MUSEUM," she would be prohibiting any other producer in the marketplace from using the term. The limitation on the registration of descriptive marks prevents such a scenario. The Lanham Act permits the registration of descriptive marks if the mark has "become distinctive" of the goods in the marketplace.[14] In order to prove that the mark has become distinctive despite being descriptive, the registration must include evidence of the mark's substantially exclusive use by the registrant and the registrant's continuous use of the mark on the goods for five years prior to the application.[15] Registration of descriptive marks is permitted solely where the mark has become closely identified with one producer's goods.[16] This acquired distinctiveness is called "secondary meaning."[17]

It can be difficult to determine if a mark is suggestive or descriptive. The main distinction is that a descriptive mark merely describes the good offered, while a suggestive mark requires that little extra bit of imaginative interpretation on the part of the consumer.

Ineligible for Protection: Generic Marks

The last category on the spectrum of distinctiveness are generic marks. These marks consist of the common descriptor of the product.[18] Because they are purely descriptive, even acquisition of a secondary meaning in the mind of the consumer cannot elevate a generic mark to being eligible for registration or protection.[19] The fact that the term was used over a course of years or that it was extensively used by the producer has no bearing; it remains ineligible for registration. Again, this goes back to the policy behind trademark law. Permitting the registration of generic terms would deprive all competitors of using the product's name.[20] A term can start out as generic (for instance, telephone or pencil), or it can become generic over time (such as escalator or aspirin). Marks that become generic lose their trademark protection.[21]

Table 6.2. The Spectrum of Distinctiveness

Type of Mark	Description	Example	Notes	Level of Protection
Arbitrary	Meaning of the mark is unrelated to the product	"APPLE" for computers "DUTCH BOY" for paint	Inherently distinctive, may be immediately registered with PTO	Strongest
Fanciful	Invented for use as a mark	"KODAK" "EXXON"	Inherently distinctive, may be immediately registered with PTO	Strongest
Suggestive	Mark requires that the consumer use his imagination to understand the nature of the goods	"GREYHOUND" for buses "PLAYBOY" for a men's magazine	Inherently distinctive, may be immediately registered with PTO	Intermediate
Descriptive	Describes the goods identified	"OPTICS OUTLET" for eyewear store "SNEAKERLAND" for shoe store	Mark must acquire distinctiveness ("secondary meaning") before it may be registered with PTO	Weakest
Generic	Purely descriptive	"MILK" "ESCALATOR" "ASPIRIN"	Not eligible for registration. A mark may start out generic, or it may become generic over time	No Protection

Further Considerations: Foreign Words and Functional Components

Foreign words are also subject to the spectrum of distinctiveness through the application of the "doctrine of foreign equivalents." This doctrine requires that modern foreign language marks be translated into their English equivalent in order to determine the mark's strength.[22] The doctrine is generally not applied to dead or obscure languages.[23] For example, imagine a company produces bottled water and wishes to use the mark "AGUA," which is Spanish for "water." Such a mark would be descriptive in this example.[24] It merely describes the product, albeit with a non-English word. Now imagine that instead of a bottled water manufacturer, it is a company that produces women's clothing that wishes to use the "AGUA" mark. In this scenario, "AGUA" would be arbitrary, as the word "water" has nothing to do with women's clothing. Application of the doctrine of foreign equivalents would suggest this mark is arbitrary and entitled to trademark protection. In comparison, imagine the bottled water company wishes to use as its mark the work "AKVO," which is Esperanto for "water." Esperanto is a constructed language with approximately one thousand native speakers worldwide.[25] This proposed mark *may* be considered suggestive when applied to a water bottle, if the trademark examiner believes Esperanto to be an obscure language when applying the doctrine of foreign equivalents.

Another consideration is the functionality doctrine, which prevents a functional component of the goods to serve as a mark. This goes to one of the purposes of trademark law, namely "to promote competition by protecting a firm's reputation. . . ."[26] If a producer could trademark a product's functional features, those features could essentially be protected by the producer's trademark monopoly forever.[27] This stifles competition and is a disadvantage to the consumer.

Further Considerations: Immoral and Scandalous Marks

Until recently, it was not possible to receive a federal trademark registration for certain "offensive" marks. This was based on a clause in the Lanham Act,[28] which stated that marks that "[consist] of or [comprise] immoral, deceptive, or scandalous matter . . ." would be "refused registration on the principal register. . . ."[29] However, two recent Supreme Court decisions have found this provision to be unconstitutional.

In the first case, the Court held that the disparagement clause was a violation of free speech under the First Amendment, as the clause was not narrowly tailored and went further than necessary to serve the government's interests.[30] In the second decision, which again considered the disparagement clause, the Court again held the clause violated free speech in regard to the registration of "immoral" marks.[31]

REQUIREMENTS TO MAINTAIN FEDERAL REGISTRATION PROTECTION

In addition to filing all necessary forms with the USPTO in a timely manner, producers must meet specific requirements to continue enjoying the benefits of federal registration. If a producer fails to meet these requirements, the mark may be canceled and federal protection lost.

Active Use and Naked Licensing

Trademark law protects marks that are being actively used in the marketplace to identify the source of goods. Therefore, a mark that has not been actively used for three years is presumed abandoned.[32] Additionally, trademark rights may be lost if the mark owner engages in so-called naked licensing, which means the mark owner failed to control the mark's use by third parties. Naked licensing is essentially permitting infringement of the mark with no concern for the creation of consumer confusion or the maintenance of the quality of goods. Such behavior weakens the mark and denies consumers the benefits of trademark law. Essentially, the law will not help mark owners who do not help themselves, requiring those who hold a mark to actively police it.[33]

Notice of Registration

Federally registered trademarks are entitled to bear a notice indicating they have obtained registration. This notice can take the form of the words "Registered in U.S. Patent and Trademark Office," the abbreviation "Reg. U.S. Pat. & Tm. Off.," or most commonly the symbol of the letter "R" inside a circle: ®.[34] Only federally registered marks should bear one of these notices. In comparison, the superscript "TM" mark, ™, indicates the owner is claiming the displayed mark is a trademark, but the mark has not been registered. Essentially, the owner is claiming common law protection of the mark.

SERVICE MARKS AND TRADE DRESS

There are two final categories that bear mention. First, service marks fall under trademark law.[35] "Services" refers to specific services offered by a business that are distinct activities offered by the business owner for the consumer's benefit. The mark used by the business owner to identify the service is a service mark. One mark may serve as both a service mark and a trademark. For instance, an exhibition title can function as both. Imagine an exhibit entitled "Capturing the Cosmos." When "Capturing the Cosmos" is used in connection with the exhibition itself, curator talks, and special events, it is a service mark, as these are all services offered by the museum. However, when "Capturing the Cosmos" is placed on T-shirts, tote bags, coffee mugs, and posters, it is a trademark, identifying the source of the goods. Service marks are categorized on the same spectrum of distinctiveness as trademarks in determining eligibility for registration and strength.[36]

The second category worth mentioning briefly is trade dress, which refers to the total packaging of a product rather than merely the placement of a mark on the product to identify goods.[37] Trade dress is a form of trademark that is entitled to the same legal protections, and it can be registered, with the limitation that the trade dress cannot be functional.[38] An example would be the McDonald's Happy Meal. While the "golden arches" themselves are a trademark, the distinctive box the Happy Meal is served in, including its color scheme and shape, are trade dress.

CONCLUSION

Trademark law provides a means for producers such as museums to protect their brand. However, as evidenced here, it is important for museums to select a trademark that is eligible for protection and not merely generic or overly descriptive without acquisition of secondary meaning. Well-chosen trademarks can help distinguish the museum in the marketplace, allowing consumers, visitors, and members to easily recognize the museum's products and positively promote the museum's brand in the marketplace. Trademark registration and ongoing maintenance can be costly and time consuming, but common law protections may offer a sufficient level of protection for institutions with less financial or staff resources.

NOTES

1. 15 U.S.C. §§ 1051-1129.
2. *Qualitex*, 514 U.S. at 163–64.
3. Ibid., 164.
4. There are other hurdles to this fictional museum adopting the "New York Metropolitan Museum" name. Perhaps most notably, the New York State Department of State, Division of Corporations will not permit the registration of a business name that is not "distinguishable" from an existing name in its Corporation of Business Entity Database. The same holds true of other states as well.
5. 15 U.S.C. § 1051.
6. Ibid. § 1091.
7. Ibid. § 1115.
8. Ibid. § 1058.
9. *Abercrombie*, 537 F.2d at 9.
10. Ibid., 9.
11. Ibid., 11.
12. Ibid.
13. Ibid., 10.
14. 15 U.S.C. § 1052(f).
15. *Abercrombie*, 537 F.2d at 10.
16. *Carter-Wallace*, 434 F.2d at 800.
17. Besides descriptive marks, there are some other types of marks that require secondary meaning to be registered with the PTO, such as marks that consist of a personal name or that consist of the title of single artistic works.
18. *Abercrombie*, 537 F.2d at 9.
19. "[N]o matter how much money and effort the user of a generic term has poured into promoting the sale of its merchandise . . . , it cannot deprive competing manufacturers of the product of the right to call an article by its name." Ibid.
20. Ibid. In an interesting twist, a federal court recently held that adding a top-level domain such as ".com" to an otherwise generic mark may provide the necessary distinctiveness to qualify for trademark registration. *Booking.com B.V. v. U.S. Patent & Trademark Office*, No. 17-2458, (4th Cir. Feb. 4, 2019). The popular website had sought federal trademarks for "BOOKING.COM" despite the word "booking" being generic in relation to the services provided by the website such as hotel reservations. The USPTO denied the registration, but the district and appellate courts found that "BOOKING.COM" was not generic, even if "booking" alone was. On appeal, the Supreme Court affirmed, explaining that "only one entity can occupy a particular Internet domain name at a time, so '[a] consumer who is familiar with that aspect of the domain-name system can infer that BOOKING.COM refers to some specific entity.'" *U.S. Patent & Trademark Office v. Booking.com B.V.*, 591 U.S. ___ (2020), quoting the Brief for Petitioners at 40. Continuing: "Thus, consumers could understand a given 'generic.com' term to describe the corresponding website or to identify the website's proprietor." *USPTO v. Booking.com*. Finally, the Court reinforced the underlying purpose of trademark law, which is to aid consumers

in distinguishing the source of goods and services. "A term styled 'generic.com' is a generic name for a class of goods or services only if the term has that meaning to consumers." Ibid.

21. 15 U.S.C. § 1127.

22. Trademark Manual of Examining Protocol § 1207.01(b)(vi).

23. Ibid. § 1207.01(b)(vi)(B).

24. See *In re Bayer Aktiengesellschaft*, 2005 TTAB LEXIS 521, finding that a mark of "ASPIRINA," Spanish for "aspirin," was merely descriptive when applied to analgesics (painkillers).

25. "Esperanto," Wikipedia at www.wikipedia.org/Esperanto.

26. *Qualitex*, 514 U.S. at 164.

27. Ibid. If the producer has actually invented the functional feature, that feature is best protected by patent law, which gives the producer/inventor a term-limited monopoly. See "Patent."

28. Lanham Act § 2(a), 15 U.S.C. § 1052(a).

29. Ibid. Prior to the cases discussed below, the USPTO would reject a mark application if the mark was "shocking to the sense of truth, decency, or propriety; disgraceful; offensive; disreputable; . . . giving offense to the conscience or moral feelings; . . . [or] calling out [for] condemnation." *In re Mavety Media Group Ltd.*, 33 F.3d 1367 (Fed. Cir. 1994), citing *In re Riverbank Canning Co.*, 95 F.2d 327, 328, 37 USPQ 268, 269 (CCPA 1938) (citations omitted).

30. *Matal v. Tam*, 582 U.S. ___ (2017). Plaintiff Simon Tam sought to register the name of his band, The Slants. The USPTO denied the application, stating the proposed mark was potentially disparaging to those of Asian descent and cited the Lanham Act's disparagement clause. After a number of appeals, the Supreme Court held unanimously for Tam in an 8-0 decision.

31. *Iancu v. Brunetti*, 588 U.S. ___ (2019). Brunetti had sought registration of the mark "FUCT," the name of his clothing brand. While Brunetti claimed the mark was pronounced by reading each letter in turn as F-U-C-T, when read together it sounds like a common English vulgarity. Relying on its decision in *Matal v. Tam*, the Court found that the Lanham Act's prohibition on the registration of "immoral" or "scandalous" words was viewpoint based and a violation of the First Amendment.

> In Tam, for example, we did not pause to consider whether the disparagement clause might admit some permissible applications (say, to certain libelous speech) before striking it down. The Court's finding of viewpoint bias ended the matter. And similarly, it seems unlikely we would compare permissible and impermissible applications if Congress outright banned "offensive" (or to use some other examples, "divisive" or "subversive") speech. Once we have found that a law "aim[s] at the suppression of" views, why would it matter that Congress could have captured some of the same speech through a viewpoint-neutral statute? *Tam*, 582 U.S., at ___ (opinion of Kennedy, J.) (slip op., at 2). But in any event, the "immoral or scandalous" bar is substantially overbroad. There are a great many immoral and scandalous ideas in the world (even more than there are swear words), and the Lanham Act covers them all. It therefore violates the First Amendment.

Iancu v. Brunetti, 588 U.S. ___ (2019).

32. Trademark Manual of Examining Protocol § 1127.

33. In an example of this that generated a great deal of amusement in the national press, in 2010 the website ThinkGeek released an April Fool's Day item on their website—Canned Unicorn Meat. In their website listing, they gave their product the tagline "the new white meat," which the National Pork Board felt was too similar to their registered trademark "THE OTHER WHITE MEAT." While ThinkGeek did not claim a trademark in the tagline, the responsibility fell to the National Pork Board to police their mark. A cease-and-desist letter was sent by NPB attorneys, which ThinkGeek posted on their now-defunct blog, garnering widespread attention. While the actions of the NPB were seen by many commentators as humorless and unnecessary, an NPB spokesperson defended their attorney's action, stating, "Clearly there's some fun being had, and we can laugh, too. . . . But in the end [the attorneys are] just following the law." Eggen, Dan. (2010, June 22). "National Pork Board Targets ThinkGeek Web Site: Blame the Unicorns." *Washington Post*. https://www.washingtonpost.com/wp-dyn/content/article/2010/06/22/AR2010062201657.html?hpid=artslot. An image of the product can be seen in Jane McEntergart's June 24, 2010, article, "ThinkGeek in Trouble for Selling Unicorn Meat," at https://www.tomsguide.com/us/think-geek-thinkgeek-april-fools-unicorns,news-7174.html. The first page of the cease-and-desist letter can be found in Allie Townsend's June 21, 2010, article,

"Think Geek Gets Cease and Desist for April Fool's Day Canned Unicorn Meat," at https://techland.time
.com/2010/06/21/think-geek-gets-cease-and-desist-for-april-fools-day-canned-unicorn-meat/.

34. Trademark Manual of Examining Protocol. § 1111.

35. Ibid. § 1053.

36. Ibid.

37. Ibid. § 1125(a), "container for goods."

38. Ibid. § 1125(a)(3).

CHAPTER 7

INTELLECTUAL PROPERTY LICENSING

Licensing is the manner in which rights in intellectual property are transferred to a person other than the owner. The main focus for this discussion will be copyright licensing, as this applies most in the museum setting. Each of the exclusive rights an owner has in their copyrighted material is best visualized as a bundle of sticks, where each stick represents a different right in the work. An individual can own one or many of the sticks independently, and ownership of the sticks is entirely separate from ownership of the actual creative object that gave rise to the sticks.[1] This means that a museum can legally own a work, such as a painting or sculpture, and not have the legal ability to act on any of the copyright rights in that work, such as producing and selling posters depicting the work.

Initially, copyright is owned by the original author or authors of the work, or, in the case of works made for hire, by the employer of the author(s). Even if the work is sold, copyright remains with that original owner unless a different agreement is reached between the parties. That separate agreement *may* be a full and complete transfer of copyright to the new owner. More likely, however, the transfer will be through a license.

Due to the fact that the rights under copyright are separate and distinct—each is its own stick—each right can be licensed individually. A license to create reproductions does not also convey a right to make derivative works, for instance. In other words, if an artist gives a museum the right to sell DVDs of the artist's short film, that does not mean the museum may also sell messenger bags featuring stills from the film. The terms of the license can and should explicitly state what is and is not permitted under the license.

COMMON TERMS FOUND IN LICENSES

Exclusive or Nonexclusive

There are a number of options and considerations when it comes to the terms of a license. The first is whether it will be exclusive or nonexclusive. An exclusive license transfers the specific right—the stick from the bundle—to the licensee, granting the licensee the right to be the only one exercising that right. Under an exclusive license, no one other than the licensee may exercise the rights of the transferred stick, including the original author(s). If the artist in our example above gives the museum an exclusive right to produce and sell DVDs of the artist's film, then no one else, including the artist, may do the same without violating the museum's exclusive license. Additionally, the artist may not purport to transfer that exclusive license to a third party, because the artist has already transferred that right to the museum exclusively. Further, regarding that specific right, the licensee has the power to prevent others from exercising that right.[2] If another company begins to produce and sell DVDs of the artist's film, the museum may sue to prevent the infringement of the museum's exclusive right.

In comparison, a nonexclusive right transfers the specific right to the licensee, but the licensor retains the right to transfer the right to additional parties or to exploit the right herself. Continuing our scenario from above, if the artist gave the museum a nonexclusive right to the museum to produce the DVDs, the artist would then be within her rights to transfer a second nonexclusive license to the competing company to do the same. Or, the artist could sell the DVDs herself. If the third-party company or artist then begins producing and selling DVDs of the film, the museum would have no remedy, since it merely owned a nonexclusive license to the right.

While this may sound like a negative situation for the museum, nonexclusive licenses are quite common and can be an advantage for all involved. For example, say a museum is producing an exhibition catalogue and wants to include a photograph of an artist's needlecrafts. The museum would seek a nonexclusive license to reproduce the work in its catalogue. There really is no reason in this scenario for the museum to seek an exclusive license. What harm would come to the museum if the needlecrafts were also reproduced in magazine articles or on the artist's website? Such exposure is beneficial to the artist's reputation and career and may also bring more visitors to the museum's exhibition. In this situation, the nonexclusive license is beneficial to both the licensor and the licensee and furthers both parties' interests.

Specific Rights Licensed

A second consideration is which rights will be transferred. Because copyright is a bundle of sticks, any one of the rights can be transferred while the owner retains the others. A license therefore must indicate which rights are being transferred to the licensee. While the museum may seek a license to reproduce images of the needlecrafts, the museum does not need to seek licenses for rights the museum will not be exploiting. Therefore, the museum here needs a fairly narrow license, not a license covering all the rights or sticks.

License Duration and Termination

The third consideration is the license's duration. While it is beneficial to most licensees to seek an unlimited duration license, meaning the license will effectively last forever, few licensors are willing to grant such a license, especially if it is an exclusive license. Instead, licensors may prefer to give a license that lasts for a limited duration, subject to renewal. This permits the parties to revisit the terms of the original license when it comes time for renewal.

Where licenses of any kind are granted for a term of decades or effectively forever, note that it will become subject to termination. Excluding works made for hire, the possibility of termination arises where the license was granted by the author and was not made by a bequest.[3]

Table 7.1. Requirements to Terminate a License Where the Original Transfer Occurred on or after January 1, 1978

Requirements to Terminate: All must be met to effect termination of the license.	Notes
The original transfer was made by the author.	The transfer was not executed in a will.
Termination is being made by the author or the author's heirs.	Who qualifies as heirs is defined in the Copyright Act and includes, among others, the author's widow or widower, the author's surviving children, and the author's surviving grandchildren.
The notice of termination must be an advance notice of future termination, must be in writing, and must be signed.	If the work was created by a single author, the author must sign.
	If the solo author is deceased, enough heirs must sign as to represent more than one-half interest in the author's termination right.
	If the work is a joint work, a majority of the authors must sign.
	If one or more authors are deceased, enough heirs must sign as to represent more than one-half interest in each author's termination right.
Termination is to be effected during the five-year period beginning at the end of thirty-five years from the original license.	If the license included the right of publication, the five-year period begins either at the end of thirty-five years of publication under the license or forty years from the execution of the license, whichever term ends earlier.
The notice must state the effective date of termination.	The effective date of termination must fall with the five-year period described above.
Notice must be served on the licensee not less than two years from termination date, and not more than ten years from termination date.	

Remember that termination does not apply to works made for hire. The transfer termination information provided here is correct as of the time of writing and may have since been amended. Consult current law or legal counsel.

Starting thirty-five years from the transfer, there is a five-year period during which termination may be effected by either the original author(s) or the heirs as defined by the Copyright Act.[4] The author(s) or heirs serve advance written notice to the licensee, stating the effective date of termination, and the notice must give the effective date of termination and must comply with the requirements set forth by the Register of Copyrights.[5] The termination date must fall within the five-year window.[6] Finally, the notice cannot be served on the licensee less than two years or more than ten years prior to the termination date.[7] Slightly different rules apply when the license included the right of publication.[8] The termination right cannot be avoided by making an agreement to not terminate in the future.[9] Once a license is effectively terminated, the rights in the license revert to the author(s) or heirs as defined by the statute.[10] However, some rights are retained by the licensee after termination, including the right to utilize derivative works that were created under the auspices of the original license.[11]

Additional Potential License Terms

The remaining considerations regarding license terms are fairly straightforward. Fourth, the license's geographic coverage must be considered. Does the license grant the licensee the right to worldwide rights, or only use in a limited geographic area? Fifth, what media does the license permit, such as print, digital, or T-shirts? Sixth, the license may limit use to black and white or color. Seventh, the license may permit reproduction in any size or only in certain sizes, whether measured in length and width or pixels. Eighth, the license may dictate in what resolution reproductions must be produced, often an attempt to maintain quality and clarity of the image. And ninth, the license can and should address what credit line, if any, should accompany the work.

Not all of these considerations will apply in every situation, and the specific situation between licensor and licensee may require discussion of topics not listed here. These are merely the considerations most likely to come into play for a museum seeking to license works.

Table 7.2. Examples of Various Considerations When Drawing Up a License

License term	Most expansive license	Limited license	Example of most expansive license	Example of limited license
Exclusivity	Exclusive	Nonexclusive	Licensor/Owner A grants an exclusive license to Licensee/Museum B in the Work titled "Bundle of Sticks."	Licensor/Owner A grants a nonexclusive license to Licensee/Museum B in the Work titled "Bundle of Sticks."
Which right(s)	All rights	Specific rights	Licensor grants all rights and privileges to Licensee, including, but not limited to, the right to publicly display, lend, reproduce, prepare derivative works.	Licensor grants Licensee the right to produce reproductions in the form of T-shirts, mugs, postcards, and magnets, and to distribute those reproductions to the public, subject to the following terms:
Duration	Unlimited duration	Limited duration	This license will exist in perpetuity,	This license will expire at the end of two (2) years from its effective date,
Geographic coverage	Worldwide	Limited geographic area	the rights granted herein are applicable worldwide,	the rights granted under this license exist solely within the continental United States and Canada,
Media	All media	Limited media	may be executed in all media, both those now in existence and unknown,	the rights may be executed in print only as enumerated above,
Color requirements	Black and white and color	Black and white or color	in both color and black and white,	in full color only,
Size	Any size	Limited sizes	in any physical or digital size,	limited in size to eight (8) inches by ten (10) inches,
Resolution	Any resolution	Certain resolutions	and in any resolution.	and only in a resolution of XXX pixels or higher.
Credit line	No credit line	Credit line	No credit line is required.	All uses must include the credit line of: "© Owner A, 2015."

The example language provided herein is for informational purposes only and does not represent legal advice as to proper language. Consult legal counsel.

Regardless of the rights transferred and the terms reached, note that any transfer of copyright ownership must be memorialized in a written document that is signed by the owner of the rights or the owner's agent.[12]

TRADEMARK AND SERVICE MARK LICENSING

Trademarks, as a form of intellectual property, may be licensed in a fashion similar to copyright. For instance, a children's museum may seek to license a particular toy to create their own version to sell in the museum store. Or a science museum may license its trademarked logo to a science-themed educational television show.

Licensing of trademarks very much mirrors the licensing of copyrights, with many of the same or similar considerations arising. Trademark owners are well advised to remember that when they give another entity the right to operate under the owner's trademark, the goodwill associated with that trademark is also transferred. A substandard product created under a museum's trademark will impact how the public views the museum, even if the museum did not produce the goods. Imagine an art museum licenses their logo to a company to create a line of silk scarves based on artworks in the museum's collection. Each scarf carries the museum's logo on the tag. The scarves are sold online and in high-end department stores nationwide. Unfortunately, they are of substandard quality, with uneven hems, irregular dimensions, and some arrive in stores with snags or pulls. Due to the quality of the scarves and the fact that the museum's logo is prominently visible on each one, it is possible the museum will be linked in the consumer's mind as producing lesser-quality goods. This is true even though the museum did not themselves select the manufacturer or cause the issues, because the placement of the museum's logo indicates a source of the goods to the consumer. The museum will be held in the consumer's mind as accountable for the substandard workmanship.

Similarly, if a science museum permits an educational television show to use its service mark,[13] the public perception will be that the science museum has had some oversight of the program and approves of the content. If the program is poorly produced, has a low production value, or contains many scientific inaccuracies, the public's perception of the museum will be impacted. Therefore, museums should be careful in the licensing of their marks, whether those are trademarks or service marks, as no amount of financial income will replace the public's good will if the museum's reputation is damaged due to the licensing agreement. As with copyrights, licensing of trademarks must be in writing and should be signed.[14]

CONCLUSION

Licensing can be a means of producing profit, marketing the museum and its collections to the public, or furthering the educational goals of the institution. When properly carried out, licenses open the collection and the institution to a whole new manner of reaching the public, such as presenting collection objects on a website, producing exhibition catalogues, or reproducing collection objects in television programs and films. However, not all licensing opportunities are positive, and licensing should be carried out with the museum's goals kept in focus and the museum's public perception to be maintained or elevated through the licensing process. With these goals in mind, a licensing program can be effectively implemented and carried out.

NOTES

1. 17 U.S.C. § 202.
2. Ibid. § 201(d)(2).
3. Ibid. § 203(a).
4. Ibid. § 203(a)(3).
5. Ibid. § 203(a)(4)(A), (B).
6. Ibid. § 203(a)(4)(A).
7. Ibid. § 203(a)(4)(A).
8. Where the license includes the right of publication, the five-year period starts at the end of thirty-five years from publication under the license or at the end of forty years from the date the license was executed, whichever ends sooner. Ibid. § 203(a)(3).
9. Ibid. § 203(a)(5).
10. Ibid. § 203(b).
11. Ibid. § 203(b)(1).
12. Ibid. § 204(a).
13. A service mark is substantially similar to trademarks under the law, but they identify the source of services in the marketplace instead of the source of goods.
14. 15 U.S.C. § 1060(a)(3).

CHAPTER 8

NONPROFIT CORPORATIONS AND TAX EXEMPTION

Most museums in America are nonprofit corporations with tax-exempt status. It is important to understand that these two categories are distinct, with different legal requirements both for creation and maintenance.

NONPROFIT CORPORATIONS

A nonprofit corporation is an incorporated organization organized and operated in a manner in which all profits are reinvested in the nonprofit purpose, as compare to being distributed to stakeholders, as in a for-profit corporation.[1] "Nonprofit" does not mean the corporation does not generate any profits. In fact, a nonprofit corporation that is not generating any profits will soon find itself out of business, as profits are necessary for the payment of expenses such as staff salaries, building mortgages, insurance, and utilities. Instead, the nonprofit corporation should be making profits to cover all its general operating expenses, and then using any additional profits after those expenses to further the corporation's nonprofit purpose, called the nondistribution constraint.

Incorporation Requirements: Articles of Incorporation and Bylaws

In order to obtain nonprofit status, the future corporation must meet the legal requirements to incorporate. Incorporation is governed by state law, so the specific requirements vary from one state to another. However, there are some general rules that will apply regardless of the state where incorporation is sought.

The organization will need to draft articles of incorporation, which will include, among other information, the organization's name, the names and addresses of the primary individuals who are establishing the organization, requirements for membership if applicable, and certain language required by the Internal Revenue Service (IRS) for when tax exemption is later sought.[2] Articles of incorporation are filed with the proper state government office, often the Department of State, which reviews and accepts them as part of the incorporation process. Articles of incorporation are a matter of public record, viewable by the general public.

The corporation may also draft bylaws, which are an internal document that details how the corporation operates, outlining rules and procedures. The bylaws, as an internal document, are easier to amend as needed, and requirements to do so should be included in the bylaws themselves. Generally, amendment is possible through a vote of the board of trustees, who are the individuals who oversee the operation of the corporation.[3] Unlike the articles of incorporation, bylaws generally do not have to be filed with the state.

Nonprofit Organizations and Attorney General Oversight

At the state level, nonprofit organizations are subject to oversight by the state's attorney general. The attorney general (AG) is the chief legal officer of the state and represents the public interest of the people in the state.[4] In relation to nonprofit and charitable organizations, the AG is mandated to investigate potential legal actions and, if necessary, commence appropriate legal actions. The AG is also charged with overseeing mergers by nonprofits as well as dissolutions.

As a public policy consideration, nonprofit organizations are understood to operate on some level for the public benefit. When a nonprofit (or charitable) organization engages in activities that go against the mission, misuses or misappropriates charitable donations, or in some other way works against the public's interest, it is the role of the AG to investigate those activities. This ensures that the benefits received by the organization by way of its nonprofit status are not abused. It also ensures that the citizens of the state can trust their donations to the organization will not be misused in some purpose other than furtherance of the organization's mission.[5]

TAX EXEMPTION

Once a nonprofit corporation is properly incorporated at the state level, it may choose to seek tax exemption at the federal level. Not all nonprofit corporations are necessarily tax-exempt. The Internal Revenue Code (IRC) has very specific requirements that must be met by the nonprofit if it is to be recognized as tax-exempt. Tax exemption is a benefit the Code bestows on certain organizations in recognition of the service they perform for society as a whole, and tax exemption is not guaranteed to corporations merely because they satisfy a particular state's requirements for nonprofit incorporation.

Categories of Tax-Exempt Organizations

There are a number of different types of tax-exempt organizations under the Internal Revenue Code. While they are all exempt from paying (many) taxes, the requirements of the application process are varied. Additionally, one large benefit that many museums enjoy—that their donors can take a deduction for their charitable contributions—does not exist for all types of tax exemption.[6.]

Most museums that have tax-exempt recognition are categorized as 501(c)(3) organizations. There are a large number of other tax-exempt categories (over twenty), but a museum that is properly organized and operated (see below) should be able to establish its qualification for 501(c)(3) status and thus enjoy both the taxation exemption and the benefit to donors.[7]

Obtaining Tax-Exempt Status[8]

An organization recognized as nonprofit at the state level may elect to pursue federal tax-exempt status. The first step in this process is the filing of IRS Form 1023, Application for Recognition of Exemption Under Section 501(c)(3) of the Internal Revenue Code. Attached to the form will be all necessary and required supporting documents, including the organizing document (such as the articles of incorporation), bylaws, and any necessary explanations or additional information.[9]

The Code provides that only certain organizations are exempt from taxation.

> Corporations . . . organized and operated exclusively for . . . charitable, . . . or educational purposes, . . . no part of the net earnings of which inures to the benefit of any private shareholder or individual, no substantial part of the activities of which is carrying on propaganda, or otherwise attempting, to influence legislation, . . . and which does not participate in, or intervene in . . . ,any political campaign on behalf of (or in opposition to) any candidate for public office.[10]

There are a number of clauses and associated tests contained within this requirement, which will be examined below.

Table 8.1. Tests for Tax Exemption for Section 501(c)(3) Organizations

Test Name	Test Components	Component Requirement
Organizational Test	Proper exempt purpose	The purpose of the organization, as stated in the founding document, must be an exempt purpose found in IRC section 501(c)(3).
	Distribution of assets upon dissolution	The founding document must require that upon dissolution, any remaining assets will be distributed to a nonprofit organization with a similar mission to the organization.
Operational Test	Proper activities	The organization's activities primarily are conducted to an exempt purpose, with allowance for an insubstantial amount of nonexempt activities. "Insubstantial" has no bright-line rule.
Private Inurement Test	No private benefit	Individuals who benefit from the activities should be the public, not a small or limited group of individuals.
Political Activities Test	Three types of political activities regulated	1. Electioneering expressly prohibited 2. Direct lobbying permitted if insubstantial enough to fall under the IRC § 501(h) safe harbor 3. Indirect (grassroots) lobbying permitted if insubstantial enough to fall under the IRC § 501(h) safe harbor
	Reflects both the organizational and operational tests	1. Looks to the organization's founding documents (organizational) 2. Looks to the organization's actual activities (operational)

An organization must successfully meet all four tests in order to obtain federal tax-exempt status.

Test One: Proper Purpose under the IRC: The Organizational Test

The Code states that a tax-exempt organization must be "organized and operated exclusively for . . . charitable, . . . or educational purposes."[11] The proper purpose of an organization is one of the primary hurdles an organization must face to obtain tax-exempt status. The test has two components: the first regarding the organization's exempt purpose and the second regarding the distribution of the organization's assets upon dissolution.

First, established within the organization's founding document, generally the articles of incorporation, the purpose of the organization must meet the limited stated purposes available in the IRC. Specifically, the purpose must be one of the stated exempt purposes found in IRC section 501(c)(3), quoted above. Therefore, the organizational test is also one of the easiest hurdles, as it is met within the four corners of the organization's founding document.

If the founding document permits the organization to carry out nonexempt activities, or if the purposes stated within the founding document are broader than those permitted by the Code, then the organizational test will not be met and the organization will not obtain tax-exempt status.[12] Further, the limited exempt purpose can only be considered if it is in the founding document itself.[13] If the limited exempt purpose is merely found in the bylaws or other documents, is stated by the organization's trustees or officers, or demonstrated by the organization's current or past activities and operations, that will not suffice to meet the requirements of the organizational test.[14]

Second, the founding document must contain provisions addressing the distribution of the organization's assets upon dissolution.[15] While dissolution of the corporation falls under the purview of the state government, the process by which assets will be distributed must meet federal requirements to obtain tax exemption.[16] In regard to dissolution, the organizational test demands that any remaining assets will be distributed to nonprofit organizations with a similar mission.[17] In other words, despite dissolution, the organization's assets must be permanently dedicated to the organization's stated exempt purpose.[18]

Test Two: Proper Activities: The Operational Test

The Code speaks to how the organization is both organized and operated. Therefore, the second test is the operational test, which looks to the actual activities of the organization in order to determine whether the organization has a proper purpose.[19] While the language of the Code requires that the organization operate *exclusively* for a properly exempt purpose, in practice, the IRS merely requires the organization be *primarily* operated for an exempt purpose.[20]

Nonexempt activities are any activities carried out by the organization that do not relate back to the organization's exempt purpose. For example, a fine art museum may have an onsite store, and the sale of the goods in that store may or may not relate back to the museum's exempt purpose. Sale of reproductions of artworks in the museum's collection would relate to the exempt purpose, but sale of celebrity gossip magazines likely would be a nonexempt activity. Because this test relates to the specific exempt purpose and activities of an individual museum, it is highly fact-specific.[21]

If the nonexempt activities only make up an insubstantial part of the organization's activities as a whole, the organization may still be entitled to exempt status.[22] However, if a substantial amount of the organization's activities are deemed nonexempt, then the organization will not be entitled to tax-exempt status no matter the quality of proper exempt activities undertaken. In this way, the operational test looks past the language in the organization's founding documents to test the manner in which the organization actually conducts itself. If the non-profit meets the organizational test but operates itself in a manner that pursues a nonexempt purpose, such as if the organization's activities are comparable to those carried out by for-profit corporations, then the operational test will not be met.

In applying the operational test, a variety of factors will be considered, including:

1. the manner by which the activities are conducted,
2. whether or not the activities are of a commercial type, and
3. the amount of profit generated.

If the activities are commercial in nature, they may still be held to be in furtherance of an exempt purpose. The test takes a holistic approach, and the existence of any of these factors is not determinative.[23]

Test Three: Ensuring a Public Benefit: The Private Inurement Test

In order to qualify for tax-exempt status, the organization must function in a manner that benefits the public, not private shareholders, limited individuals, or specific members.[24] Similar to the operational test, the private inurement test looks to the actual activities of the organization to determine if there is, in fact, a public benefit. This ensures an organization is not benefiting from the privilege of tax exemption without providing a public benefit to justify that privilege.

The private inurement test does not prohibit business transactions between insiders (such as key employees or officers) and the organization, but any such transactions should be conducted at arm's length and with full disclosure of the relationships involved.[25]

Specifically of concern to museums, the promotion of arts has been recognized by the courts as being both charitable and educational.[26] However, just as with all other organization types, museums are not guaranteed tax exemption merely because they are museums. For instance, if a museum solely exhibits artworks where all the works are available for sale through consignment arrangements with the artists, and the museum receives a 10 percent commission on all the sales, the museum would not pass the private inurement test. The artists, who are receiving 90 percent of the proceeds of sales and who are being promoted by the museum, are receiving a private benefit from the museum's principal activity.[27] In comparison, while an artist may have her reputation bolstered by inclusion of her work in a museum exhibit, which may increase the value of her works on the open market, this is a side benefit of the museum's principal activity over which the museum has no control and is removed enough from the museum's activities so as to not affect the museum's tax-exempt status.

Test Four: A Limitation on Exempt Organizations: The Political Activities Test

The final test an organization must meet if it is to be recognized as tax-exempt is the political activities test. Political activities fall into three categories: direct lobbying, indirect or grassroots lobbying, and electioneering. Direct lobbying involves the direct contacting of legislators in an attempt to impact the passage of legislation. Indirect or grassroots lobbying is where the organization encourages the public to contact legislators to do the same. Finally, electioneering is to be involved in the election process, such as by endorsing a particular candidate or campaigning against a candidate's opponent. Of these three political activities, electioneering is entirely prohibited to tax-exempt organizations.[28] Lobbying, either direct or indirect, is permitted so long as it is limited to an insubstantial degree.[29]

In application, this test reflects aspects of both the organizational test and the operational test. Reflecting back to the organizational test, the political activities test looks to the organization's founding documents to see if they expressly empower the organization to undertake prohibited political activities.[30] Likewise, reflecting back to the operational test, the political activities test also looks to the actual activities engaged in by the organization to determine whether it is engaged in prohibited activities.[31]

Organizations such as museums that intend to obtain or maintain tax-exempt status are well advised to consult legal counsel before undertaking any activities that the IRS may construe as political activities.

MAINTAINING TAX-EXEMPT STATUS

Tax-exempt organizations must file annual reporting information with the IRS.[32] For Section 501(c)(3) tax-exempt organizations, such as most museums, the annual reporting form is some version of the Form 990.[33]

Table 8.2. Forms Used to Satisfy the Annual Reporting Requirements for Tax-Exempt Organizations

Form	Name	Filing Requirements	Notes
990-N	e-Postcard	Smaller tax-exempt organizations with annual gross receipts less than or equal to $50,000 or less.	Organizations eligible to file Form 990-N may elect to file Form 990 instead.
990-EZ	Short Return of Organization Exempt from Income Tax	Organizations with • annual gross receipts less than $200,000; and • total assets less than $500,000.	Organizations eligible to file Form 990-EZ may elect to file Form 990 instead.
990	Return of Organization Exempt from Income Tax	Organizations with • gross receipts greater than or equal to $200,000 or • total assets greater than or equal to $500,000.	Organizations eligible to file Form 990-N or Form 990-EZ may elect to file Form 990 instead.
990-PF	Return of Private Foundation	Mandatory for all private foundations.	There are no financial requirements for private foundations.

Annual reporting forms are due to the IRS by the fifteenth day of the fifth month after the conclusion of the organization's accounting year.[34] If the organization cannot file by the due date, it must file a Form 8868 to request a three-month extension.[35] This three-month extension will be granted automatically, and no signature or explanation is required.[36] If the organization will not be able to file by the conclusion of the three-month extension, Form 8868 may be resubmitted, but this second three-month extension will not be automatically granted, and this second extension requires both a signature on the form and an explanation as to why the extension is required.[37]

Organizations must diligently file their annual reporting forms or risk their tax-exempt status. For all tax years beginning after December 31, 2006, tax-exempt organizations that fail to meet this filing requirement for three consecutive years are subject to an automatic revocation of their tax-exempt status.[38] Failure to electronically file when required is considered by the IRS as failure to file.[39] This automatic revocation can have a substantial negative impact on the organization, as it will need to go through the entire application process again to regain its exempt status.[40] Additionally, during the period during which tax exemption is revoked, the organization may be required to file an appropriate income tax return and pay any applicable taxes.[41] The organization will not be able to receive tax-deductible contributions during this time.[42]

CONCLUSION

Museums that are properly organized and operated receive a series of benefits in exchange for the charitable and educational services they provide to the general public. In exchange for these benefits, there are a number of constraints placed on them. To be recognized as nonprofit, they must comply with their state's incorporation requirements and the nondistribution constraint, reinvesting any proceeds back into the organization's charitable mission. The state's attorney general has oversight authority over nonprofit organizations, ensuring compliance with the state's nonprofit corporation law and any other applicable state laws or regulations.

To obtain and maintain federal tax-exempt status, the organization must be properly organized and operated, it must serve a public benefit, it must abstain from prohibited political activities, and it must comply with annual reporting requirements.

For a museum that fulfills these requirements, the benefits are numerous. The museum is waived from paying a variety of taxes. Perhaps more importantly, the museum can accept tax-deductible donations from donors, such as works of art or cash donations, which are vital to many organizations. Therefore, while the state and federal requirements may appear complex, compliance has its rewards.

NOTES

1. Besides incorporation, an organization may choose other operational schemes. It may choose to operate as an unincorporated association, which requires little paperwork but also provides little legal protection to the association and the individuals involved.

Organizations may also operate as a private foundation, which arises when a donor gives property to a trustee, with the trustee instructed to manage that property for a charitable purpose as defined by the donor. Private foundations are held to the same requirements as other nonprofit corporations when seeking federal tax exemption, including a limitation to accepted exempt purposes, proper distribution of assets upon dissolution, limitation of political activities, and prohibition on private inurement. These requirements will be discussed below in relation to nonprofit corporations in general. Private foundations differ from nonprofit corporations in that their founding documents are not filed with the state and therefore not viewable by the public. As with nonprofit corporations, private foundations are under the oversight of the attorney general, as the trust beneficiaries are the general public, which does not necessarily have standing to sue or otherwise oversee the trust's activities.

2. For an example of nonprofit incorporation documents, see the sample provided by the State of Delaware's Department of State, Division of Corporations, available as a PDF download at corp.delaware.gov/newentit09.shtml, and click on "Exempt Corporation."

3. For more information on the board of trustees, see "Chapter 9: The Board of Trustees and Their Fiduciary Duty."

4. "State" is used throughout this discussion, but attorneys general fill the same role in commonwealths and U.S. territories.

5. For an example of the role of the attorney general in charitable organization oversight, see "Chapter 9: The Board of Trustees and Their Fiduciary Duty," especially the section "The Standard of Care: Fiduciary Duties of the Board" and accompanying endnotes.

6. See IRC § 170(c) for more information.

7. *Spanish American Cultural Assoc.*, T.C. Memo 1994-510, *10.

8. This discussion provides a general overview of the application process and does not provide information on all scenarios or requirements. For a fuller discussion, see IRS Pub. 557 or consult legal counsel.

9. As of January 31, 2020, Form 1023 may only be submitted electronically.

10. IRC § 501(c)(3).

11. Ibid.

12. The organizational test, as described in the Regulations, is as follows:

An organization is organized exclusively for one or more exempt purposes only if its articles of organization (referred to in this section as its articles) as defined in subparagraph (2) of this paragraph:

(a) Limit the purposes of such organization to one or more exempt purposes; and

(b) Do not expressly empower the organization to engage, otherwise than as an insubstantial part of its activities, in activities which in themselves are not in furtherance of one or more exempt purposes.

Treas. Reg. § 1.501(c)(3)-1(b)(1)(i). Further, "[i]n meeting the organizational test, the organization's purposes, as stated in its articles, may be as broad as, or more specific than, the purposes stated in section 501(c)(3)." Ibid. § 1.501(c)(3)-1(b)(1)(ii).

13. Ibid. § 1.501(c)(3)-1(b)(2).

14. IRS Pub. 557, 25.

15. Treas. Reg. § 1.501(c)(3)-1(b)(4).

16. Due to the fact that dissolution procedures fall under state law, local law should be consulted to ensure proper adherence to statutory requirements.

17. Other options for distribution exist, as dictated by the Regulations:

An organization's assets will be considered dedicated to an exempt purpose, for example, if, upon dissolution, such assets would, by reason of a provision in the organization's articles or by operation of law, be distributed for one or more exempt purposes, or to the Federal Government, or to a State or local government, for a public purpose, or would be distributed by a court to another organization to be used in such manner as in the judgment of the court will best accomplish the general purposes for which the dissolved organization was organized.

Treas. Reg. § 1.501(c)(3)-1(b)(4).

18. IRS Pub. 557, 25.

19. "A reading of the articles of incorporation as a whole should determine the real purpose of a particular institution, but its character is not to be determined alone by the powers and purposes defined in its articles, but also by the method of transacting business." *Younger v. Wisdom Society*, 121 Cal. App. 3d 683, 688 (1981).

20. "In applying the operational test, this Court has stated that 'an organization will not be denied exemption if it partakes in activities not in furtherance of an exempt purpose so long as such nonconforming activities are insubstantial in comparison to activities which further exempt purposes'." *Spanish American Cultural Assoc.*, T.C. Memo 1994-510 at *11, citations omitted.

21. Sale of the celebrity gossip magazines in this example would not be entirely prohibited, but those sales would be subject to the unrelated business income tax (UBIT). Unrelated business income is generated by any activity that is: (1) a trade or business, that is (2) regularly carried on, and that is (3) not substantially related to furthering the exempt purpose of the organization. When unrelated business income is earned by an exempt organization, the organization must pay tax on those sales so as to not give the exempt organization an unfair advantage over nonexempt business enterprises with which the exempt organization is competing.

22. There is no bright-line rule to indicate when activities cross the threshold from insubstantial to an unallowed amount. *Spanish American Cultural Assoc. of Bergenfield*, T.C. Memo 1994-510, *13.

23. "The court can take into consideration the actual conduct of the corporation in its method of operation." *Younger*, 121 Cal. App. 3d at 688.

24. "An organization is not organized or operated exclusively for one or more of the purposes specified in subdivision (i) of this subparagraph unless it serves a public rather than a private interest.Treas. Reg. § 1.501(c)(3)-1(d)(1)(ii).

25. See also "Chapter 9: The Board of Trustees and Their Fiduciary Duty."

26. "The following are examples of organizations that, if they otherwise meet the requirements of this section, are educational: . . . Museums, zoos, planetariums, symphony orchestras, and other similar organizations." Treas. Reg. § 1.501(c)(3)-1(d)(3)(ii) Example 4.

27. This illustration is drawn from Treas. Reg. § 1.501(c)(3)-1(d)(1)(iii) Example 2. See also Revenue Ruling 71-395, 1971-2 C.B., *2 (1971), where tax exemption was denied as the organization primarily provided a private benefit:

> The cooperative gallery in this case is engaged in showing and selling only the works of its own members and is a vehicle for advancing their careers and promoting the sale of their work. It serves the private purposes of its members, even though the exhibition and sale of paintings may be an educational activity in other respects.

An organization that serves a private interest rather than a public one will not be deemed to be organized and operated exclusively for an educational or charitable purpose. Revenue Ruling 76-152, 1976-1 C.B. 151, *2 (1976).

A comparison of two other examples will illuminate the issues associated with private inurement. In the first, the IRS was asked to determine if an organization that displayed and sold art created by its members could be recognized as tax-exempt under IRC 501(c)(3). In its articles of incorporation, the organization set out its primary purpose as:

> to provide an outlet for crafts people, to provide an association of people interested in crafts who are willing to work together toward the mutual benefit in promoting the learning, participation and selling of various crafts and to promote the cultural, education and recreational enrichment of the community through crafts.

I.R.S. Priv. Ltr. Rul. 201441017 (Oct. 10, 2014). The organization had various levels of members, with fees varying based on membership level. Members would participate in art shows where they paid a booth fee to participate plus a percentage of their tag sales. Participation in the art shows was only open to members. The IRS concluded the organization did not qualify under 501(c)(3) as a tax-exempt entity. While the art shows could arguably benefit the public as a form of art education, the actual purpose of the art shows was to create a private benefit for the members. Therefore, the organization's exempt status was revoked. Ibid.

In the second example, a nonprofit organization was founded with the purpose to foster the arts through the sponsorship of public art exhibits. These exhibits were designed to display the artwork of promising but unknown artists, and the artists were selected by a panel of qualified judges. In determining the organization was eligible for exemption under 501(c)(3), some important distinctions emerge. Here, the artists were not members of the organization, but rather unknown artists not currently affiliated with art galleries. A panel of art experts selected the artists and works for inclusion. The artists were not charged a fee for inclusion in the exhibit. And finally, the organization did not sell the displayed works. Rev. Rul. 66-178, 1966-1 C.B. 138. The organization did charge a small admission fee to enter the exhibit and sold an exhibition catalogue featuring the artworks and information on the artists and how to contact them. The funds from those activities were used to pay for administrative expenses associated with the exhibition, such as hall rental fees and printing costs.

As can be seen, the first example involved an art show where all the benefits went directly to members of the organization, creating a situation where the organization's activities benefited the organization's members and not the public. In the second, while there were clearly some benefits to the artists, they were not members of the organization, and the overall intended and actual benefit of the organization's activities went to the public through the promotion of art and art education. These examples also highlight that the issues can be highly fact specific.

28. Treas. Reg. § 1.501(c)(3)-1(b)(v)(3)(ii) and Treas. Reg. § 1.501(c)(3)-1(c)(3)(iii).

29. Treas. Reg. § 1.501(c)(3)-1()(v)(3)(i) and Treas. Reg. § 1.501(c)(3)-1(c)(3)(ii), (iv). There exists a safe harbor provision in the IRC that details how much an organization can spend on direct and indirect lobbying without losing its tax-exempt status. See IRC § 501(h) for more information. While this limit on election-eering and lobbying may at first blush appear to be a constraint on free speech, it must be remembered that this constraint on political activities is a restraint voluntarily adopted by organizations when they choose to seek federal tax exemption. Congress, through the tax exemption system, is attempting to furnish a benefit to organizations that provide a charitable benefit to society, and organizations that profit from this privileged status must do so according to the rules and guidelines set forth by Congress.

30. Treas. Reg. § 1.501(c)(3)-1(b)(1)(v).

31. Treas. Reg. § 1.501(c)(3)-1(c)(3).

32. Internal Revenue Service, "Publication 557: Tax-Exempt Status for Your Organization," 11, rev'd. Jan. 2020. Publicly supported 501(c)(3) organizations (meaning they are not a private foundation) whose normal annual gross receipts total $50,000 or less are not required to meet the reporting requirements discussed here. *Id.* Those small tax-exempt organizations instead file a Form 990-N, Electronic Notice (e-Postcard) for Tax-Exempt Organizations Not Required to File Form 990 or 990-EZ. *Id.* at 11-12. If you are unsure whether your organization is eligible to file Form 990-N, consult an appropriate financial advisor or legal counsel.

33. Form 990 is the standard reporting form. Form 990-EZ is a shortened version and is available to organizations too large to file Form 990-N (the e-Postcard) yet small enough to be exempt from filing the standard Form 990.

34. IRS Pub. 557 at 11. For an organization whose accounting period coincides with the calendar year, this places the due date at May 15.

35. Ibid. at 12.

36. Ibid.

37. Ibid.

38. Ibid. at 11.

39. Ibid.

40. Ibid.

41. Ibid. at 12.

42. Ibid.

CHAPTER 9

THE BOARD OF TRUSTEES AND THEIR FIDUCIARY DUTY

In the United States, the majority of museums are organized and operated as nonprofit, tax-exempt organizations that are dedicated to a public purpose despite not being a part of the government.[1] Nonprofit corporations such as museums are governed by a group of individuals who may individually be referred to as trustees, directors, or some other term.[2] The group as a whole is the board (of trustees, of directors, etc.). Boards are self-perpetuating, meaning they do not rely on outside intervention to continue their existence, and a board remains in existence for the lifetime of the organization it oversees. Boards, just like the nonprofits they oversee,[3] are governed by the statutory and case law of the state in which the nonprofit is incorporated. Federal statutory and case law can also come into play, especially in relation to federal tax exemption and other legal issues that are governed by federal law.

With so many competing laws related to nonprofit boards, it is impossible to give a concise and comprehensive overview of all issues related to board operations. However, there are certain areas on which there is general consensus, permitting some guidance to be provided.

THE ORGANIZATION AND ROLE OF THE BOARD

Generally, a board consists of a number of individuals who oversee the nonprofit's operations during the course of their term. They work as a whole to ensure the organization is meeting its legal obligations, upholding and furthering its mission, and maintaining its ongoing institutional and financial health for the present and future. The board has both legal and ethical standards to maintain in regard to its oversight function.

Board Authorization and Organization

The board receives its authorization from the nonprofit's founding document, typically the articles of incorporation.[4] Upon filing of those articles, an initial directors meeting is held in order to adopt bylaws, elect board officers,[5] and begin the nonprofit's operations.[6] State law may regulate who is eligible to serve as a trustee, for instance limiting trustees to those over the age of eighteen.[7] State law may also direct various aspects of board operations, such as setting the number of trustees, their term length on the board, notice requirements to call a board meeting, or other matters. However, these statutory rules are often only in place if the organization's bylaws fail to address those issues, and the bylaws will prevail if they are in compliance with statutory requirements.[8]

Board members should serve a set-length term and may be permitted to serve multiple consecutive terms as permitted by the bylaws. For example, an organization may establish that trustees may serve for a three-year term, and then be permitted to serve two terms consecutively. Further, trustees may have a time period during which they have to step away from the board before returning to service. This may look like a rule that trustees serve three-year terms, may serve two consecutive terms, and may "roll off" for one term before being renominated to the board. In application, a trustee could serve for six years total (two consecutive three-year terms) and then step away from board involvement for three years before being renominated.

Board committees can be organized any number of ways, as different organizations have different needs and requirements. For instance, a noncollecting museum will have no need of an acquisitions committee. Therefore, it is impossible to state with any definitiveness what committees a board *must* have. At a minimum, the board should consider a standing executive committee and any additional committees necessary to meet the requirements of the board and provide necessary leadership to the museum. Potential committees to consider are an acquisitions or collections committee, a governance or nominating committee (to research and attract new trustees or to organize and oversee board training), an advancement committee (to seek public or private sector support and oversee fund-raising), and a finance or investment committee (to oversee annual budgets, long-term financial planning, and investments).

In recent years, some boards have added to their list of standing committees a new type: one focused on inclusion, diversity, equity, and access (IDEA)..[9] In the museum field, support for this work has come from organizations such as the American Alliance of Museums (for instance, their 2019 "Facing Change: Advancing Museum Board Diversity & Inclusion" grant program),[10] MASS Action (Museum As Site for Social Action),[11] and the Empathetic Museum.[12]

Further, an ad hoc committee may be assembled to address a specific or short-term need. An ad hoc committee may be called to oversee the recruitment and hiring of a new executive director or to organize the celebration of a landmark anniversary. An ad hoc committee may also be called to respond to an emerging situation.[13] Such a committee is intentionally short-lived and is dissolved once the assigned task or activity is accomplished.

The Role of the Board in Relation to the Nonprofit

The primary purpose of the board is to ensure the nonprofit corporation adheres to its charitable or educational mission. In this manner, it is governed not just by the organizational bylaws and relevant state law, but also by the organization's mission statement. Oversight of the nonprofit corporation falls to the board, to whom the executive director reports. As the highest level of internal oversight, the board is mandated to establish proper policies to ensure the organization is appropriately operated and managed. Further, the board must oversee how those policies are implemented by the executive director.

However, this requirement should not be interpreted to require board members to be involved in the actual day-to-day operational activities of the organization. The board should delegate daily operations to the museum's executive director, who in turn delegates tasks to appropriate employees. What remains with the board is oversight. For example, a trustee would not be expected to conduct an ongoing inventory of the museum collection. Nor would a trustee necessarily inspect collections storage regarding pest management or security access. However, the board is responsible for the overall collection, and would probably face consequences if the collection were subject to inappropriate or damaging care due to poor facilities maintenance or the hiring of inadequately trained, unprofessional staff. Additionally, if the museum staff reports issues, such as items discovered missing during an inventory or damage due to a pest infestation, the board should take appropriate action based on that information received.

There is a limitation on this ability to delegate. The board cannot delegate its essential activities. Due diligence and oversight must always be maintained (see "Duty of Care," below). As an example, while a board may bring in a financial advisor to assist with investments, especially if there are no trustees knowledgeable in that particular area, a board that engages intentionally or negligently in high-risk investments that put the organization at risk will not be shielded from responsibility and its requirement to provide active oversight and conduct its due diligence.

THE STANDARD OF CARE: FIDUCIARY DUTIES OF THE BOARD

Nonprofit boards are held to a high standard of care under the law. They are required to place the interests of the organization about their own, called a "fiduciary duty." The fiduciary duty owed to the museum by the trustees prohibits the trustees from profiting from their relationship to the museum.[14] Additionally, the trustees are mandated to ensure that the museum's activities and that properties do not stray from the charitable or educational purpose. If this sounds like a high standard, that is because it is. Fiduciary duty is the highest legal standard, and in relation to museums, it is broken down into three subsets: the duty of loyalty, the duty of care, and the duty of obedience.

Duty of Loyalty

Trustees must maintain loyalty to the organization and its mission. In exercising their powers and oversight, the trustees must operate in a manner that furthers the interests of the museum over their own interests or the interests of another person or organization.[15] This is the duty of loyalty, namely the trustees' obligation to remain at all times and in all transactions loyal to the museum's mission and purpose. Maintenance of the duty of loyalty ensures that the museum in turn remains faithful to its nonprofit status and any advantages that nonprofit status confers on the museum, including but not limited to its tax-exempt status and the public's trust.

While the duty of loyalty, as one of the fiduciary duties, is a legal requirement, there is also an ethical component. Ethical codes promulgated by the museum profession echo the duty of loyalty. The International Council of Museums (ICOM) states that "[l]oyalty to colleagues and to the employing museum is an important professional responsibility and must be based on allegiance to fundamental ethical principals applicable to the profession as a whole."[16] Similarly, the American Alliance of Museums (AAM) provides that "[n]o individual may use his or her position in a museum for personal gain or to benefit another at the expense of the museum, its mission, its reputation and the society it serves."[17]

Perhaps the worst violation of the duty of loyalty is self-dealing, where a conflict of interest arises that provides an opportunity for a trustee to profit from their relationship to the museum. An example would be where a trustee uses his connections to sell a piece of artwork from his collection to the museum, thereby financially profiting from the museum. Another example would be a trustee who is also a general contractor who takes on construction work for the museum when there has not be a proper bidding process, again allowing the trustee to profit from the museum. However, these examples highlight that activities that are unacceptable in one situation may be fully acceptable in another.

Returning to the trustee-as-contractor example, if the trustee submitted a bid for work along with other contractors, the trustee fully disclosed his relationship to the bidding company to the board, the trustee recused himself from the decision and that recusal is fully documented in the board minutes, the trustee did not have undue influence over the other trustees, and the trustee's bid was the most appropriate and competitive, then awarding the bid to the trustee *may* be considered acceptable even through the lens of the duty of loyalty.[18]

Trustees should at all times be careful to avoid any actual or perceived conflicts of interest, and they must have policies addressing such situations when they do arise.[19] Due to the fact that trustees may at times have interests that are in conflict with those of the museum, the board should adopt a conflict-of-interest policy. That policy should provide guidance as to what constitutes a conflict and should have well-thought-out procedures detailing what actions should occur when a conflict exists. Most importantly, the policy should be strictly adhered to. The conflict-of-interest policy should be part of the orientation packet received by all new trustees, a procedure should be adopted to ensure new trustees read and understand the policy, and review of the policy should occur regularly for sitting trustees.

Doctrine of Corporate Opportunity

There is a special aspect of the duty of loyalty that comes into play when a trustee learns of a potential opportunity that could be of interest to the museum. Under the doctrine of corporate opportunity, a trustee should not use their privileged position to benefit at the museum's detriment by taking advantage of an opportunity that would be available to the museum. Rather, the trustee is required to bring the opportunity before the board and allow the board a chance to either accept or decline the opportunity before the trustee can undertake the transaction on their own behalf.

A common scenario for museums in this regard has to do with trustees who collect art that is also collected by the museum. Imagine a museum collects contemporary Japanese art. Likely, at least some of the trustees will also collect contemporary Japanese art, as that shared passion is probably what drew them to involvement with the museum. Trevor Trustee learns that a painting by Takashi Murakami is going to be coming on the market, and Trevor is very interested in acquiring the work for his personal collection. This constitutes a conflict with the duty of loyalty, and specifically the doctrine of corporate opportunity. Before Trevor can purchase the painting, he must inform the board of the work's availability and allow the board to pass on that opportunity before Trevor can pursue it for himself.

Likewise, if Tracy Trustee is in the business of buying and selling investment properties and she learns that the building immediately next to the museum is going to be for sale, that real estate deal may constitute a corporate opportunity for the museum. Even if the museum does not have immediate intentions to expand, it may have such plans in the future. As a trustee, Tracy must remain ultimately loyal to the museum above her own interests, and she must present the opportunity to the museum's board before she can take advantage of it on her own behalf.

The Prohibition against Private Inurement

Also under the umbrella of the duty of loyalty is the prohibition against private inurement. This prohibition states a trustee may not use their position in order to receive institution funds in a manner that would inappropriately benefit the trustee. A trustee may receive reasonable compensation for providing goods or services to the museum (assuming the transaction was conducted in a manner in accordance with the conflict-of-interest policy). However, if the trustee is receiving an unreasonable amount of financial compensation or in some other way benefiting unreasonably from the museum, the prohibition and the duty of loyalty will have been breached.

Duty of Care

The duty of care demands the trustees take proper care of the museum and all its assets. First, the trustees must be reasonably informed about the museum and its status. Second, the trustees must exercise their own independent judgment, actively participating in decisions related to the museum's operation and maintenance.

As with the duty of loyalty, the duty of care is a legal requirement that is reinforced by museum ethical codes. Regarding collections care, ICOM states that "[museum's] collections are a significant public inheritance, have a special position in law and are protected by international legislation. Inherent in this public trust is the notion of stewardship that includes rightful ownership, permanence, documentation, accessibility and responsible disposal."[20] Likewise, AAM states that "[i]t is incumbent on museums to be resources for humankind and in all their activities to foster an informed appreciation of the rich and diverse world we have inherited. It is also incumbent upon them to preserve that inheritance for posterity."[21] Further, "stewardship of collections entails the highest public trust and carries with it the presumption of rightful ownership, permanence, care, documentation, accessibility and responsible disposal."[22]

The Business Judgment Rule

Trustees are not required to be experts in all aspects of museum operations. However, they must conduct their duties to the level expected of an ordinarily prudent person in similar circumstances. A trustee may rely on the museum's executive director, employees, and other informed professionals, so long as the trustee reasonably believes that person is a reliable source of information.[23]

The business judgment rule creates a presumption that directors' business decisions were "made in good faith and with due care."[24] It is designed to permit a certain amount of risk taking and innovation so long as business is conducted in a rational and informed manner.

Therefore, a board that approves a risky, challenging exhibition that turns out to be poorly received, critically panned, and underattended will not be held accountable for breaching the duty of care, since risk taking and innovation are to be encouraged in nonprofits. However, while the business judgment rule creates a presumption that business decisions are proper, a board that approves a risky investment of endowment funds in a highly volatile market despite warnings of a financial advisor may be found to have breached the duty of care.[25] Such risk taking is not beneficial to the organization and not excepted by the business judgment rule.

Duty of Obedience

The final fiduciary duty imposed on museum trustees is the duty of obedience. This duty requires obedience to the museum's founding documents, its mission, and its charitable or educational purpose that informs its tax-exempt status. The duty of obedience is reflected in policies and procedures, including but not limited to the collections management policy, the programming, and the fund-raising activities.

If a museum solely collects East Asian art, and that limitation is found in the museum's founding documents, its board may have violated the duty of obedience if it allocates funds to acquire Northern European Renaissance works. Similarly, if a small history museum has a mission to collect and interpret the history of a specific geographic area, the board may have violated the duty of obedience if it begins to present programming unrelated to that history.

THE STATE ATTORNEY GENERAL AND BOARD OVERSIGHT[26]

Museums are considered public trusts, and the museum trustees are "entrusted to care for and maintain a particular community's patrimony."[27] In this role, the trustees owe a fiduciary duty to the general public and not to any individual beneficiaries.[28] In other words, there are no (or very few) individual beneficiaries who can contest abuses by the trustees.[29]

The state's attorney general has the responsibility to represent the state's and public's interests regarding charitable trusts.[30] Under common law, even if the public only indirectly benefits from the charitable trust, the trust is still subject to public supervision.[31] Likewise, the attorney general has oversight of nonprofit organizations and may bring legal actions (litigation) if the nonprofit has violated its responsibilities to its public or the charitable purpose. This oversight extends to actions by nonprofits such as mergers, dissolutions, or even deaccessioning and disposal of collection objects. Members of the public, including individual donors, museum members, and staff, do not always have standing to directly bring an action against a museum, though they may bring the attorney general's attention to potential breaches by the trustees.[32]

For museums, the attorney general in the museum's state of incorporation oversees actions by the trustees. Despite this parental position, the attorney general can also be a useful resource to the museum. Many attorneys general provide resources to nonprofits, including museums, that can be helpful in establishing appropriate policies and guidelines for the board and trustees, ensuring legal compliance, and helping the museum navigate the often tricky world of the law.[33]

CONCLUSION

Museum trustees have an important responsibility, namely, to oversee the museum and ensure their collection remains as a charitable and educational force within the community in perpetuity. The trustees must ensure the collection and the nonprofit organization that oversees that collection are financially and physically secure, and that the mission of the organization is upheld through all aspects of the museum's operations and programming. This is both an ethical and a legal duty, promoted by the codes of ethics of museum professional organizations and enforced through the fiduciary duties of loyalty, care, and obedience. Museum boards that fail to meet the high standards set for them may find themselves subject to intervention by the state's attorney general's office, which represents the interests of the public who are served by the museum.

Boards must have appropriate policies and procedures in place to ensure they uphold their ethical and legal obligations. Conflict-of-interest policies, board training, and adherence to the museum's founding documents and mission will help to ensure the board properly governs the museum. Proper governance, in turn, builds public trust and keeps trustees in compliance with their legal obligations.

NOTES

1. Malaro, *Museum Governance*, 62.
2. For more information on nonprofit corporations, see "Chapter 8: Nonprofit Corporations and Tax Exemption."
3. Boards can also oversee for-profit corporations. This discussion is solely limited to nonprofit boards, specifically museum boards. *Museum* as used here is an umbrella term to include historic house museums, historical societies, and other collecting entities.
4. For more information on articles of incorporation and other issues related to nonprofit formation, see "Chapter 8: Nonprofit Corporations and Tax Exemption."
5. Such as the president, secretary, and treasurer.
6. See, for example, New York Not-for-Profit Corporation Law, N.Y. N.P.C. Law § 405(a).
7. New York Not-for-Profit Corp. Law § 701(a), with numerous exceptions unrelated to this discussion.
8. For example, New York law states that board quorum is met by "a majority of the entire board," but permits the organization's bylaws or articles of incorporation to set a higher number. Ibid. § 707.
9. Speaking to the professional higher education community but relevant to the museum profession as well, Dr. Dafina-Lazarus Stewart posed a number of questions seeking to define and describe the language used regarding diversity, inclusion, equity, and justice. Among these were:

- Diversity asks, "How many more of [pick any minoritized identity] group do we have this year than last?" Equity responds, "What conditions have we created that maintain certain groups as the perpetual majority here?"
- Inclusion asks, "Has everyone's ideas been heard?" Justice responds, "Whose ideas won't be taken as seriously because they aren't in the majority?"

Stewart, Dafina-Lazarus. (2017, March 30). "The Language of Appeasement." *Inside HigherEd*. https://www.insidehighered.com/views/2017/03/30/colleges-need-language-shift-not-one-you-think-essay.

Building on this, and focusing on the role of nonprofit boards:

> Whether in the hiring of the executive, the determination of strategy, the allocation of resources, or the goal of serving the community with authenticity, the board's leadership on diversity, inclusion, and equity matters.
>
> As stewards of the public good, all social sector organizations, regardless of mission, are called on to embrace and celebrate our common humanity, and the inherent worth of all people.

BoardSource. (n.d.) "Diversity, Inclusion, Equity." https://boardsource.org/research-critical-issues/diversity-equity-inclusion/.

10. Through this program, the AAM provided four million dollars nationwide to support training to and resources for museum boards. Grants were made to fifty-one museums, with funding backed by the Andrew W. Mellon Foundation, the Alice L. Walton Foundation, and the Ford Foundation. Also, in 2019, the AAM introduced its new "Excellence in DEAI Task Force," which works to include diversity, equity, accessibility, and inclusion (DEAI) into the AAM's existing excellence programs. Regarding the "Facing Change" grants, AAM CEO and president Laura Lott stated:

> Museum boards, in particular, set the tone for their institutions and are well positioned to be agents of change. We commend the museum directors and trustees who have committed to this program for investing in their own operations and serving as models for all museums.

American Alliance of Museums. (2019, July 23). "51 Museums Selected for Board Diversity and Inclusion Program as Part of $4 Million National Initiative." https://www.aam-us.org/2019/07/23/51-museums-selected-for-board-diversity-and-inclusion-program-as-part-of-4-million-national-initiative/.

11. Initially convened by the Minneapolis Institute of Art in 2016, MASS Action has developed a Readiness Assessment tool to assist museums as they determine their institutional readiness for equity work. Also available is a toolkit to assist institutions in working toward an environment of equity. Both are available at https://www.museumaction.org/resources.

12. The Empathetic Museum has developed a rubric-style assessment tool to aid museums and other cultural institutions to become more empathetic in their work and better reflect the values of their communities. Available at http://empatheticmuseum.weebly.com/maturity-model.html.

13. For instance, many boards organized ad hoc committees to respond to the COVID-19 pandemic and its impact on their organizations. See an example of such a committee, including its assigned purpose, at American Association of Physicists in Medicine, "Ad Hoc Committee to Respond to the Impact of the Coronavirus (COVID-19) on AAPM Meetings (AHRICM)," https://www.aapm.org/org/structure/?committee_code=AHRICM.

14. Failure to uphold the fiduciary duties can have serious and far-reaching consequences. In 2016, the New York attorney general brought an action against The Donald J. Trump Foundation and its officers, directors, and board members, including then-President-Elect Donald J. Trump and three of his children. The attorney general alleged breach of fiduciary duty and waste under the state's Not-For-Profit Corporation Law, failure to properly administer the Foundation's assets, and other causes of action.

In December 2018, the parties reached a settlement agreement wherein the Foundation was dissolved and its assets distributed to an agreed list of nonprofit organizations. In October 2019, the Trump children agreed to participate in trainings regarding the fiduciary responsibilities of board service and oversight of charitable organizations in return for the dismissal of the charges against them. Also, in October 2019, Mr. Trump agreed to pay two million dollars in damages due to his improper use of charitable assets and waste.

In her opinion for the court, Justice Scarpulla stated:

> As a director of the Foundation, Mr. Trump owed fiduciary duties to the Foundation, pursuant to N-PCL 717; he was a trustee of the Foundation's charitable assets and was thereby responsible for the proper administration of these assets, pursuant to EPTL 8-1.4. A review of the record, including

the factual admissions in the final stipulation, establishes that Mr. Trump breached his fiduciary duty to the Foundation and that waste occurred to the Foundation.

People v. Trump, 66 Misc.3d 200 (204), 112 N.Y.S.3d 467 (2019). Other actions were also taken, including the imposition of restrictions regarding Mr. Trump's ability to take part in future charitable service within the state of New York. The consequences were not limited to the individuals alone, as the Trump Foundation was itself dissolved and its assets distributed to other charities under court supervision. New York Attorney General (2019, November 7), *Press Release: AG James Secures Court Order Against Donald J. Trump, Trump Children, and Trump Foundation*, https://ag.ny.gov/press-release/2019/ag-james-secures-court-order-against-donald-j-trump-trump-children-and-trump.

15. A trustee who uses his position to benefit a third party may still be found to have breached his fiduciary duty of loyalty. The test is not whether the trustee personally benefited, but rather, whether the trustee placed the interests of another above the interests of the museum.

16. International Council of Museums, *ICOM Code of Ethics for Museums* (2004), "8.3 Professional Conduct," 41.

17. AAM, "Code of Ethics for Museums."

18. Breach of the duty of loyalty, or of any of the fiduciary duties, is highly specific as to the particular organization and the facts and circumstances of the activities undertaken. This example is provided for illustrative purposes. Consult local nonprofit corporation law before undertaking any activities that could be perceived as a breach of fiduciary duty.

19. For example, consider the "Sibley Hospital" case. There, a board effectively handed over management of the hospital's finances to two directors. Those two directors dominated the board and its executive committee, and their decisions regarding the hospital, including its finances, were routinely accepted with little oversight. Additionally, important committees, such as the finance committee, failed to meet or conduct any business for over three years. Faced with a vacuum in leadership, the board promoted an Administrator of the hospital who had little managerial experience and demonstrated less-than-satisfactory performance.

Due to such failures at the board level, a class action lawsuit was brought alleging mismanagement, non-management, and self-dealing. In order to rectify the ongoing and repeat breaches of fiduciary duty by the board as a whole and the individual trustees, the court ordered, among other remedies, the board to adopt written policies regarding its duties to the hospital and also various interests of the individual directors, including any potential conflicts of interest. This case is of special note, as it clearly states that "each director or trustee of a charitable hospital organized under the [applicable statute] has a continuing fiduciary duty of loyalty and care in the management of the hospital's fiscal and investment affairs. . . ." *Stern v. Lucy Webb Hayes National Training School for Deaconesses and Missionaries*, 381 F. Supp. 1003, 1020 (D.D.C. 1974).

20. *ICOM Code of Ethics for Museums*, 8.

21. AAM, "Code of Ethics for Museums."

22. Ibid.

23. See "The Role of the Board in Relation to the Nonprofit," above.

24. *CDX Liquidating Trust v. Venrock Assocs.*, 640 F.3d 209, 215 (7th Cir.2011).

25. The business judgment does not protect against gross negligence or fraud.

26. This section is adapted in part from the author's article, "All in a Day's Work: How Museums May Approach Deaccessioning as a Necessary Collections Management Tool," *DePaul Journal of Art, Technology and Intellectual Property* 22 (2011): 119–81 (as Heather Hope Stephens).

27. Goldstein, "Deaccession," 214.

28. Ibid.

29. Kutner and Koven, "Charitable Trust Legislation" 411.

30. Bogert, "Proposed Legislation," 633–34.

31. Kutner and Koven, "Charitable Trust Legislation," 411.

32. White, "When It's OK to Sell the Monet," 1045.

33. See, for example, the New York State Attorney General's Charities Bureau website, available at www.charitiesnys.com/home.jsp.

WORKER CLASSIFICATION

Distinguishing between an Employee and an Independent Contractor

In 2016, the nonprofit sector employed 12.3 million paid workers in the United States, representing 10.2 percent of the country's private workforce.[1] In ranking the eighteen industries that comprise the American economy, the nonprofit sector tied for third with manufacturing at 12.29 percent each. Only the retail trade (15.73 percent) and the accommodation and food services (13.28 percent) employed more workers than the nonprofit sector.[2] The nonprofit sector itself is exceptionally diverse, and the arts and recreation portion is relatively small. Again in 2016, arts and recreation (which would include most museums and related organizations) made up only 3 percent of all nonprofits, less than almost all other categories. In comparison, hospitals comprised 34 percent of all nonprofits, educational institutions 16 percent, and organizations engaged in social assistance made up 12 percent.[3]

While museums make up a small portion of the nonprofit sector, they are strong forces in the economy. In 2016, American museums contributed $50 billion to the nation's gross domestic product and supported 726,200 jobs (including 372,100 jobs directly in the museum sector).[4]

These numbers tell us that museums have a strong impact on the American economy and workforce. What the numbers do not tell us is how many of those workers are employees of their museums and how many are independent contractors. Studies have shown that between 10 and 20 percent of employers misclassify workers as independent contractors when they should be classified as employees.[5] Such misclassification can have numerous detrimental effects on the worker, as independent contractors are not eligible for many of the benefits and protections that apply to employees, such as workers' compensation, minimum wage, and overtime pay.[6] Treatment under the Federal Insurance Contributions Act (FICA) is also different, as employers are not responsible for these contributions toward independent contractors.[7] There are also financial consequences for an employer who misclassifies workers as independent contractors, as they are liable for any unpaid employment taxes for that worker.[8]

UNDERSTANDING THE CATEGORIES OF WORKERS

A museum may have workers that fall into a number of categories. Perhaps the most common categories in the museum setting are employees, volunteers,[9] and independent contractors.

As used here, an employee is understood to be a worker employed by a business or organization such as a museum. An employee is hired by the employer to perform a job in exchange for paid compensation. The employee performs the job in accordance with the employer's directions, and the work is conducted using the resources made available by the employer. For example, an employee would use an employer-provided laptop, work at an employer-provided desk, and follow guidelines developed by the employer.

Typically, an employer is required to withhold income taxes from wages paid to the employee.[10] In contrast, those same withholdings and payments are not made on the wages paid to an independent contractor.

Table 10.1. Payroll Tax Responsibilities for Section 501(c)(3) Organizations in Relation to Employees and Independent Contractors

Types of tax	Workers classified as employees		Workers classified as independent contractors	
	Responsibilities of the employer	Responsibilities of the worker	Responsibilities of the employer	Responsibilities of the worker
Federal income tax	Withholding of tax from employees' pay.	Payment of full amount owed (often through withholding).	None so long as proper documentation is provided.	Pay full amount owed.
Social Security and Medicare	Withhold half of taxes owed on employees' pay. Directly pay the other half.	Pay half of taxes owed (often through withholding).	None.	Payment of full amount of taxes owed (often through estimated tax payments).
Federal unemployment tax	None. 501(c)(3) organizations are exempt.	None.	None.	None.
State unemployment tax	Varies by state.		None.	None.

In contrast, a worker may be classified as an independent contractor if specific requirements are met. In the museum field, these independent contractors are often called consultants, independent consultants, or perhaps most commonly independent museum professionals (IMPs). These independent contractors provide a variety of highly specialized and vital services to the museum community, such as exhibit development, long-term financial or strategic planning, staff and docent training, collections management, and evaluation. Unlike an employee, an independent contractor has much more independence and control. They will use their own resources (such as a laptop or printer), work where they like (such as at a home office, rented office space, or even a public setting like a library or coffee shop), and may impose their own guidelines and requirements on the work relationship through the contract.

DETERMINING WORKER CLASSIFICATION

The first and most important aspect of worker classification that must be understood is this: An employer cannot define the relationship with a worker by unilaterally applying the label "independent contractor" to the worker. What will determine the status of the worker-employer relationship are the actual facts of the relationship, no matter what language is used between the parties.[11]

Therefore, it is important to understand how a worker is properly classified and the relevant facts and factors at play. There are two commonly used tests to determine whether a worker should be classified as an employee or an independent contractor. These are the ABC test and the common law test.[12] While workers may be classified as independent contractors if specific requirements are met, the default assumption under both tests is that workers are employees.

The ABC Test

The ABC test was developed at the state level,[13] and as such it can vary from state to state. In addition, some states only utilized a portion of the ABC test. The most common criteria under the test are:

(A) the worker is free from the control and direction of the hirer in connection with the performance of the work, both under the contract for the performance of such work and in fact;
(B) the worker performs work that is outside the usual course of the hiring entity's business; and
(C) the worker is customarily engaged in an independently established trade, occupation, or business of the same nature as the work performed for the hiring entity.[14]

Under this test, a worker will be classified as an independent contractor only if all three of these criteria are met. The ABC test starts with a presumption the worker is an employee and applies the criteria to the worker-employer relationship to determine whether the worker should instead be classified as an independent contractor.

The Common Law Test

Under the common law test, the factors to consider are (1) behavior, (2) finances, and (3) relationship.[15] **Behavior** looks to what level of control the employer exerts over the worker's behavior and whether the employer can direct and control the manner and means used by the worker to accomplish the tasks, for instance, when and where the work is done, the sequence followed in completing the work, the hiring of additional workers or assistants, or the purchase of necessary supplies or services.[16] A worker with independence in determining how to accomplish the job is more likely to be determined to be an independent contractor.

Finances considers the extent of control the employer has regarding the business aspects of the worker's conduct. For instance, if the employer provides necessary tools and supplies (laptop, copying facilities, office supplies), reimburses business expenses, and pays the worker a regular amount on a set schedule, it is likely the worker will be designated as an employee and not an independent contractor. Another consideration here is whether the worker is free to seek out additional business opportunities outside the employer-worker relationship. If the worker is advertising her services and making herself available to others in the relevant market, she is more likely to be classified as an independent contractor.[17]

Finally, **relationship** considers the actual relationship between the worker and employer. If there are written contracts outlining the scope of the work and the work will cease upon completion of a specific task or set of tasks, the worker is likely to be classified as an independent contractor. However, if the worker receives employee benefits (such as vacation pay or enrollment in a pension plan) or if the employment relationship is intended to be ongoing with no set end date or goal, the worker is likely to be classified as an employee.[18]

MAINTAINING INDEPENDENCE

Independent contractors, such as independent museum professionals, should take steps to ensure they will not conduct their activities in a manner that would result in them being classified as employees. This is important for the independent contractor, as they have invested time and resources into creating, developing, and promoting their independent business, for instance forming a business entity, acquiring insurance, having a logo designed, building a website, and advertising themselves to the profession at large as available to bring their expertise to a variety of museums and cultural institutions.[25]

Independent contractors can best ensure they will not be classified as employees by working in a manner that aligns with the tests used to determine worker classification. Maintaining a separate workspace, for instance a home office or a paid office share, continuing to hold themselves as available for hire with other employers or organizations, conducting work in a manner that is self-directed, and not participating in employee benefit programs will all aid in keeping a person's classification as an independent contractor. Independent contractors should be sure to enter into a written contract that outlines the relationship, expectations, and other vital terms (for instance, ownership of resulting intellectual property). Such preparatory steps before the commencement of the employer-worker relationship will help ensure a meeting of the minds regarding what will be produced, how, and by when, and will limit exposure to misunderstandings or risk.

Table 10.2. Criteria, Description, and Examples of the Two Tests Used to Classify a Worker as an Employee or Independent Contractor

	Common law test[19]		ABC test[20]		
Criteria	Criteria	Examples of an employee	Criteria	Description	Examples of an employee
Behavior	Does the employer direct and control the manner in which the worker does the task?	• Employer dictates where and when the work will be performed. • Employer selects and provides the equipment. • Employer dictates the sequence of tasks.	Does the employer exert control and direction over the work?	"The person is free from the control and direction of the hiring entity in connection with the performance of the work, both under the contract for the performance of the work and in fact."[21]	• Worker must follow all employer-set guidelines and regulations. • Employer sets the work schedule and related matters. • Employer exercises the degree of control a business would typically exercise over employees.
Finances	Does the employer control the business aspects of the job?	• Employer reimburses worker's business expenses. • Worker does not make their services available to the marketplace. • Employer pays worker a regular wage amount on a set schedule.	Does the worker provide a service outside the employer's usual course of business?	"The person performs work that is outside the usual course of the hiring entity's business."[22]	• Worker provides a service to the employer that is in line with the work done by employees of the business. • "[A] bakery hires cake decorators to work on a regular basis on its custom-designed cakes. . . ."[23]
Relationship	Do the employer and worker have a formalized, long-term relationship?	• The employer provides employee-type benefits (insurance, vacation pay, etc.). • The relationship is expected to continue indefinitely, regardless of completion of any specific project or completion of a specific goal.	Is the worker customarily engaged in the type of business outside of the employment relationship?	"The person is customarily engaged in an independently established trade, occupation, or business of the same nature as that involved in the work performed."[24]	• The worker does not have an established business through which they provide the services to other employers. • Worker has not taken steps to establish themselves as an independent business or advertise themselves as an independent business. For instance, the worker has not pursued incorporation, licensure, advertisements, routine offerings to provide the services, etc.

NOTES

1. At the time of writing, 2016 is the most recent year for which data is available. L. S. Salamon and C. L. Newhouse (2009). The 2019 Nonprofit Employment Report. *Nonprofit Economic Data no. 47.* Baltimore: Johns Hopkins Center for Civil Society Studies, p. 3. Available at ccss.jhu.edu.

2. Ibid., at 5.

3. Ibid., at 8.

4. American Alliance of Museums and Oxford Economic. (2017). Museums as Economic Engines: A National Study (pp.10–11, 14). Washington, D.C.: Authors. Retrieved from www.aam-us.org.

5. F. Carré (2015). *(In)dependent Contractor Misclassification* (Briefing Paper No. 403, p. 1). Washington, D.C.: Economic Policy Institute. Retrieved from https://www.epi.org/publication/independent-contractor-misclassification/.

6. Misclassification has negative impacts on parties other than the misclassified workers. Other businesses and organizations operating in the marketplace find themselves at a competitive disadvantage with employers who misclassify their workers, as they have higher costs associated with their employees. Additionally, local, state, and federal governments experience a direct impact on their income, as tax revenue is impacted by the misclassification of workers as independent contractors.

7. The Federal Insurance Contributions Act (26 USC § 3101 *et. seq.*), sometimes called payroll taxes or employment taxes. These are federal taxes paid to fund Social Security and Medicare. Employees are responsible for half the FICA tax (with the employer paying the other half). Independent consultants, however, are responsible for 100 percent of their contributions under the Self-Employment Contributions Act (26 USC § 1401-03).

8. Internal Revenue Service, Department of the Treasury. (2019, December 23). "Publication 15-A: Employer's Supplemental Tax Guide," p. 7. Washington, D.C.: Author.

9. Volunteers fall outside the scope of this discussion despite being a vital part of many museums.

10. Internal Revenue Service, Department of the Treasury. (2017, July 20). "Fact Sheet 2017-09: Understanding Employee vs. Contractor Classification." Retrieved from https://www.irs.gov/. Section 501(c)(3) organizations, while exempt from federal income tax under 26 USC 501(a), are still required to pay both Social Security and Medicare taxes unless one of two exempting situations applies: (1) the organization pays the employee less than $100 in the calendar year, or (2) the organization fits certain criteria related to churches and church-controlled organizations that have filed required IRS forms. IRS Publication 15-A at 10.

11. As explained here:

> It is well established, under all of the varied standards that have been utilized for distinguishing employees and independent contractors, that a business cannot unilaterally determine a worker's status simply by assigning the worker the label "independent contractor" or by requiring the worker, as a condition of hiring, to enter into a contract that designates the worker an independent contractor.

Dynamex Operations West, Inc. v. Superior Court of Los Angeles, 4 Cal. 5th 903 at 962 (2018).

12. At the time of writing, the common law rules were used by the IRS, the District of Columbia, and eighteen states. The ABC test (or some variation of it) was used by the Department of Labor and thirty-three states, with the state of California changing to the ABC Test following the state's Supreme Court decision in *Dynamex,* 4 Cal. 5th 903 (2018). Effective January 1, 2020, California Assembly Bill 5 codified the *Dynamex* ABC test and expanded the reach to all wage and hour Labor Code violations in the state. Since the passage of AB-5, lawsuits have been filed challenging the law as unconstitutional. These lawsuits are still pending at the time of writing. Additionally, representatives from the music industry have successfully negotiated relief for musicians, songwriters, and others in that industry who were adversely impacted by AB-5, allowing workers in the professional music industry to follow a different test for worker classification in regard to live performances and studio recordings. Jem Aswad (2020, April 17). "Musicians to Be Exempt from California 'Gig Economy' Assembly Bill 5." *Variety.* https://variety.com/2020/music/news/california-gig-economy-assembly-bill-5-ab5-musicians-1234583320/.

Finally, a new piece of legislation has been introduced in California to address the impact of AB-5 on the creative sector by, among other things, providing clarification on the "fine artist exemption." The statutory definition of a "fine artist" could have a signification impact on both the individuals and the organizations who hire them. At the time of writing, Assembly Bill 1850 had been referred to the California State Senate Standing Committee on Labor, Public Employment and Retirement.

As this is an expanding and fluctuating area of law, be sure to consult with an attorney to determine the current status of the law, especially if your organization is in California. It is foreseeable that the situation in California may impact other states as well, as states may look to California for guidance on how to amend (or not amend) their own state's laws regarding worker classification. Also note that because of the two tests being applied in different states and by different agencies, it is possible for a worker to be classified as an independent contractor by the IRS and an employee on the state level, which can impact such things as unemployment benefits.

13. Your state may use a different name for the ABC test, and the test may arise from statutory or case law. Consult a local attorney to determine the exact name, wording, and proper application of your state's version of the test.

14. *Dynamex*, 4 Cal. 5th at 916-17.

15. The IRS has long used the so-called 20-factor test to determine whether a worker should be classified as an employee. That test looks at a variety of factors to determine who (the employer or the worker) has control over each factor's activity, giving rise to its unofficial name of the "right to control" test. The factors can be understood as all falling within one of three categories: behavioral control, financial control, and the relationship between the parties. Factors considered include whose tools or equipment are used and whether the employer assigns specific duties to the worker (behavioral control), whether the worker is paid a wage/salary or a fee and whether the worker makes their services available to the marketplace (financial control), and whether the relationship is intended to be temporary versus permanent and whether the services provided by the worker fall within the employer's regular business activities (type of relationship). The 20 factors are not necessarily evenly weighed: Depending on the worker's occupation and other relevant considerations, some factors were weighed more heavily than others in the final determination. IRS Publication 15-A at 7-8.

16. Ibid., at 7.

17. Ibid., at 8.

18. Ibid.

19. Information regarding the common law test is from IRS Publication 15-A at 7-8.

20. Information and language regarding the ABC test is taken from California's Assembly Bill No. 5, which codified and expanded the *Dynamex* decision. This law went into effect on January 1, 2020. The ABC test, if applicable in your state, may use different language or may only apply part of the 3-part test.

21. Ibid. at § 2750.3(a)(1)(A).

22. Ibid. at § 2750.3(a)(1)(B).

23. *Dynamex*, 4 Cal. 5th at 960.

24. Cal. Lab. Code § 2750.3(a)(1)(C) (2020).

25. For more information on these topics, see G. C. Bonifacino, and H. H. Kuruvilla (2019). *The Business of Being an IMP* [Webinar handout and slides]. Washington, D.C.: AAM Independent Museum Professionals Network. Available at https://www.aam-us.org/professional-networks/independent-museum-professionals-network/.

UNDERSTANDING THE VARIOUS FORMS OF BUSINESS STRUCTURES

When a new business is first contemplated, it is important that careful consideration is given to how it will be legally organized. There are multiple types of business structures available, and the one chosen will impact the business' ability to grow and evolve over its lifetime. The decision is ultimately based on a number of factors, including what business structures are available in the particular state, the number of people involved in the formation, their willingness to accept personal risk and liability on behalf of the organization, and the overarching long-term goals (including whether the organization is contemplating recognition as a tax-exempt status). Overall, business structures are governed by state laws, and therefore the specifics pertaining to each type of structure will vary depending on the jurisdiction. Not all business structures are available in all states.

COMMON BUSINESS STRUCTURES

Sole Proprietorship[1]

One of the least formal business structures, a sole proprietorship is a business entity run by one person, acting on their own without partners or investors. It can only be run as a for-profit business, as nonprofit sole proprietorships do not exist under state laws. By extension, this means a sole proprietorship cannot receive tax-exempt status.[2]

A sole proprietorship has no legal separation from the individual that formed it, and therefore all income and losses related to the business are reported on the individual's personal income taxes. It is said that these profits "pass through" the business to the individual. Additionally, the individual is personally liable for the debts and liabilities of the business.

As with unincorporated associations (see below), sole proprietorships are created automatically when an individual begins to conduct business activities. And as informal structures, that automatic creation happens even if the individual does not register with their state as a business.[3]

Unincorporated Associations[4]

Another of the minimally formal business structures is the unincorporated association. Due to its streamlined and informal process, unincorporated associations are formed quite often, with the individuals involved often not even aware they have formed the association. For instance, a group of neighbors raising funds to help a family in need in their community, or engaged members organizing a fund-raiser to support scholarships to a museum's summer camp programs, or a group of college students collecting items for disaster relief have all formed an unincorporated association.

When a group of individuals decides to work together to meet some shared goal, an unincorporated association is created.[5] The name applied to this unincorporated group of people varies depending on what type of task they are seeking to accomplish. If the parties intend to gain a profit, then what they have formed is a partnership (or possibly a joint venture).[6] On the other hand, if the unincorporated association is formed to pursue a nonprofit purpose in the public interest, then a nonprofit unincorporated association is formed.

If the association wishes to be recognized as a nonprofit, it will have to comply with all the applicable state laws governing nonprofit corporations.[7] If the association successfully meets the applicable state's requirements for nonprofit recognition, it may elect next to gain tax-exempt status from the Internal Revenue Service. Whether this recognition is necessary depends on the association's particular needs and goals, as well as its annual operating revenue.[8]

Despite the ease of formation and limited financial investment associated with that formation, unincorporated associations do have drawbacks. First, unlike a more formal structure like a corporation or charitable trust, the unincorporated association has no legal existence separate from the individuals who comprise it. This means the association may not be permitted to own property or enter contracts in its own name.[9] Second, again stemming from the association having no separate legal existence, the individual members can potentially be held personally liable for the unincorporated association's debts or legal obligations.

Therefore, while a new endeavor may naturally begin life as an unincorporated association, if the association becomes a more long-term or permeant endeavor or is pursing business relationships with other entities, officially incorporating under a more stable form is preferable.

Partnership[10]

A more formal, but still easily formed, business structure is the partnership. Like the sole proprietorship, it is a type of for-profit business structure, though the partnership requires two or more parties to agree to carry on a trade or business together. These parties may be individuals or businesses. Each partner's contribution may be different and could include money, labor, property, or other assets to the partnership. In return for these contributions, each partner receives a share of the profits (or losses). The partners also each carry a share of the risk involved, as each is exposed to unlimited personal liability for the partnership's debts.

As with sole proprietorships and unincorporated associations, partnerships may be automatically created. Specifically, a partnership is automatically created at the time the parties agree to do business together and to share the partnership's profits and losses. In a general partnership,[11] if a partner decides to leave the partnership for any reason, the partnership is dissolved. At that time, all the partners equally split the partnership's assets and debts.[12]

The partnership is governed by state law, so the specific laws and regulations pertaining to partnerships will vary depending on the home jurisdiction.[13] Depending on the laws of the state, the partnership may be required to file an annual informational return. The partnership may also be required to conduct other organizational steps, such as registration of a fictitious business name with the state, signing of a partnership agreement, and obtaining any necessary licenses, permits, or zoning clearances.

As a for-profit business structure, the partnership cannot be formed as a nonprofit under state law and is not eligible for federal tax-exempt recognition.

Table 11.1.   The Common Types of Business Structures and Some Important Considerations of Each Relevant to the Museum Field.

Business Structure	Personal Liability Exists	"Pass Through" Taxation Exists	Eligible for Nonprofit Recognition
Sole Proprietorship	Yes	Yes	No
Unincorporated Association	Yes	Yes	Yes
Partnership	Yes	Yes	No
Corporation	No	No	Yes
Limited Liability Company	No	Yes[14]	Yes[15]

Corporation[16]

Requiring much more formality that the entities already discussed, the corporation is a business structure in which a legal entity is created separate from the owners. The corporation, therefore, can earn profits, be taxed, enter contracts, own property, and carry legal liability separate from the owners. The corporation can exist in perpetuity, separate from the involvement of any particular owners or investors. In other words, if a shareholder exits the corporation, the corporation continues to exist. Corporations do not "pass through" their income to owners but pay taxes directly.[17]

Generally, when people outside the museum field discuss corporations, they mean a for-profit corporation that exists to create profit for certain parties. Such a corporation may be privately held,[18] meaning it is owned by a small number of members or shareholders. Privately held companies do not offer their stock for sale to the general public. Alternatively, these companies may be publicly held,[19] where ownership shares (stocks) are traded on a stock exchange. In such a for-profit corporation, income realized is either reinvested in the company or distributed to owners/shareholders. Investors in the corporation make their investments seeking a return (profit) on that investment.

However, a properly organized corporation may receive recognition as a nonprofit entity. Such recognition would require the corporation to be organized and operated in a manner in which all the profits are reinvested into the corporation's nonprofit purpose.[20]

Both types of corporations are regulated by state law in relation to incorporation and ongoing compliance. Further, a corporation seeking nonprofit status must meet the state's legal requirements to be recognized as a nonprofit corporation. Should the nonprofit wish to do so, it may also seek tax-exempt status on the federal level.

While for-profit corporations receive oversight from their shareholders, a nonprofit corporation is subject to oversight by the state's attorney general. The attorney general is the official representative of the people within the state and receives that power of oversight from applicable state law, most often the state's nonprofit corporation statute.

Limited Liability Company[21]

Existing as a type of hybrid entity, a limited liability company (LLC) is a business structure that combines elements of corporations with elements from partnerships or sole proprietorships. Specifically, it has the pass-through taxation elements of a partnership or sole proprietorship with the limited personal liability of a corporation. The LLC provides more flexibility than the corporation and may provide certain tax benefits in some states.[22]

The LLC is a relatively young business structure, with the first statute recognizing it passing in Wyoming in 1977. While all states and the District of Columbia now have some form of LLC available under their laws, the regulations can vary wildly.[23] For instance, while most states permit an LLC to be owned by one individual, some states prohibit this practice. Additionally, some states permit an LLC to survive a member's death or resignation, while other states require such a change to dissolve the LLC and for it to be reformed with the new membership if there is not a preexisting agreement within the LLC. Depending on state law, an LLC may be operated as a nonprofit organization. However, currently the Internal Revenue Service will only recognize an LLC as a tax-exempt 501(c)(3) organization if all its members are themselves also 501(c)(3) organizations.[24]

CONSIDERATIONS FOR INDEPENDENT CONTRACTORS

Independent contractors or those considering starting an independent business should give careful consideration to the business structure they elect to use. As outlined above, this decision will impact the level of personal liability and risk assumed by the individual. Also impacted is the ability to raise capital from investments, how taxes will be assessed and paid, and the upfront costs associated with creating the business.

Independent contractors may start offering services informally and therefore find themselves running a sole proprietorship without even realizing they have started a business. Simply by entering the marketplace and offering goods and/or services—for instance, taking on a consulting job or writing a grant proposal for a nonprofit—the individual has created a sole proprietorship.

However, the sole proprietorship structure may expose the individual to more risk than they want to take on. The personal liability of the business structure means that the individual's personal assets (including her car or home) may be sought to fulfill the debts of the business. Therefore, the business owner must weigh the costs and benefits of the available business structures in their home state and determine which is the right one for them.

While many independent contractors enjoy the protections of the limited liability company, consultation with a knowledgeable attorney well versed in the state's laws will be able to help the business owner make the best choice for her particular situation and business model. The types of services offered, current financial resources, future goals, and other factors may all play a part in the ultimate decision. Additionally, consultation with an attorney can help the business owner make other decisions important to running the business,[25] such as navigating issues related to choosing and registering a business name, acquiring an employee identification number (EIN), registering for the collection and remitting of sales taxes, registration with any necessary jurisdictions (city, county, state, or foreign), compliance with local ordinances and zoning laws, and selecting and acquiring necessary insurance policies.

CONSIDERATIONS FOR MUSEUMS

Museums and other collecting and preservation organizations generally will benefit from a more formal business structure, even if the initial organization of that structure requires more financial investment and formalities. This is especially true when the organization is collecting and preserving objects with the intention of maintaining those collections for the public benefit. In that case, a more formal structure can permit a greater stability and access to resources that will permit long-term growth and permanence. For example, a community group that begins collecting the community's history and ephemera may elect to formally incorporate as a nonprofit corporation and apply for tax-exempt status as the project grows, as that would permit the corporation to enter legal relationships, purchase property, open lines of credit with banks and other creditors, and more readily raise funds through donations and grants, all while limiting the personal liability for the individuals involved.

CONCLUSION

The business structures available offer a variety of levels of complexity and protection for the individuals or businesses involved in their formation. Each offers advantages and disadvantages and can impact the business' ability to grow over its lifetime. Therefore, choosing which business structure best fits the needs of any enterprise is highly fact-specific. Complicating this is the fact that all the business structures are governed by state law, meaning the specifics of each type cannot be covered in a general text. Therefore, the best advice is to conduct thorough research into the options available in a particular jurisdiction and to follow this research up with reliance on competent and knowledgeable legal advice.

NOTES

1. As with other forms of business structures, sole proprietorships are defined and regulated under state law. Consult your jurisdiction's laws for a complete understanding of this topic.

2. This is an application of the private inurement test, which is one of the four tests applied to nonprofit organizations by the IRS when they seek tax-exempt recognition. The private inurement test ensures the organization's primary function is to benefit the public and not individuals or groups closely related to the organization. Sole proprietorships, by definition, operate for the benefit of the individual who formed the proprietorship, and therefore they fail the private inurement test.

3. Sole proprietorships may still be recommended to register with appropriate state agencies, for instance to register a business name or to collect and remit sales taxes.

4. As with other forms of business structures, unincorporated associations are defined and regulated under state law. Consult your jurisdiction's laws for a complete understanding of this topic.

5. The shared goal must be lawful.

6. Joint ventures are outside the scope of this text. Essentially, they can be understood as a business that is engaged in by two or more entities for realizing a single, defined project. Unlike a partnership, which is entered into with the purpose of conducting business generally or over an extended period of time, a joint venture is created to realize a particular project or series of projects and then naturally terminate.

7. See "In Focus: Nonprofit Corporations and Tax Exemption" for more information.

8. At the time of writing, associations with annual gross receipts not more than $5,000 did not have to file Form 1023 to operate as a 501(c)(3) tax-exempt organization.

9. Some states have legislation that does permit unincorporated associations to own property or enter contracts in their own name. See your local laws for further guidance.

10. As with other forms of business structures, partnerships are defined and regulated under state law. Consult your jurisdiction's laws for a complete understanding of this topic. This text will only discuss general partnerships. Limited partnerships (LPs) operate in a similar manner but with two "tiers" of partners—general partners, who carry all weight and responsibility of managing the business, and limited partners, who have both limited managerial control and limited exposure to financial liability. Partnerships may elect to form as an LP or an LLP at the time the partnership is formed in the partnership agreement.

11. The dissolution rules discussed here differ for a limited partnership. There, general partners may leave at any time. However, limited partners may only leave the partnership per the terms found in the partnership agreement. Unlike in a general partnership, the resignation of a partner (general or limited) does not trigger dissolution unless all the partners agree to that dissolution.

12. There is a mechanism available to avoid this automatic dissolution that can be instituted at the time of the partnership's creation. This so-called buy-sell agreement outlines the terms of a future buyout of a partner, including the buyout costs and who may execute the buyout option.

13. Most states and the Internal Revenue Service do not directly tax partnerships. Instead, profits and losses "pass through" to the partners, and the partners are each responsible to include their share of the partnership's income and losses on their personal tax returns. The amount to be taxed is based on each partner's ownership stake in the partnership as outlined in the partnership agreement. A minority of states do tax partnerships directly instead of permitting the "pass through" system to the partners. When a partnership is taxed directly, the profits to be taxed may be calculated based on the location of the partnership's principal office or on what amount of profits were earned on business conducted within that state. Consult your local law for guidance. If there is no partnership agreement, each partner will be presumed to have an equal stake.

14. Depending on the state's laws, the LLC may elect to be subject to corporate-style tax rules instead of the pass through taxation of a partnership.

15. Depending on state law, an LLC may be operated as a nonprofit organization. However, currently the Internal Revenue Service will only recognize an LLC as a tax-exempt 501(c)(3) organization if all its members are themselves also 501(c)(3) organizations. Other regulations apply for an LLC to receive tax-exempt recognition from the Internal Revenue Service. Consulting a knowledgeable attorney is recommended.

16. As with other forms of business structures, corporations are defined and regulated under state law. Consult your jurisdiction's laws for a complete understanding of this topic.

17. There is a special type of corporation, the S corporation, that *does* permit profits and limited losses to pass through the corporation to the personal income of the owners. Not all states recognize S-corps, and they do not all tax them in the same way. Consult local law.

18. Privately held corporations are also known as close corporations, closely held corporations, or private companies.

19. Publicly held corporations are also known as public companies or publicly traded companies.

20. See "In Focus: Nonprofit Corporations and Tax Exemption" for more information.

21. As with other forms of business structures, limited liability companies are defined and regulated under state law. Consult your jurisdiction's laws for a complete understanding of this topic.

22. For example, depending on the state's laws, the LLC may elect to be subject to corporate-style tax rules instead of the pass through taxation of a partnership.

23. In addition to the wide range of laws that apply to LLCs on the state level, some states recognize a hybrid form known as a low-profit limited liability company (L3C). The L3C was conceived to bridge a

perceived gap between for-profit and nonprofit organizations that is intended to better permit investment in companies that pursue a public benefit. An even more recent development than the LLC, the first L3C enabling legislation was passed in Vermont in 2008. As stated by Americans for Community Development, a professional organization that promotes L3Cs, this business model is intended to "solv[e] social problems with for profit solutions" (Americans for Community Development, "What Is the L3C?," accessed March 1, 2020. https://americansforcommunitydevelopment.org/). L3Cs combine aspects of a nonprofit (for instance, they must have a charitable or educational purpose) with aspects of a for-profit (the L3C may have owners who receive a distribution of profits similar to a dividend paid to shareholders). At the time of writing, only eight states, three federally recognized tribes, and Puerto Rico permit the incorporation of L3Cs, though they may operate in all fifty states (Americans for Community Development, "Laws," accessed March 1, 2020. https://americansforcommunitydevelopment.org/laws/).

24. Other regulations apply for an LLC to receive tax-exempt recognition from the Internal Revenue Service. Consulting a knowledgeable attorney is recommended. Additionally, the LLC seems to be the business structure favored by for-profit museums, including the Museum of Sex (New York City) and Candytopia (multiple U.S. locations). While the later example is a so-called Instagram museum, which some in the field question as being properly called a museum, it presents a glimpse at what the future holds for some for-profit museums.

25. This is a nonexhaustive list, and the necessary steps to form a specific business may include different or additional steps, depending on the business being started, the goods and/or services offered, and any applicable local laws.

FURTHER RESOURCES

BOARDS OF TRUSTEES AND GOVERNANCE

- Eisenstein, Lena. (2019, December 27). "What Is a Board Composition Matrix and Why Is It Useful?" BoardEffect. https://www.boardeffect.com/blog/what-board-composition-matrix-why-useful/.
- Lawson, Sara, Shorthand Consulting. "Board Recruitment Worksheet." 501 Commons. https://www.501commons.org/resources/tools-and-best-practices/boards-governance/board-matrix-worksheet-shorthand-consulting.
- National Council of Nonprofits. "Board Orientation." https://www.councilofnonprofits.org/tools-resources/board-orientation.
- National Council of Nonprofits. "Finding the Right Board Members for Your Nonprofit." https://www.councilofnonprofits.org/tools-resources/finding-the-right-board-members-your-nonprofit.
- Price, Nick. (2019, January 16). *Nonprofit Laws Checklist for Board Members*. BoardEffect. https://www.boardeffect.com/blog/nonprofit-laws-checklist-for-board-members/.

COLLECTIONS MANAGEMENT, DEACCESSIONING, AND DISPOSAL

- Abandoned Property: For abandoned property laws that apply to museums, see the list compiled by The Society of American Archivists, "Abandoned Property Project," https://www2.archivists.org/groups/acquisitions-appraisal-section/abandoned-property-project.
- American Alliance of Museums. "Deaccession Toolbox." Includes the "Deaccession Toolkit Resource List" and the "Collections Sustainability Rubric" and was developed by a task force with representatives from a variety of AAM Professional Networks. Available at https://www.collectionsstewardship.org/deaccession-toolbox.

- American Alliance of Museums. (2016, updated 2019). "Direct Care of Collections: Ethics, Guidelines and Recommendations." https://www.aam-us.org/wp-content/uploads/2018/01/Direct-Care-of-Collections_March-2019.pdf.
- American Alliance of Museums, Collections Stewardship. "Deaccession Toolbox." The general landing page for the Toolbox, which includes information on the joint Task Force (with members of four different AAM Professional Networks), its charge, and the overall goals, is available at https://www.collectionsstewardship.org/deaccession-toolbox.
- Yerkovich, Sally, Heather Hope Kuruvilla, and Erin Richardson. (2020, May 21). "AASLH Conversations: Deaccessioning in a Recession? Why and Why Not." [Live webinar]. American Association for State and Local History. https://learn.aaslh.org/products/live-webinar-aaslh-conversations-deaccessioning-in-a-recession-why-and-why-not.
- The Deaccession Toolbox is designed to assist "institutions of all sizes consider their work from the broader perspective of sustainability." Recognizing deaccessioning as a normal aspect of collections management, the Toolbox includes two resources:
  - "Deaccession Toolbox Resource Guide." (2019, October). A resource list that is color coded to the Collections Sustainability Rubric. Provides resources to information for institutions at all four levels of the rubric (doing well, struggling, in crisis, and hospice), such as position papers, blog posts, books, etc. https://static1.squarespace.com/static/58a5dc6cb3db2b9edd19c676/t/5ea6f8a9ceb3573cba3bccdf/1588000951705/Deaccession%2BToolbox_Resource%2BList.pdf.
  - "Collections Sustainability Rubric: Making the Right Decisions for Your Collection." (2019, October). A rubric designed to aid a museum to self-assess its overall health in relation to its collection, considering issues across areas of collections care, governance, and management. Cells of the rubric are color coded to allow reference to the Resource Guide. https://static1.squarespace.com/static/58a5dc6cb3db2b9edd19c676/t/5e17b7616bf8972d0986e26f/1578612577993/Deaccession+Toolbox_Collections+Sustainability+Rubric.pdf.
- Simmons, John E. (2018). *Things Great and Small: Collections Management Policies* (2nd). New York: Rowman & Littlefield.
- Simmons, John E., and Toni M. Kiser. (2020). *Museum Registration Methods* (6th). New York: Rowman & Littlefield.

COPYRIGHT, LICENSING, AND THE PUBLIC DOMAIN

- Center for the Study of the Public Domain. Duke University School of Law. Public domain day 2020. A partial list of works that entered the public domain in January 1, 2020, with a focus on books, music, and film. There is also a list for 2019, and it appears the list will be updated annually on January 1. Available at https://web.law.duke.edu/cspd/publicdomainday/2020/.
- Cornell University Library. Copyright Information Center. Copyright term and the public domain in the United States. A useful chart, updated annually, for determining the term of a work's copyright or its status in the public domain based on date and location

of creation, publication history, etc. Available at https://copyright.cornell.edu/public domain#Footnote_1.

- Library of Congress, United States Copyright Office: The Library of Congress produces a number of plain-language circulars addressing a wide variety of issues related to copyrights. The entire collection of circulars can be found here: https://www.copyright.gov/circs/.

- Included here are circulars that may be of use to those just beginning to work in this area or who may need a refresher for common topics relevant to museum work:

  - "Circular 1: Copyright basics." (2019). Available at https://www.copyright.gov/circs/circ01.pdf.
  - "Circular15A: Duration of copyright." (2011). Available at https://www.copyright.gov/circs/circ15a.pdf.
  - "Circular 16A: How to obtain permission." (2017). Available at https://www.copyright.gov/circs/circ16a.pdf.
  - "Circular 21: Reproduction of copyrighted works by educators and librarians." (2014). Available at https://www.copyright.gov/circs/circ21.pdf.
  - "Circular 22: How to investigate the copyright status of a work." (2013). Available at https://www.copyright.gov/circs/circ22.pdf.
  - "Circular 38A: International copyright relations of the United States." (2020). Available at https://www.copyright.gov/circs/circ38a.pdf.
  - At the time of writing, the Library of Congress is in the midst of a multi-year project of updating and renumbering the circulars. A chart tracking these updates is available here: https://www.copyright.gov/circs/circular-update-guide.pdf.

- Mannapperuma, Menesha A., Brianna L. Schofield, Andrea K. Yankovsky, Lila Bailey, and Jennifer M. Urban. (2014, May 27). *Is it in the public domain? A handbook for evaluating the copyright status of a work created in the United States between January 1, 1923 and December 31, 1977*. Berkley, CA: Samuelson Law, Technology & Public Policy Clinic, University of California, Berkeley, School of Law. Available at https://www.law.berkeley.edu/files/FINAL_PublicDomain_Handbook_FINAL(1).pdf.

- Packard, Ashley. (2013). *Digital Media Law* (2nd). Malden, MA: Wiley-Blackwell.

- *The Public Domain Review*. A digital collection of public domain works, including images, books, film, and audio, collected by type, era, and theme. Available at https://publicdomainreview.org/.

- Reilly, Samuel. (2020, February 18). Open access image libraries—a handy list. *Apollo: The International Art Magazine*. A list of museums and archives that maintain databases of public domain works available to download as high-resolution images. Available at https://www.apollo-magazine.com/open-access-image-libraries-a-handy-list/.

- Sunstein LLP. Copyright flowchart. Flowchart that can be used to determine when the copyright term will expire for eligible works. Available at https://www.sunsteinlaw.com/copyright-flowchart.

- United States Copyright Office (2019, April). "Authors, Attribution, and İntegrity: Examining Moral Rights in the United States, A Report of the Register of Copyrights." https://www.copyright.gov/policy/moralrights/full-report.pdf.

DIVERSITY, EQUITY, AND INCLUSION

- BoardSource compiles a variety of resources, including blog posts, plenary talks, research, and professional publications on their "Diversity, Inclusion, Equity" website at https://boardsource.org/research-critical-issues/diversity-equity-inclusion/.
- The Empathetic Museum. "Maturity Model." An assessment tool to aid museums and other cultural institutions to become more empathetic in their work and better reflect the values of their communities. Available at http://empatheticmuseum.weebly.com/maturity-model.html.
- MASS Action. "Readiness Assessment." Used to determine a museum's readiness to engage with equity work. Includes tools to assist in the identification of areas ready for growth and opportunity. Available at https://www.museumaction.org/resources.
- MASS Action. "Toolkit." A guide that provides an introduction to diversity, equity, and inclusion theory and steps toward practical practice, including worksheets and reading lists. Intended to serve as a tool to assist museums to works toward creating greater equity within the museum field. Available at https://static1.squarespace.com/static/58fa685dff7c50f78be5f2b2/t/59dcdd27e5dd5b5a1b51d9d8/1507646780650/TOOLKIT_10_2017.pdf.
- National Council of Nonprofits curates a number of resources for nonprofits seeking to enter or further develop their institutional practices regarding diversity, equity, and inclusion work on their "Why Diversity, Equity, and Inclusion Matter for Nonprofits" webpage at https://www.councilofnonprofits.org/tools-resources/why-diversity-equity-and-inclusion-matter-nonprofits.

ETHICS

- American Alliance of Museums, *Code of Ethics for Museums* (1993, amended 2000), https://www.aam-us.org/programs/ethics-standards-and-professional-practices/code-of-ethics-for-museums/.
- The American Alliance of Museums maintains a link library of codes of ethics for various parts of the museum professions as well as the ethical codes for specific job functions within the profession. Available at https://www.aam-us.org/programs/ethics-standards-and-professional-practices/ethics/.
- American Association for State and Local History, *AASLH Statement of Standards and Ethics* (rev'd 2018), http://download.aaslh.org/AASLH+Statement+of+Standards+and+Ethics+-+Revised+2018.pdf.
- Association of Art Museum Directors, *Professional Practices in Art Museums* (2009), https://aamd.org/sites/default/files/document/2011ProfessionalPracitiesinArtMuseums.pdf.
- International Council of Museums, *Checklist on Ethics of Cultural Property Ownership* (2011), https://icom.museum/wp-content/uploads/2018/07/110825_Checklist_print.pdf.
- International Council of Museums, *ICOM Code of Ethics for Museums* (2004), https://icom.museum/wp-content/uploads/2018/07/ICOM-code-En-web.pdf.

- International Council of Museums, *ICOM Code of Ethics for Natural History Museums* (2013), https://icom.museum/wp-content/uploads/2018/07/nathcode_ethics_en.pdf.
- King, Elaine A., and Gail Levin. (2006). *Ethics and the Visual Arts*. New York: Allworth Press.
- Yerkovich, Sally. (2016). *A Practical Guide to Museum Ethics*. New York: Rowman & Littlefield.

FASB UPDATE

- American Association for State and Local History. "Valuing History Collections." Position paper explaining the AASLH opinion in regard to the practice of capitalization of collections. Prepared by a working group of members of the AASLH Standards & Ethics committee. Available at http://download.aaslh.org/AASLH+Valuing+History+Collections+Position+Paper+May+2020.pdf.
- Financial Accounting Standards Board. (n.d.). *Accounting Standards Update 2019-03: Not-For-Profit Entities (Topic 958): Updating the Definition of Collections.* fasb.org/cs/ContentServer?c=FASBContent_C&cid=1176172408217&d=&pagename=FASB%2FFASBContent_C%2FCompletedProjectPage.
- Tysiac, Ken. (2019, March 21). "FASB modifies definition of 'collections.'" *Journal of Accountancy.* journalofaccountancy.com/news/2019/mar/fasb-definition-of-collections-201920838.html.

FUND-RAISING AND DEVELOPMENT

- Association of Fundraising Professionals. *The donor bill of rights*. Available at https://afp-global.org/donor-bill-rights.
- Exponent Philanthropy. (2017). *A Toolkit for Funders: Great Funder-Nonprofit Relationships*. http://www.exponentphilanthropy.org/wp-content/uploads/EXP_FFSI_Toolkit.pdf.
- National Council of Nonprofits. "Ethical Fundraising." https://www.councilofnonprofits.org/tools-resources/ethical-fundraising.
- National Council of Nonprofits. "Gift Acceptance Policies." https://www.councilofnonprofits.org/tools-resources/gift-acceptance-policies.

MANAGEMENT

- Genoways, Hugh H., Lynne M. Ireland, and Cinnamon Catlin-Legutko. (2017). *Museum Administration 2.0*. New York: Rowman & Littlefield.
- Lord, Gail Dexter, and Barry Lord. (2009). *The Manual of Museum Management* (2nd). Lanham, MD: AltaMira Press.

MUSEUM LAW AND ART LAW

- Courtney, Julia [Ed.] (2015). *The Legal Guide for Museum Professionals*. New York: Rowman & Littlefield.
- Jones, Michael E. (2016). *Art Law: A Concise Guide for Artists, Curators, and Art Educators*. New York: Rowman & Littlefield.
- Legal Issues in Museum Administration annual conference (live and webcast). https://www.ali-cle.org.
- Malaro, Marie C., and Ildiko Pogány DeAngelis. (2012). *A Legal Primer on Managing Museum Collections* (3rd). Washington, D.C.: Smithsonian Books.

MUSEUM LIFECYCLES: CREATION TO CLOSING

- Internal Revenue Service: Lifecycle of an Exempt Organization. Provides links to information relevant to tax-exempt organizations from initial organization to dissolution. Available at https://www.irs.gov/charities-non-profits/life-cycle-of-an-exempt-organization.
- Klein, Janice. (2018, November 13). *Making a good end: How to close a museum.* Includes links to the original webinar audio file, the presentation slides, and a handout that provides a number of important resources for museums as they prepare for closure, including ethical considerations, increasing museum resiliency to difficult situations, and guidelines on how to properly dissolve a nonprofit corporation. Available at https://www.connectingtocollections.org/close-a-museum/.
- At the time of writing, the American Association for State and Local History is in the process of updating their position paper "When a History Museum Closes." Dissemination is expected in late 2020 or early 2021.

NONPROFIT ORGANIZATIONS, TAX EXEMPTION, AND RELATED ISSUES

- The National Association of Attorneys General maintains a list of all the attorneys general (all fifty states plus American Samoa, the District of Columbia, Guam, and Puerto Rico). States attorneys general have general oversight of nonprofit organizations and often include valuable informational documents, sample forms, educational and training opportunities, and links to relevant statutes and regulations. Find the comprehensive list, with links to individual offices of attorneys general, at https://www.naag.org/naag/attorneys-general/whos-my-ag.php.
- Internal Revenue Service Form 1023 is used to apply for tax-exempt status under Section 501(c)(3). Some organizations can submit a streamlined version, Form 1023-EZ, if they meet certain requirements including budgetary limits. Information about both forms, including how to determine Form 1023-EZ eligibility and instructions for both forms, is maintained by the IRS on their website "About Form 1023, Application for Recognition of Exemptions Under 501(c)(3) of the Internal Revenue Code," available at https://www.irs.gov/forms-pubs/about-form-1023.

- Specific information about the streamlined Form 1023-EZ application, including a link to instructions and an eligibility worksheet, is maintained by the IRS at "About Form 1023-EZ, Streamlined Application for Recognition of Exemption Under Section 501(c)(3) of the Internal Revenue Code" at https://www.irs.gov/forms-pubs/about-form-1023-ez.
- Internal Revenue Service: StayExempt. The IRS website for organizations seeking to acquire and maintain 501(c)(3) tax-exempt status. Available at https://www.stayexempt.irs.gov/.
- Internal Revenue Service: Small to Mid-Sized Tax Exempt Organization Workshop is a website with a number of interactive presentations on topics such as how to apply for and maintain 501(c)(3) status, deductions for charitable contributions, the Form 990, and unrelated business income. Available at https://www.stayexempt.irs.gov/home/resource-library/virtual-small-mid-size-tax-exempt-organization-workshop.
- Internal Revenue Service: Supporting Organizations—Requirements and Types. An overview of the tests a supporting organization must satisfy as well as the types of classifications of these organizations based on the relationship test. Available at https://www.irs.gov/charities-non-profits/charitable-organizations/supporting-organizations-requirements-and-types.
- Internal Revenue Service: Form 990 Series Which Forms Do Organizations File. This site details the various versions of the Form 990 and what the requirements are for each. Links are provided to the individual forms. Available at https://www.irs.gov/charities-non-profits/form-990-series-which-forms-do-exempt-organizations-file-filing-phase-in.

TRADEMARK REGISTRATION AND MAINTENANCE

- The United States Patent and Trademark Office maintains an online library of forms, videos, and instructional materials regarding trademarks. Information on how to apply, what paperwork to file, what fees to pay, the timeline of the process, and other useful information is compiled on their website at https://www.uspto.gov/trademark.
- Search for trademarks using the online Trademark Electronic Search System (TESS) at http://tmsearch.uspto.gov/bin/gate.exe?f=tess&state=4809:p32d1m.1.1.
- Contact the Trademark Assistance Center
  - Toll-Free 1-800-786-9199
  - Local 1-571-272-9250 (press 0)
  - Email TrademarkAssistanceCenter@uspto.gov

WORKER CLASSIFICATION

- Internal Revenue Service. (2017, July 20, updated July 8, 2020). FS-2017-09: Understanding employee vs. contractor designation. Provides an overview of the issues related to worker classification with links to additional resources. Available at https://www.irs.gov/newsroom/understanding-employee-vs-contractor-designation.

WORKER CLASSIFICATION: CALIFORNIA SPECIFIC

- Bogatin, M. J., Kyle Kate Dudley, and Alma Robinson, with Sanam Rafiq. (2020). *Life after AB5: A Toolkit.* California Lawyers for the Arts. Provides an overview of AB-5 and resources for California employers and workers. Available at https://calawyersforthearts .org/resources/Documents/AB5%20ToolKit_February%202020.pdf.
- Californians for the Arts. *About AB5.* A website maintaining a number of resources related to AB-5, from understanding what the law is to how it applies in a wide variety of situations. Available at https://www.californiansforthearts.org/ab-5.
- Gonzalez, Assemblywoman Lorena. (n.d.). AB5: Stop the misclassification of workers. Fact sheet from the office of Assemblywoman Gonzalez, author of California AB-5. Available at https://d3n8a8pro7vhmx.cloudfront.net/arts4bayarea/pages/241/attachments/ original/1573860784/AB.pdf?1573860784.

BIBLIOGRAPHY

CASES AND STATUTES

Abercrombie & Fitch Co. v. Hunting World, Inc., 537 F.2d 4, 9 (2d Cir. 1976).

Advisory Council on Historic Preservation, 54 U.S.C. §§ 304101-112.

American Antiquities Act of 1906, 16 U.S.C. §§ 431-33.

Archaeological Resources Protection Act, 16 U.S.C. § 470aa-mm.

Arts and Artifacts Indemnity Act, 20 U.S.C. §§ 971 *et. seq.*

Ashcroft v. Free Speech Coalition, 535 U.S. 234 (2002).

Berne Convention for the Protection of Literary and Artistic Works art. 2(6), Sept. 9, 1886, 1161 U.N.T.S. 3.

Booking.com B.V. v. U.S. Patent & Trademark Office, No. 17-2458, (4th Cir. Feb. 4, 2019).

Brief for the Association of Art Museum Directors, et. al. as Amici Curiae Supporting Petitioner, *Kirtsaeng v. John Wiley & Sons, Inc.*, 568 U.S. 519 (2013) (No. 11-697)

Cal. Civ. Code § 986, "California Resale Royalty Act."

Cal. Civ. Code § 987, "California Art Preservation Act."

California Assembly Bill 5, "Worker Status: Employees and Independent Contractors." (2019–2020).

California Assembly Bill 1850, "Worker Classification: Employees and Independent Contractors." (2019–2020).

Campbell v. Acuff-Rose Music, Inc., 501 U.S. 569 (1994).

Carter v. Helmsley-Spear, Inc., 861 F. Supp 303 (S.D.N.Y. 1994).

Carter-Wallace, Inc. v. Procter & Gamble Co., 434 F.2d 794, 800 (9th Cir. 1970).

Cassirer v. Thyssen-Bornemisza Collection Found, No. 19-55616 (9th Cir. Aug. 17, 2020).

Castillo v. G&M Realty L.P., 18-498-cv (L) (2d Cir. 2020).

CDX Liquidating Trust v. Venrock Assocs., 640 F.3d 209 (7th Cir. 2011).

Cohen v. G&M Realty L.P., Case No. 13-CV-05612(FB)(RLM) (E.D.N.Y. Jun. 13, 2018), *aff'd Castillo v. G&M Realty L.P.*, 18-498-cv (L) (2d Cir. 2020).

Community for Creative Non-Violence v. Reid, 490 U.S. 730 (1989).

Convention on Cultural Property Implementation Act, 19 U.S.C. §§ 2601-2613.

Convention on the Means of Prohibiting and Preventing the Illicit Import, Export, and Transfer of Ownership of Cultural Property, Preamble, Nov. 11, 1970, 823 U.N.T.S. 231.

Copyright Act of 1909, Pub. L. 60-349 § 10 (*repealed by* the Copyright Act of 1976).

Copyright Act of 1976, 17 U.S.C. §§ 101 *et. seq.*

Copyright Term Extension Act of 1998, Pub. L. 105-298.

Council of the European Communities. (1993, November 24). Council Directive 93/98/EEC of 29 October 1993 Harmonizing the Term of Protection of Copyright and Certain Related Rights.

Curation of Federally Owned and Administered Archaeological Collections, 36 C.F.R. Part 79.
Dynamex Operations West, Inc. v. Superior Court of Los Angeles, 4 Cal. 5th 903 (2018).
Eldred v. Ashcroft, 537 U.S. 186 (2003).
Endangered Species Act, 16 U.S.C. §§ 1531-44.
Federal Insurance Contributions Act, 26 U.S.C. §§ 3101 *et. seq.*
Fourth Estate Public Benefit Corp. v. Wall-Street.com, 586 U.S. ___ (2019).
Gilliam v. American Broadcasting Companies, 538 F.2d 14 (2d Cir. 1976).
Grosz v. Museum of Modern Art, 772 F.Supp.2d 473, 476 (S.D.N.Y. 2010).
Harper & Row v. Nation Enterprises, 471 U.S. 539, 565 (1985).
Holocaust Expropriated Art Recovery Act of 2016, Pub. L. No. 114-308, 130 Stat. 1524 (2016).
Hopi Tribe v. Trump, No. 1:17-cv-02590-TSC (*amended compl. filed* D.D.C. Nov. 8, 2019).
Iancu v. Brunetti, 588 U.S. ___ (2019).
In re Bayer Aktiengesellschaft, Trademark Trial and Appeal Board, 2005 TTAB LEXIS 521 (2005).
In re Celia Clarke, Trademark Trial and Appeal Board, 17 U.S.P.Q.2D (BNA) 1238 (1990).
In re Mavety Media Group Ltd., 33 F.3d 1367 (Fed. Cir. 1994).
Internal Revenue Code, 26 U.S.C. §§ 1 *et. seq.*
I.R.S. Priv. Ltr. Rul. 201441017 (Oct. 10, 2014).
Justice for Uncompensated Survivors Today Act, Pub. L. 115-171.
Kelley v. Chicago Park Dist., 635 F.3d 290, 299 (7th Cir. 2011).
Kelly v. Arriba Soft Corp., 280 F.3d 934 (9th Cir. 2002) withdrawn and re-filed at 336 F.3d 811 (9th Cir. 2003).
Lanham Act, 15 U.S.C. §§ 1051 *et. seq.*
Martin v. City of Indianapolis, 192 F.3d 608, 611 (1999).
Miller v. California, 413 U.S. 15, 20 (1973).
National Historic Preservation Act, 16 U.S.C. §§ 470 *et. seq.*
National Museum of the American Indian Act of 1989, 20 U.S.C. § 80q.
Native American Graves Protection and Repatriation Act, 25 U.S.C. §§ 3001-13.
National Register of Historic Places, 54 U.S.C. §§ 302101-108.
New York v. Ferber, 458 U.S. 747 (1982).
N.Y. Not for Profit Corp L § 402 (2014).
Osborne v. Ohio, 495 U.S. 103 (1990).
People v. Trump, 66 Misc.3d 200 (204), 112 N.Y.S.3d 467 (2019).
Perry Education Assoc'n. v. Perry Local Educators' Assocn., 460 U.S. 37, 70-71 (1983).
Phillips v. Pembroke Real Estate, 459 F. 3d 128, 129 (1st Cir. 2006).
Piarowski v. Illinois Community College, 759 F.3d 625, 632 (7th Cir. 1985).
Protection of Archaeological Resources Uniform Regulations, 36 C.F.R. Part 296.
Protection of Historic Properties, 36 C.F.R. Part 800.
Pueblo of San Ildefonso v. Ridlon, 103 F. 3d 936 (10th Cir. 1996).
Qualitex Co. v. Jacobson Products Co., Inc., 514 U.S. 159, 162 (1995).
Restatement (2nd) of Contracts.
Rev. Rul. 66-178, 1966-1 C.B. 138.
Rev. Rul. 71-395, 1971-2 C.B. (1971).
Rev. Rul. 76-152, 1976-1 C.B. 151, *2 (1976).
Rev. Proc. 90-12, 1990-1 C.B. 471.
Roth v. United States, 354 U.S. 476, 487 (1957).
Salinger v. Random House, Inc., 811 F.2d 90, 95-96 (2d Cir. 1987).
Serra v. United States Gen. Servs. Admin., 847 F.2d 1045, 1047 (2d Cir. 1988).
Sony Corp. of America v. Universal City Studios, Inc., 464 U.S. 417 (1984).
Spanish American Cultural Assoc. of Bergenfield v. Comm'r, T.C. Memo 1994-510 (1994).
State Historic Preservation Programs, 54 U.S.C. §§ 302301-304.
Stern v. Lucy Webb Hayes National Training School for Deaconesses and Missionaries, 381 F. Supp. 1003, 1020 (D.D.C. 1974).
Texas v. Johnson, 491 U.S. 397 (1989).
Towell v. Comm'r, T.C. Summary Opinion 2010-141 (2010).
Uniform Commercial Code.

United Nations Educational, Scientific and Cultural Organization, Convention for the Protection of Cultural Property in the Event of Armed Conflict with Regulations for the Execution of the Convention. The Hague, May 14, 1954.

United Nations Educational, Scientific, and Cultural Organization, Convention for the Protection of Cultural Property in the Event of Armed Conflict, First Protocol to the Convention for the Protection of Cultural Property in the Event of Armed conflict 1954, May 14, 1954.

United Nations Educational, Scientific, and Cultural Organization, Convention for the Protection of Cultural Property in the Event of Armed Conflict, Second Protocol, Mar. 26, 1999.

United States Constitution.

United States v. Eichman, 496 U.S. 310 (1990).

U.S. Patent & Trademark Office v. Booking.com B.V., 591 U.S. ___ (2020).

Visual Artists Rights Act of 1990, 17 U.S.C. § 106A.

Wallace Computer Systems, Inc. v. Adams Business Forms, Inc., 837 F.Supp. 1413, 1416 (N.D. Ill. 1993).

Ward v. Rock Against Racism, 491 U.S. 781, 798-99 (1989).

Younger v. Wisdom Society, 121 Cal. App. 3d 683 (1981).

Zuckerman v. Metropolitan Museum of Art, 928 F.3d 186 (2d Cir. 2019).

Zuckerman v. Metropolitan Museum of Art, 140 S.Ct. 1269 (2020), *cert. denied* (U.S. March 2, 2020) (No. 19-942).

ARTICLES, TEXTS, AND RELATED

Advisory Council on Historic Preservation, "About the ACHP."

Advisory Council on Historic Preservation, *Protecting Historic Properties: A Citizen's Guide to Section 106 Review* (Washington, D.C.: Advisory Council on Historic Preservation).

Advisory Council on Historic Preservation, "Working with Section 106."

Ahmad, Yahaya, "The Scope and Definitions of Cultural Heritage: From Tangible to Intangible," *International Journal of Heritage Studies* 12 (May 2006): 292.

American Alliance of Museums. (2019, July 23). "51 Museums Selected for Board Diversity and Inclusion Program as Part of $4 Million National Initiative."

American Alliance of Museums. (2018). "Alliance Reference Guide: Developing an Institutional Code of Ethics."

American Alliance of Museums. (1993, revised 2000). Code of Ethics for Museums.

American Alliance of Museums, "Core Documents."

American Alliance of Museums. (2016, April). *Direct Care of Collections: Ethics, Guidelines and Recommendations* [White paper]. Washington, D.C.

American Alliance of Museums. (n.d.). Museum Facts & Data.

American Alliance of Museums, "Recommended Procedures for Providing Information to the Public about Objects Transferred in Europe during the Nazi Era" (Washington, D.C.: American Alliance of Museums, 2013).

American Alliance of Museums, "Statement on the Deaccessioning by the Delaware Art Museum and the Action Taken by the AAM Accreditation Commission."

American Alliance of Museums and Oxford Economic. (2017). Museums as Economic Engines: A National Study. Washington, D.C.

American Association for State and Local History. (2018). *Statement of Standards and Ethics.*

American Association for State and Local History. (2020). *Valuing History Collections.* Nashville, TN: Author.

American Association for State and Local History. *When a History Museum Closes* (2nd edition). *Forthcoming.*

American Association of Physicists in Medicine, "Ad Hoc Committee to Respond to the Impact of the Coronavirus (COVID-19) on AAPM Meetings (AHRICM)."

Americans for Community Development, "Laws."

Americans for Community Development, "What Is the L3C?"

Art Dealers Association of America, "Code of Ethics and Professional Practices."

Association of Art Museum Directors. (2010, June 9, amended October 2015). AAMD Policy on Deaccessioning.

Association of Art Museum Directors. (2018, May 25). "Press Release: AAMD Statement on Sanction of Berkshire Museum and La Salle University Art Museum."

Association of Art Museum Directors, "Association of Art Museum Directors Sanctions Delaware Art Museum."

Association of Art Museum Directors. (2020, April 15). "Press Release: AAMD Board of Trustees Approves Resolution to Provide Additional Financial Flexibility to Art Museums During Pandemic Crisis."

Association of Art Museum Directors. (2011). *Professional Practices in Art Museums.* New York. https://aamd. org/sites/default/files/document/2011ProfessionalPracitiesinArtMuseums.pdf.

Aswad, Jem. (2020, April 17). "Musicians to Be Exempt from California 'Gig Economy' Assembly Bill 5." *Variety.*

Blue Shield International.

BoardSource. (n.d.). "Diversity, Inclusion, Equity."

Bonifacino, Ginny Cascio, and Heather Hope Kuruvilla. (2019). *The Business of Being an IMP* [Webinar handout and slides]. Washington, D.C.: AAM Independent Museum Professionals Network.

Buck, Rebecca [edited and updated by John E. Simmons and Toni M. Kiser], "Found-in-Collection," in *Museum Registration Methods* [6th].

Carré, F. (2015). *(In)dependent Contractor Misclassification* (Briefing Paper No. 403). Washington, D.C.: Economic Policy Institute.

College Art Association, "Statement Concerning the Deaccession of Works of Art."

Commission for Art Recovery, established 1997, New York, NY, http://www.commartrecovery.org/index.php.

"College Strips Off Kozlowski Name." *CNN Money*, Aug. 18, 2005, https://money.cnn.com/2005/08/18/news/ newsmakers/kozlowski_seton/

Creative Commons, "CC0: 'No Rights Reserved.'"

Cultural Property Advisory Committee, Bureau of Educational and Cultural Affairs, U.S. Department of State, https://eca.state.gov/cultural-heritage-center/cultural-property-advisory-committee.

Daly, Karen, "Provenance Research in Museum Collections: An Overview," in *Museum Registration Methods* [6th].

Department of the Treasury, Internal Revenue Services. (Reviewed 2017, September 10). Internal Revenue Manual Part 25, chapter 18.8, section 1. Basic Principles of Community Property Law. "Exhibit 25.18.1-1 "Comparison of State Law Differences in Community Property."

Department of the Treasury, Internal Revenue Service, "Form 8283: Noncash Charitable Contributions" (rev'd Nov. 2019).

Department of the Treasury, Internal Revenue Service. (2017, July 20). Fact Sheet-2017-09: Understanding Employee vs. Contractor Classification.

Department of the Treasury, Internal Revenue Service, "Notice 2020-65: Relief with Respect to Employment Tax Deadlines Applicable to Employers Affected by the Ongoing Coronavirus (COVID-19) Disease 2019 Pandemic."

Department of the Treasury, Internal Revenue Service, "Publication 15-A: Employer's Supplemental Tax Guide," (2019, December 23).

Department of the Treasury, Internal Revenue Service, "Publication 526: Charitable Contributions" (2019).

Department of the Treasury, Internal Revenue Service, "Publication 557: Tax-Exempt Status for Your Organization" (revised January 2020).

Department of the Treasury, Internal Revenue Service, "Publication 561: Determining the Value of Donated Property" (revised Feb. 2020).

Department of the Treasury, Internal Revenue Service, "Publication 1771: Charitable Contributions: Substantiation and Disclosure Requirements" (rev'd March 2016).

Desvallées, André, and François Mairesse [eds.], *Key Concepts of Museology*, trans. Suzanne Nash (International Council of Museums, 2010).

Eggen, Dan. (2010, June 22). "National Pork Board Targets ThinkGeek Web Site: Blame the Unicorns." *The Washington Post.*

Eizenstat, Stuart E. (1998, December 3). Concluding statement, Washington Conference on Holocaust-Era Assets, Washington, D.C.

European Parliament and the Council of the European Union, "On the Resale Right for the Benefit of the Author of an Original Work of Art," June 6, 2001, Council Directive 2001/84/EC.

European Union, "On the Resale Right for the Benefit of the Author of an Original Work of Art," Council Directive 2001/84/EC.

Federal Bureau of Investigation, "National Stolen Art File (NSAF)."

Federal Bureau of Investigations, "Protecting your Treasures: Advice from Our Art Theft Expert."

Financial Accounting Standards Board, Norwalk, CT, https://www.fasb.org/home.

Financial Accounting Standards Board. (n.d.). *Accounting Standards Update 2019-03: Not-For-Profit Entities (Topic 958): Updating the Definition of Collections.*

Financial Accounting Standards Board, "Statement of Financial Accounting Standards No. 116: Accounting for Contributions Received and Contributions Made" (Norwalk, CT: Financial Accounting Foundation, 1993).

Fischer, Charles. (2010). *Easements to Protect Historic Properties: A Useful Historic Preservation Tool with Potential Tax Benefits.* Washington, D.C.: National Park Service, Technical Preservation Services.

German Lost Art Foundation, Results of the Specialist Conference, November 26–29, 2018, Berlin, Germany.

Gleason Bogert, George, "Proposed Legislation Regarding State Supervision of Charities," *Michigan Law Review* 52 (1954): 633–34.

Gold, Marc S., and Stefanie S. Jandl, "Why the Association of Art Museum Directors's [*sic*] Move on Deaccessioning Matters So Much" (18 May 2020), *The Art Newspaper.*

Goldstein, Jason R., "Note, Deaccession: Not Such a Dirty Word," *Cardozo Arts and Entertainment Law Journal* 15 (1997): 213–48.

Honan, William H. (1991, March 30). "Soviets Reported to Hide Looted Art." *The New York Times.*

International Council of Museums, *ICOM Code of Ethics for Museums* (2004).

International Institute for the Unification of Private Law (UNIDROIT), established 1926, Villa Aldobrandini, Rome, Italy, https://www.unidroit.org/

Jokilhto, J. [comp.], International Centre for the Study of the Preservation and Restoration of Cultural Property Working Group "Heritage and Society," *Definitions of Cultural Heritage: References to Documents in History,* 1990, revised Jan. 15, 2005.

Kirkland, Jesse. (2019, December 4). "In 2024, Mickey Mouse Will Finally Enter the Public Domain—Sort of." *The Blog of the NYU Journal of Intellectual Property and Entertainment Law.*

Kutner, Luis, and Henry H. Koven, "Charitable Trust Legislation in the Several States," *Northwestern University Law Review* 61 (1966): 411–425.

Kuruvilla, Heather Hope, "All in a Day's Work: How Museums May Approach Deaccessioning as a Necessary Collections Management Tool," *DePaul Journal of Art, Technology and Intellectual Property* 22 (2011) (published as Heather Hope Stephens).

Legal Information Institute, Cornell University, established 1992, https://www.law.cornell.edu/.

Lord, Gail Dexter, Forward Planning and the Cost of Collecting.

Malaro, Marie C., "Deaccessioning: The American Perspective," in *A Deaccession Reader,* ed. Stephen E. Weil (Washington, D.C.: American Association of Museums, 1997).

Malaro, Marie C., *Museum Governance: Mission, Ethics, Policy* (Washington, D.C.: Smithsonian Institution Press, 1994).

Malaro, Marie, and Ildiko Pogány DeAngelis, *A Legal Primer on Managing Museum Collections* [3rd] (Washington, D.C.: Smithsonian Books, 2012).

McEntegart, Jane. (2010, June 24). "ThinkGeek in Trouble for Selling Unicorn Meat." *Tom's Guide.*

Merret, Helen, The Association of Registrars and Collections, "Old Loans: Out of Sight, Out of Mind [information session write-up]."

Morris, Martha, and Antonia Moser, "Deaccessioning," in *Museum Registration Methods* [5th], ed. Rebecca A. Buck and Jean Allman Gilmore, 100–108 (Washington, D.C.: The AAM Press, 2010).

National Association of Attorney Generals, "Who's My AG?"

National Conference of State Historic Preservation Officers, "What Is a State Historic Preservation Officer (SHPO)?"

National Endowment for the Arts, "Arts and Artifacts Indemnity Program: Domestic Indemnity," http://arts.gov/artistic-fields/museums/arts-and-artifacts-indemnity-program-domestic-indemnity.

National Endowment for the Arts, "Arts and Artifacts Indemnity Program: International Indemnity," http://arts.gov/artistic-fields/museums/arts-and-artifacts-indemnity-program-international-indemnity.

National Historic Landmarks Program, National Park Service, U.S. Department of the Interior, Washington, DC, https://www.nps.gov/orgs/1582/index.htm.

National Park Service, Archaeology Program. (n.d.). "The Archaeological Resources Protection Act of 1979 (ARPA)," excerpting Francis P. McManamon, *Archaeological Method and Theory: An Encyclopedia*, (Linda Ellis, ed.) (New York: Garland Publishing Co., 2000), 62–64.

National Park Service, "Archaeology Program: Curation of Federally Owned and Administered Archaeological Collections (36 C.F.R. 79)."

National Park Service, "Determining the Eligibility of a Property for National Historic Landmark Designation."

National Park Service, National Register of Historic Places, "What Is the National Register of Historic Places?"

National Park Service, "National Register of Historic Places Program: Research."

National Park Service, "National Historic Landmarks Program."

National Park Service, U.S. Department of the Interior, Washington, DC, https://www.nps.gov.

National Trust for Historic Preservation. (n.d.). Established October 26, 1949, Washington, DC. https://savingplaces.org/

National Trust of Historic Preservation. (2017, December 6). "Broad Coalition Sues to Stop Trump Administration's Unlawful Dismemberment of the Bears Ears National Monument."

Nazi-Era Provenance Internet Portal, "The Nazi-Era Provenance Internet Portal Project."

New York Attorney General. (2019, November 7). *Press Release: AG James Secures Court Order Against Donald J. Trump, Trump Children, and Trump Foundation.*

New York State Office of the Attorney General, "Charities: Guides & Publications," http://www.charitiesnys.com/guides_advice_new.jsp.

O'Donnell, Nicholas. (2020, August 18). "'Moralistic Preening' and Broken Commitments under the Washington Principles: Ninth Circuit Chastises Spain for Keeping Nazi-Looted Pissarro but Rules Painting Will Not Return to Cassirer Family." Art Law Report.

O'Hare, Michael. (2005). *Capitalizing Art Museum Collections: Awkward for Museum but Good for Art and for Society.* Association for Public Policy Analysis and Management Research Conference, Washington, D.C, November 2005.

Pogány DeAngelis, Ildiko [updated and edited by John E. Simmons and Toni M. Kiser], "Old Loans and Museum Property Laws," in *Museum Registration Methods* [6th].

Roca-Hachem, Rochelle. "UNESCO and UNIDROIT: Cooperation in the Fight Against Illicit Traffic in Cultural Property." *Uniform Law Review* 10 (August 2005): 536–42. doi: 10.1093/ulr/10.3.536.

Salamon, L. S., and C. L. Newhouse. (2009). The 2019 Nonprofit Employment Report. *Nonprofit Economic Data no. 47.* Baltimore: Johns Hopkins Center for Civil Society Studies.

Simmons, John E., "Collections Management Policies," in *Museum Registration Methods* [6th].

Simmons, John E., *Things Great and Small: Collections Management Policies* [2nd] (New York: Rowman & Littlefield, 2018).

Simmons, John E., and Toni M. Kiser, "Acquisitions and Accessioning," in *Museum Registration Methods* [6th].

Simmons, John E., and Toni M. Kiser [eds.], *Museum Registration Methods* [6th] (New York: Rowman & Littlefield, 2020).

Society of American Archivists, The, "Abandoned Property Project."

Spiegler, Howard N. (2001). "Recovering Nazi-Looted Art: Report from the Front Lines." *Connecticut Journal of International Law, 16*(2), 297–312.

Stewart, Dafina-Lazarus. (2017, March 30). "The Language of Appeasement." *Inside HigherEd.*

Sungaila, Mary-Christine, William Feldman, and Marco A. Pulido. (2020, March 11). "Holocaust-Era Art and Property Recovery Claims after 'Zuckerman.'" *The Recorder.*

Terezín Declaration on Holocaust Era Assets and Related Issues.

Townsend, Allie (2010, June 21). "Think Geek Gets Cease and Desist for April Fool's Day Canned Unicorn Mean." *Time.*

Trump, Donald. (2020, August 8). "Memorandum: Deferring Payroll Tax Obligations in Light of the Ongoing Covid-19 Disaster."

United Nations Educational, Scientific and Cultural Organization, "Permanent Delegation of Nigeria to UNESCO."

United Nations Educational, Scientific and Cultural Organization (UNESCO), established November 16, 1945, Paris, France, https://en.unesco.org/.

United States Copyright Office. (2019, April). "Authors, Attribution, and Integrity: Examining Moral Rights in the United States, A Report of the Register of Copyrights."

United States Copyright Office, "Circular 1: Copyright Basics" 2012.

United States Copyright Office, "Circular 30: Works Made for Hire" (rev'd Sept. 2017).

United States Copyright Office, "Orphan Works and Mass Digitization: A Report of the Register of Copyrights," June 2015.

United States Copyright Office, Office of the Register of Copyrights, "Resale Royalties: An Updated Analysis" (2013).

United States Department of State, Office of the Special Envoy for Holocaust Issues, Bureau of European and Eurasian Affairs (March 2020), "Justice for Uncompensated Survivors Today (JUST) Act Report."

United States Trademark Reg. No. 11210, filed Apr. 7, 1884, reg. issued May 24, 1884, Samson Rope Technologies, Inc., Ferndale, WA.

United States Patent and Trademark Office, "Trademark Manual of Examining Protocol" (October 2018).

Wex Law Dictionary. (n.d.). Cornell Law School, Legal Information Institute. https://www.law.cornell.edu/wex.

White, Jennifer L., "When It's OK to Sell the Monet: A Trustee-Fiduciary-Duty Framework for Analyzing the Deaccessioning of Art to Meet Museum Operating Expenses," *Michigan Law Review* 94 (1996): 1045–66.

World Intellectual Property Organization. Established 1967, Geneva, Switzerland. https://www.wipo.int/portal/en/.

World Jewish Restitution Organization (WJRO). (n.d.). "Guidelines and Best Practices for Restitution."

Yerkovich, Sally, *A Practical Guide to Museum Ethics* (Rowman & Littlefield, 2016).

INDEX

first sale doctrine, 63–64, 191–92;
fixation, 64–65, 190;
and ideas, 190;
infringement, 73, 199–200;
joint work, 79, 192;
licensing, 81, 215–20;
versus moral rights, 84, 141–42;
notice of registration, 192, 194;
novelty, 190;
originality, 190;
orphaned works, 99;
ownership of exclusive rights under, 192;
pre-1978 works, 194–95;
pseudonymous work, 106, 193;
public display right, 107–8, *191*, 191–92;
public domain, 108–9, 193;
Public Domain Day, 195–96;
public performance right, 110, *191*;
publication, 15, 193–94, 217;
registration, 192, 194;
reproduction right, 63–64, 108, 117, *191*;
subject matter of, 190;
tangibility, 190;
versus trademarks, 35;
work made for hire, 144–45, 192;
works of authorship, 145–56
Copyright Act of 1909, 194–95
Copyright Clause, 35;
and fair use, 201
Copyright Duration Directive 93/98/EEC. *See*
Copyright Term Extension Act
Copyright Term Extension Act, 195–96
corporation, 35, *251*, 251–52;
nonprofit corporation, 221
Corpus Juris Civilis. *See* civil law
co-tenant. *See* tenancy in common
COVID-19
Deferring Payroll Tax Obligations in Light of
the Ongoing COVID-19 Disaster, 156n268
response of the Association of Art Museum
Directors, 186n22
CPIA. *See* Convention of Cultural Property
Implementation Act
Creative Commons, 108–9
CTEA. *See* Copyright Term Extension Act
cultural heritage, 36
cultural patrimony. *See* cultural heritage
cultural property. *See* cultural heritage
Cultural Property Advisory Committee, 32, 37;
bilateral agreement, 15–16;
Convention on Cultural Property
Implementation Act, 32
culturally affiliated objects. *See* Native American
Graves Protection and Repatriation Act

Curation of Federally Owned and Administered
Archaeological Collections, 37–38
customs regulations. *See* Endangered Species Act
cy pres doctrine, 38–39;
versus doctrine of equitable deviation, 48
See equity

deaccession, 39, 179–84;
versus accessioning, 180;
and capitalization of collections, 18–19;
and conflicts of interest, 29;
and direct care of collections, 43–44, 182–83;
versus disposal, 179;
donor notification of, 181, 185n11;
ethics of, 173–74, 181;
and Financial Accounting Standards Board,
60–61, 183;
legality of, 173;
reasons to, 180–81;
of restricted gift, 181;
and sanctions, 176n8;
tax consequences of, 77–78;
written policy, 181
See also proceeds from deaccessioning
dealer, 39–40
declaratory
judgment, 40
relief. *See* equity
deduction, 41, 49;
IRS Form 8283, 78;
partial gift, 99–100;
qualified appraisal, 110–11;
qualified appraiser, 111–12;
recapture of, 116;
token benefit, 113, 132–33, 169n11
defective title. *See* title
Deferring Payroll Tax Obligations in Light of the
Ongoing COVID-19 Disaster, 156n268
delivery. *See* gift
derivative work, 41–42, *191*
descriptive mark, 42, *209*;
secondary meaning, 42;
versus suggestive mark, 125
determination letter. *See* Internal Revenue Service
Form 1023
detrimental reliance, 105
direct care of collections, 43–44, *43*, 182–83;
AAMD moratorium on sanctions of April 2020,
156n264;
See FASB Update No. 2019-03
direct lobbying. *See* political activities test
director. *See* trustee
disclosure statement, 44–45;
fair market value, 58–59;

exclusive rights (copyright) *191*:
  derivative work, 41–42;
  distribution right, 46–74;
  public display 107–8;
  public performance 110;
  reproduction, 117
exclusive use, right of. *See* title
exportation regulations. *See* Endangered Species Act
express agent. *See* agent
express contract. *See* contract
express warranty. *See* warranty of title

facts-and-circumstances test, 58
fair market value, 58–59
fair use doctrine, 59, 201–2;
  and the Copyright Clause, 201;
  four factors of, 201;
  and statutory damages, 202–3
fanciful mark, 59–60, 208, *209*
FASB Update No. 2019-03, 60–61, 183
Federal Bureau of Investigations, 91
Federal Insurance Contributions Act, 61–62, *242*
federal law, *20–21*:
  tax exempt, 126–27.
  See categories of law
  See statutory law
fee simple, 62, *115*
FICA. *See* Federal Insurance Contributions Act
fiduciary duty, 63;
  board of trustees, 22, 233–36;
  and closing of the museum, 23;
  and the collection, 3;
  and conflicts of interest, 29, 234;
  doctrine of corporate opportunity, 47, 234–35;
  duty of care, 52–53, 235;
  duty of loyalty, 53, 233–34;
  duty of obedience, 25, 53–54, 236;
  prohibition against private inurement, 104, 235
Financial Accounting Standards Board. *See* FASB
  Update No. 2019-03
first refusal. *See* sunset clause
first sale doctrine, 63–64, 191–92;
  necessary elements, 64;
  and the public display right, 64, 191–92;
  and the reproduction right, 63–64
fixation, 64–65, 190
  Berne Convention for the Protection of Literary
    and Artistic Works, 15
Form 990. *See* Internal Revenue Service
found-in-collection, 23, 65;
founding documents:
  articles of incorporation, 8–9, 221–22, 224;
  bylaws, 18, 222;
  code of ethics, 24–25;

mission statement, 84
four unities, 161n377
  See joint tenancy
Fourth Estate Public Benefit Corp. v. Wall-Street.com,
  204n14
fractional gift. *See* partial gift
freedom of speech, 66
functionality doctrine, 66–67, 210;
  and patent, 66–67
funerary objects. *See* Native American Graves
  Protection and Repatriation Act
future interest, 67

general charitable purpose. *See cy pres* doctrine
generic mark, 68, 209, *209*
gift, 38;
  versus contract, 30, *30;*
  promised, 105
Gilliam v. American Broadcasting Companies,
  161n389
good faith:
  effort. *See* old loans;
  purchaser, 132.
  See also warranty of title
grantee. *See* easement
grantor. *See* easement
grassroots lobbying. *See* political activities test
gross-receipts organizations, 164n476.
  See private foundation
Grosz v. Museum of Modern Art, 158n306
guarantee, 69

Hague Convention. *See* Convention for the
  Protection of Cultural Property in the Event of
  Armed Conflict
Harper & Row v. Nation Enterprises, 168n557
HEAR Act. *See* Holocaust Expropriated Art
  Recovery Act
historic preservation, domestic:
  Advisory Council on Historic Preservation,
    89–90;
  Antiquities Act, 6;
  Cultural Property Advisory Committee, 32, 37;
  Curation of Federally Owned and Administered
    Archaeological Collections,;
  easement, 37–38;
  historic preservation easement, 23–24, 69
  National Historic Landmarks Program, 89;
  National Historic Preservation Act, 88–89;
  National Monument Act. *See* Antiquities Act;
  National Register of Historic Places, 88;
  Native American Graves Protection and
    Repatriation Act, 36, 91–92;
  Protection of Historic Properties, 90;

ABOUT THE AUTHOR

Heather Hope Kuruvilla is a museum professional with special interests in the areas of intellectual property, museum administration, board fiduciary responsibility, community development and engagement, and the ethical and thoughtful approach to necessary deaccessioing. She studied museum professions, focusing on museum registration, at Seton Hall University, where she was awarded a Master of Arts with Distinction. In addition to her Juris Doctor degree, she holds a Certificate in Intellectual Property: Art and Museum Law from DePaul University College of Law.

Heather's past research interests include the intersection of ethics and the law in museum deaccessioning and the impact of the Visual Artists Rights Act on museums. Her seminar article on deaccessioning was awarded honorable mention in the 2011 Lawyers' Committee for Cultural Heritage Preservation student writing competition. Since 2015, she has been a consultant for the Institute of Museum Ethics, providing guidance and feedback to museum professionals.

In addition to writing and publishing, Heather is an experienced speaker and presenter. She has spoken on the topics of museum deaccessioning, museum law and ethics, and moral rights at the meetings of the American Association for State and Local History, the Mid-Atlantic Association of Museums, the New Jersey History and Historic Preservation Conference, the Institute of Museum Ethics, and as a visiting lecturer at Wheaton College (Norton, Massachusetts).

Contributing to the museum profession, she co-presented the "Business of Being an IMP" webinar for the American Alliance of Museums' Independent Museum Professionals Network on business concerns such as formation issues, taxes, liability, and contracts.

Most recently, Heather has had the pleasure to serve on the Standards and Ethics Committee of AASLH. As part of that service, she recently took part in a working group to produce the new position paper, "Valuing History Collections." That paper was introduced in the webinar "Deaccessioning in a Recession? Why or Why Not." Heather has since joined a newly formed working group at AASLH reviewing the organization's paper providing guidance on what to do when a history museum closes its doors, an unfortunately necessary update in light of the ongoing COVID-19 worldwide pandemic.

Heather is the recipient of numerous awards, including the CALI Award for Excellence for Senior Research Seminar: Cultural Property at DePaul University, the Bernard B. and Gloria L. Rinella Endowed Scholarship, the Art Law Award from DePaul Center for Art, Museum & Cultural Heritage Law, and the DePaul Faculty/Staff Endowed Scholarship. She has been recognized as a scholar by the Leopold Schepp Foundation. As a student, Heather clerked for the Honorable Arlander Keys of the Northern District of Illinois and the Honorable LaQuietta Hardy-Campbell of the Circuit Court of Cook County. Upon graduation, Heather clerked for the Honorable Melvin Gelade of the Superior Court of New Jersey, Middlesex Vicinage.

During the course of her education, Kuruvilla held positions with a number of well-respected organizations in the areas of museum education, museum registration, and intellectual property management, including the Chicago History Museum, the Chicago Public Art Group, the Newark Museum, Philadelphia Volunteer Lawyers for the Arts, and Save Ellis Island. Her past volunteer experience includes serving as a brief grader and judge for the National Cultural Heritage Law Moot Court Competition, database volunteer with the Holocaust Art Restitution Project, extern supervisor with the Douglass College Extern Program, volunteer with the Douglass Alumnae Recruitment Team, Board Secretary for the Georgian Society, and Troop Leader for the Girl Scouts of Eastern Pennsylvania.

Heather is a past interim director of the Meadowlands Museum (Rutherford, New Jersey) and a former instructor in the Museum Professions program at Seton Hall University. Currently, she lives in Berks County, Pennsylvania, with her husband and daughter. She teaches in the graduate arts administration programs at Kutztown University of Pennsylvania and the University of Kentucky, training the next generation of arts administrators in areas related to ethics and the law, community engagement, governance and leadership, and diversity, equity, and inclusion. Recently, Heather has been reading more on the manners in which communities preserve and present their own narratives and histories outside of the formal museum setting. In her free time, Heather enjoys reading, traveling, crochet, and tending to her ever-expanding vegetable garden.